JEWISH LAW

JEWISH LAW

ITS INFLUENCE ON THE DEVELOPMENT
OF LEGAL INSTITUTIONS

by

JACOB J. RABINOWITZ

Associate Professor of Jewish Law
The Hebrew University
Member of the New York Bar

40109

BLOCH PUBLISHING COMPANY

NEW YORK

1 9 5 6

PRINTED BY TWERSKY BROTHERS, NEW YORK 52, N. Y.

Published through the generosity of

LOUIS M. RABINOWITZ

PREFACE

The role of the Jewish legal tradition in the development of law in the world has been almost entirely overlooked, although marks of a powerful influence of Jewish legal ideas and practices are discernible throughout the civilized world, from ancient times to the late Middle Ages. Except for the first chapter and parts of chapters II and IV, which concern Oriental law in general, the studies in this volume deal with the evidence of this influence.

Jewish influence in the realm of law asserted itself, mainly, through legal forms which were used by Jews in the lands of their dispersion and which were copied by their non-Jewish neighbors. It is for this reason that the influence can be traced with a high degree of certainty. The form into which a given legal insitution is cast, unlike its substance, bears the stamp of individuality. A literal translation of a legal formula from one language into another often betrays the source from which the formula was copied.

Throughout the ages legal formulae have been of great importance in the development of legal institutions. The law of property and the law of obligations, the two branches of the law which play an important part in shaping the destinies of every society, are to a very large extent the product of the ingenuity of the legal draftsman. To cite but one outstanding example: the modern law of negotiable instruments is ultimately traceable to a new legal formula which was introduced in the later Middle Ages.

For the ancient period, I have drawn heavily upon the Bible — the narrative and the other non-legal parts thereof — the Aramaic papyri of the 5th century B. C. E. and the Talmud, in all of which I have found unmistakable signs of a substantial continuity of the same legal tradition. For the Middle Ages, my main reliance has been upon the Talmud and upon forms of legal instruments.

The Aramaic papyri, to the study of which a substantial part of this volume is devoted, deserve special comment. For various reasons, these papyri, mostly documents of a legal nature stemming from the Jewish military colony of Elephantine on

the Nile, have been treated by legal historians as though they
were an isolated episode in the history of law, hardly worth their
attention. As will be shown in the following pages, this attitude
on the part of students of ancient law is entirely unjustified.
These papyri, especially the Brooklyn Museum collection, contain
so much that is of paramount importance for the history of law
in the Ancient World that a study of them from the legal point
of view is imperative. Much that is obscure in Assyro-Babylonian,
Egyptian and Hellenistic law will receive fresh light from these
documents. Moreover, a legal analysis of these documents will
yield information that is of great importance not only to the
legal historian but also to the Biblical scholar, the philologist
and the general historian.

The lines of specialization, which, with the vast accumulation of
knowledge, historical and philological scholarship must of necessity
follow, do not correspond to the historical realities. The professional scribes of Elephantine who wrote their legal documents
in Aramaic probably knew, and perhaps also wrote, Egyptian
as well, and the Egyptian scribes probably knew something
of the legal style and formulae which were in use by their
brethren whose medium was Aramaic. But the modern Egypto-
logist is usually not versed in Aramaic and the Aramaic scholar
usually does not know any Egyptian, and neither of them is
trained to discern the significance of legal terms and phrases
which are often pregnant with meaning. The student of the
Aramaic papyri hardly ever draws upon demotic legal documents
and the demotist is hardly aware of the existence of the Aramaic
papyri. The result, in each case, is a partial picture which, very
often, is misleading.

Still more oblivious to the existence of the Aramaic papyri
are students of juristic papyri written in the Greek language.
Here too the historical realities are in sharp contrast with the
lines of specialization which are usually followed by modern
scholarship, and the result is not a very happy one. To illustrate:
The oldest extant papyrus written in the Greek language is a
marriage contract from Elephantine (P. Eleph. 1), dated 311/310
B. C. E. This document, which has been thoroughly discussed

by the foremost papyrologists and which has been classified by them as a "purely Greek" form of marriage contract, contains a provision to the effect that the husband shall not marry another woman or have children by another woman. None of these papyrologists apparently knew that an Aramaic papyrus (Cowley 15), also from Elephantine, of the year 440 B. C. E. contains precisely the same provision, which of course casts considerable doubt upon the purely Greek character of P. Eleph. 1.

Some of the material presented in this volume has already appeared in various periodicals, such as Jewish Social Studies, Harvard Theological Review, University of Pennslyvania Law Review, Cornell Law Quarterly, Law Quarterly Review, Speculum and Biblica. The volume also contains some parts of a course of lectures which was delivered by me at the Hebrew Unversity in Jerusalem during the 1950-51 academic year.

I owe a debt of profound gratitude to Mr. Louis M. Rabinowitz whose generosity, coupled with an abiding interest in Jewish scholarship, has made the publication of this volume possible. Thanks are also due to him for a helpful suggestion regarding the title of the volume. To Dean Emeritus Frank H. Sommer and to Professor Herman A. Gray of New York University School of Law, both of them devoted friends and inspiring teachers, I am indebted for constant encouragement. To my friend Leo Guzick, Esq., I am indebted for some helpful suggestions. To Dr. Joshua Bloch, the former Chief of the Jewish Division, and to Mr. Abraham Berger, its present Chief, and to Dr. John L. Mish, Chief of the Oriental Division, and to his Assistant Mr. Francis Paar, of the New York Public Library, and to their respective staffs, I am indebted for assistance, so readily extended to me, in the use of the facilities of that library. Finally, like all other students of legal history, I am indebted to Professor Emil G. Kraeling for that magnificent volume of *The Brooklyn Museum Aramaic Papyri,* which he so ably edited, translated and provided with commentary and historical introduction.

J. J. R.

CONTENTS

Page

CHAPTER I

EARLY ROMAN LAW AND BIBLICAL LAW

In a recent article [1] on the subject of the relationship between Roman law and Oriental law, Volterra, after an exhaustive survey of the literature and the various views on this much debated subject, arrives at the conclusion that so far as early Roman law is concerned there is no evidence of any Oriental influence upon the development of its institutions.[2] In this chapter we shall present some evidence tending to show that early Roman law, in its main institutions, *was* influenced by Oriental law, and that the Bible is an important source for the study of this influence. This evidence will be discussed under four main headings: 1. Public law. 2. Family law. 3. The law of property. 4. The law of obligations.

Public law.

Foedus ferire and foedus firmare. There is a striking resemblance between the expressions *foedus ferire* [3] and *foedus firmare*,[4] used in Latin in the sense of concluding a treaty, and the expressions לכרות ברית and להקים ברית used in the Bible [5] in the same sense. As to ברית Albright [6] correctly says that its primary meaning is *bond, fetter*. A similar primary meaning (bond) is given by Latin etymological dictionaries for *foedus*.[7] The correspondence between כרת (to cut) and *ferire* (to cut) is quite obvious, and that between להקים (to make firm, establish)

---

[1] E. Volterra, *Introduction à l'histoire du droit Romain dans ses rapports avec l'Orient,* AHDO, 4 (1949), p. 117ff.

[2] *Ibid.,* p. 146ff.

[3] See Ch. T. Lewis, *A Latin Dictionary for Schools,* s. v. *ferio.*

[4] See *ibid.,* s. v. *firmo.*

[5] See GB, 116a-b, s. v. ברית.

[6] See BASOR, no. 121 (Feb. 1951), p. 22, n. 6.

[7] See Ch. T. Lewis, *ibid.,* p. 1183, s. v. 1 FID.

1

and *firmare* (to make firm, establish) is no less obvious. Bickerman,[8] who has noted the similarity between כרת ברית and *foedus ferire*, speculates concerning the significance of the symbolism of which these phrases are expressive. But he says nothing about להקים ברית and *foedus firmare*, nor does he even as much as hint that these phrases may be indicative of Oriental influence upon the basic concepts of an incipient international law in ancient Rome.

Conubium and Commercium. These terms, meaning the rights of intermarriage and commercial intercourse, respectively, are usually found together in Roman sources.[9] Speaking of *conubium* and *commercium*, A. N. Sherwin-White says:

> "These complementary rights formed an essential part of *ius Latii*. Their development, unparalleled in the Ancient World until the later stages of some Greek cities, belongs to the period before the growth of large States in Latium, and was encouraged by the continental environment of the numerous small *populi* of the plain-dwellers, *Latini*".[10]

However, a reference to Gen. 34:8-10 will reveal that *conubium* and *commercium* are not unparalleled in the Ancient World. This passage reads:

וידבר חמור אתם לאמר שכם בני חשקה נפשו בבתכם
תנו נא אותה לו לאשה. והתחתנו אתנו בנתיכם תתנו
לנו ואת בנותינו תקחו לכם. ואתנו תשבו והארץ תהיה
לפניכם שבו וסחרוה והאחזו בה.

> ("And Hamor spoke with them, saying: 'The soul of my son Shechem longeth for your daughter. I pray you give her unto him to wife. And make ye marriages with us; give your daughters unto us, and take our daughters unto you. And ye shall

---

[8] E. Bickerman, *Couper une alliance*, AHDO, 5 (1950), 133ff.

[9] See Mommsen, *Römisches Staatsrecht*, III, 1 (3 Aufl.), 632-634; A. N. Sherwin-White, *The Roman Citizenship*, 80ff., 103ff., 107.

[10] See the article *Commercium* by A. N. Sherwin-White in Oxford Classical Dictionary, p. 222.

dwell with us; and the land shall be before you;
dwell and trade ye therein, and get you possessions
therein' ".).

This is evidently an offer to conclude a treaty of *conubium*
and *commercium* . The parallelism is so obvious and so striking
that it requires no comment.

It is to be noted that the phrase והאחזו בה ("and get you
possessions therein") probably refers to the right to acquire landed
property as an incident of the right of *commercium*. Under Roman
law, too, only citizens and persons belonging to a group having
the right of *commercium* could acquire an *ager privatus*.[11]

Family law.

Coemptio. One of the forms of Roman marriage is known
under the name of *coemptio*.[12] The name clearly implies that this
form of marriage was, at least in legal contemplation, akin to
purchase.   It also seems to imply, as some late Roman texts
suggest,[13] mutuality of purchase, so to speak, the wife being
purchased by the husband and the husband by the wife. Buckland
frowns upon this suggestion, saying that mutuality of purchase
is "not a necessary implication of the word *coemptio* and in itself
improbable".[14] However, a reference to Oriental sources will
reveal that the idea of mutuality of purchase in marriage is not
at all far-fetched. Careful study of certain Babylonian and
Hebrew sources will show that this idea was quite pronounced
among the Babylonians and the Hebrews and that it found
expression in unmistakable language patterns going back to the
period of the First Babylonian Dynasty. In a number of Baby-

---

[11] See M. Kaser, *Die Typen der römischen Bodenrechte in der späteren
Republic,* Zeitschrift der Savigny-Stiftung für Rechtsgeschichte, Rom. Abt., 62
(1942), 74, n. 238.

[12] See *Gai Inst.* 1, 112; W. W. Buckland, *A Text-Book of Roman Law,* p.
119.

[13] See Bruns, *Fontes Iuris Romani Antiqui* (7th ed.), 2, 74, 76. See also
F. de Zulueta, *The Institutes of Gaius,* II, 35.

[14] Buckland, *ibid.,* p. 119, n. 9.

lonian marriage documents the bride is said to be given to the
husband, or taken by him, into *wifehood* and *husbandhood* (*ana
aššutim u mututim*).[15] This expression is clearly indicative of a
mutual relationship implying a certain degree of equality between
husband and wife. The transaction is a two-sided one. The man
takes the woman into wifehood and gives himself to her into
husbandhood. The expression certainly does not square with
the notion of marriage as a purchase of the bride by the husband
as though she were a chattel. One does not buy a slave into
masterhood-slavehood; one simply buys a slave.

The two-sidedness of the transaction is also apparent in
the marriage formula in the Aramaic papyri. In three marriage
documents of 449,[16] 440 [17] and 420 [18] B. C. E., respectively, the
formula reads: הי אנתתי ואנה בעלה (She is my wife, and I
am her husband). A similar marriage formula is also implicit
in Hos. 2:4 היא לא אשתי ואנכי לא אישה (She is not my wife,
and I am not her husband) which, as Blau [19] has correctly
pointed out, is a divorce formula using *contraria verba* to the
formula of marriage.

The expression *to give into wifehood-husbandhood* of the
Old-Babylonian marriage documents was, in the course of time,
shortened into *to give into wifehood,* and in this form it appears
in the three marriage documents in the Aramaic papyri mentioned
above. Cowley no. 15.3 (440 B.C. E.), for example, reads:
אנה [א]תית ביתך למנתן לי [ל]ברתך מפטיה לאנתתו ("I came to
your house that you might give me your daughter Miptahiah

[15] See UAR, nos. 2.5, 31.5, 33.5, 35.3.

[16] APK, no. 2.3-4.

[17] APC, no. 15.4.

[18] APK, 7.4.

[19] See L. Blau, *Die Jüdische Ehescheidung* I, 25; II, 15. The mutuality
of the relationship between husband and wife is expressed in clear terms in
some Middle-Assyrian marriage contracts. (See M. David and E. Ebeling,
Assyrische Rectsurkunden, no. 1). These contracts contain a provision which
in the editors' German translation reads: *Solange sie* (husband and wife) *leben
werden sie einander... Ehrfurcht erweisen.* Cf. p. 179, below.

into wifehood"). It is most remarkable to find an exact replica of the expression *to give into wifehood* in Roman sources. We are referring to the expression *in matrimonium dare,* the word *mater* meaning wife, married woman,[20] and *matrimonium* meaning wifehood.

It will perhaps be argued that all of the above similarities between the Oriental and the Roman institutions are but co-incidences, the result of independent parallel development along similar lines. However, we must keep in mind a sharp distinction between parallelisms in substance of legal institutions and those in form. The former may well arise as a result of parallel development, whereas the latter are indicative either of borrowing by one system from the other or of a common source. A form such as *to give into wifehood,* for example, is not likely to arise in two different cultural areas spontaneously and independently. Furthermore, as we shall presently see, in the case of marriage by *coemptio* the parallelisms noted above fit into a larger scheme, where, again, form points to an Oriental origin.

The contract of *emptio-venditio,* of which *coemptio* is a special type, also seems to be of Oriental origin. Pringsheim [21] calls attention to the similarity between the Roman *emptio-venditio* and the Greek ὠνὴ καὶ πρᾶσις, adding that "in Rome as in Greece the term is ancient". For Greece he cites, among other sources, Herodotus 1,153. With respect to the Roman *emptio-venditio* he says:

> "The assumption that the two-sided term was caused by the classical creation of two actions (empti-venditi) and not used before is unproved and improbable. The Roman term has the same root as the Greek one. Nobody knows if the one was influenced by the other".[22]

---

[20] See A. Walde, *Lateinisches etymologisches Wörterbuch* (3rd ed., 1951), v. II, p. 49.

[21] GLS, 111f., 114.

[22] *Ibid.,* 114, n. 3.

It is significant that the two-sided term for the contract of sale — מקח וממכר (purchase and sale) — also occurs in the Mishnah and in other Talmudic sources.[23] That this is a Semitic language pattern can hardly be doubted.[24]

As for Greece, there are, as will be shown in ch. 3, below, other indications of Oriental influence in the realm of the law of sale. As for Rome, we shall show in a subsequent section of this chapter that *mancipatio per aes et libram* has a close parallel in the Bible. For the present, we shall only indicate that the very terms *emptio* and *venditio*, etymologically, point to an Oriental origin. The primary meaning of *emere* is *to take*[25] and *venditio* (*venumdare*) contains the verb *dare* (to give). Similarly, the Hebrew לקח and the Accadian *leqû*, the primary meaning of both of which is *to take* are used in the sense of *to buy*, and the Hebrew נתן (to give) and Accadian *nadânu* (to give) are used in the sense of *to sell*.[26]

Divorce. The bill of divorce is called in the Bible (Deut. 24:1; Isa. 50:1; Jer. 3:8) ספר כריתות, which literally means *document of cutting*. This Biblical term apparently represents a linguistic relic of an ancient ceremonial by which divorce was accompanied. In the formula of divorce of the Sumerian family law (*ana ittišu*, tablet 7, col. 2.50) it is stated that the husband

---

[23] See, e g., Mishnah, BM 4:10; Tosefta Shabbath 9:13 (ed. Zuckermandel, 120).

[24] Cf. UAR, p. 8; GB, 389b. See also p. 25, below.

[25] See Ch. T. Lewis, *ibid.*, p. 1183a, s. v. EM. See also A. Ernout et A. Meillet, *Dictionnaire étymologique de la langue latine* (3rd ed., 1951), v. I, p. 347, where it is stated that there is perhaps Greek influence here, for λαμβάνω (to take) is attested in Sicily in the sense of *to buy*. Is not there Oriental influence in both?

[26] See GB, 389b. With respect to *venum*, one of the components of *venumdare*, Latin etymological dictionaries (See A. Walde, *ibid.*, II, 754; Ernout et Meillet, *ibid.*, II, 1276) tell us that it is a cognate of a Sanskrit word meaning *price*. This makes the composite word *venumdare* strikingly similar to the Hebrew נתן בכסף (give for silver, a price), used in the sense of *to sell*. See Gen. 23:9; Deut. 2:28. For the Accadian equivalent of this phrase, see C. Bezold, *Babylonisch-assyrisches Glossar*, 193b.

cut off the hem of the wife's garment. It seems that as a result of this ceremonial the document of divorce came to be called *document of cutting off*. In Roman sources divorce is called *discidium, a cutting asunder*. (See lexica s. h. v.), which is strikingly similar to the Biblical term. In addition to *discidium, dimittere* (to send away) and *domo expellere* (to drive out of the house), used in Roman sources in the terminology of divorce, have a close parallel in ושלחה מביתו (and he sendeth her out of his house) of Deut. 24:1. Also similar to this Biblical phrase is the Roman divorce formula *baete foras* (go out).[27] Cf. further ויצאה מביתו (and she departeth out of his house) in Deut. 24:2.

The Law of Property

Mancipatio. On the subject of *mancipatio* in the Bible, we shall quote some Biblical passages which, when properly understood, speak for themselves.

Jer. 31:30-31 (31-32), reads:

הנה ימים באים נאם ד' וכרתי את בית ישראל ואת
בית יהודה ברית חדשה. לא כברית אשר כרתי את
אבותם ביום החזיקי בידם להוציאם מארץ מצרים אשר
המה הפרו את בריתי ואנכי בעלתי בם נאם ד'.

("Behold, the days come, saith the Lord, that I will make a new covenant with the house of Israel, and with the house of Judah; not according to the

---

[27] See E. Levy, *Der Hergang der römischen Ehescheidung*, p. 19. Cf. *ina bíti u-še-ṣi-šu* (from the house he put her out) in the Sumerian divorce formula (*ana ittišu*, tablet 7, col. 3.3); הוציאו (they put out their wives) in Ezra 10:3, 19; והאיש מוציא...יוצאת האשה (the wife departs...and the husband puts her out) in Mishnah, Yebamoth 14:1 — all of which is technical language of divorce in Oriental sources covering a period of about two millenia. On the parallelisms between the Jewish and Sumerian divorce formulae, see my article "divorce" in the Biblical Encyclopedia (Hebrew), v. II, p. 551ff. The subject of divorce in Jewish and Roman law is discussed at length by B. Cohen in his article *Concerning Divorce in Jewish and Roman Law* (Proceedings of the American Academy for Jewish Research XXI [1952], p. 1ff.), but the author does not touch upon matters of form.

covenant that I made with their fathers in the day
that I took them by the hand to bring them out
of the land of Egypt; forasmuch as they broke My
covenant, although I was a lord over them, saith
the Lord").

The phrase "I took them by the hand" is used here in the
sense of taking formal possession, such as one would take when
acquiring ownership of a slave, as in the Roman *mancipatio*,
and the phrase ואנכי בעלתי בם, which should be rendered as
"although I had acquired ownership of them" rather than
"although I was a lord over them", refers to this formal act.

Isa. 41:9, reads:

אשר החזקתיך מקצות הארץ ומאציליה קראתיך ואמר
לך עבדי אתה בחרתיך ולא מאסתיך.

("Thou whom I have taken hold of from the ends
of the earth, and called thee from the uttermost parts
thereof, and said unto thee: 'Thou art My servant',
I have chosen thee and not cast thee away".

The phrase "and said unto thee: 'Thou art My servant'" is
strongly suggestive of the formula "Hunc ego hominem ex iure
Quiritium meum esse aio" which, under the Roman procedure,
the transferee was required to pronounce at the time of taking
formal possession of the slave.[28] Similarly, ואחזק בידך ("and

---

[28] *Gai Inst.* I, 119, 121. See also H. F. Jolowicz, *Historical Introduction to
Roman Law* (2nd ed., 1952), 140, 145. The full formula reads: Hunc ego
hominem ex iure quiritium meum esse aio isque mihi emptus esto hoc aere
aeneaque libra. In de Zulueta's (*The Institutes of Gaius*, I, p. 39) English
translation: "I declare that this slave is mine by Quiritary right, and be he
purchased to me with this bronze ingot and bronze scale". This formula has
been called by de Zulueta (*ibid.*, II, p. 59) "an enigma". "Its first clause" —
he says — "appears to state an untruth, its second to confess the untruth".
See also Buckland, *ibid.*, p. 237, who says that the form "looks illogical".
However, if we assume, as appears from Isa. 41:9 and as seems reasonable,
that the formula was pronounced by the transferee at the time of his grasping
the slave by the hand, which followed the weighing of the bronze on the
scales, there is nothing illogical in the formula. The transferee declares that
the slave is his by Quiritary right and then proceeds to state the ground for his

have taken hold of thy hand") in Isa. 42:6 probably refers to the formal act of taking possession.

At still another point there is a striking parallel in the Bible to the Roman *mancipatio*. An essential part of the procedure was the weighing of the copper (the price) on the balances — *mancipatio per aes et libram*.[29] A similar procedure — except that instead of copper, silver was used as the price — is described in Jer. 32:10, in connection with the purchase by the prophet of the field of Hanamel: ואכתב בספר ואחתם ואעד עדים ואשקל הכסף במאזנים ("And I subscribed the deed, and sealed it, and called witnesses, and weighed him the money in the balances").

Nexum mancipiumque in the Twelve Tables. Table VI, 1, reads: "*Cum nexum faciet mancipiumque, uti lingua nuncupassit, ita ius esto*". The meaning of the combination *nexum mancipiumque*, which has been much discussed by historians of Roman law,[30] still remains obscure. In the light of certain Oriental parallels, we believe that it refers to two stages in the process of transfer of property which were originally separate and distinct and which later became merged. These two stages were: 1. Payment of the price by the transferee to the transferor. 2. Taking possession of the property by the transferee. According to Koschaker, under Sumerian law the transfer of property involved precisely these two stages — *Preiszahlung und Besitzergreifung*.[31] A close parallel to the rule of Sumerian law is reflected in the story of the purchase of the Cave of Machpelah. Gen. 23:16-20, reads:

"And Abraham hearkened unto Ephron; and Abra-

---

assertion: "he *is* purchased to me with this bronze ingot and bronze scale" There is authority for reading *est* instead of *esto* in the formula, See de Zulueta, *ibid.*, I, p. 38, n. 5 and p. 206, n. 4

[29] See *ibid.*, I, 122.

[30] See K. F. Thormann, *Der doppelte Ursprung der Mancipatio* (Münchener Beiträge zur Papyrusforschung und antiken Rechtsgeschichte, 33), p. 175ff.

[31] P. Koschaker, *Eheschliessung und Kauf nach alten Rechten*, Archiv Orientalni, 18, 3 (1950), p. 214.

ham weighed to Ephron the silver, which he had
named in the hearing of the children of Heth, four
hundred shekels of silver, current money with the
merchant. So the field of Ephron, which was in
Machpelah, which was before Mamre, the field,
and the cave which was therein, and all the trees
that were in the field, that were in all the border
thereof round about, were made sure unto Abraham
for a possession (למקנה, more precisely, for a
purchase) in the presence of the children of
Heth, before all that went in at the gate of his city.
And after this, Abraham buried Sarah his wife in
the cave of the field of Machpelah before Mamre —
the same is Hebron — in the land of Canaan. And
the field, and the cave that is therein, were made
sure unto Abraham for a possession of a burying-
place by the children of Heth".

The two stages in the process of transfer of property are clearly
discernible here. Twice it is said that the field was made sure
unto Abraham — once after Abraham weighed the silver to
Ephron, that is after payment of the price, and then again
after he buried Sarah, that is after he took possession of the
field. The first time it is said that the field was made sure unto
him *as a purchase* (למקנה), and the second time that it was
made sure unto him *as a burial possession* (לאחזת קבר).

The two terms מקנה (purchase) and אחוזה (possession),
used in the above passage from the Bible in connection with
the two stages in the process of the transfer of the field of
Machpelah, are of particular significance as showing the way
to the solution of the problem of the meaning of *nexum mancipiumque* in the Twelve Tables. In several texts quoted by
Thormann [32] the term *nexum* is used in the same sense as
the Hebrew term מקנה is used in the phrase מקנת כסף,
that is as the ground on which a person's rights in certain

---

[32] Thormann, *ibid.*, 252ff.

property rest. Particularly revealing in this respect is the phrase "nexa atque hereditates" (property acquired by purchase and property acquired by inheritance) in Cic. pro Caec. XXXV, 102. There is thus a remarkable correspondence between *nexum* (purchase) and *mancipium* (possession), on the one hand, and מקנה (purchase) and אחוזה (possession) on the other. As to *mancipium* and אחוזה, there is a further correspondence between them. In early Roman law landed property and slaves were considered *res mancipi*.[33] Similarly, in the Bible the term אחוזה is used with respect to landed property [34] and slaves.[35]

The Law of Obligations.

Stipulatio. Two of the words, the utterance of each of which in proper form had, under Roman law, the effect of producing a binding promise on the part of the person who uttered it, were *spondeo* and *promitto*. [36] Both of these terms are explained as relics of what originally was a religious ritual, namely the taking of an oath accompanied by a certain ceremony. *Spondeo* is believed to be a cognate of the Greek σπένδω meaning *to make libations* and to point to the making of libations on the occasion of taking an oath,[37] and *promitto* is taken to mean

[33] *Gai Inst.* II, 14a.

[34] See, e. g., Gen. 17:8; 23:4.

[35] See Lev. 25:45-46. The Hebrew אחז, like the Accadian *aḫâzu*, means to take hold of, to seize. See GB, 24a. The Latin *capio* has a similar meaning. Jolowicz, *ibid.*, 140 suggests that originally land was not included within the category of *res mancipi.* "It has been pointed out" — he says — "that the ceremonial of mancipation is not at all appropriate to a conveyance of land, because it includes the grasping of the thing to be acquired by the transferee and the grasping of land is an impossible, or at least an undignified, gesture". However, the force of this argument is vitiated by the fact that אחוזה (that which is seized) is used in the Bible, as *mancipatio* is used in Roman law sources, with respect to both land and slaves, although the Hebrew term, like the Roman, is not appropriate to land.

[36] *Gai Ins.* III, 92.

[37] See F. Leifer, *Die Herkunft von Sponsio und Stipulatio,* Bulletino dell'-Istituto di Diritto Romano, 1936, p. 163.

to put forth and to point to putting forth the hand when taking an oath.[38]

The above explanation of *spondeo* and *promitto* is anything but convincing. As to *spondeo*, it is most peculiar to find that this highly technical term, which, as we are told, was borrowed by a secular jurisprudence from the realm of religion, came to be the chief component of the word *respondeo*, with the very plain and homely meaning of *to answer*. Did not the Romans have a word with this meaning before *spondeo* could be used as a component for such a word? [39] As to *promitto*, the word does not mean to put forth but to *set in view, before*,[40] which is something quite different.

The writer believes that a simple explanation of the two terms under discussion may be had, if we assume an Oriental origin of the early Roman law of obligations. There is in Babylonian law a word — *apâlu* — which is widely used as a technical term in the law of obligations and the non-technical meaning of which is *to answer*. This at once reminds one of *spondeo*, which seems to have been used in similar manner. In view of the importance for our discussion of the various shades of meaning in which the Babylonian term is used, we shall quote an authority on Babylonian law on this point:

> "Die primäre Bedeutung dieses Zeitwortes ist nach den Wörterbüchen 'erwidren, antworten', doch tritt diese Bedeutung in der Rechtssprache der Urkunden hinter eine zweite zurück, die auch in 279 K. H. über die Gewährleistung des Verkäufers vorliegt. Es bezeichnet nämlich in den altbabylonischen Rechtsquellen *apâlu* die Erfüllung einer Verbindlich-

---

[38] See R. Dekkers, *Des méfaits de la stipulatio*, Révue internationale des droits de l'antiquité, 4, 368f. See also F. de Zulueta, *The Institutes of Gaius*, 2, p. 152.

[39] Ernout et Meillet (*ibid*, II, 1136) state that at first *respondeo* was used in the sense of *to promise in return* and then it came to be used in the sense of *to answer to a question* — a rather unusual semantic development.

[40] See Ch. T. Lewis, *ibid.*, s. v. *promitto*.

keit durch Leistung des Geschuldeten ohne Rücksicht
auf den Verpflichtungsgrund, bedeutet also: 'leisten,
erfüllen, erstatten, begleichen' und dort, wo die Leistung nicht erwähnt ist, einfach: '(den Gläubiger)
befriedigen' .. Das in der sumerischen Fassung der
Vertragsklausel an Stelle von *apâlu* häufig vorkom-
mende *b-gì-gì* ist nach Poebel, MVAG 26 S. 50f.
das Kausativum bezw. Transitivum aus *gì-gì*, 'umkehren, sich umwenden, zurückkommen', und bedeutet neben 'umkehren machen' auch 'zurückgeben,
erstatten, ersetzen' ".[41]

(The primary meaning of this verb, according to the
dictionaries, is 'respond, answer', but in the legal
language of the documents this meaning gives way
to a second one, which also appears in sec. 279 of
the Code of Hammurabi concerning the seller's warranty. In the Old-Babylonian legal sources *apâlu*
signifies the fullfilment of an obligation through
performance without regard to the ground of the
obligation, it means, that is, 'perform, fullfil, restore,
pay' and, where the nature of the performance is
not mentioned, simply 'satisfy (the creditor)' ...
The Sumerian *b-gì-gì*, which, in contracts drawn up
in Sumerian, occurs often instead of *apâlu*, is, according to Poebel, MVAG 26, p. 50f., the causative,
respectively the transitive of *gì-gì*, 'return, turn
around, come back' and means, along with 'cause to
return', also 'give back, restore, replace'.)

An equivalent of the Accadian *apâlu* and of its Sumerian
counterpart occurs also in the Bible. We are referring to the word
להשיב, the causative — *hifil* — of שוב. This word, in both the *qal*
and the *hifil*, has exactly the same basic meanings as the intran-
sitive and causative, respectively, of the Sumerian term referred

[41] M. San-Nicolo, *Die Schlussklauseln der altbabylonischen Kauf-und
Tauschverträge*, 150-152.

to by San-Nicolo, שוב meaning *to return, to come back* and להשיב
to restore, to bring back.[42] In combination with דבר (word),
להשיב is also used in the Bible, as *apâlu* is used in Accadian,
in the sense of *to answer*.[43] There is thus a definite affinity
between these Hebrew, Accadian and Sumerian words as far as
their basic meanings are concerned, and upon a close examination
of certain Biblical passages it appears that this affinity extends
also to the technical-legal meanings of these words. In Gen. 42:37
להשיב is used in the sense of *to restore pursuant to an obligation*.
תנה אותו על ידי ואני אשיבנו אליך — says Reuben to Jacob who
is unwilling to send Benjamin to Egypt. This is legal language
par excellence. תנה אותו על ידי means give him upon my
guarantee — the Hebrew יד (hand) being used here, as the
Accadian *qâtu* (hand) is used in Babylonian legal terminology,[44]
in the technical sense of guarantee — and ואני אשיבנו אליך means
and I will restore him to you pursuant to my obligation.
להשיב is also used in the Bible in the sense of *to pay a debt*.
In Ez. 18:7 חבולתו חוב ישיב means *his debt he pays*.
חבולתו is apparently derived from the Accadian *ḥubullu* (debt)[45]
and ישיב corresponds to the Accadian *apâlu* (to pay). A similar
combination — *ḥubullam apâlu* — meaning *to pay a debt* occurs
in an Old-Babylonian source.[46] Finally, להשיב is used a number
of times in the Bible in the sense of *to pay tribute*.[47]

From the foregoing it appears that in Sumerian, in Accadian
and in Biblical Hebrew, respectively, a word meaning *to return,
to bring back* and, derivately, *to answer* came to be used in
technical legal language in the sense of *to restore pursuant to an
obligation, to pay*. Is it not reasonable therefore to suppose that

[42] See GB, 810a-812b.

[43] See *ibid.*

[44] See P. Koschaker, *Assyrisch-babylonisches Bürgschafts*recht, 15; C. Bezold, *Assyrisch-babylonisches Glossar,* 24a-b.

[45] See Bezold, *ibid.,* 118b.

[46] See L. Waterman, *Business Documents of the Hammurabi Period,* American Journal of Semitic Languages, 30, 57.6.

[47] See, e.g., 2 Kings 3:4; 2 Chron. 27:5.

spondeo, like *respondeo*, means *to answer* and that in the
language of the law of obligations it means *to restore pursuant
to an obligation, to pay?* This supposition is strengthened by the
fact that the basic meaning of the word *recipio*, which is used in
Roman sources synonymously with *spondeo* and *promitto*, like
that of the Hebrew להשיב and the Sumerian *b-gì-gì*, is *to bring
back.*[48]

As to *promitto*, the writer believes that the technical meaning
of this term is but an extension of its basic meaning of *to set in
view, before*. In the language of the law of obligations it means
to set before the obligee, that is at his disposal, that which is
promised. Here, too, a reference to Oriental sources is most
illuminating. A similar expression is used in the Bible and in the
Talmud in a similar sense. We are referring to the expression
להציג לפני (to set before) which occurs in Judah's undertaking
to bring Benjamin back to his father from Egypt. Gen. 43:9 reads:
אנכי אערבנו מידי תבקשנו אם לא הביאותיך אליך והצגתיו לפניך
והטאתי לך כל הימים. ("I will be surety for him; of my hand
shalt thou require him; if I bring him not unto thee, and set
him before thee, then let me bear the blame forever"). That the
expression והצגתיו לפניך ("and set him before thee") is technical
language of obligation is indicated by the fact that precisely the
same expression in Aramaic — ואוקים קדמך (and I will set
before thee) — occurs in BT, Baba Metzia 15a, in the formula
of a warranty clause in which the seller undertakes that in case
a claim is asserted against the property by a third party he will
clear it of the claim and *set* it *before* the buyer. Again, in Baba
Metzia 104a the same expression occurs in the cropsharing
tenant's undertaking to *set* the crop *before* the landlord.

Qatam nasâḥu, שמוט יד and *manum depellere*.

Cuq[49] has noted the remarkable similarity between the ex-

---

[48] See Ch. T. Lewis, *ibid.*, s. v. *recipio*.

[49] E. Cuq, *Études sur le droit babylonien, les lois assyriennes et les lois
hittites*, 294ff.

pressions *qatam nasâḥu* (to remove the hand) in some Old-Babylonian documents and *manum depellere* in Roman sources. In both cases the expressions are used with respect to a surety who intervenes on behalf of the debtor and removes, as it were, the hand of the creditor from him.[50] These expressions point to the right of the creditor to seize the defaulting debtor for the purpose of making him work off the debt — *manus iniectio* in Roman law.[51] A similar expression, in similar connection, occurs in Deut. 15:2 וזה דבר השמטה שמוט כל בעל משה ידו אשר ישה ברעהו לא יגש את רעהו ואת אחיו. This verse is to be translated as follows: This is the manner of the release: Every creditor (בעל משה) who demands aught of his neighbor (אשר ישה ברעהו) shall remove his hand (שמוט ידו); he shall not make his neighbour and his brother work (לא יגש ברעהו ובאחיו).

---

[50] *Ibid.*
[51] *Ibid.*

CHAPTER II

THE PEREGRINATIONS OF A LEGAL FORMULA

In several documents from Susa [1] all of them representing gifts of property by husband to wife, there occurs, with some variations, a formula which concerns the wife's power to dispose of the property in question. In the first volume of the *Actes Juridiques Susiens* (no. 131.30f.), due to a scribal error in the document, Scheil completely missed the meaning of the formula. In this document the formula reads: *sa-ar- ta-ra-a-mu ta-na-di*. This was translated by Scheil as "le roi que tu aimes, tu l'exalteras", which hardly makes any sense at all. However, in a document (no. 379.39f.) published by him three years later, where a similar formula occurs, Scheil gave a nearly correct translation of the formula. On the basis of the reading in this document, he suggested an emendation of the text in no. 131.30 and changed his original translation thereof accordingly.

In no. 379.39. the formula reads: *a-šar ta-ra-a-mu a-na a-li-ik ar-ki i-ta-ad-di-in*. This is translated by Scheil as *où elle voudra à qui viendra après, elle redonnera*. In a note to this formula, he says: "*Ašar tarâmu* 'où elle voudra', c'est-a-dire 'à qui elle voudra': *râmu* a le sens atténué de 'vouloir, préférer' sans plus. De même *ina narâmišu* signifie 'de son gré', c'est évidemment la même expression qui se lit no. 131.30, où il faut restituer [*a*]-*sa-ar- ta-ra-a-mu ta-na-di* 'elle appliquera où elle voudra'. *Nadânu* et *nadû* semblent confondus dans ces passages".

The writer believes that *râmu* is used in the above formula not in any attenuated sense, but in the original sense of "to love", as a mother loves a child, and that this formula is in complete

---

[1] *Actes Juridiques Susiens, Mémoires de la délégation en Perse*, XXII, no. 131.30; XXIV, nos. 378.9f., 382bis. 24f.

agreement with section 150 of the Code of Hammourabi, where precisely the same word is used in the same sense. This section, in Meek's translation, reads:

> "If a seignior, upon presenting a field, orchard, house, or goods to his wife, left a sealed document with her, her children may not enter a claim against her after (the death of) her husband, since the mother may give her inheritance to that son of hers whom she likes, (but) she may not give (it) to an outsider"[2]

In substance, this law provides, to use modern legal phraseology which fits the case admirably, that where a husband makes a gift of property to his wife by a writing (probably to take effect after his death), the wife is to have a life estate in the property, together with a limited power of appointment of the remainder after her death to that one of her sons whom she loves best. The brief *ašar tarâmu* clause in the Susa deeds of gift by husband to wife means exactly what section 150 of the Code of Hammourabi provides, namely, that the woman is to enjoy the property during her lifetime, and that she shall have the power to leave it after her death to that one of her sons whom she loves best.

Further support for our interpretation of the *ašar tarâmu* clause is found in an Egyptian document of the Twelfth Dynasty (ca. 1800 B. C. E.).[3] In this document, as in the Susa documents referred to above, a husband makes a gift of property to his wife, with the provision that "she shall give it to any she desires of her children". Interestingly enough, according to Sethe,[4] the

---

[2] James B. Pritchard, *Ancient Near Eastern Texts relating to the Old Testament*, p. 172. In the light of the *ašar tarâmu* clause in the Susa documents, it seems that this section of the Code of Hammourabi was either adopted from an older code or represents a codification of customary law.

[3] F. Ll. Griffith, *The Petrie Papyri, Hieratic Papyri from Kahun and Gurob*, pl. XII, p. 32.

[4] Sethe-Partsch, *Demotische Bürgschaftsurkunden* (Abhandl. d. Sächs. Ak. d. Wiss., phil-hist. Kl., 32), p. 41.

exact meaning of the Egyptian word which is rendered by Griffith somewhat freely as "to desire", is "to love". There is thus an almost complete parallelism between this provision, on the one hand, and the *ašar tarâmu* clause of the Susa deeds and section 150 of the Code of Hammourabi, on the other.

While originally the *ašar tarâmu* clause was used only in gifts of property by husband to wife and conferred upon the wife a limited power to leave the property to one of her sons, in the course of time this clause came to be used generally in deeds of conveyance of property and to mean an unlimited power to dispose of the property.[5] Accordingly, the word *râmu* in this clause acquired the meaning of "to desire". It is in this modified sense that an exact replica of the *ašar tarâmu* clause is found in the Aramaic papyri.[6] In Cowley, no. 8, for example, in which one Mahseiah makes a gift of property to his daughter Miptahiah, there occurs the following clause:אנתי שליטה בה מן יומא זנה ועד עלם ובניכי אחריכי למן זי רחמתי תנתנן (you have full rights over it from this day for ever, and your children after you. To whom you wish you may give it).

It is quite obvious that the words למן זי רחמתי תנתנן are but an Aramaic version of the *ašar tarâmu itaddin* clause. What

---

[5] The *ašar tarâmu* clause is used in this sense in a fragment of a deed from Susa quoted by Scheil (*Mémoires* etc., v. XXIV, p. 74), which reads: *a-ša -ar ta-ra-a-mu i-ta-di-in a-na ši-mi i-ta-di-in*. This is translated by Scheil as follows: "Où elle voudra elle donnera (ce bien, en cadeau); elle peut le donner contre un prix (c'est-a-dire le vendre)". The donee is given the general power to dispose of the property, by way of gift or by way of sale, to whomsoever she wishes.

The change in the meaning of the formula occurred perhaps in the following manner: first the formula, as in 379.39f., contained the phrase *ana alik arki* (to him who will come after, that is to one of her children after her death), then, as in 131.30, this phrase, for the mere sake of brevity, was left out, but the formula still retained its original meaning, and finally the abbreviated formula acquired the meaning of a general power to dispose of the property.

[6] APC, nos. 8.9, 13.8, 25.9. It should be noted that, as far as the writer was able to ascertain, nothing even remotely resembling this clause is found in the demotic Papyri.

is not so obvious is that by this clause the donee is given the
general power to dispose of the property at will, and that רחם =
râmu is used here in the sense of "to desire". But this becomes
abundantly clear from an examination of Cowley, no. 13, another
deed of gift by Mehaseiah to Miptahiah, which was written by
the same scribe as no. 8. In the main part of this document, lines
7-8, the scribe, with the conservatism so characteristic of his
profession, adheres faithfully to the archaic formula, saying:
דילכי הו ולבניכ[י] מן אחריכי ולמן זי רחמ[תי] תנתננה.
However, at the end of the document, line 16, where the
substance of this formula is repeated, he reverts to the usual
Aramaic, substituting the verbs צבי (to desire) and יהב (to give)
for רחם and נתן. He writes: דילכי הו עד עלם ולמן זי תצבין הבהי.
It requires a great deal of courage on the part of a scribe
to deviate from an old legal formula, consecrated by a long
tradition. But once some brave soul among the professional
scribes musters up enough courage to make a change dictated
by reason, though at first hesitatingly, using both the old and
the new form, the rest of his brethren begin to imitate him, until
finally the old form disappears and only the new remains. As
we shall presently see, this is apparently what happened in the
case of צבי and רחם in our formula.

The word צבי also occurs in what seems to be an adaptation
of the above-quoted Aramaic legal formula in Dan. 4, 14 (17). 22
(25). 29 (32), which reads: די שליט עליא במלכות אנושא ולמן די
יצבא יתננה. (that the most High ruleth in the kingdom of men,
and giveth it to whomsoever he will). Note the correspondence
between this verse and the formula from the Aramaic papyri.
In both the key-word שליט occurs and in both the power to
dispose of a thing at will is given as the main indicium of ownership of the thing. The author of the Book of Daniel apparently
adopted, without much change, a cliche from the legal formulary
which was common in his day. That this is so is indicated by the
fact that in 5,21 he apparently became aware that the formula
he was using did not quite fit his purpose, since the "kingdom of
men" is not a piece of property which is "given", and he changed

the formula to read: די שליט עליא במלכות אנשא ולמן די יצבא יהקים עליה (that the most high God ruleth in the kingdom of men, and that He appointeth over it whomsover he will).

A most remarkable parallel to the formula under discussion, as it appears in the Aramaic papyri, occurs in a source where one would least expect to find it. We are referring to Aristotle, Rhet. 1361a, where the following definition of ownership is given: τοῦ δὲ οἰκεῖα εἶναι ὅταν ἐφ' αὐτῷ ἦ ἀπαλλοτριῶσαι ἦ μή· λέγω δὲ ἀπαλλοτρίωσιν δόσιν καὶ πρᾶσιν (To have ownership of a thing is to be able to alienate it or not; by alienation I mean gift or sale). Long before Aristotle formulated this definition of ownership the scribes of Yeb, using precedents which were already then centuries old, prepared the way for it in pragmatic fashion. As we have seen above, in conveyances of property they invariably inserted a clause stating that the grantee shall have power to give the property to whomsoever he will. In Brooklyn 12,[7] a deed of conveyance of a house dated 402 B. C. E., it is stated (lines 23-24) that the grantee shall have power *to give or to sell* the house to whomsoever he will, which fully corresponds to the Aristotelian definition of ownership.

Is the parallelism just mentioned the result of a coincidence? The writer believes that it is not. There was apparently considerable traffic of ideas, especially in matters legal, between the Jewish colony of Elephantine and Greece, probably through the ancient Greek port of Naucratis in Egypt. This will perhaps account also for the Greek technical terms ἀρραβών (earnest) ὠνὴ καὶ πρᾶσις (purchase and sale) and for the expressions *buy for silver* and *sell for silver,* which will be discussed in the next chapter.

In the case of Aristotle's definition of ownership there is, in addition to the parallelism noted above, another indication of the influence of Aramaic legal terminology. The word ἀπαλλοτρίωσις (alienation), in the sense of *transfer, conveyance,* seems to be an Aramaism. Its equivalent in Aramaic — מרחק (alienation) — is useα a number of times in the Aramaic papyri in the same sense. It is highly significant that the Aramaic מרחק and the Greek ἀπαλλοτρίωσις as technical legal terms meaning conveyance of property, are each derived from a word meaning *strange,* the Aramaic word being [8] רחיק and the Greek being ἀλλότριος Conveyance of property is viewed as an estrangement of the grantor from the property conveyed. Thus, in Cowley 13.[9]7 (447 B. C. E.), a deed of conveyance of a house, the grantor says: זנה ביתא יהבתה לכי ורחקת מנה (this house I give to you and I am estranged from it). Similarly, in Brooklyn 3.[10] 10-11 (437

---

[8] The word רחיק is used a number of times in the Aramaic papyri in the sense of stranger and also in the sense of removed. See APC, 310 (Index) s. v. רחק

[9] APC, 37.

[10] APK, 154. Cf. P. BGU 405.11-13=SP 56 (release of a claim to a share in an instrument for grinding corn, dated 348 C. E.): "I accordingly acknowledge that I have no share in the afore-said instrument for grinding corn *but am estranged and alienated from it*" (ἄλλα ξένον με εἶναι καὶ ἀλλότριον αὐτῆς). It is not unlikely that the origin of the demotic *document of cession* is to be sought in the ספר מרחק (document of being estranged, distant) of the Aramaic papyri. Under Egyptian practice during the Ptolemaic period two documents were used to effect a sale of property — a *document of sale* and what Griffith calls a *document of cession.* See GCD, 118, 126. The Greek translation of these terms is συγγραφὴ πράσεως (document of sale) and συγγραφὴ ἀποστασίου (document of being distant), respectively. Griffith states that the earliest known example of a document of cession is one of the reign of Darius III, and, after mentioning the possibility that this type of document was introduced in Egypt under Greek influence, he says: "but *a priori* it seems more probable that it was a native growth, perhaps stimulated by the presence of business-like and influential foreigners in the country". It seems that the two documents referred to above correspond to the two stages in the conveyance of property — payment of the price and delivery of possession — which, as has been shown above (p. 9f.), are clearly discernible in the story of the purchase of the Cave of Machpelah. See also p. 140f., below.

In the light of what has been said above a troublesome passage in Cicero, *Topica* V, 28, may be satisfactorily explained. This passage reads: Abalienatio est eius rei quae mancipi est aut traditio alteri nexu aut in iure cessio... Hubbell's translation (H. M. Hubbell, tr., *Cicero, De inventione, de optimo genere oratorum, topica* [The Loeb Classical Library], p. 401) is as follows: "*Abalienatio* (transfer of property according to the forms of civil law) of a

B. C. E.), also a deed of conveyance of a house, the house is referred to as ביתא זנה זי אנחן זבן ויהבן לך ורחקן מנה (this house
which we sell and give to you and are estranged from it).

It should also be noted here that the verb רחק (to be far,
removed), with the preposition מן (from) referring to a person,
is used in the Aramaic papyri in the sense of *to release* or *renounce*
a claim against the person. In Cowley 14[11] (441 B. C. E.), which
Cowley calls "settlement of claim", and which should rather be
called "release of claim", the maker of the document says:
ורחקת מנכי מן יומא זנה ועד עלם (And I am removed from you
from this day and forever). In the endorsement the document is
called ספר מרחק (document of removal). Again, in Cowley 20.[12]
9-10 (420 B. C. E.), another release of a claim, the makers say
רחיקן אנחנה מנך מן יומא זנה ועד עלם (we are removed from
you from this day and forever). Significantly enough, the noun
ἀπαλλαγή (removal) is used by Demosthenes (33.3) in the sense
of a *release* and the verb ἀπαλλάττω (to remove) is used by him
(36. 25) in the sense of *to release*. This verb is also used in the
same sense by Plato, *The Laws*, 768c, and 915c.

Such, then, are the peregrinations of a legal formula: from
the Susa documents, through the Aramaic papyri, to Aristotle and
the Book of Daniel.

---

thing which is *mancipi* is either transfer with legal obligation (*mancipatio*) or
cesssion at law (fictitious suit)...". It seems that this passage is an adaptation
from that part of Aristotle's definition of ownership, quoted above, in which
alienation is defined. It should be translated into English as follows: "*Abalienatio*
of a thing which is *mancipi* is either transfer with purchase (See p. 10f., above)
or cession at law". It should be noted in this connection that three of the
Aramaic papyri (Cowley 6, 14, 25) which bear the designation ספר מרחק
on the *verso* are renunciations of rights to certain property, made by one party
to another before a court, that is they are *in iure cessiones*.

[11] APC, 42.
[12] *Ibid.*, 57f.

CHAPTER III

THE ARAMAIC PAPYRI AND GREEK LAW

In addition to the parallelisms between the Aramaic papyri and Greek sources discussed in the preceding chapter, there are some other evidences of contact between Greek law and early Jewish law. At least in the case of one important legal institution, that of *earnest*, there can be little doubt that it was taken over from a Jewish source. The Greek term — ἀρραβών — by which the institution is known, is derived, with but little change in form, from the Hebrew ערבון (pledge).[1] Speaking of this institution, San-Nicolo,[2] while recognizing its Semitic origin and the Hebrew derivation of the term by which it is designated in Greek sources from the 4th century onward, for some reason uses the vague geographical term *Syria* to indicate the place of its origin. However, no amount of equivocation can gloss over the fact that Gen. 38:17, where the term ערבון occurs, is a Jewish, not a Syrian, source. It seems that the Jewish colony of Elephantine was the medium through which the Hebrew term was conveyed to the Greeks. The term occurs in Cowley 10. 9 (456 B. C. E.) and Cowley correctly points to its Hebrew origin.

It is interesting to note in this connection that in the case of another legal institution, that of the double document, San-Nicolo[3] mentions *Syria and Palestine* as its possible source, citing Jer. 32:10ff. and adding that the "Aramaic" colonists of Elephantine may have brought this type of document from their home country to Egypt. It hardly needs to be said that the

---

[1] See GLS, 335; M. San-Nicolo, *Beiträge zur Rechtsgeschichte im Bereiche der Keilschriftlichen Rechtsquellen*, 201f. According to San-Nicolo, the term does not occur in Babylonian or Assyrian sources.

[2] *Ibid.*

[3] *Ibid.*, 128f. See p. 155f., below.

prophet Jeremiah was not a Syrian and that his compatriots, the colonists of Elephantine, were not Arameans.

Another indication of Oriental, possibly Jewish, influence on Greek law, again in the realm of the law of sale, may be seen in the term ὠνὴ καὶ πρᾶσις (purchase and sale). Pringsheim discusses at length this two-sided term, which occurs already in Herodotus 1, 153, and speculates on its legal significance.[4] An exact counterpart of this two-sided term — מקח וממכר (purchase and sale) — occurs quite frequently in the Mishnah and in other Talmudic sources.[5] That this is a Semitic language pattern can hardly be doubted. It corresponds to the Accadian *nadânu u maḥâru* (to give and take), to the Hebrew נשא ונתן (to carry away and to give) and to the Aramaic נסב ויהב (to take and give).[6]

Finally, an idiomatic expression, once more in the realm of sale, which occurs quite frequently in the Bible and twice in the Aramaic papyri seems to have found its way into Greek sources. The expression זבן בכסף (buy for silver, money) occurs in Brooklyn 9.3 and 12.4. This obviously corresponds to the familiar Biblical idiom קנה בכסף (buy for silver, money) and מכר בכסף (sell for silver, money).[7] This idiom, which sounds so natural to a student of the Bible, sounds strange to a student of ancient Greek law, when he finds it used in ancient Greek sources. It will be instructive to quote a recognized authority on the Greek law of sale on this point. "Sometimes" — says Pringsheim — "it does not seem sufficient to speak of selling, buying, sold. These terms are combined with that for the price, with ἀργύριον. The meaning of this strange usage is: to sell for money, to buy for money, bought for money".[8] Surely, when a Hebrew or an Aramaic idiom is translated literally into Greek it sounds an unfamiliar note in the strange milieu.

[4] GLS, 111ff.

[5] See, e. g., Mishnah, *Baba Metzia* 4:8; Tosefta, *Shabbath* 9:13 (ed. Zuckermandel, 120).

[6] See GB, 389b.

[7] See, e. g., Deut. 21:14; Isa. 43:24; Jer. 32:25, 44.

[8] GLS, 100.

CHAPTER IV

BROOKLYN 5 AND MANUMISSION WITH PARAMONE IN GREECE.

Brooklyn 5[1] is a deed of manumission, dated 427 B. C. E., in which one Meshullam b. Zakkur, a Jew of Yeb, manumits his woman slave *Tpmt* and her daughter Yehoyishima under an arrangement whereby the woman and her daughter are to serve (פלח) and support ((סבל)) the manumitting master and his son Zakkur after him during their respective lifetimes "as a son supports his father". This arrangement is, as Kraeling correctly points out,[2] similar to the Greek manumission with *paramone,* numerous examples of which occur in the Delphi inscriptions and elsewhere.[3] Kraeling also mentions a Babylonian document which "provides service to former master and mistress by the manumitted slave for the rest of their lives, but their children are declared not entitled to it"[4]

The fact that the same socio-legal institution, in substance, is found in Babylonia during the period of the First Dynasty, among the Jews of Elephantine in the 5th century B. C. E., and in Greece from the beginning of the 2nd century B.C.E., and probably earlier, is more than suggestive of the continuity, at least with respect to the institution of slavery, of Babylonian customary law in the Ancient World over a long period of time. But we need not rely upon similarity in substance alone. More significant are the similarities in form, in the language patterns into which the institution of manumission with a provision for

[1] APK, 180f.

[2] *Ibid.,* 186.

[3] See W. L. Westermann, *The Paramone as General Service Contract,* Journal of Juristic Papyrology, 2(1948), 9f.

[4] APK, 186.

continuing service is cast in Babylonia, among the Jews of Elephantine and in Greece. Besides the document of manumission with a provision for continuing service mentioned by Kraeling, there are several other Old-Babylonian manumission documents with a provision that the manumitted slave support his master during the latter's lifetime.[5] The *terminus technicus* which is used in these documents in the sense of *support* is *naśû* (= Hebrew נשא), the primary meaning of which is *to carry*.[6] In Brooklyn 5, the term used in the same sense is סבל, the primary meaning of which is likewise *to carry*.[7] The interchangeability of נשא and סבל stands out in bold relief in Isa. 46:4 (ואני אשא ואני אסבל) which, as the writer has pointed out elsewhere,[8] seems to have been adopted from legal phraseology of manumission documents.

In the Old-Babylonian document mentioned by Kraeling and referred to above, the freedwoman's duty of continuing service to her master and mistress during their respective lifetimes is expressed by the idiomatic phrase *to stand before*. In Ungnad-Koschaker's German translation: "Solange Wêdum-libur und Nin-Utu-mu leben, wird sie vor ihnen stehen".[9]

A similar idiom — עמד לפני — occurs a number of times in the Bible [10] and is rendered by the Targum by שמש. In Dan. 7:10 the terms קום קדם (to stand before) and שמש (to serve, attend to) occur side by side: אלף אלפים ישמשונה ורבו רבון קדמוהי יקומון. In Ex. 24:13 and in Nu. 11:28, the Hebrew משרת is rendered by the LXX as ὁ παρεστηκώς (one who stands by, beside) and by the Targum משמשנא (servant, attendant).

What has been said above with respect to the phrase *to stand before* leads us to a consideration of the exact meaning and origin of the Greek παραμένειν which is used in the Delphi inscriptions and elsewhere as a *terminus technicus* for the freed-

---

[5] See UAR, nos. 23, 24, 27, 29.
[6] See GB, 522b.
[7] See *ibid.*, 535a.
[8] Journal of Biblical Literature. 73 (1954), 237.
[9] A. Ungnad und P. Koschaker, *Hammurabis Gesetz*, 6, no. 1427.
[10] See, e. g., Nu. 16:9 and Deut. 10:8.

man's duty of continuing service to his master. Koschaker, discussing the legal significance of manumission with paramone, says:

> "Die Paramone legt, was schon im Worte enthalten ist, dem Freigelassenen die Verpflichtung auf, 'bei' dem Freilasser zu 'bleiben'. Das bedeutet juristisch die Aufhebung seiner Freizügigkeit, um so mehr als die Paramone in der Regel mit seiner Aufnahme in die Hausgemeinschaft des Freilassers verbunden ist. Daher wird umgekehrt die Vollfreiheit durch Redewendungen bezeichnet, die Gewicht darauf legen auszudrücken, dass der Freigelassene nicht bloss tun kann, was er will, sondern auch bleiben und gehen kann, wo und wohin er will".[11]

> (The paramone imposes upon the freedman, what is already implicit in the word, the duty of 'remaining by' the manumitter. Legally, this means that he is deprived of his freedom of movement, all the more so since the paramone is as a rule connected with his reception into the household of the manumitter. By way of contrast, full freedom is characterized by expressions which lay stress upon the fact that the freedman may not only do what he will but that he may also stay or depart wherever and whither he will).

However, in the light of the parallels discussed above, particularly of the Old-Babylonian manumission document with a provision for continuing service, it would seem that the crucial word παραμένειν is to be rendered as *stand by, beside,* and not as *remain by,* and that in manumission documents and the like it is used, as its Accadian, Hebrew and Aramaic equivalents are used, in the sense of *to serve, attend to.* The primary meaning of παραμένειν, , like that of παριστάναι, as given in Liddell-Scott-Jones, *Greek-English Lexicon,* is: *to stand by, beside.*

---

[11] KRU, 25.

While Koschaker's interpretation of παραμένειν as *remain by* is, as shown above, somewhat inaccurate, he seems to be right in his assertion that manumission with *paramone* involved the reception of the freedman into the manumitter's household and the consequent limitation upon his freedom of movement. This was probably due to the fact that originally in Babylonia adoption of the slave by the master was the usual method of effecting manumission. Traces of this method are still discernible in Brooklyn 5[12] and 7[13]. In Brooklyn 5.11-12 it is stated that *Tpmt* and Yehoyishima are to support Meshullam and his son Zakkur "as a son supports his father". In Brooklyn 7.4-5 Yehoyishima is given in marriage by her "brother" Zakkur. Zakkur was not Yehoyishima's natural brother, as she was apparently begotten by Ananiah b. Azariah, *Tpmt's* husband, and not by Meshullam b. Zakkur. Meshullam's son Zakkur was styled Yehoyishima's "brother" by reason of the relationship which was created between them by the manumission of Yehoyishma on the part of Meshullam.[14] Traces of manumission by adoption have also been noted by Welles for Greece.[15]

The limitation upon the freedman's freedom of movement

---

[12] APK, 180.

[13] *Ibid.* 204.

[14] With regard to Zakkur's "brotherhood" to Yehoyishma, see APK, 201. All of the difficulties noted there by Kraeling are resolved, if we assume that this "brotherhood" was not one of blood.

The institution of manumission by adoption is also reflected in Brooklyn 8 (416 B.C.E.). In this document Uriah b. Mahseiah promises to Zakkur b. Meshullam not to reduce to slavery the boy Yedoniah, whom Meshullam had given to Uriah by another instrument, but that the boy shall be his, Uriah's, son. It is interesting to note that in P. Oxy. 1206, a Greek papyrus of 325 C.E. representing a deed of adoption of a two-year-old boy, there is (lines 10-11) a similar provision that the boy shall not be reduced to slavery, though no manumission was involved there, the boy having been "well-born". Cf. Ex. 21:8: לעם נכרי לא ימשל למכרה (to sell her unto a foreign people he shall have no power). Like selling *trans Tiberim* in ancient Rome, selling "unto a foreign people" means selling into outright slavery.

[15] See C. Bradford Welles, *Manumission and Adoption*, AHDO 3 (1949), 507f.

under manumission with *paramone* is, as Koschaker suggests, the reason why in Greek manumission documents with full freedom to the slave there usually occurs a formula granting the manumitted slave freedom "to go whither he pleases" (ἀποτρέχειν οἷς κα θέλῃ). [16] Interestingly enough, this formula has striking parallels in ancient Semitic sources. In the Middle-Assyrian Laws, tablet A, col. IV, l. 70 it is said of a woman who is free of marital and parental ties that "she may go whither she pleases" (*ašar ḥaditûni tallak*).[17] Similarly, in P. Sayce-Cowley G. (Cowley no. 15), ll. 25, 28-29, it is said of a divorced woman "and she may go whither she pleases" (זי אן[ל] ותהך[18] צבית). In the Aramaic papyrus, as in the Middle-Assyrian Laws, this formula implies freedom from parental control as well as from the marital tie. That this is so may be seen from the marriage document of the above-mentioned Yehoyishma (Brooklyn 7), in which it is stated (line 28) that in case of divorce she "shall go to her father's house" (ותהך לבית אבוה),[19] that is to the house presided over by her "brother" Zakkur by whom she was given in marriage. Miphtahiah, the bride in Cowley 15, was a freeborn woman and therefore upon being divorced would become free from both the marital ties and parental authority, while Yehoyishma was a freedwoman who upon being divorced would become free of the marital tie only, returning to the house of her *paterfamilias* to whom she owed the duty of *service* and *support*.

In addition to the term παραμένειν the Greek manumission documents show some other marks of Oriental influence. Koschaker [20] has called attention to the parallelism between the formula in Greek manumission documents without *paramone*, and in releases from *paramone*, granting the slave, or the freedman,

[16] See KRU, 25, n. 4.

[17] See G. R. Driver and John C. Miles, *The Assyrian Laws*, 224, 403. See also *id., The Babylonian Laws*, vol. I, 398, n. 6.

[18] APC, 45.

[19] APK, 206.

[20] KRU, 74.

authority over himself (κυριεύειν αὐτοσαυτοῦ) and the formula in a certain Old-Babylonian manumission document in which a woman manumits her woman slave on condition that she (the freedwoman) support her (the mistress) during her lifetime, adding that upon the mistress's death the freedwoman "is free, belongs to herself" (*el-li-it ša ra-ma--ni-ša ši-i*).[21] The writer has pointed out elsewhere [22] that the formula of this Old-Babylonian document, in both of its parts, is discernible in Jer. 34:16:

ותשבו ותחללו את שמי ותשבו איש את עבדו ואיש את שפחתו אשר

שלחתם חפשים לנפשם — and that an almost exact replica thereof occurs in Mishnah Gittin 9:3, where it is stated: ("The essential גופו של גט שחרור הרי את בת חורין הרי את לעצמך formula of a writ of emancipation is, Lo, thou art a freedwoman; lo, thou belongest to thyself").

The Legal Niceties Involved in Manumission

In Brooklyn 5.8-10, there occurs the following formula:

ואנתי שביקה מן טלא לסמשא ויהישמע ברתכי וגבר אחרן לא שליט עליכי ועל יהישמע ברתכי ואנתי שביקה לאלהא.

This is translated by Kraeling as follows: "and thou art freed before(?) the Sun, as well as Yehoyishma, thy daughter, and another man shall not have power over thee and over Yehoyishma, thy daughter, but thou art freed to the god". Taking the word סמשא as referring to Shamash, the sun-god, Kraeling [23] has drawn from this formula some rather unfounded conclusions concerning the religion of the Jews of Elephantine, casting doubt upon the purity of their monotheism. However, a careful analysis of this clause, in all of its parts, will reveal that it does not contain the slightest suggestion of the recognition of the divinity of Shamash by the Jews of Elephantine.

In the first place, מן טלא לסמשא does not mean "before the

---

[21] UAR, n. 29.

[22] See BIES, 12 (1953), 101. A résumé of the article in English is given by R. Taubenschlag in Journal of Juristic Papyrology, VII-VIII (1954), p. 385.

[23] APK, 87, 178.

Sun", but "from shadow (darkness) to sunshine", slavery having
been associated with darkness and freedom with sunshine.[24]
Indeed, it may very well be that the Aramaic and late Hebrew
שמש (to serve, to attend to), the etymology of which is obscure,[25]
is traceable to the institution of manumission which was conceived
of as a release from darkness to sunshine and which involved,
as a transitional stage, the freedman's becoming his master's
servant, attendant, instead of his slave.

As to the phrase אנתי שביקה לאלהה, its legal significance
will become clear only upon a correct understanding of the
meaning and import of the key-word שבק. In his comment
upon this word, which also occurs in line 4 of Brooklyn 5,
Kraeling says: "This verb ordinarily means 'to leave' as in A. P.
27:1, 'We did not leave our posts', but in legal texts it must have
a special nuance, as our papyrus shows".[26] But legal terms require
more precise definition in order to understand their import. In
legal terminology, the Aramaic שבק, like the Accadian *ezêbu*
and the Hebrew עזב, means *to abandon, to abandon control and
authority over someone.* The Accadian, Hebrew and Aramaic
words, respectively, occur in this sense in the legal terminology
of divorce — which is closely related to that of manumission —
in the Code of Hammurabi, sec. 138, and elsewhere,[27] in Isa. 60:15

---

[24] See S. Smith, *Isaiah Chapters XL—LV,* The Schweich Lectures, 1940
(1944), 55 and 164, n. 28. Cf. מעבדות לחרות . . . ומאפלה לאור גדול (from
slavery to freedom . . . and from darkness to great light) in Mishnah *Pesahim*
9:5. This point, as well as most of the other points concerning Brooklyn 5,
was made by the writer in a paper entitled *Some Legal Aspects of the Brooklyn
Museum Aramaic Papyri,* read before the American Academy for Jewish Research on Oct. 23, 1954. The same point was made independently by H. L.
Ginsberg (Journal of the American Oriental Society 74, 158) and by Z. Falk
(Journal of Jewish Studies, October, 1954).

[25] See GB, 849b, 928b.

[26] APK. 183.

[27] See UAR, 522. Cf. the term *šûzubûtu* in the tablets from Alalakh which
is very aptly rendered by Speiser (Journal of the American Oriental Society
74, p. 21) as "freed-man", from Accadian *ezêbu* (to abandon).

In P. Petr. I 16(1), a fragmentary papyrus representing a will from
Crocodilopolis dated 237 B.C.E., there is a provision by which the testator

(עזובה ושנואה) and in Mishnah, Gittin, 9:3, where the bill of divorce is referred to as אגרת שבוקין (letter of abandonment).

The phrase אנתי שביקה לאלהה is in line with the legal conception of the act of manumission as abandonment of the slave by the master. The master could not grant liberty to the slave as a gift of his (the slave's) own self, because the slave had no legal capacity to acquire such gift. Whatever the slave acquired belonged to his master. All the master could therefore do was *to abandon* the slave. But if he just abandoned him, without more, another person might take possession of the slave. The master therefore abandoned the slave to God so as to prevent others from taking possession of him. This is the meaning of the phrase וגבר אחרן לא שליט עליכי ועל יהישמע ברתכי ("and another man shall not have power over thee and over Yehoyishma, thy daughter") which immediately precedes the phrase under discussion. A similar idea is perhaps implicit in Lev. 25:55:

כי לי בני ישראל עבדים עבדי הם אשר הוצאתי אותם מארץ מצרים.
("For unto Me the children of Israel are servants; they are My servants whom I brought forth out of the land of Egypt: I am the Lord your God".)

apparently manumits his slave, named Semele, and her children. The operative word which is used in the document (line 15) in the sense of *to manumit* is καταλείπω (to leave, abandon) — a word which is not found anywhere else used in this sense. This has given rise to differences of opinion among papyrologists as to the nature of the provision in question. Contrary to the opinion of Mahaffy, the editor of the Petrie papyri, who takes the provision to be one of manumission, Arangio-Ruiz (*La successione testamentaria secondo i papiri greco-egizii*, 102) holds that by this provision the testator did not manumit Semele and her children but constituted them heirs of his property. See also Kreller, *Erbrechtliche Untersuchungen auf Grund der graeco-ägyptischen Papyrusurkunden* 352, n. 34. It seems that the solution of the difficulty lies in the fact that καταλείπω in the sense of *to manumit* is a literal translation of the Aramaic שבק (to leave, abandon) which is used in Brooklyn 5 in this sense. It is to be noted that in P. Petr. I 16(1) there is a provision for a *paramone* of the manumitted slave during the lifetime of the testator. This makes it strikingly similar to Brooklyn 5 in which the manumision is also to take effect after the manumitter's death (line 4: שבקתכי במותי) and in which there is also a provision for *paramone*.

In his discussion of "the essential character of manumission", Buckland says:

> "Manumission is not transfer of *dominium;* it is creation of a *civis,* and release not merely from ownership, but from the capacity of being owned. This seems a better way in which to express the matter than to speak, as Karlowa does, of the acquisition of personality. The Romans of an early age did not think of the matter, still less would they have felt Karlowa's difficulty that if the slave is a mere *res* he cannot acquire, and manumission is an impossibility. This sort of subtlety is of a later time, as is his solution that the man acquires by virtue of a derivative personality, based on that of his master".[28]

It seems, however, that this sort of subtlety is an ancient one. Indeed, the form of manumission known as *manumissio inter amicos* was apparently designed to overcome precisely this difficulty of the slave's lack of capacity to acquire anything, including his own liberty. It was for this reason that manumission was effected through the intervention of a third party. In Brooklyn 5, it was God to whom the slave was abandoned; in the Greek manumissions from Delphi, it was the god Apollo to whom the slave would be sold;[29] and at a later time, in the Mishnah and in Roman sources, a human being, apparently a friend of the master and the slave, would be called upon to serve as an intermediary between them for the purpose of effecting manumission of the slave. There are two documents from Egypt representing manumissions *inter amicos* extant, one of 221[30] and the other of 291 [31] C. E., and in both of them a large ransom is

---

[28] W. W. Buckland, *The Roman Law of Slavery* (1908), 715.

[29] See the article by W. L. Westermann cited in n. 3, above.

[30] P. F. Girard, *Textes de droit romain* (5th ed., 1923), 854.

[31] P. Oxy. 1205. The phrase *inter amicos* is generally interpreted as meaning "before witnesses". See W. W. Buckland, *A Text-Book of Roman Law* (2nd ed. 1950), 77. But F. Schultz (*Classical Roman Law,* 84) interprets this

paid to the manumitting master by a third party, In Mishnah
Kiddushin 1:3, it is stated:

עבד כנעני נקנה בכסף ובשטר ובחזקה וקונה את עצמו
בכסף ע"י אחרים ובשטר ע"י עצמו, דברי רבי מאיר.
וחכמים אומרים, בכסף ע"י עצמו ובשטר ע"י אחרים
ובלבד שיהא הכסף משל אחרים.

("A Canaanitish bondman is acquired by money
or by writ or by usucaption; and he acquires himself by money through others and by writ (of
manumission) through himself. So Rabbi Meir. But
the Sages say: By money through himself or by
writ (of manumission) through others, provided
that the money is that of others".)

We shall not enter here into a discussion of the reason for
the difference of opinion between Rabbi Meir and the Sages.
It is sufficient for our purpose to point out that with respect
to manumission "by money" Rabbi Meir's opinion fully accords
with the practice found in the two manumission documents just
mentioned.

Greek Terms in the Aramaic Papyri

While some of the characteristic features of the institution
of slavery in Greece point to an Oriental origin, it seems that as
a result of an active commerce between the Jews of Elephantine
and Greeks, the former adopted and used some Greek terms
pertaining to slavery. This gives us a clue to the understanding

---

phrase as meaning *inter dominum et servum ut inter amicos*. It would perhaps
be more correct to say *inter dominum et servum et tertiam partem ut inter amicos*. The whole procedure seems to have been a friendly arrangement between the
master, the servant and the third party. It is hardly believable that in each of
the two cases of manumission *inter amicos*, of which the documents are extant,
the cne of 221 and the other of 291 C. E., the third party was some
philantropist who supplied the ransom money out of his own pocket. It is
far more reasonable to suppose that the money came out of the slave's pocket,
and that the third party acted only as a straw man whose sole function was
to make the transaction conform to the legal niceties involved in the grant of
liberty to a slave.

of two significant terms occurring in Brooklyn 12[32] (402-401 B. C.E.) which have puzzled Kraeling and others. This document is a deed of conveyance of certain house property by Anani b. Azariah and his wife *Tpmt*. In line 24 thereof the woman is referred to as ותפמת אנתתי זי הות גוא למשלם בר זכור which is rendered by Kraeling as "and *Tmpt*, my wife, who was hand-maiden(?) to Meshullam b. Zakkur'.

Kraeling indulges in a good deal of speculation with respect to the difficult word גוא. He cites the expression גויא מהימנא from the Palmyrene inscriptions (Jean Cantineau, *Inventaire des inscriptions de Palmyre*, 1, no. 193) and the Jewish Aramaic גוא (belly) and tentatively arrives at the meaning of "slave concubine or handmaiden?".[33] However, the solution of the difficulty is very simple: the Aramaic word does not mean here "belly" or "hand-maiden"; it means *body*, one of its common meanings.[34] As is well known, the Greek word σῶμα (body) is often used in the sense of slave.[35] גוא (body) in the sense of slave is thus a literal translation of the Greek σῶμα. Similarly, גויא מהימנא in the Palmyrene inscriptions means *faithful slave*.[36] Cf. לא כן עבדי משה בכל ביתי נאמן הוא (My servant Moses is not so; he is trusted in all My house) — Nu. 12:7.

In line 11 of the same document *Tpmt* is referred to as פריפת of Meshullam b. Zakkur. In his comment on this word Kraeling says: "It is new that *Tpmt* is called פריפת (or פדיפת) of Meshullam b. Zakkur. Erichsen suggests connecting the word with demotic *pr-ip.t*, 'workhouse', and thinks it designates the slave as an inmate of it".[37] However, Erichsen's suggestion cannot

---

[32] APK, 270f.

[33] *Ibid.*, 278f.

[34] See JDT, 216a *s. v.*

[35] See Liddell-Scott-Jones, *A Greek-English Lexicon s. v.*

[36] F. Rosenthal's (*Die Aramäistische Forschung seit Th. Nöldekes Veröffent-lichungen*, 98, n. 2) explanation of the term as representing a euphemistic description of a eunuch ("Der Getreue, zum Innern des Hauses Gehörige") is as untrue as it is ingenious.

[37] APK, 277.

be considered acceptable. At the time of the writing of this document (402-401 B. C. E.) *Tpmt* was no longer a slave. She had long since been enfranchised by Meshullam b. Zakkur, as shown by Brooklyn 5,[38] which is dated some 25 years before Brooklyn 12. The word seems to be a transcription into Aramaic of the Greek θρεπτή a word which is especially used with respect to slaves reared in a house.[39] Even after *Tpmt* was manumitted she did not cease to be a θρεπτή of Meshullam b. Zakkur.

It should be noted here that in our document (ll.5 and 14), which, as noted above, is a deed of conveyance of house property, the price paid for the property is expressed in Greek staters (כסף יון סתתרי 6), which is a sure indication of Greek influence. Greek influence is also discernible in the Aramaic papyri at a somewhat earlier time than the date of Brooklyn 12. In Cowley 20. 4 (420 B. C. E.); 27. 4 (c. 412 B. C. E.); 30. 5 (408 B. C.), there occurs a word פרתרך which, as is apparent from the context, signifies a title of a high official. Cowley, who transcribes this word as *fratarak*, says with respect thereto: "From OP (Old-Persian) *fratara* 'prior superior', and so 'governor'.[40] Since the official in question was Persian, Cowley concluded that the title he bore must also be Persian. It did not occur to him that a Persian official might bear a Greek title. It seems, however, that the word is to be transcribed as *protarche,* and that it is the Greek title πρωτάρχης.[41]

---

[38] *Ibid.,* 178f.

[39] See Liddell-Scott-Jones, *ibid., s. v.* Cf. חניכיו ילידי ביתו in Gen. 14:14.

[40] APC, 59.

[41] The importance of Brooklyn 5 as putting an entirely new aspect on the question of manumission in Greece may be illustrated by a reference to A. Cameron's article *Inscriptions Relating to Sacral Manumission and Confession* in Harvard Theological Review XXXII (1939), 143ff. At p. 146 the author says: "The practice of attaching conditions to manumission is typically Greek", which, of course, it is not. At p. 145 he cites a manumission inscription from Edessa in which "the slave is to support his mistress and remain with her till her death", which is precisely the condition attached to the manumission in Brooklyn 5 and in the Old-Babylonian manumission documents. Finally, at p.

The adoption and use of Greek terms by the Jews of Elephantine in the 5th century B. C. E. seems to indicate that the traffic of ideas between Greeks and the Jews of Elephantine, to which reference has been made above, moved in both directions.

155 he cites "sacral manumissions" in which verbs meaning *to release* (to the deity) are used. This corresponds to אנתי שביקה לאלהה (you are abandoned, released, to God) of Brooklyn 5.10.

CHAPTER V

MARRIAGE CONTRACTS IN ANCIENT EGYPT IN THE LIGHT OF JEWISH SOURCES

In an article [1] published some years ago, the present writer called attention to a remarkable similarity between a certain clause occurring in some demotic marriage contracts of the late Ptolemaic period and Mishnah Ketubot, 9,5. The clause in question reads: "I shall not be able to require an oath from thee in the house of judgment on account of the right of thy woman's property above (named), saying 'thou didst not bring them to my house in thy hand'" (Adler Dem. 14 and Ryl. 16). The pertinent part of Mishnah, Ketubot, 9,5, reads: "If he declared to her in writing, 'I will require of thee neither vow nor oath,' he may not exact of her an oath. . ." (Danby, The Mishnah, p. 258).

Upon further study and research, the writer has found that the above similarity between the demotic marriage contracts and the Mishnah does not represent an isolated instance of parallelism between marriage contracts from Egypt, demotic and Greek, and Jewish sources, Biblical and post-Biblical, bearing on the subject of marriage, but that from the late 4th century B. C. E. onward there is a whole series of such parallelisms.

We shall begin with the demotic marriage contracts. A document of the reign of Alexander IV reads, in part, as follows:

> "If I abandon thee as wife, and hate thee, and love (?) another woman more (?) than thee, I will give (thee) 10 (pieces of) silver, making 50 staters,

[1] Jacob J. Rabinowitz, *Some Remarks on the Evasion of the Usury Laws in the Middle Ages*, Harvard Theological Review, v. XXXVII, p. 52, n. 5.

making 10 (pieces of) silver again. My eldest son
is thine eldest son, the owner of all of everything
that belongeth to me and of those things that I shall
gain, of house, land, revenue (?), slave, female slave,
silver, copper, clothing, ox, ass, small cattle, property
in any chamber (?)."[2]

An analysis of the contents of this portion of the document
and of the technical terms used therein will reveal that it follows
closely Deut. 21, 15-17:

"15. If a man have two wives, the one beloved, and
the other hated, and they have borne him children,
both the beloved and the hated; and if the first-born
son be hers that was hated; 16. then it shall be, in
the day that he causeth his sons to inherit that
which he hath, that he may not make the son of
the beloved the first-born before the son of the
hated, who is the first-born; 17. but he shall acknowledge the first-born, the son of the hated, by
giving him a double portion of all that he hath; for
he is the first-fruits of his strength; the right of the
first-born is his."

In the first place, the word for *hate* is used in the Bible and
in the Aramaic papyri in the technical sense of *divorce*. To quote
from Cowley:[3] "שנא ... is a legal term for 'divorce.' Staerk
quotes an Egyptian document of the fourth century B. C. in
which 'hate' is similarly used. In Hebrew cf. Deut. 21, 15, etc."
The word *hated* in Deut. 21, 15, as Cowley, quite correctly, seems
to suggest, means *divorced*. The phrase *"hate thee and love
another woman"* in the demotic document thus corresponds to
the phrase "the one beloved and the other hated" in Deut. 21, 15.

---

[2] F. Ll. Griffith, *Catalogue of the Demotic Papyri in the John Rylands
Library*, v. III, pp. 114-115. The sum of 50 staters is strikingly similar to the
50 shekel of the Biblical *mohar,* which in post-Biblical times developed into the
ketubah. See Liddell-Scott-Jones, *Greek-English Lexicon* s. v στατήρ, citing Matt
17:27, where the shekel is referred to as a stater.

[3] APC, p. 28.

Secondly, the term *abandon* is characteristic of the technical language of divorce in Accadian (ezêbu), Hebrew (עָזַב) and Aramaic (שבק). The Accadian term occurs, for example, in the Code of Hammurabi, sec. 138,[4] the Hebrew term, in combination with *hated,* in Isaiah, 60, 15, and the Aramaic, in the formula of divorce quoted in Mishnah, Gittin, 9, 3, where the bill of divorce is referred to as אגרת שבוקין (letter of abandonment).[5]

Finally, the provision "My eldest son is thine eldest son" cannot but mean that even if the husband divorces his wife and marries another woman, the first-born son of the first wife, and not that of the second wife, shall be deemed the first-born son of the husband with respect to the right of inheritance. This, it will readily be seen, is but a paraphrase of Deut. 21, 16-17, quoted above.

Another demotic marriage contract which bears several marks of a close relationship with Jewish sources, this time post-Biblical, is one dated in the year 176 B. C. E. This document reads, in part, as follows:

> "Hath said X to Y 'Thou hast given me 50 silver (pieces) of the treasury of P'tah refined ... it is thou who shalt be entitled to the security (?) of thy bread and clothing, and it shall be at my charge, and I will give it thee without being able to say to thee 'Receive thy endowment.' On the day when thou preferrest to receive it, I will give it to thee on it. Everything that I have or shall acquire (is) the pledge of thy endowment."[6]

There are several clauses in this document which correspond to the Jewish *ketubah* (marriage settlement). In the first place, the amount of 50 sliver (pieces) corresponds to the amount of 200 zuz = 50 shekel prescribed in Mishnah, Ketubot, 1, 2, as

---

[4] See also UAR, p. 522.

[5] See JDT, p. 1515b. Danby (DM, p. 319) renders this term somewhat less precisely as "letter of dismissal".

[6] H. Thompson, *A Family Archive from Siut,* p. 25.

the marriage settlement for a virgin. This amount is based upon the Biblical *mohar*, which was likewise 50 shekel.[7] Secondly, the husband's obligation to furnish food and clothing to the wife has an exact counterpart in Talmudic sources, where it is said to be based on Exod. 21, 10. (See below.) Thirdly, the clause in which the husband pledges all his property for the wife's endowment has a close parallel in the Talmud. Indeed, this clause can hardly be understood without the aid of the Talmudic parallel. What is meant by the provision that the husband shall not be able to say to the wife "Receive thy endowment"? What would be the purpose of the husband's saying so? What possible end could the husband accomplish by forcing upon his wife payment of the endowment before she demanded it? The answer to these questions is found in a Talmudic passage which purports to relate the history of the Jewish *ketubah,* and which reads as follows:

> "At first they used to give merely a wrttien undertaking in respect of the *ketubah* of a virgin for two hundred *zuz* and in respect of that of a widow for a *maneh,* and consequently they grew old and could not take any wives. It was then ordained that the amount of the *ketubah* was to be deposited in the wife's father's house. At any time, however, when the husband was angry with her he used to tell her, 'Go to your *ketubah.*' It was ordained, therefore, that the amount of the *ketubah* was to be deposited in the house of her father-in-law ... Still, whenever the husband had occasion to be angry with his wife he would say to her, 'Take your *ketubah* and go.' It was then that Simeon b. Shetah ordained that the husband must insert the pledging clause, 'All my property is mortgaged to your *ketubah.*' "[8]

From this passage it appears that the pledging clause was

---

[7] See Exod. 22:15-16; Deut. 22:29.
[8] BT, *Kethubot.*

introduced in order to prevent quick divorce by the husband in a fit of anger. When the amount settled by the husband upon the wife is kept as a trust fund and is readily available, it is always easy for the husband to refer the wife to the fund and dismiss her. However, when the husband, instead of laying aside a trust fund for the wife, assumes an obligation towards her and pledges his property therefor, he cannot easily dismiss her, for it is not always easy for him to raise the cash necessary to discharge the obligation and free his property from her lien. Accordingly, in the demotic document quoted above, the husband in effect says to the wife: "I shall not be able to dismiss you by saying 'Take your endowment and go'; all my property is pledged for your endowment."

It should be noted that on the whole the demotic document under discussion seems to confirm the Talmudic tradition relating to the development of the Jewish marriage settlement, though in one point, that ascribing the introduction of the pledging clause to Simeon b. Shetah (1st century B. C. E.) this tradition seems to be inaccurate. The pledging clause was apparently introduced in the Jewish *ketubah* long before the time of Simeon b. Shetah.

It may well be, however, that Simeon b. Shetah, who, according to a Talmudic tradition (PT, Nazir, 5:3), fled from the wrath of Alexander Jannaeus, spent some time in exile in Egypt, where he became acquainted with the pledging clause in the marriage document which had been in use there for a long time, and that upon his return to Palestine he introduced this clause into the marriage document of Palestinian Jewry.

We now come to a consideration of some marriage contracts from Egypt written in Greek. Three such marriage contracts of the pre-Augustan era — P. Eleph. 1 (311 B. C. E.), P. Gen. 21 (2nd century B. C. E.) and P. Tebt. 104 (92 B. C. E.)—contain a provision to the effect that it shall not be lawful for the husband to marry another wife or to have children by another woman. In P. Eleph. 1, lines 8—9, for example, this provision reads:

μὴ ἐξέστω δὲ Ἡρακλείδηι γυναῖκα ἄλλην ἐπεισάγεσθαι
ἐφ' ὕβρει Δημητρίας μηδὲ τεκνοποιεῖσθαι ἐξ ἄλλης
γυναικὸς

Taubenschlag,[9] relying upon these papyri, states: "... the
express prohibition of polygamy in many Greek marriage contracts
of the pre-Augustan era must be regarded as proof that even
Greek parties were not legally forbidden to practice polygamy."
But the question arises: from whom did the Greeks in Egypt
adopt the practice of legal polygamy, which was unknown in their
homeland? One might be inclined to say that this practice,
together with the express provision in the marriage contract
prohibiting it, was adopted by the Greeks from the Egyptians.
However, the question of whether or not the practice of polygamy
was permissible among the ancient Egyptians is itself a debatable
one.[10] Besides — and this is of decisive importance for the solution
of the problem of the origin of the provision under discussion —
none of the available demotic marriage contracts contains anything even remotely resembling such a provision.

The solution of the problem of the origin of the provision
in question in the Greco-Egyptian marriage contracts is furnished
by the Aramaic papyri stemming from the Jewish military colony
in Elephantine. Two of these papyri, representing marriage con-

---

[9] R. Taubenschlag, *The Law of Greco-Roman Egypt in the Light of the
Papyri*, p. 78.

[10] In support of the opinion that polygamy was permissible in ancient
Egypt, Taubenschlag (*ibid.* p. 78, n. 4) cites Erman (Z f. äg. Sp. XXX, 63)
to the effect that the secondary wife was called in ancient Egypt *hated* (*msdt*)
and that in Rabbinic literature the secondary wife was called *enemy*. With
respect to *enemy*, there are two inaccuracies in Erman's assertion. First, the
term צרה, which he undoubtedly had in mind, does not mean *secondary wife*,
but *rival*. When a man has two wives, one is the צרה (rival) of the other.
Secondly, the word צרה in this sense is Biblical, not only Rabbinic. It occurs
in I. Sam. 1:6. With respect to the term *hated*, as applied to a wife in ancient
Egypt, it seems, in view of the evidence discussed in the text of this chapter,
that its correct meaning is *divorced*, not *secondary*.

tracts dated 441[11] and 420[12] B. C. E., respectively, contain a provision which is almost identical with that of the Greco-Egyptian marriage contracts. In the first one of these papyri, it reads: "And I shall have no right to say I have another wife besides Miphtahiah and other children than the children whom Miphtahiah shall bear to me." It is quite apparent that this provision, in both of its parts, that relating to marrying another woman and that relating to having children by another woman, is substantially the same as that quoted above from P. Eleph. 1. That such similarities do not occur by chance hardly needs to be said.

Another provision in the above-mentioned Greco-Egyptian marriage contracts which bears a striking resemblance to Jewish law and practice on the subject is that in which the husband undertakes to supply the proper necessaries to the wife. In P. Eleph. 1, this provision reads: παρεχέτω δὲ Ἡρακλείδης Δημητρίαι ὅσα προσήκει γυναικὶ ἐλευθέραι πάντα. In the other two Greek papyri mentioned above the provision in question is more elaborate. In P. Tebt. 104 it reads: τὰ δὲ [δ]έοντα π[ά]ντα καὶ τὸν [ἱμ]ατισμὸν καὶ τἆλλα ὅσα προσήκει γυναικὶ γαμετῆι παρεχέσθω Φιλίσκος Ἀπολλωνίαν. . . . This is in close agreement with what is known from the Talmud on the subject of the husband's obligations towards his wife. These obligations are derived by the Tannaim [13] from that part of Exod. 21, 10, which reads: "her food, her raiment, and her marriage duty shall he not diminish." There are three items in this passage — *food, raiment,*

---

[11] APC 15.31-33. The similarity between this provision in the Aramaic papyrus and the corresponding provision in P. Tebt. 104 has already been noted by Cowley at p. 50.

[12] APK 7. 36.

[13] BT, *Kethubot,* 47b; *Mekilta de Rabbi Ishmael* (ed. Lauterbach), v. 3, p. 27. in accordance with the Talmudic interpretation of Exod. 21:10, the standard form of the Jewish *ketubah* contains a clause enumerating the three items of marital duty. See Maimonides, *Mishneh Torah, Ybbum Ve-Halitzah,* 4, 33. For an English translation of this form, see McClintock and Strong, *Cyclopedia of Biblical, Theological and Ecclesiastical Literature,* v. 5, p. 776.

and *marriage duty* — the last item, having reference to intimacy between husband and wife. When we examine closely the provision just quoted from P. Tebt. 104 it appears that there too three items are enumerated, namely, *necessaries, clothing,* and *whatever else is proper for a wedded wife.* The last item is apparently a veiled allusion to intimacy between husband and wife. There is thus a striking similarity between this provision and Exod. 21, 10, as traditionally interpreted in Jewish law. This similarity becomes a virtual identity when we compare the provision in question with Exod. 21, 10, as rendered by the LXX. The Hebrew שארה is rendered as τὰ δέοντα, כסותה is rendered as τὸν ἱματισμόν, and ועונתה is rendered as καὶ τὴν ὁμιλίαν αὐτῆς.

What are the conclusions to be drawn from all of the above parallelisms? There are, of course, three possibilities, namely: 1. That these parallelisms are due to the fact that both Egyptian and Jewish jurists and scribes derived their legal rules and formulae from a common source. 2. That the Jews copied from the Egyptians. 3. That the Egyptians copied from the Jews. The writer believes that, upon the evidence, the last possibility is the one that is indicated. He has been led to this belief by the following considerations:

1. The Book of Deuteronomy preceded the fourth century B. C. E. marriage contract from Egypt, quoted above, by centuries, and during these centuries there is apparently nothing in Egyptian marriage contracts resembling the clauses of this contract.

2. The provision in the Aramaic marriage contracts stemming from the Jewish military colony in Elephantine concerning the husband's marrying another woman and having children by another woman preceded the similar provision in the Greek marriage contract of 311 B. C. E., also from Elephantine, by over a century, and no such provision appears in demotic marriage contracts of any period. As is well known, the practice of polygamy was legally permissible among the Jews during the Biblical period and after. A special provision in the marriage contract prohibiting such practice was therefore in order. To this day, among Oriental Jews, who do not recognize the post-

Talmudic ban against polygamy known as the *herem de-Rabbenu Gershom,* a special provision against the practice of polygamy by the husband is usually inserted in the *ketubah.*

3. The LXX translation of the difficult passage in Exod. 21, 10 is, as indicated above, entirely in agreement with the tannaitic interpretation of this passage. It would be straining one's imagination to the extreme to say that the authors of the LXX seized upon a formula that was being used by Greek scribes in drawing up marriage contracts in order to render the passage in question into Greek, and that thereafter this rendering became the traditional Jewish interpretation of the passage. It is far more reasonable to suppose that Jewish scribes in Egypt, in drawing up marriage contracts in the Greek language, inserted into these contracts a clause concerning the husband's duties towards his wife which was based upon Exod. 21, 10, as rendered by the LXX, and that this clause was later copied by non-Jewish scribes.

In any event, the possibility that the parallelisms noted above are the result of mere chance need not be considered at all. Whatever the precise conclusion to be drawn from them, these parallelisms are certainly significant and should not be ignored by students of the history of the Jewish people during the two or three centuries that preceded the Christian Era.

CHAPTER VI

BROOKLYN 7 AND GRECO-EGYPTIAN MARRIAGE DOCUMENTS OF THE PTOLEMAIC PERIOD.

In his introductory remarks to Brooklyn 7, which was written in the year 420 B. C. E., Kraeling says that "this is the most elaborate of the known Aramaic marriage documents",[1] as indeed it is. The document contains some new clauses which are not found in Papyrus Sayce-Cowley G. (Cowley 15), a marriage document dated in the year 440 B. C. E.[2] In one important clause our document makes it possible to establish the correct reading of a crucial word in Cowley 15, which was incorrectly restored by Cowley.

The Clausula Salvatoria in the Aramaic Papyri

In Cowley 15.29-31 there occurs the following clause: ו[הן] יקום על מפתחיה לתרכותה מן ביתה זי אסחור ונכסוהי וקנינה ינתן לה כסף כרשן 20 ויע[די] לה דין ספרא זנה This is translated by Cowley as follows: "But if he should rise up against Miphtahiah to drive her out from his, Ashor's, house and his goods and chattels, he shall give her the sum of 20 kerashim, and the provisions of this deed shall be annulled, as far as she is concerned". It is quite obvious that, from the legal point of view, the last part of the clause — "and the provisions of this deed shall be *annulled* as far as she is concerned" — does not make much sense. Luckily, there is a parallel clause in Brooklyn 7.30-32 in which the word corresponding to that which in Cowley 15 was restored as [יע[די reads יעבד (ויעבד לה דין ספרא זנה). This at once puts a new aspect on the entire clause. We

[1] APK, 201.
[2] APC, 44f.

have here what is known as a *clausula salvatoria*,[3] that is a
provision that in case of a breach of the terms of the agreement
by its maker he shall pay a certain amount of money as a
penalty and shall *nevertheless* be bound to abide by the terms
of the agreement. The import of the clause in Cowley 15.
29-31, then, is: If Ashor ejects Miphtahiah from his house and
property, he shall pay her 20 kerashin as a penalty and shall
nevertheless be bound to "do unto her the law of this document",
that is to perform according to the terms of the agreement.

It was through the recognition by the writer of the clause
under discussion as a *clausula salvatoria* that Kraeling was able
to read the word ויעבד correctly and to translate and interpret
the clause with tolerable accuracy, although, not being a jurist,
he did not fully grasp its significance. In his comment on the
word ויעבד, he says: "Jacob Rabinowitz calls my attention to
the survival of this sort of thing in much later times; see *Sefer
Haschtaroth, Dokumentenbuch von Rabbi Jehudah ben Barsillai
aus Barcelona*, C. J. Halberstam, ed. (Berlin, 1898), No. 72,
though the verbiage differs."[4] "This sort of thing" is the *clausula
salvatoria*, which appears most clearly and unmistakably in the
form cited from the Formulary of R. Jehudah b. Barzillai. This
is a form of an affiancing document (שטר שידוכין), in which the
fiancée's father stipulates that he is to give his daughter in
marriage to the fiancé, and to provide her with a certain dowry,
by a certain date, with a provision that if he (the father) does
not perform according to the stipulation, he shall be bound to
pay a certain penalty to the fiancé "and withal to perform the
stipulation" (ועל הכל להשלים לו התנאי). The writer pointed
out this form particularly to Professor Kraeling because it
illustrates the persistence and longevity of legal formulae. But
of course the *clausula salvatoria* is known from the Greco-

---

[3] See R. Taubenschlag, *The Law of Greco-Roman Egypt in the Light of
the Papyri* (1944), v. 1, 277. See also A. Berger, *Die Strafklauseln in den
Papyrusurkunden*, 47f., 81f., 130.

[4] APK, 218.

Egyptian papyri of well over a thousand years before the time
of the Formulary of R. Jehudah b. Barzillai. And let it be said
here at once that certain linguistic characteristics of the Greco-
Egyptian *clausula salvatoria,* together with some other evidence,
which we shall presently discuss, point to the Aramaic papyri as
the ultimate source of this clause.

The *clausula salvatoria* occurs quite frequently in the Aramaic
papyri,[5] old and new, although its true nature has hitherto remained unrecognized by scholars who have dealt with these
documents. Cowley's translation of the passages containing this
clause is inaccurate and misleading. In Cowley 6, for example,
there occurs the followig provision:

לא אכהל אגרנך דין ודבב אנה וברלי וברה לי אח ואחה
לי קריב ורחיק על ארקא זך אנת וברלך וברה לך אח ואחה
לך קריב ורחיק זי יגרנך בשמי על ארקא זך ינתן לך כסף
כרשן 20 הו עשרן באבני מלכא... וארקא אפם זילך.

"I shall have no power to institute suit or process
against you, I and my son and my daughter, brother
and sister of mine, relative and stranger, concerning
this land, (against) you and your son and your
daughter, brother and sister of yours, relative and
stranger. Whoever. sues you in my name concerning
this land, shall pay you the sum of 20 (twenty)
karash royal weight, ... and the land is assuredly
yours."[6]

The key-word in this provision — אפם — has been misunderstood by Cowley. It does not mean *assuredly;* it means *in
addition, moreover.* The import of the provision, then, is: in case
the validity of the conveyance is contested, the contestant is to
pay a penalty *and in addition* the conveyance shall remain valid —
a *clausula salvatoria,* pure and simple. At the writer's suggestion,[7]

---

[5] See, e. g., Cowley 5.8; 6.13; 8.15, 21.

[6] APC, 16f.

[7] See APK, 162. On purely philological grounds, N. H. Torczyner (Tur-
Sinai) arrived at a similar meaning of the word some forty years ago. See his
Die Entstehung des semitischen Sprachtypus (1916), 75.

Kraeling rendered the word אף‌ם, which occurs also in the Brooklyn papyri, as *moreover,* but he was unaware of the legal pattern involved in the clause.

To return to Brooklyn 7. The precise nuance of the expression ויעבד לה דין ספרא זנה, in this document and in Cowley 15, eluded Kraeling. This expression has a close parallel in the Book of the Covenant, whereas the parallels cited by Kraeling [8] are not altogether relevant. There can hardly be any doubt that it corresponds to כמשפט הבנות יעשה לה (according to the law (or manner) of the daughters he shall do unto her) of Ex. 21:9. The Aramaic יעבד לה (he shall do unto her) corresponds to the Hebrew יעשה לה, both of which mean *he shall perform in her favor.* Interestingly enough, the Greek word ποιεῖν (to do) in the sense of perform in accordance with an agreement appears in the *clausula salvatoria* in the Greco-Egyptian papyri of the Ptolemaic period. In P. BGU 998 [9] (101 B. C. E.), for example, a sale of a house by one Psenmenches to one Peteesis, there occurs a clause which, in Hunt and Edgar's English translation, reads:

> "... and that neither Psenmenches himself nor any of his assigns shall take proceedings against Peteesis or any of his assigns; and if anyone does so, the proceedings shall be invalid and in addition the aggressor shall straightway forfeit a penalty of 8 talents of copper and a fine consecrated to the Crown, of 160 drachmae of coined silver, and he shall be none the less bound to conform to the above terms".[10]

The phrase which is rendered by Hunt and Edgar as "to conform to the above terms" reads in the original ποιεῖν κατὰ [τὰ] προγεγραμμένα and should be rendered instead as "to perform according to the above terms", the word ποιεῖν (to do) in this

---

[8] APK, 217.

[9] This is one of the papyri from Gebelên. On these papyri, see chapter 8, below.

[10] SP, 89.

context, like the Hebrew עשׂה (to do) and the Aramaic עבד
(to do) in similar context, meaning *to perform*.[11]

That the clause quoted above from P. BGU 998 is an
adaptation of a formula going back to the Aramaic papyri may
be seen from the fact that it contains a not too skilful fusion
of two types of the *clausula salvatoria* found in the Aramaic
papyri, one in deeds of conveyance and the other in marriage
documents. The former type is characterized by the word אפם
(in addition, moreover), while the latter is characterized by the
word ויעבד (and he shall perform). In deeds of conveyance
it is stated that in case of a contest of the validity of the conveyance the contestant is to pay a certain penalty and *in
addition* the conveyance shall remain valid. It is not stated
there that the maker of the document shall nevertheless *perform*,
because, the conveyance having been made, there is nothing for
him to perform. In marriage documents, on the other hand,
it is stated that if the maker of the document acts in contra-
vention of the terms of the document he is to pay a certain
penalty *and* perform in accordance with the terms of the document, because, unlike a deed of conveyance the operation of
which is complete at once upon its execution and delivery, a
marriage document is one of an obligatory nature looking to
the future, with obligations under it yet to be performed. In
P. BGU 998, a deed of conveyance of a house, and in other
documents of this group, both types are combined, although the
second type is altogether superfluous and meaningless in such
a document, since there is nothing to perform under it.

Brooklyn 7.30-32 and Cowley 15.29-31, and Greco-Egyptian Marriage Contracts

There is also a close parallel in the Greco-Egyptian papyri
of the Ptolemaic period to Brooklyn 7.30-32 and Cowley 15.
29-31, in another respect. In P. Gen. 21.6 (2nd century B. C.
E.) and in P. Tebt. 104.22 (92 B. C. E.), both of them

---

[11] See p. 104, below. P. BGU 998 stems from Gebelên.

marriage contracts, there is a provision that the husband shall not eject μὴ ἐγβάλλειν the wife. Mitteis interprets this provision as meaning that the husband undertakes not to divorce the wife. To quote from his *Grundzüge der Papyruskunde,* p. 217:

> "Einseitige Scheidung durch den Mann ἀποπομπή muss natürlich als Verstoss gegen seine Verpflichtung zum μὴ ἐγβάλλειν mit den oben genannten Rechtsnachteilen belegt worden sein; diese Verpflichtung wäre ja inhaltslos, wenn er sie durch Scheidungserkläung jederzeit illusorisch machen konnte, und damit stimmt es überein, dass die Ehekontrakte von einseitiger Scheidung durch den Mann nie weiter sprechen während eine solche durch die Frau wiederholt erwähnt wird. Diese Scheidung durch die Frau ἀπαλλαγή gilt nicht als Verletzung ihrer Treupflicht, wird also nicht mit dem Verlust der Dos und überhaubt mit keiner Vermögensstrafe bedroht".
>
> (Unilateral divorce by the husband, as a violation of his obligation *not to eject,* naturally must have entailed the penalties mentioned above. This obligation would indeed be meaningless, if the husband could at any time render it illusory through a declaration of divorce. Accordingly, the marriage contracts never speak any more about unilateral divorce by the husband, while such divorce by the wife is repeatedly mentioned. Divorce by the wife is not deemed a breach of her duty of faithfulness and therefore does not draw a threat of the loss of her dowry or of any other property loss.

With all due respect to the great scholar that Mitteis was, the writer must say that his interpretation of the provision in question leads to a paradox: divorce of the wife by the husband *is* a breach of the duty of marital faithfulness; divorce of the husband by the wife *is not.* The correct interpretation of this provision is that it refers to unlawful ejection of the wife by the husband, and not to lawful divorce. Direct support for this interpretation is found in Brooklyn 7.30-32 and Cowley 15.29-31. In Brooklyn 7.21-28 and in Cowley 15.22-29, there are provisions for divorce by either party, and in Brooklyn 7.30-32 and Cowley 15.29-31, as we have seen above, the husband undertakes that "if he should rise up against the wife to drive her out (לתרכותה) from his house and his goods and chattels, he shall give her the sum of 20 kerashim". Cowley correctly interprets the last provision as having reference to unlawful ejection and not to lawful divorce.[12] The same is true of the μὴ ἐγβάλλειν provision in P. Gen. 21.6 and P. Tebt. 104.22. It refers to unlawful ejection and not to lawful divorce. Other parallels between Gen. 21 and Tebt. 104 and the marriage contracts in the Aramaic papyri will be discussed below.

Brooklyn 7.37-40

The expression ויעבד לה דין ספרא זנה, together with the parallel expression in Ex. 21:9, noted above, will help us understand the rather obscure clause contained in lines 37-40 of Brooklyn 7, which reads:

ואף לא יכהל עניניה ולא יעבד דין חדה ותרתין מן נשי
כנותה לי[ה]וישמע אנתתה והן לא יעבד כות שנאה הי
[ו]יעבד לה דין שנאה ואף [ל]א תכהל יהוישמע ולא
תעבד דין חד ו[ת]רין לעניניה בעלה והן לא תע[ב]ד
לה שנאהי.

This is translated by Kraeling as follows:

> "And moreover Ananiah shall not be able to go to law in cooperation with(?) one or two of the wives of his companions with respect to Yehoyishma his wife. And if he does not act thus, divorced she is. He shall do to her the law of divorce. And moreover, Yehoyishma shall not be able to go to law in cooperation with(?) one or two (men)...with respect to Ananiah her husband. And if she does

---

[12] APC, 49f

not act (thus) toward him, he has divorced her".

Commencing on lines 37-39, Kraeling [13] says that Anani is forbidden from cooperating with one or two of the wives of his "colleagues" (implying that he was a member of some *collegium*) in a legal action against his wife, and adds that the nature of this legal action is not apparent from the document.

The truth of the matter, however, is that there is not the slightest reference to any legal action or lawsuit in this clause. As in line 32, עבד דין does not mean here *to take legal action;* it means *to perform in accordance with the law* (or rather *manner*). Furthermore, Kraeling ignored entirely the double negative לא יכהל... ולא יעבד, which must mean *he shall not be able not to do,* that is, he is bound to do. This error, in turn, led him to a forced interpretation of the phrase והן לא יעבד כות (and if he does not act thus), which clearly implies that in what precedes Ananiah is required *to do* a certain thing, and not *to refrain from doing it.*

The correct translation of the above clause is:

> "And also, Ananiah shall not be able not to do
> unto Yehoyishma, his wife, (according to) the
> manner of one and two of the wives of his friends.
> And if he does not do thus it is (ground for)
> divorce, and he shall do unto her the law of
> divorce. Also, Yehoyishma shall not be able not to do
> unto Ananiah, her husband, (according to) the
> manner of one and two. And if she does not do
> (thus), it is (ground for) divorce".

Thus understood, the clause, in both of its parts, contains a euphemism for cohabitation. The husband shall not refuse cohabitation with the wife in accordance with custom (the manner of one or two of the wives of his friends), and the wife shall not refuse cohabitation with the husband in accordance with custom (the manner of one and two). It seems that the word דין in the sense of manner (*Art und Weise*) is a translation of the

---

[13] APK, 219.

Hebrew משפט, which has this nuance in Ex. 21:9 and else-where.[14]

It should be noted that in lines 36-37 of Brooklyn 7, immediately preceding the clause under consideration, there is a provision that Ananiah shall not take another wife besides Yehoyishma. Perhaps there is some connection between this provision and the one about Ananiah's duty of cohabiting with Yehoyishma which follows it. Perhaps, too, in the light of these two provisions, Gen 31:50 אם תענה את בנתי ואם תקח נשים על בנתי is to be interpreted, as it is interpreted in BT *Kethubot* 47b, as meaning "if you will cohabit with my daughters, and if you will take wives besides my daughters".

It should also be noted that at a later day the tannaim regarded cohabitation as one of the three main duties — the other two being sustenance and clothing — which the husband owes to his wife, basing this on Ex. 21:10 שארה כסותה ועונתה לא יגרע For cohabitation they used a euphemism — דרך ארץ[15] (the way of the world) — which is somewhat similar to the one used in Brooklyn 7.

P. Eleph. 1.4-5 and Brooklyn 7.37-38.

In his comment on Brooklyn 7.37-38, Kraeling says:

> "The wife cannot join forces with one or two men (presumably colleagues) in legal action against Anani. In the Greek marriage contract published by Rubensohn, Elephantine Papyri, No. 1, ll. 7-9, three men on whom both parties agree function as judges before whom husband or wife must prove their accusations".[16]

In the light of what has been said above, there is of course no similarity whatsoever between Brooklyn 7.37-40 and the provision concerning three judges in P. Eleph. 1 (311 B. C. E.).

---

[14] See GB, 473a, where, among others, the following meanings of the word are given: *Gewohnheitsrecht, Sitte, Gebrauch, Art u. Weise.*

[15] See *Mekilta de Rabbi Ishmael* (ed. Lauterbach), v. 3, 27.

[16] APK, 220.

There is, however, another provision in P. Eleph. 1 which resembles Brooklyn 7.37-38. In P. Eleph. 1.4-5 there occurs the following clause: "and Heraclides shall supply to Demetria all that is proper for a freeborn wife".[17]

What precisely is meant by "all that is proper for a freeborn wife" is difficult to determine from this papyrus alone.[18] However, several other papyri of a later period containing a similar clause, couched in similar language but more elaborate, shed considerable light on the meaning of the clause in P. Eleph. 1.4-5 In P. Tebt. 104.16-18, for example, it is stated: "All necessaries and clothing and whatever else is proper for a wedded wife Philiscus shall supply to Apollonia".[19] There are three items enumerated here, namely: necessaries, clothing, and whatever else is proper for a wedded wife. The last item is apparently a veiled allusion to cohabitation. As has been pointed out above,[20] these three items correspond to שארה כסותה ועונתה of Ex. 21:10, as rendered by the LXX. It is therefore not unlikely that in P. Eleph. 1 "all

---

[17] SP, 3.

[18] It is perhaps not without significance that in the phrase כמשפט הבנות יעשה לה (according to the law of the daughters he shall do unto her) of Ex. 21:9, which, under Jewish law, forms the basis of the husband's obligations toward his wife, the word בנות (daughters) seems to be used in the sense of *freeborn women*. The words בן (son) and בת (daughter) seem to have a similar meaning in Ex. 21:31. The Targum renders בנות in Ex. 21:9 as בנת ישראל (daughters of Israel) and בן and בת in Ex. 21:31 as בר ישראל (a son of Israel) and בת ישראל (a daughter of Israel), respectively. Ex. 21:9, as rendered by the Targum, has a most striking parallel in a Middle-Assyrian document of adoption (M. David and E. Ebeling, *Assyrische Rechtsurkunden*, no. 5), in which the adopting father undertakes that he will not ill-treat the adopted girl, but that he will treat her "as his daughter, an Assyrian" (*ki-i marti-su(?)-ma as-su-ra-i-e*). In both places, the similar expressions apparently mean a *freeborn woman*.

The words "son" and "daughter" in the sense of *freeborn son* and *freeborn daughter* call to mind the Latin *liberi* (children) which is believed to be related to *liber* (free) and to mean *freeborn children*. Cf. E. Benveniste *Liber et liberi*, Revue des études latines 14 (1936), 51ff.

[19] SP, 7. See p. 45f., above.

[20] See p. 46, above.

that is proper for a freeborn wife" includes cohabitation. This is all the more likely in view of the other parallels between the Aramaic papyri and P. Eleph. 1, which will be discussed below.

P. Eleph. 1.6-7 and Brooklyn 7.33-34.

Brooklyn 7.33-34, reads: להן לא שליטה יה[וישמע ל[הבעלה This is translated by בעל אהרן בר מן עניני והן תעבד כות שנאה הי. Kraeling as follows: "But Yehoyishma shall not have power to cohabit with(?) another man beside Anani, and if she does thus, she is divorced". The word להבעלה seems to be a *niphal* of בעל, as in Hebrew, and not an Aramaic *haphel*, as Kraeling [21] supposes, since the sense requires a passive mode. Cf. Isa. 62:4 (וארצך תבעל); Pr. 30:23 (תחת שנואה כי תבעל).

A provision similar to that of Brooklyn 7.33-34, is contained in P. Eleph 1.6-7, where it is stated:

> ἐιὰν δέ τι κακοτεχοῦσα ἁλίσκεται ἐπὶ αἰσχύνῃ τοῦ ἀνδρὸς
> Ἡρακλείδου Δημητρία στερέσθω ὧμ προσενέγκατο
> πάντων
>
> ("If Demetria is discovered doing any evil to the shame of her husband Heraclides, she shall be deprived of all that she brought").[22]

Although a circumlocution is used here, it seems clear that the reference is to misconduct on the part of the wife amounting to adultery. In P. Tebt. 104 and P. Gen. 21 and in the marriage documents from Alexandria of the time of Augustus, which will be discussed in the next chapter and which follow pretty much the pattern of P. Eleph. 1, the language in this respect is direct and specific. There is in these documents a provision that the wife shall not cohabit with another man (μήδ' ἄλλῳ ἀνδρὶ συνεῖναι).

It is perhaps not without significance that a circumlocution similar to that of P. Eleph. 1 is used in Deut. 24:1, a verse dealing with the subject of divorce. This verse reads:

כי יקח איש אשה ובעלה והיה אם לא תמצא חן בעיניו

---

[21] APK, 218.
[22] SP, 3.

כי מצא בה ערות דבר וכתב לה ספר כריתות ונתן בידה
ושלחה מביתו.

("When a man taketh a wife, and marrieth her,
then it cometh to pass, if she find no favor in his
eyes, because he hath found some unseemly thing
in her, that he writeth her a bill of divorcement,
and giveth it in her hand, and sendeth her out of
his house").

An old Jewish tradition reported in the Mishnah interprets
ערות דבר, which is rendered by the LXX as ἄσχημον πρᾶγμα
(a shameful thing), as unchastity. In Mishnah, Gittin, 9:10,
it is stated:

בית שמאי אומרים לא יגרש אדם את אשתו אלא אם
כן מצא בה דבר ערוה, שנאמר כי מצא בה ערות דבר.
ובית הלל אומרים אפילו הקדיחה תבשילו, שנאמר כי
מצא בה ערות דבר.

("The school of Shammai say: A man may not
divorce his wife unless he has found unchastity in
her, for it is written, *Because he has found in her
indecency in anything.* And the School of Hillel
say: He may divorce her even if she spoiled a dish
for him, for it is written, *Because he hath found in
her indecency in anything*").[23]

Still more significant in this respect is a certain stylistic peculiarity
in P. Eleph. 1.6-7. It is stated there that "If Demetria is
discovered (ἁλίσκηται) doing any evil to the shame of her husband
Heraclides etc.", whereas the more direct and natural way of saying
this would undoubtedly have been "If Demetria does any evil
etc.", Why "is discovered doing"? The answer, it seems, is that
the clause is an adaptation of כי מצא בה ערות דבר (because he
discovered in her a shameful thing) of Deut. 24:1.

In ch. 5 the writer has called attention to the striking
similarity between the provision in Cowley 15.31-32, against
the husband's marrrying another woman and having children by

---

[23] DM, 321.

another woman, and the provision of P. Eleph. 1.8-9, to the
same effect. He has also shown there that a certain demotic
marriage contract of the reign of Alexander IV contains a
provision which it but a paraphrase of Deut. 21:15-17, and
that the sum of 50 staters payable by the husband to the wife,
according to this contract, in case of divorce corresponds to the
Jewish *ketubah* which developed from the Biblical *mohar* of 50
shekel. In a demotic marriage contract of 169 B. C. E. the
endowment sum is even expressed in shekelss. In Revillout's
French translation: "Je t'ai donné 10 argenteurs, en sekels 50".[24]

All of this, in its cumulative effect, points to a powerful
influence of the Jewish legal tradition, as represented by the
Aramaic papyri and by later developments, upon the form and
contents of the Egyptian marriage contract, demotic and Greek,
during the Ptolemaic period. It may very well be therefore that
in Brooklyn 7.37-38 and 7.33-34 and in Eleph. 1.4-5 and 1.6-7,
we hear an echo of Ex. 21:10 and Deut. 24:1, respectively.

Double Documentation of Marriage in Egypt.

In the light of what has been said above about the influence
of the Jewish legal tradition upon Egyptian marriage documents
during the Ptolemaic period the perplexing problem of the double
documentation of Egyptian marriage [25] during this period will
receive its satisfactory solution. The two documents — the
συγγραφὴ ὁμολογίας and the συγγραφὴ συνοικισίου — correspond
to the שטר ארוסין (document of betrothal) and שטר נישואין
(document of marriage),[26] respectively. From P. Par. 13 (c. 157
B. C.E.) it appears that in Egypt the second document would
be drawn up within a year from the time the first one was
drawn up. To explain the interval between the drawing up of
the two documents, the theory has been advanced that this
interval represented a sort of trial period during which the parties

[24] Revue égyptologique 1, 93—94, quoted in MRV, 269, n. 4.

[25] See H. J. Wolff, *Written and Unwritten Marriages in Hellenistic and Postclassical Roman Law*, 7ff.

[26] See Mishnah, Baba Bathra, 10:4.

to the marriage were to decide whether they wished to confirm
their marriage, which was only a trial marriage (*Probeehe*),
by drawing up a second document making it permanent.[27] However, a far more satisfactory explanation of the year's interval
is found in Mishnah Ketuboth 5:2. With classic terseness and
simplicity it is stated there:

נותנין לבתולה שנים עשר חדש משתבעה הבעל לפרנס
את עצמה. וכשם שנותנין לאשה כך נותנין לאיש לפרנס
את עצמו ולאלמנה שלשים יום.

(A virgin is given 12 months, after the husband has
made a request upon her, to provide for herself —
and just as the woman is given (time) so is the
man given (time) — and a widow is given 30 days.)

Marriage is a serious matter requiring extensive preparations,
particularly on the part of the bride who is to be provided with
a dowry and a trousseau. The period of one year between
betrothal and marriage was required by the bride for just that
purpose.

The statement in the Mishnah with respect to the time
given to the man is ambiguous. It does not definitely appear
how much time he is given. It is reasonable to suppose, however,
that the man required less time 'to provide for himself" than the
woman. A period of 30 days notice to the groom is provided for
in P. Freib. III 26. 29, 30 (Philadelphia, 179—178 B. C. E.).
Speaking of this group of papyri, Wolff says:

"The problem of this group of sources lies in the
fact that the husband regularly pledges himself to
make with his wife a second contract ... within
thirty business days after he has been requested
by her to do so. In what relation would the second
act have been to the first?"[28]

The answer to Wolff's query seems to be that the second act
recorded the marriage, while the first recorded the betrothal.

---

[27] See MGP, 200ff.
[28] Wolff, *ibid.*, 22.

There is one detail in the provision about the 30 days notice to the husband which strengthens the supposition that this provision originated among Jews. We are referring to the term "business days". This term would hardly have been used unless the people who used it were observing *non-business days* at regular and frequent intervals. This would seem to fit no other group of people in Egypt during the second century B. C. E. than Jews. Cf. יום המעשה (the day of work) in 1 Sam. 20:19 and ששת ימי המעשה (the six days of work) in Ez. 46:1.

Married Couple's Mutual Rights of Succession and Matrimonial Regime.

In this chapter and in the preceding one we have shown that the Greek marriage contracts of the Ptolemaic period in Egypt exhibit a number of striking similarities with the marriage contracts of the Aramaic papyri. On the basis of the evidence presented in these chapters, it can be said without hesitation that there is hardly a clause in the Greco-Egyptian marriage contracts of the Ptolemaic period which does not have a close parallel in the Aramaic papyri. We shall conclude by pointing out one more such parallel, this time not in a marriage contract but in one closely related to the marital status.

P. Eleph. 2 (284 B. C. E.) is an agreement between husband and wife concerning the rights of succession to their property after the death of either of them. The first two clauses of this agreement, in Hunt and Edgar's English translation, read:

> "Should aught happen to Dionysius, he shall leave all his property to Callista and she shall be owner of all the property so long as she lives. Should aught happen to Callista while Dionysius is alive, Dionysius shall be owner of the property . . .".[29]

Similar clauses are contained in Brooklyn 2.10-13 (449 B. C. E.), the oldest marriage contract in the Aramaic papyri. These clauses read:

[29] SP, 237.

מחר או יום אחרן ימות עניה תמת הי שליטה בכל נכסן
זי יהון בין עני ותמת ותמת מחר או יום אחרן תמות תמת עני
הו שליט [...] בכל נכסן זי יהוון בין תמת ובין עני.

Kraeling's translation is as follows:

"If tomorrow or another day Ananiah should die,
Tamut shall have power over all the goods which
there may be between Anani and Tamut. If tomorrow
or another day, Tamut should die, Anani — he —
shall have power over all the goods which there
may be between Tamut and Anani".[30]

The similarity between Brooklyn 2 and Eleph. 2 is not limited
to substance alone; it extends to some details in form as well.
It will be noted that, in true chivalrous fashion, the contingency
of the husband's death is stated first in both documents. But
more important is the similarity between the terms used for
ownership in each of the two documents.[31] In the Aramaic
document it is הי שליטה, which Kraeling, quite correctly, renders
as "she shall have power", and in the Greek document it is
κυρίαν εἶναι which similarly means "she shall have power".

Incidentally, the wording of the clauses just quoted from
Brooklyn 2 seems to indicate that the matrimonial regime which
prevailed among the Jews of Elephantine in the 5th century B.C.E.
was that of community of goods between the spouses. The phrase
"the goods that there may be between Anani and Tamut" points
in this direction. With respect to this phrase, Kraeling, with an
insight all the more remarkable in view of the fact that he is a
non-jurist, says: "An interesting formulation appears in 'the
goods which may be between Tamut and Anani' — evidently the
joint possessions acquired after marriage, hardly just those now
existing."[32] It is interesting to note in this connection that a

---

[30] APK, 142. See also Cowley 15.17-22 (APC, 45f.); Brooklyn 7.28-30
(APK, 206f.).

[31] The same is true of the two other Aramaic papyri cited in the preceding
note.

[32] APK, 148.

similar inference concerning the matrimonial regime under which the parties lived is drawn by Wolff[33] from the wording of the clauses just quoted from P. Eleph. 2.

Community of goods between the spouses is also implicit in the clause in the Aramaic papyri providing against the unlawful ejection of the wife by the husband. It will be recalled that in this clause it is provided that the husband shall not eject the wife from "his house and his goods and chattels" (מן ביתה ונכסוהי וקנינה), which can hardly mean anything else than that the wife is legally entitled to own the property in common with her husband.

---

[53]. *Ibid.*, p. 15, n. 41. It is not unlikely that the clause often found in the Greco-Egyptian marriage contracts of the Ptolemaic period to the effect that husband and wife shall own (κυριεύειν) their property in common is also ultimately traceable to the Aramaic papyri. In P. Tebt. 104, for example, the clause in question, in Hunt and Edgar's English translation, reads: Apollonia shall live with Philiscus, obeying him as a wife should her husband, owning their property in common with him" (SP, 7). See also Wolff, *ibid.*, 13.

CHAPTER VII

THE ARAMAIC PAPYRI AND THE GREEK PAPYRI
FROM ALEXANDRIA

In the group of papyri from Alexandria of the time of Augustus there are seven marriage contracts (BGU 1050-1052, 1098-1101) in which, as in Eleph. 1, Gen. 21 and Tebt. 104, the provisions follow rather closely those of Brooklyn 7 and of the Jewish marriage document of a later day. As in Brooklyn 7, the husband undertakes not to eject the wife and not to marry another woman.[1] As in the Jewish marriage document of a later day, the husband undertakes to provide *necessaries and clothing* for the wife, the phrase used τὰ δέοντα πάντα καὶ τὸν ἱματισμὸν being identical with that in Ex. 21:10, as rendered by the LXX.[2] Also as in Brooklyn 7, the wife is prohibited from cohabiting with another man.[3] All of this seems to point to the Jewish legal tradition as the source of these documents. Indeed, it may very well be that the parties to these documents were Jews. Schubart has demonstrated that the papyri from Alexandria all stem from the same notarial bureau or law office.[4] In a number of these papyri representing deeds of sale and leases of real property it is stated that the property involved is located in the Delta quarter,[5] which, as is well known, was largely populated by Jews. It is therefore not unreasonable to suppose that the clients of the

[1] See p. 54, above.
[2] See p. 46, above.
[3] See p. 58, above.
[4] See W. Schubart, *Alexandrinische Urkunden aus der Zeit des Augustus*, Archiv fur Papyrusforschung 5, 47ff.
[5] See *ibid.*, 37.

notary or lawyer from whose archive the papyri stem were, for the most part, Jews.

Double Documentation of Marriage in Alexandria

Upon the hypothesis that the parties to the marriage documents from Alexandria were Jews, a peculiar feature of these documents will perhaps be satisfactorily explained. We are referring to the provision that within five business days (ἐν ἡμέραις χρηματιζούσαις πέντε) from the time of demand made by one of the parties upon the other a second document is to be drawn up before a board of priests ἱεροθύται With regard to the purpose of having a second document drawn up before the board of priests and the function the priests performed in connection therewith there is nothing but guesses which have very little to commend them.[6] As to the term five *business days,* Schubart,[7] quite frankly, says that he fails to understand its significance.

The reader will recall what has been said above with respect to the use of the term *business days* as pointing to people who were observing *non-business days* at regular and frequent intervals. This would seem to fit no other group in Alexandria during the age of Augustus except Jews. As to the drawing up of a second document before a board of priests, it may also be explained in terms of Jewish law and custom. Intermarriage between certain classes of people was forbidden according to Jewish law.[8] The prohibition affected priests in a very vital manner. The offspring of a union between a priest and a woman of one of the forbidden classes were forever tainted. The male offspring were not qualified to perform the priestly functions, and the female offspring were

---

[6] See MGP, 212; Schubart, *ibid.,* 78; S. G. Huwardas, *Beiträge zum griechischen und gräkoägyptischen Eherecht der Ptolemäer-und frühen Kaiserzeit,* (Leipziger Rechtswissenschaftliche Studien, Heft 64), 21, 27; H. J. Wolff, *Written and Unwritten Marriages in Hellenistic and Postclassical Roman Law,* 34ff.

[7] *Ibid.,* 79.

[8] See Mishnah, Kiddushin 4:1.

not eligible to marry priests.[9] In order to prevent forbidden unions, it would be appropriate to have some board pass upon the qualifications of the prospective husband and wife. It would also be appropriate that such a board should consist of priests since they were the people who formed the superior class, so to speak, and who were most vitally concerned in the matter of keeping family strains pure. It may well be therefore that the custom developed among Alexandrian Jews to have the marriage document [10] (שטר נישואין), which followed the betrothal document (שטר אירוסין),[11] drawn up before a board of priests.

[9] See *ibid.* 3:12; 4:6.

[10] In the Alexandrian papyri the second document is similarly called marriage document (περὶ γάμου συγγραφή). In P. BGU 1050. 24ff. it is stated that the marriage document to be drawn up before the *hierothytai* is to contain a provision concerning the disposition to be made (probably of the property of the spouses) in case of the death of either during the existence of the marriage. See Schubart, *ibid.*, 78f. and Wolff, *ibid.*, 36. Precisely the same provision is contained in all of the three marriage documents in the Aramaic papyri — Cowley 15, Brooklyn 2 and 7 — now extant. See p. 62f., above.

[11] A careful analysis of the provision about the groom's duties toward the bride in the so-called "marriage documents" from Alexandria will reveal that these documents, like the Jewish שטר אירוסין (document of betrothal), do not relate to marriage but to betrothal. In P. BGU 1052, for example, this provision reads: "From now Apollonius son of Ptolemaeus shall furnish to Thermmion all necessaries and clothing like to a wedded wife (ὡς γυναικὶ γαμετῇ). It will be noted that in this formula the third item — whatever else is proper for a wedded wife — contained in P. Tebt. 104 and P. Gen. 21, is missing, although in other respects these documents from Alexandria follow closely the pattern of P. Tebt. 104 and P. Gen. 21. The reason for the omission is that the wedded life of the couple was not to begin until after the second document had been drawn up, which corresponds to the state of אירוסין (betrothal), as distinguished from נישואין (marriage), under Jewish law. In line with this explanation is the emphasis upon the immediate taking of effect of the groom's obligation to furnish necessaries and clothing to the bride. In the absence of a specific agreement between the parties modifying the customary law in this respect, this obligation would come into force only after the marriage took place. See Mishnah Ketubot 5:2. Hence, the emphasis "from now", which would otherwise be entirely superfluous. Also pointing in the same direction is the expression "like to a wedded wife", which seems to indicate that the woman was not in reality a wedded wife but only to be

Reference to a "court of priests" (בית דין של כהנים) is also contained in the Mishnah [12] in a passage dealing with the *ketubah,* although it does not appear there what precisely the functions of this court were.

Strong support for the supposition that the Alexandrian *hierothytai* were a board of Jewish priests whose function it was to keep records of marriages may be seen in Josephus, *Contra Apionem* I, 7 (ed. Niese 30-33). According to Josephus, Jewish priests in Egypt, as well as in other countries where Jews lived, kept records of marriages for the purpose of establishing the eligibility of the offspring to marry priests. Speaking of the priestly order and the purity of its lineage, he says:

> "Not only did our ancestors in the first instance set over this business (of keeping records) men of the highest character, devoted to the service of God, but they took precautions to ensure that the priests' lineage should be kept unadulterated and pure. A member of the priestly order must, to beget a family,

treated as such with respect to necessaries and clothing. Cf. Wolff *ibid,* 37f. The inference drawn by Wolff from the opening sentence of these documents that the wedded life of the couple had already begun when the document was drawn up seems to be due to a misinterpretation of this sentence. In P. BGU 1052, in Hunt and Edgar's English translation (SP, p. 11) it reads: "Thermion and Appollonius son of Ptolemaeus agree that they have come together to share a common life (συνεληλυθέναι ἀλλήλοις πρὸς βίου κοινωνίαν). The phrase "agree that they have come together" does not make much sense. In a contract an agreement means a promise to do something in the future, and not unanimity as to a past event. The correct translation of the sentence seems to be as follows: "Thermion and Appollonius son of Ptolemaeus acknowledge that they have *agreed* upon a common life". The verb συνέρχομαι means here, as elsewhere, *to agree.* See PWB *s. h.v.*

Incidentally, the phrase πρὸς βίου κοινωνίαν, which is rendered by Hunt and Edgar as "to share a common life", literally means for a life's partnership. It is perhaps not without significance that in a clause from the *kethubah* quoted in PT Kethuboth 7:6 the marital status is also referred to as a *partnership* (שותפות). See J. N. Epstein, *Notizen zu den jüdisch-aramäischen Papyri aus Assuan,* Jahrbuch der jüdisch-lit. Gesellschaft, 1908, p. 369.

[12] See Mishnah, Kethubot 1:5.

marry a woman of his own race, without regard to her wealth or other distinctions; but he must investigate her pedigree, obtaining the genealogy from the archives and producing a number of witnesses. And this practice of ours is not confined to the home country of Judea, but wherever there is a Jewish colony there too a strict account is kept by the priests of their marriages;[13] I allude to the Jews in Egypt and Babylon and other parts of the world in which any of the priestly order are living in dispersion".[14]

The *hierothytai* are also mentioned in P. Fay 22, a fragmentary papyrus from Ptolemais of the first century C. E. apparently dealing with the subject of divorce.[15] This document seems to prescribe that in case of divorce a declaration containing the names of the parties, their fathers' names and the date of the divorce be addressed to the *heirothytai* and deposited by them in a chest (κιβωτός). [16] Registration of divorces would be a most appropriate function of a board of Jewish priests, who would have to keep a record of divorces, since a Jewish priest was forbidden to marry a divorced woman (Lev. 21:7). It is not unlikely therefore that P. Fay 22, which is badly mutilated at the beginning, represents a set of rules concerning divorce which was promulgated by some Jewish authority and which applied only to Jews.

The Papyri from Alexandria and Jewish Sources.

To return to the papyri from Alexandria. There is an almost certain indication in one of these papyri that the notary who drew

---

[13] The word "their" in the translation is without warrant in the original which reads περὶ τοὺς γάμους (of marriages). The priests had to keep records of all marriages in order to determine the eligibility of the offspring to marry priests.

[14] H. St. J. Thackaray, tr., (The Loeb Classical Library), *Josephus,* vol. I, 174ff.

[15] See Schubart, *ibid.,* 77.

[16] See Huwardas, *ibid.,* 21.

it up, or the form from which he copied, followed a model which, at least with respect to one clause, goes back to the Aramaic papyri. BGU 1127 (19 B. C. E.) is an agreement for the sale of a shop for melting gold. The seller, who has received part of the purchase price, agrees to make the definitive transfer of the shop through the registry office upon receipt of the balance of the price by a certain date. In line 20 it is stated: "And Apollonios (the seller) shall not be allowed to say: 'I have not received'" (καὶ μηι ἐξῖναι τῷ 'Απολλωνίῳ λέγειν οὐκέτι παρείληφα). Pringsheim [17] has noted the striking similarity between this clause and Old-Babylonian clauses to the same effect, quoting from UAR, 115, as follows: "andererseits schützt sich zuweilen der Käufer durch eine besondere Klausel gegen eine etwaige Ableugnung des Geldempfanges seitens des Verkaüfers: 'Das Geld haben wir nicht bekommen, werden wir nicht sagen, vor Zeugen haben wir es erhalten'". However, much nearer in time and place to BGU 1127 than the Old-Babylonian deeds of conveyance are the Aramaic papyri, and in these papyri there is still closer approximation to the clause in question than in the Old-Babylonian deeds. The following are examples: Cowley 5,[18] a deed of grant of building rights dated 471 B. C. E., lines 11-12:

ואנא קוניה לא אכהל אמר למחסה לאמר תרעא זך לא
זילך הו ולא תנפק בשוקא זי בינין ובין בית פפטעונית
מלחא.

("And I Koniya shall not be allowed to speak to Mahseth saying: 'This gateway is not yours, and you shall not go out (by it) into the street which is between us and the house of Peftconith, the boatman'".)

Cowley 10,[19] a loan agreement dated 456 B. C. E., lines 11-12:

---

[17] GLS, 319, n. 5.

[18] APC, 11.

[19] *Ibid.*, 30. For another clause in the Alexandrian papyri which has a close parallel in the Aramaic papyri, see p. 125f., below.

ולא אכל אמר לך שלמתך בכספך ומרביתה וספרא זנה
בידך.

("And I shall not be allowed to say to you I have
paid you your money and the interest thereon".)
The correspondence between these clauses and the clause in line
20 of BGU 1127, quoted above, is obvious and requires no
comment.

Another characteristic feature of BGU 1127 which has a
striking parallel in a Jewish source is the provision (lines 28-38)
that in case the seller would not accept the balance of the price
within the time specified in the agreement, the purchaser may
deposit the money in an authorized bank to the seller's account
and have the property transferred to himself through the registry
office. A procedure which is similar in conception and design to
this provision is reported in the Mishnah in the name of Hillel the
Elder. Under Biblical law (Lev. 25:29), the seller of house
property situated within a walled city has a right to redeem the
property by paying back the purchase price to the purchaser within
a year from the time of the sale. In connection with this law
it is stated in Mishnah Arakhin 9:4:

בראשונה היה נטמן יום י"ב חדש שיהא חלוט לו. התקין
הלל הזקן שיהא חולש את מעותיו בלשכה²⁰ ויהא שובר
את הדלת ונכנס אימתי שירצה הלה יבא ויטול את
מעותיו.

"Beforetime the buyer used to hide himself on the
last day of the twelve months so that the house
might be his for ever; but Hillel the Elder ordained
that he that sold it could deposit his money in the
Temple Chamber, and break down the door and
enter, and that the other, when he would, might
come and take his money".

A procedure similar to that of BGU 1127 and the "ordinance
of Hillel" is also found in BGU 1158 (9 B. C. E.). A creditor,

²⁰ In BT *Arakhin* 31b the reading is ללשכה, which, as wil be shown below,
is correct.

who has received a conveyance of certain land by way of a mortgage for a debt of 80 drachmae, agrees to reconvey the land to the debtor upon payment of the debt within a twelve-month period. In case the debtor tenders payment and the creditor refuses to reconvey the property, the debtor is authorized to deposit the money in a bank to the creditor's account and recover the property.

There is internal evidence in the Mishnah to the effect that the "ordinance of Hillel" is somehow related to the Alexandrian practice. The word חולש, which Danby, quite correctly, renders as *deposit,* has caused considerable difficulty to commentators and lexicographers alike.[21] It does not occur in this sense in any other Talmudic source. The verb חלש occurs in Ex. 17:13 — ויחלש יהושע את עמלק — and here too the verb has caused difficulty.[22] The noun חלש occurs in Talmudic sources in the sense of *lot, ballot,* that is, that which is cast down. It seems that the basic meaning of the verb is *to throw down* and hence *to strike down* with a weapon, and that in the latter sense the verb is used in Ex. 17:13. A similar semantic development occured in the case of the Greek καταβάλλω (to throw down), which is used already in the Iliad 2,692 in the sense of *to strike down* with a weapon, *slay.*[23] Interestingly enough, the same Greek word is also used in the sense of *to deposit, pay,*[24] exactly as חלש is used in the "ordinance of Hillel". While the semantic development from *to throw down* to *to strike down with a weapon* may be considered natural and is likely to occur in two unrelated languages independently, the development from the former meaning to that of *to deposit, pay* is probably peculiar to the Greek language. It is therefore not unreasonable to suppose that in the only place in the Mishnah where we find חלש used in the sense of *to deposit* it represents a Grecism. That this is so is further

---

[21] See Kohut, *Aruch Completum* and JDT, *s. v.*

[22] See GB, *s. v.*

[23] See Liddell-Scott-Jones, *A Greek-English Lexicon, s. v.*

[24] See *ibid.*

indicated by the preposition ל (to, into) following the verb חלש,
which corresponds to the Greek usage of the verb καταβάλλω
in the sense of *to deposit* with the preposition εἰς (to, into).[25]

Incidentally, the close connection between the Alexandrian
practice referred to above and the "ordinance of Hillel", together
with other evidence,[26] makes it highly probable, as has been

---

[25] See *ibid.*

[26] The *prosbol*, introduced by Hillel for the purpose of circumvening the
Biblical law of the "year of release" (Mishnah, Shebiith 10:3), is a Greek
technical term προσβολή taken over from the procedure of execution against
a defaulting debtor which is known to have prevailed in Hellenistic Egypt.
See R. Taubenschlag, *The Law of Greco-Roman Egypt in the Light of the
Papyri*, I, 208, n. 21. One is not likely to use a foreign technical term unless
he is familiar with the foreign procedure of which it is a part.

In Tosefta, Kethuboth 4:9 (ed. Zuckermandel, 264f.) it is reported that
when the question of the effect of betrothal upon the status of the bride arose
among "the people of Alexandria", Hillel, upon the basis of the formula of the
kethuba which was in use by the Jews of Alexandria, decided that betrothal
alone did not constitute the bride the groom's wife. The plain inference from
this report is that Hillel was in Alexandria at the time when the matter came
before him and that he occupied there a position of authority.

Hillel is reported in Sifra, introduction (ed. Weiss 3a) and Tosefta, Sanhedrin 7:11 (ed. Zuckermandel, 427) to have applied seven rules of interpretation of Scripture (מדות). It has been suggested that these rules of interpretation were derived from Hellenistic rhetoric. See D. Daube *Rabbinic Methods
of Interpretation*, Hebrew Union College Annual 22, 239ff. Whether or not
Hillel, or those who preceded him, in formulating the rules of interpretation,
availed himself of similar rules of Hellenistic rhetoric must still be considered
an open question. The evidence presented by Daube of a Greek derivation
of the rules of interpretation seems inconclusive. It does seem, however, that
these rules were formulated in a Greek-speaking milieu, probably among the
Jews of Alexandria. The very term מדה in the sense of *rule* is a Grecism.
The Greek μέτρον the basic meaning of which, like that of the Hebrew מדה,
is *measure*, is also used in the sense of *rule*. See Liddell-Scott-Jones, *A Greek-
English Lexicon*, s. h. v. Another highly significant Grecism, which occurs in the
Talmudic terminology pertaining to the rules of interpretation, is the word דון.
The basic meaning of this word is *to decide, render judgment,* but when used
in connection with the rules of interpretation it means *to compare, draw an
inference.* See JDT, s. h. v. In the latter sense it is a translation of the Greek
συγκρίνω (to compare). This Greek word occurs in the Greco-Egyptian papyri
from the 3rd century B. C. E. onward also in the sense of *to decide, render*

suggested by Kaminka,[27] that Hillel the Elder hailed from Alexandria, and not from Babylonia as is generally supposed. Particularly significant in this respect is the Grecism noted above. It seems that Hillel was bilingual and that his second language was Greek. It may well be that the designation "Babylonian" is equivalent to that of "Persian of the Epigone" (See below).

Persians of the Epigone and Jews.

There is further evidence to the effect that many of the parties to the agreements represented by the papyri from Alexandria were Jews, although they are not designated as such but as Persians of the Epigone. In a large number of these papyri representing loan agreements (BGU 1054, 1055, 1150 II, 1156, 1158, 1162, 1167 III, 1170, 1171, 1172) it is stated that the loan is made without interest (ἄτοκος), but that if the debtor fails to pay the debt when due, he is to pay a penalty of ½ the amount of the loan, together with interest at the rate of 2 drachmae per mina per month for the overtime. There seems to be no other reason for the no-interest stipulation except that the parties were observing the Pentateuchal prohibition against the taking of interest. Interest was disguised in the form of a penalty for non-payment on the due date plus interest for arrears. As the writer has pointed out elsewhere,[28] a similar device for the evasion of the prohibition against the taking of interest was used by Jews in the Middle Ages and a medieval Jewish authority held that according to the strict letter of the law the use of the device is permissible but that it is to be frowned upon as an evasion and violation of the spirit of the law.

Precisely the same device for the evasion of the law against

judgment. See PWB, s. h. v. and cf. S. Lieberman, *Hellenism in Jewish Palestine,* 59.

[27] See A. Kaminka, *Hillel's Life and Work,* Jewish Quarterly Review 30 (N. S.), 107ff.

[28] See Jacob J. Rabinowitz, *Some Remarks on the Evasion of the Usury Laws in the Middle Ages,* Harvard Theological Review 37 (1944), 49ff.

the taking of interest as that which was used in the loan agreements from Alexandria was also used some 160 years earlier in P. Tebt. 817 (182 B. C. E.), in which both parties were Jews and are designated as such. This device was also used by the people figuring in the Adler papyri, who, like the debtors in the loan agreements from Alexandria, are designated as Persians of the Epigone.[29] The no-interest provision in the loan agreements in the Adler Papyri has led E. N. Adler to conclude that the people figuring therein were observing the Pentateuchal prohibition against usury.[30]

Wilcken[31] has objected to Adler's conclusion concerning the no-interest provision in the Adler papyri, pointing to P. Tebt 818 of 174 B. C. E., a loan agreement between two Jews, in which it is specifically stated that the loan is to bear interest at the rate of two drachmae per mina per month. From this agreement, he argues, it appears that Jews in Hellenistic Egypt were influenced by non-Jews with respect to the taking of interest, rather than the reverse. He offers no explanation, however, for the no-interest provision either in P. Tebt. 817 or in the Adler papyri, except quoting some generality from Werner Sombart's *Die Juden und das Wirtschaftsleben*, 285, about loans having generally been made without interest in the early stages of development of society — which, even if it be true, has no application whatsoever to the situation in Hellenistic Egypt in the 2nd and 1st centuries B. C. E.

As to Wilcken's argument from P. Tebt. 818, the writer believes that it is fallacious. This document contains much more than appears on the surface. The Jewish lender did not disregard the Pentateuchal prohibition against usury. At least in form, he endeavored to abide by it, using a device, or rather a combination of two devices, which resulted in a considerable profit

---

[29] E. N. Adler, J. G. Tait, F. M. Heichelheim and F. Ll. Griffith, editors, *The Adler Papyri*, Introduction by E. N. Adler, 1.

[30] *Ibid.*, 5f. See also F. Heichelheim, *Jewish Influence in the Adler Papyri*, Harvard Theological Review 35 (1942), 35ff.

[31] See *Archiv für Papyrusforschung* 13, 218ff.

to him, but which, from the formal point of view, was not violative of the law against usury. It is recited in the document that the amount of the loan represents the balance owed by the debtor to the creditor of an advance towards a retail business in partnership (εἰς προσβολὴν κοινῆς ἐργασίας μεταβολικῆς), [32] made by the latter to the former. On the basis of this recital, the editors of the Tebtunic papyri, quite correctly, call this document "Renewal of a loan". The original advance and the renewal, both, were devices for the evasion of the law against usury. In Mishnah, Baba Metzia 5:4 it is stated: אין מושיבין חנוני למחצית שכר. ("None may set up a shopkeeper on condition of receiving half the profit"). Advancing money towards the opening of a retail business, with a provision that the party receiving the money share his profits with the party advancing it, was apparently a common practice engaged in for the purpose of evading the law against usury. The Sages of the Mishnah ultimately declared this practice unlawful as savoring of usury, but among the Jews of Egypt in the 2nd century B. C. E. it was apparently still considered lawful. As to the interest on the renewal, it was not considered violative of the law, since interest on arrears was in the nature of a penalty [33] and the amount of the debt had already become due before the renewal was made, that is the interest on the renewal was in effect interest on arrears. In this manner, the lender probably made a handsome profit both on the original advance and on the renewal without violating the letter of the law as it was then understood.

Tscherikover,[34] who likewise disagrees with Adler's conclusion

---

[32] The editors of the Tebtunis Papyri render this phrase as "as an advance towards a money-changing(?) business in partnership". However, in a note they say: μεταβολικῆς is ambiguous, since μεταβόλος and μεταβολή may be concerned either with money-changing or small retail trade". In the light of Mishnah Baba Metzia 5:4, quoted in the text, it seems that the word is used here in the latter sense.

[33] Cf. V. Tscherikover, *Jewish Religious Influence in the Adler Papyri,* Harvard Theological Review 35, 28, n. 10.

[34] *Ibid.,* 25ff.

concerning Jewish influence on the people figuring in the Adler papyri, has attempted an explanation of the no-interest provision in these papyri other than in terms of Jewish influence. However, as the writer has stated elsewhere, his explanation fails to carry conviction.

> "As a rule" — says Tscherikover — "heavy fines were agreed on in case of failure to repay punctually as provided in the contract. In many cases the loans were granted for one or two months or other short periods, and the wording of many contracts suggests that it was expected at the date of the agreement that the debt would not be repaid on the fixed day. If the loans were not repaid new contracts were drawn up providing for payment of the fines stipulated in the original agreement, and the interest paid under the name of such fine would be higher than the usual quota of between 4% and 24% allowed by the royal 'diagramma'. We may therefore suppose that in many cases loans without interest were an artful method of extorting from the borrower more interest than was allowed by the law of the country".

To this the writer [35] has retorted:

> "If the penalty had been intended solely to bring to the lender a higher rate of interest than the one he was legally permitted to charge, the provision for a penalty would have been made in addition to a provision for the payment of interest within the permissible range . . . The question that arises in the writer's mind is: why did the lender have to advance the loan without interest at all, even if the term of the loan was a very short one, when he could have provided for interest payments up to the allowable limit, and in addition thereto he could have made provision for a penalty for the purpose of

---

[35] See article cited in n. 28, above, 56ff.

increasing his profit beyond that limit? In other words, why did the lender have to run the risk of having the loan repaid before the term of the bond expired, when he could have avoided that risk and accomplished his purpose at the same time by a combined interest-penalty clause?"

Furthermore, short term loans, with interest probably disguised in the form of a penalty, were apparently in vogue among the Jews of Alexandria during the time of Philo. In *De Virtutibus*, 122, discussing the subject of slavery, Philo says:

"As for debtors, who through temporary loans (ἐξ ἐφημερινῶν δανείων) have sunk into bearing both the name and the painfulness which their cruel situation entails... he would not allow them to remain forever in their evil plight but gave them total remission in the seventh year".[36]

Commenting on the expression which he renders as "temporary loans", Colson says: "If this is right and reference is to loans which the borrower expects and promises to pay shortly, it is an unusual sense for the word, though it is applied to brief and shortlived men and things".[37] In the light of the practice revealed by the papyri from Alexandria Philo's words assume a new significance. The reference is to short term loans which the borrower promises, but *does not expect,* to pay within a short period of time. Such loans, which, in disguised form, bear a high rate of interest, are likely to lead the borrower to insolvency and, ultimately, to debt bondage. Philo was apparently speaking in terms of the practice that prevailed in his day among the Jews of Alexandria.

In one of the papyri from Alexandria, BGU 1115 of the year 13 B. C. E., there occurs another device which was apparently used for the purpose of overcoming the prohibition against the taking of interest. In this document it is stated that the loan is given without interest, but it is provided that the lender shall

---

[36] F. H. Colson, tr., *Philo,* vol. 8 (The Loeb Classical Library), 236f.
[37] *Ibid.,* 237, n.b.

reside in the borrower's house. The borrower is designated as a
Persian of the Epigone. His house, in which the lender was to
reside, was situated in the Delta, which, as noted above, was the
Jewish quarter of Alexandria. This device for the evasion of the
prohibition against the taking of interest was apparently used also
by Jews in Palestine during the Mishnaic period, and the Sages of
the Mishnah declared it unlawful as savoring of usury. In Mishnah
Baba Metzia 5:2 it is stated: המלוה את חברו לא ידור בחצרו חנם
("The creditor may not dwell without charge in the debtor's
courtyard").

It will perhaps be objected that the presence in BGU 1115
of the provision that the lender shall reside in the borrower's
house does not necessarily mean that the parties were Jews, since
such a provision also occurs in a number of other papyri. The
answer to this objection is that, rather than impairing its force,
these papyri add cogency to the argument. In most of these
papyri [38] the borrowers are designated as Persians of the Epigone.
Is this accidental? The writer believes that it is not. It has
already been noted by papyrologists that many of the persons
designated in the papyri as Persians of the Epigone were Jews.[39]

---

[38] See documents cited in R. Taubenschlag, *The Law of Greco-Roman
Egypt in the Light of the Papyri*, 218, n. 15.

[39] While non of the persons designated as Persians of the Epigone bears an
Iranian name, some of them bear distinctly Jewish names. See Zucker's article
in Pauly-Wissova, *Real-Encyclopädie der classischen Altertumswissenschaft*,
XIX, 1, p. 916. It seems that Jews came to be designated as Persians and
Persians of the Epigone because many of them were descendants of soldiers
who came to Egypt in the Persian army of occupation. Cf. *ibid.*, p. 914f. On
this point the Letter of Aristeas contains significant information. In §13
(R. H. Charles, *Apocrypha and Pseudoepigrapha of the Old Testament*, II, 98),
we read: "And even before this time (i. e. the time of Ptolemy I) large
numbers of Jews had come into Egypt with the Persian...". In P. S. I, 488.10
(257 B. C. E.) there is mention of a Syro-Persian quarter in Memphis. It is not
unlikely that the reference is to a quarter inhabited by Jews, as Jews were
often classed as Syrians in documents of Greco-Roman Egypt. See H. I. Bell,
Cults and Creeds in Greco-Roman Egypt, 35.

In P. Grenf. II 15 (139 B. C. E., Thebaid) — a deed of conveyance of
certain property by a woman which follows the formula invariably found in the

But is is quite likely that this designation, generally, conceals Jews or persons who embraced the Jewish faith.

papyri from Gebelên and the neighboring districts (See ch. 8, below) — the husband of the seller is referred to as Πέρσης τῶν Πτολεμαίου καὶ τῶν υἱῶν With respect to this designation, Grenfell and Hunt (*New Classical Fragments and Other Greek and Latin Papyri*, 33) say: "The whole phrase, we suggest, means 'a Persian belonging to the class whcih consists of those settled by Ptolemy I and their descendants'". In the light of the passage quoted above from the Letter of Aristeas, it is not unlikely that the reference is to Jews who came to Egypt during the reign of Ptolemy I.

In three papyri from Gebelên — P. Lond. 218 (111 B. C. E.?), 879 (123 B. C. E.), 881 (108 B. C. E.) — there occurs the designation Πέρσης τῶν προσγράφων (a Persian of those added to the register). Grenfell and Hunt (*ibid.*), referring to this "obscure phrase", say that it points to an addition or additions made to the privileged class of Persians of the Epigone, though at what period is quite uncertain". In the writer's opinion, it is quite possible that the phrase has reference to persons whose names were added to the register of Jews after they had embraced the Jewish faith. Cf. Ez. 13:9 ("...neither shall they be written in the register of the house of Israel"). This will perhaps also explain the cases cited by Pringsheim (GLS, 160, n. 2) and Taubenschlag (Journal of Juristic Papyrology, VI, 300f.) in support of Tait's fiction theory of the designation "Persian of the Epigone".

In some papyri of the 3rd century B..C. E. from Tebtunis (P. Tebt. 814.7, 16; 815, Fr. 7.2) there occurs the phrase Πέρσης τῶν ἐπέργων This phrase is rendered by Hunt and Smyly as "Persian under employ", which is obviously vague. It seems to the writer that the phrase is a constriction of τῶν ἐπὶ τῶν ἔργων (of those who are over the works, that is, of the superintendents of the royal works). If this is so, then the designation bears a striking resemblance to אשר על המלאכה (those that are over the work, that is, the superintendents) in I Kings, 5:30, which refers to the superintendents of Solomon's works. Cf. the rendering of this phrase by the LXX.

H. I. Bell (*Cults and Creeds in Graeco-Roman Egypt*, 33) rejects the suggestion made by Adler that the parties to the loan agreements without interest were "God-fearing men who followed the Jewish law as it seemed good to them". He says, however, that "it does seem at least possible that a Jewish custom may have influenced the current practice in a region in which the Jews had long been settled and had in the past enjoyed a position of some authority". This explanation can hardly be considered satisfactory. Advancing loans without interest is not a mere matter of folkways and customs which are likely to be taken over by one group of people from another. Such a practice is not likely to be adopted by any people unless there is a compelling reason,

The problem of the national origin of the Persians of the Epigone and of their legal status in Egypt has been widely discussed by papyrologists, but has defied solution.[40] In an exhaustive study on the subject, Pringsheim [41] analyzes a large number of documents in which the designation Persian of the Epigone occurs and discusses at length the characteristic features of these documents. It so happens that all of these features have striking parallels either in the Aramaic papyri or in Jewish legal practice of a later day. We shall touch upon these briefly, listing them *seriatim*.

1. The so-called ἀγώγιμος clause. In this clause it is provided that in case of default by the debtor the creditor may take him into bondage and hold him until the debt is paid.[42] This,

such as a religious conviction, for its adoption. To be sure, there is abundant evidence in these papyri of pagan practices by the people figuring therein. But this may be due to syncretism, traces of which are also found elsewhere among Jews in Egypt during the late Ptolemaic period. See Bell, *ibid.* 33f.

[40] See L. Wenger in Archiv für Papyrusforschung 13, 310, and the literature cited there.

[41] F. Pringsheim, *Die Rechtsstellung der* Πέρσαι τῆς ἐπιγονῆς Zeitschrift der Savigny-Stiftung für Rechtsgeschichte, Romanistische Abteilung, 44(1924), 396-526

[42] See *ibid.*, 411ff.

In P. Petr. III 7, a will from Crocodilopolis dated 238/37 B.C.E., lines 11-17, in Mahaffy's English translation, read as follows:

"I leave all my possesions to my wife Eirene, the daughter of Asclepiades, of Cyrene, and to Demo my daughter by Eirene, together with my slaves Parthemion and Myrine, females ..., males, and according to the bill in the public registry Apollonius a foreigner, who is also called, in the Syrian language, Jonathan, who owes me 150 dr. in silver".

The word, which is here translated as "a foreigner" is παρεπίδημος which occurs in the LXX Gen. 23:4 as the rendering of the Hebrew תושב (a sojourner). In the context in which it occurs in the papyrus the word is obviously difficult. Why was it thought necessary or expedient to indicate in the will that Apollonius-Jonathan was "a foreigner" or "a sojourner". Kreller (*Erbrechtliche Untersuchungen auf Grund der graeco-ägyptischen Papyrusurkunden,* 252) is justifiably sceptical of the rendering "a foreigner", referring to Apollonius as "ein auswärtiger Schuldner(?)". The solution of the difficulty, as appears from Philo, *De Virtutibus,* 122, quoted above, was the Jewish legal practice in Alexandria.

2. The so-called πίστις clause. In this clause the debtor apparently waives his right to resort to the protection of the *strategos* against the exactions of the creditor.[43] A similar waiver of the right to resort to the protection of officials occurs in Cowley 10, a loan agreement of 456 B. C. E. In lines 12-14 of this document it is stated: ולא אכל אקבל עליך קדם סגן ודין לם ("And I shall not be allowed to לקחת מני ערבן וספרא זנה בידך. complain against thee before governor or judge saying 'thou hast taken a pledge from me', while this deed is in thy hand' ".).

3. In many of the documents of an obligatory nature in which the obligor is designated as Persian of the Epigone it is stated that the obligation is to be discharged ἄνευ δίκης καὶ κρίσεως, which literally means *without lawsuit or judgment.*[44] This, undoubtedly, is a translation of the stereotyped phrase ולא דין ודבב (without judgment and lawsuit) occurring numerous times in the Aramaic papyri.[45]

At this point the writer begs to be permitted a digression. The phrase דין ודברים, which corresponds to the דין ודבב of the

the writer believes, is to be sought in a special nuance of the Hebrew word תושב of which the Greek term is a literal translation. This Hebrew word is sometimes used to denote a person who dwells in his creditor's house working off a debt. The word is used in this sense in the phrase תושב כהן (a sojourner of a priest) in Lev. 22:10 and perhaps also in Lev. 25:35 and 40. Cf. *The Middle Assyrian Laws,* Tablet A, col. 6.40f. (Driver-Miles, *The Assyrian Laws,* 412). Jonathan, who was obviously Jewish, was in debt bondage, working off a debt of 150 drachmae which he owed to the testator. This would seem to indicate that in the third century B. C. E. in Egypt Jews were subject to debt bondage, and the fact that the term by which the person in debt bondage is denoted seems to be a Hebraism points to the conclusion that the institution was especially applicable to Jews.

[43] See *ibid.,* 499. See also F. Woess, *Das Asylwesen Aegyptens in der Ptolemäerzeit* (Müncherner Beiträge zur Papyrusforschung und antiken Rechtsgeschichte, Heft 5), 184ff.

[44] See *ibid.,* 502f.

[45] See e. g., Cowley 6.12; 8.12,14; Brooklyn 1.5; 3.13,14; 5.15.

Aramaic papyri, occurs in the Mishnah [46] and also in Jewish medieval documents,[47] whence it apparently found its way in the later Middle Ages into non-Jewish documents. Rabel[48] has called attention to the parallelism between the phrase ἄνευ δίκης καὶ κρίσεως which becomes very frequent in the papyri of the late Byzantine period and the phrase *sine omni strepitu iudicii et querele* occuring in some 15th century documents from Germany quoted by Kisch.[49] However, he makes no attempt whatsoever to account for the interval of almost a thousand years between the late Byzantine papyri, where the Greek phrase occurs frequently, and the 15th century documents from Germany where the Latin phrase occurs. This interval certainly calls for an explanation. The explanation, it seems, is that the Jewish formulary is the source of both the Greek and the Latin phrases. It would seem that, as a matter of sound methodology, Rabel and Kisch should have given some thought to the possibility of the influence of the Jewish formulary upon the form of loan agreements in 15th century Germany. Had they done so, they would have discovered that the clauses *mit und ohne Recht* and *mit oder an gericht* (with or without court), which occur in loan agreements of the same period written in German [50] and to which Rabel likewise calls attention, were also copied from the Jewish formulary. Similar clauses occur in Jewish forms [51] of the Middle Ages, and a 13th century Jewish authority,[52] in a responsum, discusses the legal effect of such a clause authorizing the lender to levy execution בבית דין ושלא בבית דין (in court and without court).

[46] Mishnah, Kethubot, 9:1.

[47] See, e. g., ספר השטרות of R. Jehudah b. Barzillai, no. 44; M. Davis, ed., *Hebrew Deeds of English Jews before 1290*, 206.

[48] E. Rabel, *Papyrusurkunden der öffentlichen Bibliothek der Universität zu Basel* (Abhandl. d. königl. Gesellschaft d. Wiss. zu Göttingen, Philologisch-hist. Kl. N. F. XVI, 3 (1917), 83.

[49] G. Kisch, *Die Pfändungsklausel*, Zeitschrift der Savigny-Stiftung fur Rechtsgeschichte, germanistische Abt., 35, 41ff.

[50] See *ibid.*, 60.

[51] See A. Gulak, אוצר השטרות, no. 216.

[52] See Responsa of R. Asher b. Yechiel, ch. 68, sec. 13.

In a document from Dura-Europos, Dura Pg. 22.25 (204 C. E.) published by Welles,[53] there occurs the phrase ἄνευ λόγου καὶ κρίσεως, which is obviously but a variation of ἄνευ δίκης καὶ κρίσεως. Welles has noted some remarkable parallelisms between the legal documents from Dura-Europos and Greco-Egyptian documents of the late Byzantine period.[54] One of these is the phrase ἄνευ λόγου which occurs in Greco-Egyptian documents very late only.[55] Anyone familiar with Biblical Hebrew and Aramaic will at once recognize that λόγος (word) is used in this phrase in the sense of *lawsuit,* and that it is a literal translation of the Hebrew דבר, which is used in the Bible in this sense,[56] or of the Aramaic דבב, which is used in the Aramaic papyri in a similar sense.

The formula *without lawsuit or process* thus has a long history. From the Aramaic papyri of the 5th century B. C. E. to the Greco-Egyptian documents of the Ptolemaic period, to Dura Pg. 22 of 204 C. E., to the Greco-Egyptian documents of the late Byzantine period, to Jewish medieval documents and, finally, to 15th century documents from Germany. In all probability, it was the people "scattered and dispersed among all the nations" that were responsible for the wide dissemination of this legal formula and its continuance over a period of two millenia.

4. In many of the documents of an obligatory nature in which the obligor is designated as a Persian of the Epigone it is provided that the obligation is to be discharged ἄνευ πάσης ὑπερθέσεως

---

[53] C. Bradford Welles, *Die zivilen Archive in Dura, Münchener Beiträge zur Papyrusforschhung und antiken Rechtsgeschichte,* Heft 19(1934), 379ff.

[54] *Ibid.,* 386, n. 6.

[55] Welles, *ibid.,* also calls attention to the term καθαροποιεῖν (to clear) which is used in Dura Pg. 23.19 (180 C.E.) and also in the Greco-Egyptian papyri of the late Byzantine period in the sense of clearing property of adverse claims. As will be shown below (p. 170), this term too is probably a translation from the Aramaic.

[56] Cf. דבר להם יחיה כי in Ex. 18:16 Cf. also דברים בעל in Ex. 24:14. The latter phrase corresponds to *be-el a-wa-ti-šu* in the Series *ana ittiisû,* tablet 7, col. 1, 1.51, which is rendered by Landsberger (*Materialen zum summerischen Lexicon,* I, 94) as *seinem Prozessgegner.*

(without any delay).[57] A similar provision is contained in medieval Jewish forms of documents of an obligatory nature,[58] where it seems to be designed to overcome the rule of Talmudic law that a defaulting debtor be given by the court 30 days of grace within which to satisfy the debt.[59] How far back this rule of Talmudic law goes is difficult to determine, but it may well be a very old one.

The theory has been advanced by Tait [60] that the designation Persian of the Epigone, which in the Roman period occurs only in the description of the obligor in documents of an obligatory nature, was in many cases but a fiction which was resorted to in order to subject the obligor to the stricter rules of execution which applied to Persians of the Epigone. He bases his theory, principally, upon BGU 1142, one of the papyri from Alexandria, Oxy. 271 and Lips. 120, where it is stated that the obligors styled themselves (χρηματίζειν) Persians of the Epigone.[61] Pringsheim [62] rejects this theory insofar as documents other than those from Alexandria are concerned on the ground that in Ptolemaic and Roman Egypt an unauthorized change of name or designation was strictly forbidden, which makes it extremely unlikely that a fiction involving an unauthorized change of designation should have become general.

It is quite apparent that Pringsheim's objection to the fiction theory applies with the same force to the documents from Alexandria as to all other documents. But with regard to the Alexandrian documents he was driven to the reluctant acceptance of the fiction theory [63] by the fact that in all of these documents of an obligatory nature the obligors are designated as Persians

---

[57] See the articles by Pringsheim cited in n. 41, above, 502f.
[58] See A. Gulak, *ibid.*, no. 213 *et seq.*
[59] See Mishnah, Baba Kama 8:6; BT, Baba Metzia, 118a.
[60] J. G. Tait in Archiv fur Papyrusforschung 7, 175ff.
[61] *Ibid.*, 179f.
[62] See his article cited in n. 41, above, 517ff.
[63] *Ibid.*, 525.

of the Epigone, while from the names they bear it appears that they are a diversified group, as far as national origin is concerned, including Greeks, Romans and Egyptians. Pringsheim [64] also considered the possibility that the Persians of the Epigone of the Alexandrian documents were Jews, and presented some cogent arguments in favor of this possiblity. But he decided in favor of the fiction theory for the reason which has just been stated. However, the writer believes that the names are by no means an indication that the parties were not Jewish, and, besides, it is quite possible that some of these parties became Persians of the Epigone by embracing the Jewish faith. This, incidentally, will perhaps explain the cases, noted above, in which it is stated that the parties *styled themselves* Persians of the Epigone. In these cases the parties were perhaps not Persians of the Epigone by birth but acquired that status by embracing the Jewish faith.

Persians of the Epigone and Agraphos Gamos.

One of the unsolved problems of the law of the Roman period in Egypt is that of the nature and origin of the *agraphos gamos* (literally, unwritten marriage).[65] The writer believes that the solution of this problem is to be sought in the customs and law relating to marriage which prevailed among the Jews during this period and which are reflected in Talmudic sources. In the writer's opinion, *agraphos gamos* means marriage without a *kethubah,* that is without an obligation on the part of the husband to pay to the wife a certain amount of money — a minimum of 200 *zuz* in the case of a virgin and 100 *zuz* in the case of a widow — if he should divorce her.[66] In some cases this obligation must have been so onerous that it virtually precluded divorce. As a result, the custom apparently developed that by agreement between husband and wife at the time when their joint life began the assumption of the obligation by the husband to pay to the

[64] *Ibid.*
[65] See Wolff, *ibid.,* 48ff.
[66] See Mishnah, Kethuboth 1:2.

wife the amount of the *kethuba* in case of divorce was postponed
to a future time. Rabbi Meir (c. middle of the 2nd century
C. E.) condemned this practice and enunciated the rule:
כל הפוחת לבתולה ממאתים ולאלמנה ממנה הרי זו בעילת זנות.
(If one assumes an obligation of less than 200 *zuz* for a virgin
or less than a mina for a widow, it is a fornication).[67] However,
with respect to this rule of Rabbi Meir it is stated in the Talmud:
זו דברי רבי מאיר אבל חכמים אומרים משהא אדם את אשתו שתים
ושלש שנים בלא כתובה. (This is the opinion of R. Meir, but
the Sages say: 'A man may live with his wife for two or three
years without a ketubah' ").[68] From this statement it appears
that the Sages were not just laying down a theoretical rule but
that they were referring to an actual practice to which they gave
their approval. The purpose of this practice, in the cases in which
it was resorted to, apparently was to allow a sufficient trial
period of two or three years to elapse before the husband em-
barked upon the heavy obligation of the *ketubah* which would
make divorce virtually impossible for him.

In the Greco-Egyptian papyri, there is a series of documents
of the first and second centuries which attest to a practice similar
to the one alluded to in the Talmud and referred to above.
In these documents couples who are already living as husband
and wife in *agraphos gamos* establish a new basis for their union
in which a *pherne* — the equivalent of the Hebrew *ketubah* — is
invariably constituted. Wolff [69] cites ten such documents, and
it so happens that in seven of these the grooms are designated
as Persians of the Epigone.[70] Of the remaining three documents,
two [71] are of the latter part of the second century, when the
designation Persian of the Epigone is no longer used in legal

[67] *Ibid.*, 5:1.
[68] BT., Kethubot, 57a.
[69] *Ibid.*, 58, n. 205.
[70] PSI 36a, Ryl. 154, BGU 183, 232, 251, 252, CPR 28.
[71] BGU 1045, PSI 450 *recto*, col. I.

documents, and one [72] is mutilated at the beginning. This points
to the conclusion that the *agraphos gamos* in Egypt in the first
and second centuries C. E. was an institution peculiar to Persians
of the Epigone, and the fact that a similar institution is found
among the Jews in Palestine during the same period furnishes
further proof of some relationship between Persians of the Epigone
and Jews.

A further indication of some connection between Jewish
marriage customs and the *agraphos gamos* of the papyri is furnished by P. Oxy. 267 of the year 36 C. E., the oldest document
attesting an *agraphos gamos*. In this document the weaver
Tryphon, son of Dionysios, a Persian of the Epigone, acknowledges
to Saraeus, daughter of Apion, that he has received from her a
"loan" of 72 drachmas, consisting of 40 silver drachmas, one pair
of earrings worth 20 drachmas, and one dress worth 12 drachmas,
"to which nothing at all has been added". The meaning of the
phrase "to which nothing at all has been added" can only be
understood in the light of a Talmudic parallel to which Gulak [73]

---

[72] Oxy. 265.

[73] A Gulak, *Das Urkundenwesen im Talmud im Lichte der griechisch-
ägyptischen Papyri und des griechichen und römischen Rechts,* 65. The liberal
appraisal of the dowry was probably due to a desire to make it appear that
the bride was richly endowed. It seems that in keeping with this desire to
make it appear that the parties were no mere paupers the custom developed
in some places to name in the *kethubah* an amount which was double of what
was actually agreed upon between the parties. As a result of this custom, R.
Jose the Galilean (1st half of 2nd century C. E.) enunciated the rule that
in a place where they are wont to double the *kethubah* the wife collects only
one-half thereof: מקום שכופלין כתובה אינו (אינה?) גובה אלא מחצה (Tosefta,
Kethuboth 4:13, ed. Zuckermandel 265).

Incidentally, the custom referred to by R. Jose the Galilean affords a
satisfactory explanation of a puzzling feature in Brooklyn 2 (449 B. C. E.),
the oldest of the three marriage documents in the Aramaic papyri now extant.
In the text of the document the total of the bride's dowry is given as 7 *shekels*
and 7½ *hallur*, whereas in the endorsement it is given as 1 *karsh*, 5 *shekels*.
Commenting on the discrepancy, Kraeling (APK, 150) says:

> "In the text we heard the value of the goods was 7 shekels
> and 7 hallur...Here in the endorsement her assets are doubled.

has already called attention. According to Mishnah, Ketuboth 6:3, one-fifth of the total is to be deducted from the appraised value of the articles brought to the husband by the wife, the custom apparently having been to appraise these articles liberally. However, if the parties stipulated that the appraised value is to be considered the true value (שום במנה ושוה מנה), the stipulation is to be given effect. This is apparently what is meant by the phrase "to which nothing at all has been added" in P. Oxy. 267. The parallelism between this phrase in the papyrus, on the one hand, and the Mishnah, on the other, can hardly be due to chance. Both point to the same custom —- that of a liberal appraisal of the articles—to the same rule growing out of this custom — that of a deduction from the appraised value — and, finally, to the same stipulation designed to overcome this rule.

The *agraphos gamos* is also referred to in Pg. Dura 22 of the year 204 C. E.[74] From this Wolff concludes that it was a Greek institution.[75] However, this conclusion is unwarranted. The occurrence of the institution in Dura-Europos proves perhaps that it was not Egyptian, but it does not prove that it was Greek. In view of the evidence discussed above, the "people scattered

> She may thus have brought in some cash money, disclosed belatedly, or received wedding presents. The increase was taken into account in this way".

Without the aid of the Tosefta, quoted above, a modern commentator could hardly arrive at the true reason for the discrepancy. It seems that at first the exaggeration, which was resorted to for the purpose of ostentation, was confined to the endorsement on the back of the document, which remained visible after the document was sealed, but that as time went on — perhaps as a result of changes in the external characteristics of the document — it came to be incorporated in the text itself. It is regrettable that the endorsements in the two other marriage documents in the Aramaic papyri are lost. See APC, 50 and APK, 222. It is not unlikely that they would have revealed discrepancies similar to that of Brooklyn 2.

[74] See C. Bradford Welles, *Die zivilen Archive in Dura,* Münchener Beitrage zur Papyrusforschung und antiken Rechtsgeschichte, Heft 19, 389ff.

[75] Wolff, *ibid.,* 50.

and dispersed among the nations of the world" is more likely to have been the source of this institution, both among the Persians of the Epigone of Egypt and in Dura-Europos. It is not without significance in this connection that Pg. Dura 22 contains a phrase which is characteristic of documents in which Persians of the Epigone are parties and which is undoubtedly a translation from the Aramaic.[76]

[76] See p. 82, above.

CHAPTER VIII

THE ARAMAIC PAPYRI AND THE PAPYRI FROM GEBELEN.

The papyri from Gebelên, of which the Adler papyri are a part, contain a large number of deeds of sale, dated between 140 and 88 B.C.[1] These documents all follow a set form. They begin (leaving out of consideration the date-formula) with a statement that A has sold certain property (described by bounds). This is followed by a statement that B has purchased the property for a certain price, which is named, and then follows a clause the meaning of which is not altogether clear. The following is an excerpt from such a document:

ἀπέδοτο Πετεῆσις Πατῆτος Πέρσης . . . τὴν ὑπάρχου-
σαν αὐτῷ οἰκίαν . . . ἐπρίατο Πελαίας Εὐνόου χα(λκοῦ)
(ταλάντου) α· προπωλητὴς καὶ βεβαιωτὴς τῶν κατὰ τὴν
ὠνὴν ταύτην πάντων Πετεῆσις ὁ ἀποδόμενος, ὃν ἐδέξατο
Πελαίας ὁ πριάμενος.[2]

The English translation by Hunt and Edgar reads:
"Peteesis son of Pates, Persian . . . has sold the house belonging to him . . . Pelaeas son of Eunous has bought it for 1 talent of copper. Negotiator and guarantor of all the terms of this deed of sale: Pateesis the vendor, who has been accepted by Pelaeas the purchaser".[3]

Even a cursory reading of the last clause of this document

---

[1] A list of 36 such documents is given by A. B. Schwarz in *Homologie und Protokoll* (Festschrift für Zitelmann, 1913), 8, n. 2. Additional documents are listed in GLS, 194, n. 5.

[2] P. Amh. 51.22-29.

[3] SP, 85.

will reveal that it bristles with difficulties. What is meant by the phrase "negotiator of the terms of this deed of sale", and what is the meaning of the *acceptance* of the vendor by the buyer? Pringsheim[4] following Mitteis,[5] maintains that the term προπωλητής which is rendered by Hunt and Edgar as *negotiator,* means literally previous seller, that is the seller's seller, and he offers an ingenious explanation of this term in our clause as well as of the whole clause. Originally, he asserts, the person who would normally be the guarantor of the sale of property was he who sold the property to the seller. Later on, the buyer "became more and more willing to accept the warranty of the vendor, and eventually this acceptance became stereotyped". The term προπωλητής then, is synonymous with βεβαιωτής meaning guarantor, and the acceptance of the vendor by the buyer refers to the acceptance of the latter by the former as guarantor.

It seems to the writer that Hunt and Edgar's rendering of the term προπωλητής as *negotiator* is to be preferred to that of Pringsheim and Mitteis, although, as we shall presently see, it does not fully convey the meaning of this term. The clause in question seems to be a concise summary, in objective form, of the contents of a *Zwiegesprächsurkunde* in the form of an offer by the vendor stating the terms of the sale and of an acceptance of the offer by the buyer. The term προπωλητής means the person who started the negotiations leading to the sale — the offeror — and the acceptance refers to the acceptance of the vendor's offer by the buyer.

The *Zwiegesprächsurkunde* is a type of document which became frequent in Babylonia during the late Persian period.[6] It recites, in direct discourse, the offer by one of the parties, and, in objective form, the acceptance by the other party. These recitals are followed by a statement of the legal consequences

---

[4] GLS, 439.

[5] MGP, 188.

[6] See J. Kohler und A. Ungnad, *Hundert ausgewählte Urkunden* aus der *Spätzeit des babylonischen Schrifttums,* 73f.; M. San-Nicolo, *Beiträge zur Rechtsgeschichte im Bereiche der keilschriftlichen Rechtsquellen,* 152; 219, n. 1.

of the offer and acceptance. The following is an excerpt from the English translation of such a document dated in the 37th year of the reign of Artaxerxes I (429 B.C.E.):

> "X, son of Y, spoke of his own free will to A, son of B, thus: 'My orchard and uncultivated land and the orchard and uncultivated land of C, my deceased uncle (literally, brother of my father), ... all I will give to thee for sixty years for rent and for planting it with trees, hold thou the orchard for a rent of twenty gur of dates per annum and the uncultivated land for planting it with trees. Whereupon A, son of B, accepted his offer (literally, hearkened unto him), and for sixty years he took over (literally, held) the orchard and the uncultivated land, his (i. e., X's) portion and the portion of his deceased uncle C, the orchard part for a rent of twenty *gur* of dates per annum, and the uncultivated part for planting it with trees. Each year in the month of Tishri, A shall pay the twenty *gur* of dates to X, as rent of that property.
>
> From the month of Nisan of the 37th year of King Artaxerxes that property is held for sixty years for rent and for planting it with trees by A, son of B".[7]

San-Nicolo cautiously suggests that this new type of document, which is fundamentally different from the old type which had been in use in Babylonia for a period of over two millenia, was perhaps brought there from the West together with the new writing material of papyrus and parchment.[8] As the writer has shown elsewhere,[9] there is a strong possibility that the *Zwiege-*

---

[7] UPBE, Series A, v. 9, 36-38.

[8] San-Nicolo, *ibid.,* 160.

[9] Asaf Anniversary Book (Jerusalem, 1953), 433f. (Hebrew). In this article I have shown that in the portion of the form of a deed of conveyance quoted in BT, Baba Metzia 15a the last phrase וצבי זבונא דנן וקביל עלוהי means "and this purchaser agreed and accepted (the seller's offer)" — which makes it

sprächsurkunde was introduced in Babylonia by exiles from Judea. The pattern of the *Zwiegesprächsurkunde* is discernible already in the story of the purchase of the cave of Machpelah by Abraham, and this type of document was used extensively, probably exclusively, by Jews throughout the Talmudic period.[10] In one legal form, that of the *kethubah* (marriage document), it is used by Jews to this day.[11]

The parallelism between the *Zwiegesprächsurkunde* and the story of the purchase of the cave of Machpelah is fully apparent even from the English translation, which reads:

> "And Ephron answered Abraham, saying unto him: 'My lord, hearken unto me: a piece of land worth four hundred shekels of silver, what is that betwixt me and thee? bury therefore thy dead.' And Abraham hearkened unto Ephron; and Abraham weighed to Ephron the silver, which he had named in the hearing of the children of Heth, four hundred shekels of silver, current money with the merchant. So the field of Ephron, which was in Machpelah, which was before Mamre, the field, and the cave which was therein, and all the trees that were in the field, that were in all the border thereof round about, were made sure unto Abraham for a possession in the presence of the children of Heth, before all that went in at the gate of his city". (Gen. 23: 15-18).

There is here a recital of the offer by Ephron, in direct discourse, of the acceptance by Abraham, in objective form, and a statement of the legal consequences of the offer and acceptance. Particularly revealing is the expression *he hearkened unto him* (Hebrew שמע = Accadian *šemû*), which is used in both the

---

strikingly similar to the last phrase in the deeds of conveyance from Gebelên.

[10] See, e. g., Mishnah, Kethubot 4:8-12.

[11] See *Jewish Encyclopedia*, v. 7, 472; McClintock and Strong, *Cyclopedia of Biblical, Theological and Ecclesiastical Literature*, v. 5, 776.

Babylonian document and the Biblical story in the technical legal sense of *he accepted his offer.*

Pringsheim, in his discussion of the type of deed of sale represented by the Gebelên papyri, referring particularly to the form "A has sold — B has purchased", says that "perhaps Egyptian influence explains that form".[12] However, in the light of what has been said above, it seems that the form "A has sold — B has purchased" is fully in keeping with the pattern of the *Zwiegesprächsurkunde,* which was in the mind of the draftsman. With respect to this type of document, San-Nicolo says:

> "Das juristisch wichtigere ist aber dabei die für das babylonisch-assyrische Urkundenwesen ganz ungewohnte Hervorhebung des *Konsensualmomentes* beim Vertragsabschluss . . . "

In the Gebelên papyri, too, the two-sidedness of the transaction, the *consensus* between the parties, comes to the fore.

In the Aramaic papyri, as in demotic legal documents, the maker of the document generally speaks in the first person, in direct discourse, to the person in whose favor the document is made. With but one exception which occurs in the Brooklyn collection and which we shall presently discuss, there is no reference in the Aramaic papyri to an offer by one party and an acceptance by the other. This may be due to the fact that not until the Brooklyn papyri were published was there any Aramaic papyrus representing a deed of sale available. Fortunately, the oldest papyrus in the Brooklyn collection, no. 1 of 451 B. C. E., represents just such a deed and it does contain a reference to an offer by one party and an acceptance of the offer by the other. This document [13] has been misinterpreted by Kraeling, and the writer must admit that he is partly responsible for the misinterpretation. The seller's statement in the document begins as follows:

יהבת לי כסף שקלן 5 בדמי הירא זילך זי קבלת עלי בגו.

The crucial words upon which the interpretation of the document

---

[12] GLS, 104.
[13] APK, 132f.

depends are קבל על. Kraeling took these words to mean "lodge a complaint" and accordingly he translated the passage just quoted as folows: "Thou hast given me silver, 5 shekels, as the price of the *hira* of thine about which thou didst bring complaint against me". When the writer, at the invitation of Professor Kraeling, first inspected the papyrus, he agreed with him that the words קבל על in the above passage mean "to lodge a complaint" and suggested that the document represents a sale in the form of a fictitious suit. Upon further consideration, however, the writer is convinced that this view is erronous. The purpose of making a transfer of property in the form of a fictitious suit is to afford greater security to the transferee by invoking the high authority of the court in aid of the transfer. This being so, it is unthinkable that in a document representing a transfer in such form the name of the court, or of the judge, before which, or before whom, the transfer was made should not be mentioned at all. The conclusion is therefore inescapable that the document represents an ordinary sale, and not one in the form of a fictitious suit.

As to קבל על, it does not mean in the above passage "to lodge a complaint" but "to agree, accept an offer". Accordingly, the passage should be rendered thus: "Thou hast given me silver, 5 shekels, the price of the *hira* on which I agreed". As the writer has shown elsewhere,[14] the words קבל על are used a number of times in the Talmud in the sense of "to agree, to accept an offer". In Maccabees I, 6:60, we read:

καὶ ἤρεσεν ὁ λόγος ἐναντίον τοῦ βασιλέως καὶ τῶν ἀρχόντων, καὶ ἀπέστειλεν πρὸς αὐτοὺς εἰρηνεῦσαι, καὶ ἐπεδέξαντο.

"And the saying pleased the king and the leaders,

---

[14] See his article cited in n. 9, above, at p. 436, n. 7. If קבל על is taken to mean *agree*, the correction suggested by Kraeling (APK, 133, 136) of קבלת עלי, instead of קבלת עליך, in line 6 of Brooklyn 12 becomes unnecessary. Purchase and sale being a bilateral transaction, the term *agree* applies to the buyer as well as to the seller.

and he sent unto them to make peace; and they accepted thereof".[15]

The word ἐπεδέξαντο in the sense of "they agreed to, accepted the offer", seems to be a literal translation of קבלו עליהם. Interestingly enough, the word ἐπιδέχεσθαι is used in the same sense in P. Amh. 31, 1.12, one of the papyri from Gebelên.

From the foregoing discussion it appears that the emphasis upon the two-sidednes of the transaction, upon the offer and acceptance, in sale is common to the Greek papyri from Gebelên and to Jewish sources, Biblical and Talmudic. It is probably not without significance in this connection that the demotic papyri from Gebelên, covering about the same period of time and stemming from the same group of people as the Greek papyri from this locality, contain some clauses which have striking parallels in the Mishnah.

Marriage Documents from Gebelên

In all of the available marriage documents from Gebelên there is a clause which reads: "I shall not be able to require an oath from thee in the house of judgment on account of the right of thy woman's property above (named), saying 'thou didst not bring them to my house in thy hand' ".[16] In Mishnah, Ketubot, 9:5, it is stated: "If he declared to her in writing, 'I will require of thee neither vow nor oath', he may not exact of her an oath. . . ". The similarity between this passage from the Mishnah and the clause just quoted from the demotic marriage document is quite obvious and suggests some relationship between them. How is this similarity to be accounted for? Were some of the clauses of the demotic marriage document from Gebelên copied from a Jewish model? There is some indication that this was the case.

In some of the marriage documents from Gebelên there is

---

[15] R. H. Charles, *Apocrypha and Pseudoepigrapha of the Old Testament*, v. 1, 90.

[16] GCD, 134. Cf. p. 39, above.

a clause which, in Griffith's English translation, reads: "If I abandon thee as wife, and hate thee and approach(?) another woman than thee, I will give unto thee the hair(?) of these X pieces of silver and Y (measures of) wheat(?) which I have given unto thee as a bridal gift".[17] As the writer has shown above,[18] the words for *abandon* and *hate* are technical terms of divorce in Accadian, Hebrew and Aramaic, and when used in this sense in demotic they seem to have been borrowed from a Semitic source, probably Jewish. In addition to these terms, the word for *approach,* which is used in this demotic document in the sense of *have sexual intercourse* and which puzzled Griffith, has an exact parallel in the Bible. קרב (come near, approach) is used numerous times in the Bible in precisely the same sense. Following are some examples:

ואבימלך לא קרב אליה (Now Abimelech had not come near her) — Gen. 20:4; את האשה הזאת לקחתי ואקרב אליה ולא מצאתי לה בתולים (I took this woman, and when I came nigh to her, I found not in her the tokens of virginity) — Deut. 22:14; ואקרב אל הנביאה ותהר ותלד בן (And I came near the prophetess; and she conceived and bore a son) — Isa. 8:3.

Finally, in the writer's opinion, the phrase "I will give unto thee the hair etc" is highly significant in this respect. What is the meaning of "the hair" in this phrase? Griffith suggests that it means "full and precise weight (to the hair)",[19] which is obviously strained. The writer believes that the awkward phrase is the result of a misreading and mistranslation by some scribe of a Hebrew word. The scribe had before him the word שער meaning *current value, market price* and he misread it as שער meaning *hair,* which has the identical spelling, and translated accordingly.

A Deed of Gift from Gebelên.

Another parallel to the Mishnah occurs in Ryl. dem. 17

---

[17] *Ibid.*
[18] See p. 40, above.
[19] GCD, 134, n. 6.

(118 B.C.E.), a deed of gift of a house from Gebelên, which contains the following clause: "I have given it unto thee: it is thine: it is thy house built and covered in, fully provided with beams and doors comprising a chamber(?), a forecourt, and a staircase(?) below upward, (described) above".[20] What is rendered by Griffith as "below upward, (described) above" probably corresponds to עוּמְקָא וְרוּמָא‎ אָ‎ (the depth and the height, that which is below and that which is above) clause which, as appears from Mishnah, Baba Bathra, 4:2, was a regular feature of the deed of conveyance of house property.

The above parallel between Ryl. dem. 17 and Mishnah, Baba Bathra, 4:2 assumes special significance in view of the fact that the scribe who wrote that document seems to have been Jewish. At the end of the document it is stated: "Written by Espnuti, son of Zeho, writing in the name of the priests of Sobk, lord of Amur, of the 5 orders". Commenting on the name Espnuti, Griffith says: "Meaning 'belonging to God'; it suggests a Jewish monotheist".[21]

The Deeds of Cession or Renunciation from Gebelên

There is a group of papyri, mostly stemming from Gebelên and neighboring districts in the Thebaid, which represent renunciations of rights to property as well as renunciations of personal rights.[22] Schwarz [23] states that these renunciations cannot be considered a peculiarity of the local notarial style, since such a renunciation is also found in P. Hib. 96 of the year 259 B.C.E. As has been stated above,[24] the ספר מרחק‎ (document of removal, renunciation) is used in the Aramaic papyri in precisely the same double sense of cession of rights to

---

[20] Ibid., 144.

[21] Ibid., n. 10. It is perhaps not without significance that the same scribe wrote Ryl. dem. 20 (GCD, 149f.) and Ryl. dem. 22 (GCD, 151f.), two marriage documents from Gebelên of 116 and 115-108 B.C.E., respectively.

[22] A list of these papyri is given by Schwarz, ibid., p. 11, n. 5.

[23] Ibid., p. 11.

[24] See p. 23, above.

property and release of personal claims. As to P. Hib. 96, a mutual general release of claims by two parties to one another, it is perhaps not without significance that one of the parties is designated as a Jew and the other was probably also a Jew.

How is the affinity between the papyri from Gebelên, Greek and demotic, and Jewish sources to be explained? The answer to this question, the writer believes, may well shed considerable light upon the problem of the national origin of the people figuring in the papyri from Gebelên who, as noted above, are designated as Persians of the Epigone.[25]

---

[25] See p. 75, above. For further similarities between this group of papyri and Jewish sources, see ch. 16, n. 42.

CHAPTER IX

THE DEMOTIC PAPYRI OF THE PTOLEMAIC PERIOD AND THE ARAMAIC PAPYRI

In Brooklyn 12, a deed of sale of house property, the property is described, in lines 3-5, as follows:

ביתן זי זבן בכסף מן בגזשת בר פלין כספיא הו ביתה זי
ינבולי בר מסדי כספי זי ביב הו מהחסן.

This is rendered by Kraeling as follows:

> "Our house which we bought with silver from Bagazust b. Plyn, 'silverman', that is the house of Yanbuli b. Misdai 'silverman', which in Yeb he possessed".[1]

In his comment on the second הו in line 4, he suggests that it might be an error for הוה, since, as he says, "an indication of the past would be desirable".[2] However, when the technical meaning of the term מהחסן is properly understood, it becomes obvious that "an indication of the past" would be quite incongruous. מהחסן means a tenant, that is a person holding property of which someone else is the owner. The last part of the above-quoted description, beginning with הו ביתה, should therefore be rendered as follows: "That is the house of which Yanbuli b. Misdai the 'silverman' is a tenant". The sellers were not in possession of the property which they sold. It was therefore thought desirable to mention in the description of the property the name of the person who was in actual possession.

The method of describing property by naming, in addition to the owner, the person who is in possession thereof, is also found

---

[1] APK, 270ff.
[2] Ibid., 275.

frequently in the demotic papyri of the Ptolemaic period. In British Museum 10523 [3] (296-295 B.C.E.), for example, a loan on a mortgage of a house, the house is described as follows:

> "... my house, which is built and roofed, (and) which is in the Northern district of Thebes in The-House-of-the-Cow, whose (boundries) are: (to) its south — the house of the joiner(?) of the house of Amen Kludj son of Djufachi, which is in the possession of Petenefhopet son of Aludj".

It is to be noted that the word מהחסן (holder), without specifying what is held, appears frequently in the Aramaic papyri in the description of persons. In Cowley 7.2, for example, we read: ("Said Malchiah b.Josh-אמר מלכיה בר ישביה ארמי מהחסן ביב-ibiah, holder in Yeb").[4] In a note, Cowley says: "מהחסן the regular word for 'holding property' ".[5] More precisely, he should have said "the regular word for holding property of which some-one else is owner". It seems that when the term מהחסן, without more, is used in the description of a person it means *a tenant of royal land,* that is a holder of an allotment, title to which remained vested in the king.

The Brooklyn Museum Aramaic papyri furnish another striking parallel to the demotic papyri of the Ptolemaic period. In Brooklyn 12.2, one Anani b. Azariah is described as "Lhnah (servant?) of Yahu the god who dwells in Yeb the fortress" (שכן יב ברתה).[6] Commenting on the words שכן יב (who dwells in Yeb), Kraeling says that this usage is astonishingly like the

---

[3] S. R. K. Glanville, ed, *Catalogue of Demotic Papyri in the British Museum,* 10ff. See also Br. Mus. 10527 (*ibid.,* 29ff.); H. Thompson, *A Family Archive from Siut,* 28ff., 41ff. A similar description of property also occurs in Greek papyri from Gebelên. See, e. g., Adler Gr. 5, col. II. 8; 16.7,9; 20.12.

[4] APC, 19f. See also Cowley 8.2; 16.2.

[5] *Ibid.,* In Roman sources, too, the term "possessor", without mere, was used to designate a holder of *ager occupatorius.* See M. Kaser, *Die Typen der römischen Bodenrechte in der späteren Republik,* Zeitschrift der Savigny-Stiftung für Rechtsgechichte, Rom. Abt., 62 (1942), 27.

[6] APK, 271.

Biblical "usage in such passages as Deut. 33:16 שכני סנה, Ps. 135:21 שכן ירושלים and probably reveals the impact of Palestinian theology".[7] Precisely the same usage occurs in demotic papyri of the Ptolemaic period. The formula of an oath in Adler dem. 17, 19, 28 [8] and Ryl. dem. 36 [9] begins as follows: "As Sobk liveth who resteth here and every god who resteth with him". In a complaint in court, the complainant speaks "before her lords, the judges of the priests of Wepwoi and the gods who dwell with him".[10] The similarity between the phraseology in these demotic documents and the Biblical usage referred to by Kraeling speaks for itself. An appraisal of the significance of this parallelism from the point of view of the history of religion is outside the scope of this work. We are concerned here only with its significance from the point of view of style.

The two parallels between the Aramaic papyri and the demotic papyri of the Ptolemaic period, discussed above, concern incidental matters which do not bear upon the substance of the documents in which they occur, although their significance as pointing to the influence of the style of the Aramaic papyri upon that of the demotic document of the Ptolemaic period is perhaps so much the greater for that. We shall now turn our attention to some of the points which bear more directly upon the substance of the document in the main two types of legal document — the loan agreement and the deed of sale.

The loan agreement.

The opening clause in Br. Mus. 10523, the loan agreement referred to above [11] reads: "Thou hast 3 silver (pieces) and six kite, that is 18 staters, that is 3 silver (pieces) and six kite again,

---

[7] APK, 274.

[8] *The Adler Papyri*, 95, 96f., 107.

[9] GCD, 161.

[10] H. Thompson, *ibid.*, 12f. See also E. Revillout in Revue egyptologique 4(1886), 133ff., 140.

[11] See n. 3, above.

against me". Sethe-Partsch,[12] referring to the phrase which is rendered by Glanville as "thou hast against me", mention the possibility that this phrase is to be rendered as "thou hast *with me*" (*du hast bei mir*). When so rendered, the phrase fully corresponds to Deut. 15:3 — ואשר יהיה לך עם אחיך תשמט ידך ("but whatsoever of thine is with thy brother thy hand shall release"), which is technical legal language. It is interesting to note that similar technical language occurs in a Nabataean contract from the Dead Sea Region published by Starcky.[13] In fragment A. 10, the phrase מה די לך עמי (literally, what you have with me) is used in the sense of *what I owe you.*

Another clause in Br. Mus. 10523 reads: "I shall not be able to say: 'I have satisfied thee therewith (i. e. I have paid in full); I have performed for thee the rights of the writing above".[14] The first part of this clause also occurs in Cowley 10,[15] a loan agreement of 456 B. C. E. In ll. 11-12 thereof it is stated: ולא אכל אמר לך שלמתך בכספך ומרביתה וספרא זנה בידך. ("And I shall not be able to say to you 'I have paid you your money and the interest thereon, while the writing is in your hand' ".). The similarity between the two clauses is obvious, and there is a strong probability that the Aramaic version is the original one. This is shown by the phrase "I shall not be able" which is used in both the Aramaic and the demotic documents in the sense of *I shall not be allowed.* The Hebrew יכל is used in the double sense of *being able,* physically, and of *being allowed,* legally.[16] When coupled with the negative לא, the word is used numerous times in the Bible, as its equivalent is used in the Aramaic papyri, in the latter sense. Following are some examples:

---

[11] K. Sethe und J. Partsch, *Demotische Urkunden zum ägyptischen Bürgschaftsrecht* (Sächsische Akad. d. Wiss., Abhandl., philol.-hist. Kl. 32[1920]), 211f.

[13] J. Starcky, *Un contract nabatéen sur papyrus,* Revue Biblique 61(1954), 161ff.

[14] See n. 3, above.

[15] APC, 30f.

[16] See GB, 299b-300a.

לא תוכל לאכל בשעריך מעשר דגנך ("Thou art not allowed to eat within thy gates the tithe of thy corn") — Deut. 12:17; לא יוכל לבכר את בן האהובה על פני בן השנואה הבכור ("he is not allowed to make the son of the beloved the first-born before the son of the hated who is the first-born) — *ibid.*, 21:16; לא תוכל להתעלם ("thou art not allowed to hide thyself") — *ibid.*, 22:3. It is to be noted that לא תוכל and לא יוכל in these passages are rendered by the Targum as לית לך רשו (thou hast no authority) and לית ליה רשו (he has no autority), respectively. This would seem to indicate that לא יכל in the sense of *not being allowed, not having authority* is a Hebraism.

The second part of the clause just quoted from Br. Mus. 10523 does not occur in the Aramaic papyri. But it, too, was apparently copied from an Aramaic model. The expression "I have performed for thee the right of the writing" seems to be a translation of עבדת לך דין ספרא זנה ("I have done unto thee the law of this writing") which corresponds to ויעבד לך דין ספרא זנה of Brooklyn 7 and Cowley 15, and which, as noted above,[17] has a close parallel in Ex. 21:9.

Another Aramaism seems to be contained in the following clause of the loan agreement: "I shall not be able to say 'I have given thee new money therefor without (an) official (? — lit. 'proved') receipt' ". Sethe-Partsch,[18] referring to the word which is rendered by Glanville as "official", say: "auf den füssen stehen — bestätigen. Demnach würde bei uns frei etwa zu übersetzen sein: ohne eine Zahlung (surkunde), die bestätigt, anerkannt d. h. beweiskräftig ist' ". It so happens that the "somewhat free" translation — *bestätigt* (confirmed) — proposed by Sethe-Partsch is the correct one, although they did not know what precisely this "confirmation" represented. The writer believes that a reference to Talmudic terminology and legal procedure will fully solve the puzzle both from the philological and the legal points of view. The word קיום, which, literally means a

---

[17] See p. 51, above.
[18] *Ibid.*, 194f.

causing to stand and which, as we shall presently see, is used in the Aramaic of the Targum in the sense of *oath,* is also used in Talmudic sources in the sense of *confirmation,* particularly in the phrase קיום שטרות (confirmation of documents).[19] In the case of the Talmudic "confirmation of documents" we are not in the dark at all as to its nature and purpose. The Mishnah supplies us with precise information on this point. אין קיום השטר אלא בחותמיו (there is no confirmation of the document except by its signers) — says the Mishnah.[20] Under Talmudic law, a legal document derived its probative force from the signatures of the witnesses appearing thereon. It was therefore incumbent upon a party proferring a document and relying thereon to prove the genuineness of the witnesses' signatures. A document, the probative force of which has been established by proving the genuineness of the witnesses' signatures, is called in Talmudic terminology שטר מקוים a *confirmed document,* literally, a document which *has been made to stand.* This is probably also the meaning of the word which has puzzled Egyptologists and which Sethe-Partsch render as *bestätigt.* The word seems to be an Aramaism and hence the Egyptologists' puzzlement.

From what has been said above concerning "confirmation of documents" it appears that under Egyptian law of the Ptolematic period rules strikingly similar to those which we find later in Talmudic sources prevailed with respect to the use of documents as proof in courts of law. This affords a clue to the understanding of a certain legal term occurring in a Greek papyrus of 116 B.C.E., which has defied correct interpretation by papyrologists. In P. Tor. I, IV, 17ff., which represents a record of a trial, it is stated: "And from the law of the country [the advocate recited] sections according to which if one produces in court a document without *styriosis* (μὴ ἐστυριωμένην) it is not to be used, and if one produces a false document it is to be torn up". It is the term *styriosis* occuring in this passage which forms the *crux interpretum.*

---

[19] See, e. g., BT, Kethuboth 21b, 28a; Baba Bathra 40a.
[20] Mishnah, Gittin 2:5.

Preisigke defines it as "a legally binding act touching contracts, the nature and meaning of which is unknown".[21] Now the fact that the rule about *styriosis* is followed by the rule concerning the tearing up of false documents indicates that *styriosis* was a procedure by which the genuineness of documents was established and without which the document was inadmissible in evidence. As stated above, such a procedure, similar to the Talmudic קיום שטרות, did in fact prevail under Egyptian law of the Ptolemaic period. Furthermore, the companion rule to that about *styriosis* — the one about false documents — also has an exact parallel in the Talmud. Under Talmudic law too a false document was to be torn up by the court.[22]

The Deed of Sale

One of the clauses (14) in the demotic deed of sale of the Ptolemaic period, in Griffith's English translation, reads:

> "The oath, the causing to stand that shall be de-
> manded of thee in the court of justice — in the
> name of the right conferred by the above writing
> which I have made unto thee, to cause me to make
> it: I will make it without citing any patent(?),
> any word in the land against thee".[23]

There are in this clause three Aramaisms which are discernible even in translation. We shall begin with the last one — "without citing any patent, any word in the land against thee". This is so clearly an adaptation of ולא דין ודבב (without lawsuit or process, literally without lawsuit or word), which occurs numerous times in the Aramaic papyri,[24] that one wonders how the parallelism between the two phrases could escape the attention of demotists.

The phrase "in the name of", in the sense of *concerning,*

---

[21] Eine die Verträge betreffende rechtsverbindliche Handlung, deren Art und Bedeutung unbekannt ist". — PWB, s. v. στυρίωσις.

[22] See BT, Baba Bathra 168b., and cf. p. 364, below.

[23] GCD, 121.

[24] See, e g., Cowley 8.21-22; 9.15; 15.29. Cf. p. 82, above.

with respect to, on account of is similarly an Aramaism. It is a
literal translation of בשם (literally, in the name of) which is
used in the Aramaic papyri in the same sense of *concerning, with
respect to, on account of.* The following is an example:

זי ירשנכי דין ודבב אנתי ובר וברה לכי ואיש זילכי בשם
ארקא זך זי יהבת לכי.

("Whoever shall institute against you suit or process,
against you or son or daughter of yours or any one
belonging to you on account of this land which I
give to you").[25]

The phrase "in the name of" in the sense of *on account of*
also occurs in another clause (13) of the demotic deed of sale,
which reads:

"Every writing that has been made concerning them
and every writing that has been made for me concerning them, and all writings in the name of which
I am entitled to them (the property): thine are
they and the rights conferred by them. Thine is
that to which I am entitled in their name (i. e. in
the name of the writings)".[26]

It seems that, in addition to "in the name of", this clause
contains another Aramaism. In a note to the word 'entitled'
in this clause, Griffith says: "The word here translated 'entitled'
is perhaps stronger in meaning, implying full justification in the
courts of law".[27] What Griffith says about this word fits perfectly
the Aramaic, and the late Hebrew זכאי.[28] The literal meaning
of this Aramaic word, like that of its equivalent נקי [29] is *clear,
pure.* Derivatively, the word came to mean — again like its

---

[25] Cowley 8, 11.11-13 (APC, 22). Cf. משום (on account of) in Mishnaic
Hebrew. See JDT, 1535b-1536a.

[26] GCD, 121.

[27] *Ibid.,* n. 4.

[28] See JDT, 398a-299b.

[29] See GB, 520a-b.

Hebrew equivalent — *free of guilt, obligation*. Finally, it came to mean *having a right, entitled*.[30]

To return to clause 14. The phrase "the causing to stand" is a synonym of *oath* and should be rendered into English as *affirmation*. It is a literal translation of the Aramaic קיום (a causing to stand), by which the Targum [31] renders the Hebrew word שבועה (oath).

Clause 6 of the demotic deed of sale contains a statement by the vendor to the effect that the price has been received by him in full. It reads: "I have received their price in silver from thee, complete without remainder".[32] A similar statement is contained in Brooklyn 12 [33] (402 B.C.E.). The vendors, after stating that the price (naming the amount) was given to them, continue וטיב לבבן בגו זי לא אשתאר לן עליך מן דמיא (1.6). This is rendered by Kraeling, as follows: "and our heart is satisfied therewith, that there is not outstanding to us against thee any part of the price". It seems that this clause was an innovation introduced by the resourceful Haggai b. Shemaiah, the scribe who wrote Brooklyn 12, for it does not appear either in Brooklyn 1 (451 B.C.E.) or in Brooklyn 3 (437 B.C.E.), the two other deeds of sale in the Brooklyn Museum collection.

The Marriage Document.

The problem of the relationship between the Jewish marriage document and its demotic counterpart of the Ptolemaic period has already been discussed above.[34] We shall therefore limit ourselves here to a discussion of some sidelights on this problem.

In P. Cairo 30601, a demotic marriage document of 231/230 B.C.E., there occurs a clause which, in Edgerton's English trans-

---

[30] See n. 28, above.

[31] See, e. g., Targum Onkelos to Lev. 5:4; Nu. 30:11. Cf. נשבעתי ואקימה לשמר משפטי צדקך (Ps. 119:106), which should be rendered into English as "I have sworn and affirmed to keep thy righteous judgments".

[32] GCD, 120.

[33] APK, 270f.

[34] See p. 39f., above.

lation, reads: "If I marry another woman than thee, I will give thee 10 (deben) of silver. . .".[35] In a note [36] Edgerton says that the word used in the original for "marry" literally means "sit [with]". Curiously enough, an idiom very similar to that of "sit" in the sense of "marry" occurs several times in the Books of Ezra and Nehemiah.[37] In Ezra 10:2, for example, we read: ונשב נשים נכריות מעמי הארץ ("and we have married foreign women of the peoples of the land").The causative of ישב (sit) is used in this verse in the sense of "marry".

The word "sit" in the sense of "marry" is also used in Ostrakon Louvre 8112 of the Ptolemaic or Roman period. This is a formula of a "woman's oath" which, in English translation, reads:

> "Text of the oath which A(woman) is to make in the gate of Jeme, in the Temple of Montu. . . to B(man): 'By the Bull of. . . who dwells here and (by) every god who dwells here with him, I have not lain, I have not arrived with (any) man, since the sitting which I made with you in year 22, down to today. There is no falsehood in the oath'. If she makes the oath, he shall be without claim on her and shall give her 4 talents 100 (deben)".[38]

It will be noted that in addition to "sitting" in the sense of "marrying", the above document contains another idiom, namely "arriving" in the sense of "having sexual intercourse". Again, a Hebrew parallel is most illuminating. ביאה (arrival) is used in Mishnaic Hebrew [39] in the sense of "sexual intercourse", and

---

[35] W. F. Edgerton, *A Clause in the Marriage Settlements*, Zeitschrift fur ägyptische Sprache und Altertumskunde, 64,60.

[36] *Ibid.*, n. 4.

[37] Ezra 10:2, 14, 17, 18; Neh. 13:23.

[38] W. F. Edgerton, *Notes on Egyptian Marriage, Chiefly in the Ptolemaic Period* (University of Chicago Studies in Ancient Oriental Civilization, no. 1), 19.

[39] See JDT, 169a.

the verb בּוא (come, arrive) with אֶל (to)[40] or עַל (upon)[41] is used in the Bible in similar sense.

We now come to a phrase in the above document which has caused difficulty to Edgerton and which, when viewed in the light of a Biblical parallel, presents no difficulty at all. In her oath the woman says: "I have not lain, I have not arrived with (any) man etc". To this Edgerton remarks: "The absence of the word *ky*, 'other' is very striking... Had the couple had no relations even with each other since the year 22? Had the man been absent from home during the entire interval, or had one or both parties taken a vow comparable to that of the Christian couple in Zoega, *Catalogus codicum Copticorum Manuscriptorium...?*"[42] It seems, however, that these speculations are quite unnecessary. The explanation for the absence of the word for "other" in the formula is much simpler than all that. In Biblical Hebrew שָׁכַב (lie) usually means "to have *illicit sexual intercourse*".[43] The word for "other" in the formula would therefore be quite superfluous. Indeed, it is not unlikely that the whole demotic "woman's oath" was patterned after the oath to which, according to the Bible (Nu. 5:19ff.), a woman who was suspected by her husband of infidelity was to be subjected. It is not without significance in this connection that in the Biblical oath-formula there occurs the phrase אִם לֹא שָׁכַב אִישׁ אֹתָךְ ("if no man have lain with thee"), which is strikingly similar to the phrase "I have not lain with (any) man" in the demotic formula.

---

[40] See Gen. 16:2; 30:3.
[41] See Gen. 19:31; Deut. 25:5.
[42] *Ibid.*, p. 19, n. 7.
[43] See Robinson, *A Hebrew and English Lexicon of the Old Testament* (5th ed., 1854), 1059.

CHAPTER X

THE CLOSING FORMULA OF BROOKLYN 10 AND OF THE GRECO-EGYPTIAN PAPYRI.

Brooklyn 10.[1] which was written in 402 B.C.E., is a deed of gift of a house by a father to his daughter. At the end of the document (lines 15-17), before the attestation by scribe and witnesses, there occurs the following formula:

אף לא יכלון ינפקון עליכי ספר חדת ועתיק בשם ביתא
זנה זי תחומוהי מנעל כתב בספרא זנה זי יהנפק כדב הו
זנה ספרא זי אנה עניני כתבת לכי הו יצב.

Kraeling's translation of this formula is as follows:

"Moreover, they shall not be able to put forth against thee a document new or old in the name of this house of which the boundaries were written above in this document. Whoever causes to go forth (a document), a lying one it is. This document which I, Anani, wrote to thee is valid".

A similar formula occurs in Cowley 8.[2]15-18, also a deed of a house by a father to his daughter, which was written in 460 B.C.E., that is 58 years earlier than Brooklyn 10. The formula in Cowley 8 reads:

ולא יכהלון יהנפקון עליכי ספר חדת ועתיק בשמי על
ארקא זך למנתן לאיש אחרן זך ספרא זי יהנפקון עליכי
כדב יהוה לא אנה כתבתה ולא יתלקח בדין וספרא זנה
בידכי.

Cowley's translation is as follows:

". . .and they shall have no power to produce against

---

[1] APK, 247f.
[2] APC, 21f.

you any deed new or old in my name concerning
this land to give it to any one else. Any deed
which they produce against you will be forged. I
shall not have written it and it shall not be accepted
by the court while this deed is in your hand".

It will be noted that the two formulae quoted above are
virtually identical, with this important qualification: the last
part of the formula in Brooklyn 10 (זנה ספרא...הו יצב) is new.
This phrase in Brooklyn 10 was apparently added by the scribe
for emphasis by way of contrast. *That* document is false, nul
and void, but *this one* is valid. This is evident from the position
of the word זנה before ספרא, instead of after it, in the phrase.
The words זנה ספרא should be rendered into English something
like "this document here", as contrasted with "that document
there".

There is still another difference between the above formulae
in Cowley 8 and Brooklyn 10, not in contents but in the relative
position of the formula in each of the two documents. While
in Cowley 8 the formula occurs in the middle of the document,
in Brooklyn 10 it occurs at its end. It is not unlikely that Haggai
b. Shemaiah, the scribe who wrote Brooklyn 10 and who was
apparently an experienced hand at writing legal documents, was
the one who for the first time added the new phrase to the old
formula. Having done this, it apparently occurred to him that
a phrase like "this document is valid" is an appropriate one on
which to end the document, and he therefore transposed the whole
formula from the middle of the document to its end.

Some support for the supposition that Haggai b. Shemaiah
was the inventive spirit who introduced the new phrase in the
form of deeds of gift may be seen in Brooklyn 9 [3] (404 B.C.E.),
also a deed of gift written by the same scribe about two years earlier
than Brooklyn 10. As in Brooklyn 10, the formula occurs there
at the end of the document, and, again as in Brooklyn 10, a new
phrase is added there which means substantially the same as

[3] APK, 235f.

the new phrase in Brooklyn 10 but is somewhat different in form.
The formula in Brooklyn 9.21-22 reads:

אַף לֹא יכהילון ינפקון עליכי ספר חדת ועתיק להן ספרא

זנה זי אנה עבדת לכי הו מיחב.

This is rendered by Kraeling as follows:

> "Moreover, they shall not be able to bring forth
> against thee a document, new or old, except this
> document which I made out to thee. Guilty he is".

The rendering of מיחב as "Guilty he is" does not make any sense.
Kraeling failed to perceive the pattern of the formula which is
the same as in Brooklyn 10.15-18. A comparison of the two
formulae makes it certain that מיחב in Brooklyn 9 corresponds
to יצב in Brooklyn 10 and that הו מיחב is not a separate sentence
but part of the phrase להן ספרא זנה זי אנה עבדת לכי הו מיחב,
which phrase is to be rendered as "but this document which I
made out for thee is the valid one". מיחב apparently means
the same, or nearly the same, as יצב, and is probably an Egyptian
word. Haggai b. Shemaiah, who gave the new twist to the
formula, must have been looking for a word meaning *valid* or
firm, and not being able at the moment to think of the appropriate Aramaic word, he used an Egyptian word. But two
years later he found the appropriate Aramaic term — יצב — and
used it.

It seems that Haggai b. Shemaiah's inventiveness, in the
course of time, gave rise to a new development which he could
not even imagine at the time when he first deviated from the set
formula giving it a new twist. In a large number of Greco-Egyptian
papyri, beginning with P. Eleph. 1 of 311 B.C.E., there occurs a
closing formula — ἡ συγγραφὴ κυρία ἔστω (the contract shall be
valid) or some slight variation thereof — which is called by
papyrologists the *kyria*-clause.[4] This formula, it will readily be
seen, corresponds to the closing formula זנה ספרא הו יצב (this
document is valid) of Brooklyn 10. Indeed, in the older Greco-
Egyptian papyri such as Eleph. 1 and 2, the correspondence is

---

[4] See MRV, 178; OPU, 103f.

even in emphasis—this contract here—the formula reading there: ἡ δὲ συγγραφὴ ἥδε κυρία ἔστω (this contract here shall be valid). The word ἥδε (this here) does not properly belong in the formula unless this briefer formula was taken out of a context such as lines 15-17 of Brooklyn 10.

It has been asserted by papyrologists[5] that the *kyria*-clause was brought to Egypt by Greek settlers. They point to Demosthenes, Or. 35, contra Lacrit. §13, where the following closing formula is quoted from a loan agreement:

κυριώτερον δὲ περὶ τούτων ἄλλο μηδὲν εἶναι τῆς συγγραφῆς

(About these matters nothing else shall be more valid than this contract).

Even a superficial inspection of the respective formulae will convince any unprejudiced observer that while the Greco-Egyptian formula bears some resemblance to the one quoted by Demosthenes, it is a twin sister of the Aramaic formula in Brooklyn 10. As to the formula in Demosthenes, it looks very much like a condensed paraphrase of the longer formula in the Aramaic papyri, of which the formula זנה ספרא ... הן יצב is a part, and which is to the effect that any other document relating to the same matter is false, nul, but this one is valid. In other words: nothing else about these matters is more valid than this document.

Although Haggai b. Shemaiah, the scribe who wrote Brooklyn 10 in 402 B.C.E., used a Greek term in one case and translated one into Aramaic in another [6] only nine months after he wrote Brooklyn 10, it will hardly be maintained that the longer formula in Brooklyn 10 is, itself, an adaptation of a Greek formula. The larger part of the longer formula, as we have seen above, occurs already in Cowley 8.15-18, of 460 B. C. E., and the addition זנה ספרא ... הן יצב was apparently made by Haggai himself to lend greater stylistic force to the old formula by way of emphasis.

Furthermore, the formula in Cowley 8.15-18, as well as other

---

[5] See *ibid.*
[6] See p. 36f., above.

parts of this document, have striking parallels in the legal documents of Susa, a collection of documents belonging to a period in the history of Susa corresponding to that of the First Babylonian Dynasty. In a deed of gift from Susa,[7] which was apparently to take effect after the donor's death, it is stated: "ki-ir-ba-na ša pa-ni u wa-ar-ki iḥ (?)-pi-ma a-na(sal) Na-ru-ub-t ma-ar--ti-šu id-di-iš-ši. In Scheil's French translation: "toute donation d'avant et après, il a annulé, et à sa fille Narubti il a donné".

It seems that among the Jews of Elephantine in the 5th century B.C.E., as in Susa well over a millenium earlier, the above formula was used primarily in deeds of gift. In the course of time, the use of the formula stating that other documents relating to the matter are void and this document is valid, or only the last part thereof, was extended to other types of legal documents. It was apparently at this stage of the development that the borrowing of the formula by Greek notaries occurred.

That Greek notaries made an adaptation of the above-mentioned Aramaic formula as it finally emerged from the hands of Haggai b. Shemaiah appears also from the closing formula in a loan agreement from Arkesine (2nd century B.C.E.), quoted by Mitteis,[8] which reads:

τῆς δὲ συγγραφῆς τῆσδε . . . μηδὲν εἶναι κυριώτερον μήτε νόμον μήτε ψήφισμα μήτε δόγμα μήτε στρατηγὸν μήτε ἀρχήν.

(Nothing is to be more valid than this document, neither law, nor ordinance, nor decree, nor strategos, nor magistrate).

This is to be compared with Brooklyn 10.12-17:

זי ירשנכי דין ודבב ויקבל עליך ועל בניכי לסגן ומרא
להעדיה ביתא זנה מן קדמיכי בחיי ובמותי יחוב וינתן

---

[7] AJS, no. 285.11-14. The documents from Susa contain several formulae which have striking parallels in the Armaic papyri. See p. 126, below.

[8] MRV, 178, n. 4, citing Bulletin de correspondance hellenique VIII, 23f. Cf. Demosthenes, Or. 35, 839.

לכי ועל בניכי אביגדן כסף כרשן 30 באבני מלכא ואנתי
אם שליטה בביתא זנה זי תחומוהי כתבן בספרא זנה
ויהך בדן ולא יצדק אף לא יכלון ינפקון עליכי ספר חדת
ועתיק בשם ביתא זנה זי תחומוהי מנעל כתב בספרא
זנה זי יהנפק כדב הו זנה ספרא זי אנה ענני כתבת לכי
הו יצב.

Note particularly the parallelism between ומרא לסגן in the
Aramaic formula and μήτε στρατηγὸν μήτε ἀρχήν in the Greek
formula.

The formula of Cowley 8.15-18, which, as we have seen
above, goes back to the Susa tablets of about 2000 B.C.E., is a
good illustration of the tenacity and persistence of a good legal
formula over a long period of time and of the ease with which
such formulae gained currency in widely separated areas of the
world. A close approximation to this formula appears in the
ספר השטרות (Formulary) of R. Jehudah b. Barzillai of Barcelona
(ed. Halberstam, Berlin, 1898), no. 11, and a still closer one in
Marculfi Formularum Liber II (a Frankish collection of legal
forms compiled about the middle of the 7th century), no. 3.[9]

In the Formulary of R. Jehudah b. Barzillai the formula
reads:

וכל כתב וקיום כתוב בכל לשון שיצא על מתנה זו כדי
לבטלה כולה או מקצתה, יהא אותו כתב וקיום בטל
ומבוטל ודלא למיעבד ביה דינא, ולא יהא בו כח לא
בדיני ישראל ולא בדיני אומות העולם.

(And as to any writing and affirmation, written in
any language, that may be produced against this gift
to avoid it, in whole or in part, — that writing or
affirmation shall be nul and void, and judgment
shall not be rendered pursuant thereto either under
the laws of Israel or under the laws of the nations
of the world).

The substance of this formula is obviously the same as that of

[9]K. Zeumer, ed., *Formulae Merovingici et Karolini Aevi* (MGH, Legum
Sectio V), 74f. See also Formulae Turonenses, no. 16 (*ibid.*, 135f.).

Cowley 8.15-18, and at one point there is a striking similarity between the two formulae in form as well. I am referring to the expressions לא יתלקח בדין in Cowley 8.17 and ודלא למיעבד ביה דינא in R. Jehudah's form, both of which mean, to use modern legal phraseology, it shall not be admissible in evidence.

The Frankish formula reads:

> "Quod si aliquos instrumentus de ipsas villas de nomen nostrum in adversitate predicti monasterii quolibet ordine conprehensus, aut anterius vel posterius prenotatus, quod nos nec fecimus nec facire rogavimus, a quemcumque preter istum, quem firmissimun volumus esse, quoque tempore fuerit ostensus nullum sorciatur effectum, nisi vacuus et inannis appareat".

> (That if at any time any instrument concerning these farms, besides this one which we desire to be most firm, in whatever order, whether prior or subsequent, expressed, which we did not make nor asked to make, will be produced by anyone against the aforesaid monastery, it shall have no effect, but shall be found nul and void).

Note particularly the phrase *aut anterius aut posterius,* which corresponds to חדת ועתיק (new and old) of Cowley 8.16, in reverse order. Note also that the Latin formula is a poor copy of a good original, and that, as is often the case, the mistakes of the copyist betray the source from which he copied. The word *quod* (which) in the phrase *quod nec fecimus, nec facire rogavimus* makes it appear that the declaration of "no effect" refers only to those documents which the makers of the present one "did not make, nor asked to make", and not to those which they did make or asked to make, which of course makes no sense and defeats the real purpose of the clause. In Cowley 8.17, it is said with reference to any "new and old" document לא אנה כתבתה (not I wrote it), that is it shall be deemed forged, which makes perfect sense. The author of the Frankish formula apparently had before him a model which contained this Aramaic phrase, or a translation thereof. Having failed to understand its import, he introduced into his formula a mutilated form of the phrase in a place where it does not belong and where it makes no sense.

To return to the closing formula of Brooklyn 9 and 10 and of the Greco-Egyptian papyri. A similar formula is mentioned in BT, Baba Bathra, 160b and in PT, Gittin, 9:8, the words used in the former source being שריר וקיים (valid and firm) and those in the latter being קיים שריר וברור (firm, valid and established). Gulak,[10] who noted the similarity between the Greco-Egyptian and Talmudic formulae, states that this similarity points to the conclusion that a closing formula in legal documents "was common to the various legal systems of that time". This statement, which is obviously vague, evades the issue. The problem is: How did it happen that the Greco-Egyptian documents from the early Ptolemaic period down to the late Byzantine period, on the one hand, and the Jewish document of the Talmudic period, on the other, exhibit a closing formula which is couched in substantially the same words? The Brooklyn Museum Aramaic papyri furnish the answer. In both cases the formula is probably traceable to the Aramaic papyri, more specifically, to that resourceful Haggai b. Shemaiah, scribe of Yeb.

The Execution-Clause in the Greco-Egyptian Papyri of an Obligatory Nature

The loan agreement quoted in Demosthenes' speech and the document from Arkesine, mentioned above, bring us to a consideration of the execution-clause in these documents and in the Greco-Egyptian papyri.[11] The gist of this clause is that the creditor is authorized, in case of default by the debtor, to take pledges, without resort to legal action, from all of the

[10] A. Gulak, *Das Urkundenwesen im Talmud in Lichte der griechisch-aegyptischen Papyri und des griechischen und roemischen Rechts* (1935), 26f.

[11] See MRV, 404f. ; MGP, 119f.

debtor's property, as if on the strength of a judgment. In Demosthenes' speech this clause reads:

> παρὰ ᾿Αρτέμωνος καὶ ᾿Απολλοδώρου ἔστω ἡ πρᾶξις τοῖς δανείσασι καὶ ἐκ τῶν τούτων ἁπάντων, καὶ ἐγγείων καὶ ναυτικῶν, πανταχοῦ ὅπου ἂν ὦσι καθάπερ δίκην ὠφληκότων καὶ ὑπερημέρων ὄντων.

> (The creditors shall have the right of execution upon Apollodoros and Artemo and upon all their property, on land and on water, wherever it may be found, as if judgment had been rendered against them and they had defaulted thereon.).

A similar clause is contained in many Greco-Egyptian papyri beginning with P. Eleph. 1 of 311 B. C. E., the earliest extant Greco-Egyptian papyrus, down to Byzantine times. In P. Eleph. 1.12-13, it reads:

> ἡ δὲ πρᾶξις ἔστω καθάπερ ἐγ δίκης κατὰ νόμον τέλος ἐχούσης Δημητρίᾳ καὶ τοῖς μετὰ Δημητρίας πράσσουσιν ἔκ τε αὐτοῦ Ἡρακλείδου καὶ τῶν Ἡρακλείδου πάντων καὶ ἐγγαίων καὶ ναυτικῶν.

> (Demetria and those aiding Demetria to exact payment shall have the right of execution, as if derived from a legally decided action, upon the person of Heraclides and upon all the property of Heraclides both on land and on water).

The close resemblance between the two formulae is obvious and leaves no doubt as to the relationship between them. On the surface, therefore, it would seem that the clause in question was brought to Egypt from Greece. There is, however, strong evidence to the effect that the execution-clause, like its companion *kyria*-clause, is traceable to the Aramaic papyri.

Another execution-clause which occurs in some Greco-Egyptian papyri of the early Ptolemaic period is that in which it is provided that "execution shall be as for debts owed to the king" (πρᾶξις ὡς πρὸς βασιλικά) [12] The effect of this clause is the same

---

[12] See MGP, 120.

as that of the καθάπερ ἐκ δίκης clause, namely it authorizes the
creditor to take pledges without resort to legal action, as in the
case of a debt owed to the crown. A similar clause occurs in the
Bauer-Meissner Aramaic Papyrus of 515 B.C.E.,[13] to which we
shall still have occasion to refer in another connection. This is
an agreement between landlord and tenant for a cropsharing
tenancy, in which the landlord warrants the land to the tenant
against adverse claims and undertakes that in case a claim is
asserted against the land by a third party, he shall clear it of the
claim, and that if he does not clear it, he shall give an equivalent
thereof to the tenant. The relevant portion of this agreement
reads·

10.　　אקם ואנקה ואנתן [לך וה]ן לא קמת ...
ונקת ונתנת לך אתננהי לך [מן ח]לקי למלך מן
... בלעדי מלת מלך

The phrase מן בלעדי מלת מלך, literally "without a word of the
king", clearly means "without an order of the king". In this
context, it most likely refers to an order of execution or judgment
issued by the king.[14] Thus understood, the phrase fits in well
with what immediately precedes it and will help us restore
correctly the illegible word in line 11 which was restored by
Bauer and Meissner as מן. It should be restored instead as
כמו=כם (like). The portion quoted from the document should
therfore be translated as follows:

> "... I will rise up and clear(it) and give(it) to
> thee. And if I do not rise up and clear(it) and
> give(it) to thee, I will give it (an equivalent there-
> of) to thee, like my portion to the king, without a
> word of the king".

That we have here an execution-clause, similar to the

---

[13] H. Bauer und B. Meissner, *Ein aramäischer Pachtvertrag aus dem 7.
Jahre Darius I*, Sitzungsberichte d. Preuss. Akad. d.Wiss. XXXI (1936), 414-424.

[14] On the use of מבלעדי in the sense of *without the will or order*, see GB,
102a, citing 2 Kings, 18:25; Isa. 36:10; Jer. 44:19. Is מן בלעדי in the papyrus
a Hebraism?

πρᾶξις ὡς πρὸς βασιλικά of the Greco-Egyptian papyri of the early Ptolemaic period, is beyond any doubt, and the date of the agreement is 515 B.C.E.

The description of the property out of which execution may be had as "on land and on water", which occurs in both P. Eleph. 1 and in Demosthenes' speech, is interesting. It has been asserted that this description "fits the conditions of the maritime Greek cities but not the Egyptian scene".[15] However, the writer entertains some doubts as to its Greek origin. It is quite obvious that the description is intended to be all-inclusive — all property wherever it may be found. It so happens that a description of property which is similarly intended to be all-inclusive occurs already in Cowley 15 [16] of 441 B.C.E. In lines 17-20 of this document there occurs the following clause:

מחר או יום א[חר] ימות אסחור ובר דכר ונקבה לא
איתי לה מן מ[פטח]יה אנתתה מפתחיה הי שליטה
בביתה זי אסחור ונכס[והי] וקנינה וכל זי איתי לה
על אנפי ארעא כלה.

("To-morrow or another day (if) Ashor should die and there is no child male or female belonging to him by Miphtahiah, his wife, Miphtahiah has a right to the house of Ashor, his goods and his chattels and all that he has on the face of the earth, all of it".)

It is quite possible that at some time after 441 B.C.E. it occurred to some cautious scribe that a description of property as "all that he has on the face of the earth" was not sufficient, since one might also have property on water, and he therefore added the words "and on water" to the formula. Similar caution is displayed by Jewish medieval scribes in their description of the property out of which a debt may be collected. They use the formula תחות כל שמיא (under the whole heaven),[17] which of

[15] GLS, 30, n. 1.

[16] APC, 45f.

[17] See, e. g., ספר השטרות לרב האי בר שרירא גאון, ed. Asaf (Supplement to *Tarbitz,* 1.3), no. 3, 1.18. Cf. Job 41:3.

course includes all property, both on land and on water. Indeed, it may very well be that the latter formula is much older than the Middle Ages.

It will perhaps be objected that the date of Demosthenes' speech (ca. 340 B.C.E.) is too early for influence from the Aramaic papyri to have asserted itself in the legal formulae therein. There are, however, several possible answers to this objection. In the first place, no one really knows how fast and how far such formulae traveled in antiquity. Secondly, as has been shown above,[18] early Greek law exhibits a number of other points of affinity with the law reflected in the Aramaic papyri, making the supposition of some traffic of ideas in matters legal between Greeks and the Jews of Elephantine at an early time highly probable. Finally, on philological grounds, it is held by some classical scholars [19] that the legal formulae contained in the speeches of the Attic orators are not part of the original speeches but were inserted therein at a much later time by the grammarians in conformity with the usage that was current in their times.

[18] See p. 21, above.

[19] See MRV, 405, citing C. Wachmuth, *Oefentlicher credit in der hellenistischen Welt der Diadochenzeit,* Rhein. Mus. f. Philologie (XL 1885), 301f. With particular reference to the form of the loan agreement quoted in *Contra Lacrit.,* see also F. Blass, *Die attische Beredsamkeit* (2nd ed., 1893), 562, n. 4.

CHAPTER XI

BROOKLYN 12 AND THE KYRIEIA CLAUSE OF THE GRECO-EGYPTIAN PAPYRI

Brooklyn 12,[1] which was written in 402-401 B.C.E., is a deed of sale of a house. We have already dealt with some aspects of this document. We shall now turn our attention to one of its main constituent parts. Lines 22-24 of the document read:

מן תמה תנפק ותנעל ביתא זנה זי משחתה ותחומוהי
כתיב בספרא זנה אנת עני שליט בה מן יומא זנה ועד
עלמן ובניך שליטן אחריך ולמן זי רחמת תנתן או זי
תזבן לה בכספ.

Kraeling's translation is as follows:

> "From there thou shalt go forth and go in to this house, of which the measurements and boundaries are recorded in this document. Thou, Anani, shalt have power over it from this day unto forevermore, and thy children shall have power after thee, and to whomsoever thou wilt thou mayest give it and to whom thou wilt sell it for money (thou mayest sell it".

This translation is somewhat inaccurate and conceals a feature of the document which is of paramount importance in the history of law. The words מן תמה תנפק ותנעל ביתא זנה, which are rendered by Kraeling as "From there thou shalt go forth and go into this house," should rather be rendered as "From now thou shalt go out and go in(to) this house." There can hardly be any doubt that the words תנפק ותנעל correspond to the familiar Hebrew idiom לצאת ולבוא [2] and that these words

---

[1] APK, 268f.
[2] See GB, 87a.

are used here in the sense of *thou shalt take possession*. As to
מן תמה, it seems, on the basis of parallels which we shall
presently discuss, that it means here *from now, henceforth*.
תמה (=Hebrew שם) occurs in Biblical Aramaic [3] in the spatial
sense of *there, here* only. But its Hebrew equivalent is used in
the Bible [4] in both the spatial and the temporal sense. In the
clause under discussion, תמה also seems to be used in the latter
sense.

The permission given by the grantor to the grantee to take
possession *from now* has striking parallels in Jewish legal forms
of the Middle Ages. In the ספר השטרות of R. Jehudah b.
Barzillai, no. 26 (a form of a deed of sale of landed property),
for example, there occurs the following clause:

ומעכשיו ילך פלוני זה ויזכה ויחזיק ויקנה שדה זו
שמכרתי לו ויעשה בו כל הפצת נפשו.

("And *from now* N shall go and acquire right and
take possession and acquire this field which I have
sold to him and shall do therewith all his heart's
desire".)

The word מעכשיו (from now) occurs already in the Babylonian Talmud [5] in connection with the permission of the vendor
to the vendee to take possession of the property sold to him.
Still more striking are the parallels to Brooklyn 12.22-24, which
are found in Greco-Egyptian deeds of conveyance from about
the end of the 1st century B.C.E. onward. These deeds usually
contain a clause, called by Schwarz [6] the *kyrieia*-clause, in which
the grantor authorizes the grantee to take possession and be owner
(κρατεῖν καὶ κυριεύειν) of the property conveyed "from now for

---

[3] See *ibid.*, 930b.

[4] See *ibid.*, 839a-b. See also Jer. 50:9, where משם, like מן תמה in our
document, seems to be used in the sense of *henceforth*.

[5] Kethubot, 82a.

[6] See, *e. g.*, P. BGU 1129.20f. (13 B. C. E.) and 1130.13 (4 B. C. E.).
See also OPU 170ff. It is significant that the oldest deeds containing this
formula belong to the group of papyri from Alexandria discussed in ch. 7,
above.

all time" (ἀπὸ τοῦ νῦν εἰς τὸν ἀεὶ χρόνον). The part of this clause in which the grantee is authorized to take possession (κρατεῖν)   of the property *from now* corresponding to מן תמה תנפק ותנעל ביתא זנה (from now thou shalt go out and go in(to) this house) in 1.22 of Brooklyn 12, and the part in which he is authorized to be master, owner, (κυριεύειν) of the property corresponds to אנת עני שליט בה מן יומא זנה ועד עלמן (thou Anani art ruler over it from this day forever). The similarity between the *kyrieia*-clause of the Greco-Egyptian papyri and the corresponding clause in the Aramaic papyri — which, for the sake of brevity, we shall call the *shallit*-clause—is quite obvious. What is not so obvious is that the *shallit*-clause is of Jewish origin. Although the Aramaic papyri stem from a Jewish military colony in Egypt and the parties to the legal transactions evidenced by these papyri are, for the most part, Jews, the possibility that these Jews followed Egyptian legal forms cannot be ignored. Nor can we leave out of consideration the possibility that the legal formulae in the Aramaic papyri are of Babylonian origin. Indeed, Kraeling [7] asserts that a combination of Babylonian and Egyptian influence fully accounts for these formulae. However, the problem of the origin of the legal formulae contained in the Aramaic papyri will not be solved by such flat assertions. What is needed is a careful analysis of these formulae and a comparison of their contents and form with Babylonian, with demotic, and, above all, with Jewish legal formulae, Biblical and post-Biblical. At this juncture, the writer will attempt to make such a comparison and analysis with respect to one clause—the *shallit*-clause in deeds of conveyance. But before doing this he begs to be permitted a digression.

Kraeling [8] invokes the analogy of the English common law and contemporary American legal documents to prove Babylonian influence upon the legal formulae in the Aramaic papyri. To the writer it seems that this analogy may be invoked with

[7] See APK, 50, 52.
[8] See *ibid.*

greater cogency to prove Hebrew influence upon these formulae. If we found a collection of documents containing such characteristic terms and expressions as "to wit", "dower", "judgment of peers", and "to X and to his heirs forever", we would undoubtedly be justified in concluding that the style of these documents was influenced by that of the common law of England. Why, then, should we not be justified in drawing a similar conclusion, *mutatis mutandis*, from such characteristically Hebrew terms and expressions as [12] לך ולבניך אחריך [11], בעדה [10], מהר [9], לאמר occurring frequently in the Aramaic papyri?

[9] The word occurs frequently in the Aramaic papyri, and Cowley (APC, 13) says that it is a Hebraism. Kraeling (APK, 134) doubts this and cites a letter from Ashur (M. Lidzbarski, *Wissenschaftliche Veröffentlichung d. deutschen Orient-Gesellschaft* 38, Tafel I, 1.8), where this word occurs. But he fails to mention Lidzbarski's highly significant remark (at p. 11) that this and other "Canaanisms" in the Aramaic of the Assyrian and Babylonian documents tend to prove that the mother tongue of the scribes who brought the new alphabetic script to Assyria and Babylonia was not Aramaic.

In any event, it is inaccurate to talk of *Reichsaramäisch* or of "official Aramaic" as the source of the legal formulary used by the Jews of Elephantine. A legal formulary does not come into being at the behest of some bureaucrat. It takes a very long time for it to develop, and when it is developed, if it is to remain effective and vital, it must be constantly guarded against deterioration at the hands of incompetent practitioners. It must also possess a high degree of flexibility in order to enable it to meet new situations as they arise. All this requires that the function of drawing up legal documents be exercised by a highly competent professional group. A study of the Aramaic papyri shows that the Jewish notaries of Elephantine constituted such a group. Very ancient elements there certainly are in the Aramaic papyri. As has been shown in ch. 2, above, a certain formula in these papyri exhibits unmistakable signs of a legal tradition going back as far as the Susa tablets of about 2000 B.C.E. But the notaries of Elephantine did not follow their ancient models blindly. It is enough to lay side by side the marriage document of 440 B.C.E. (Cowley 15) and the one of 421 B.C.E. (Brooklyn 7) for any unprejudiced observer to see the vast difference between them and the development of new and important clauses that occurred during the interim. Sometimes it is even possible to trace important innovations to an individual — Haggai b. Shemaiah by name — as in the case of the clause which forms the topic of ch. 10.

[10] See Kraeling's remarks at APK, 209.

To return to the *shallit*-clause of the Aramaic papyri. In
an extensive search of Old-Babylonian and Neo-Babylonian, as
well as Assyrian, deeds of conveyance the writer has failed to
discover any clause corresponding to the *shallit*-clause. Only in
one collection of cuneiform documents, that from Susa,[13] is there a
parallel to one part of the *shallit*-clause—to the formula ולמן זי
רחמת תנתן (to whomsoever thou wishest thou mayest give it)—-
but not to the other parts thereof. On the other hand, the *shallit*-
clause has close parallels in the Bible. Its main part bears a
striking resemblance to a verse which occurs three times in the
Book of Daniel—4:14 (17), 22 (25), 29 (32)—and which reads:

די שליט עליא במלכות אנושא ולמן די יצבא יתננה

[11] Cowley renders the phrase קום בעדה as "rise up in the congregation"
and succinctly and quite correctly says: "בעדה, Hebrew. Borrowed as a
technical term". (APC, 49). The phrase occurs in the Aramaic papyri, old
and new, in connection with divorce. Divorce being a judicial proceeding,
it had to take place before the congregation which performed judicial functions.
That the Hebrew עדה performed such functions appears most clearly from
such verses in the Bible as Nu. 35:12 (עד עמדו לפני העדה למשפט) and 24
(ושפטו העדה). Rosenthal's suggestion, cited by Kraeling (APK, 147), that
בעדה be rendered as "on his own (or her) behalf" is plainly incomprehensible.
Why "rise up on his own behalf"? Why not simply "rise up"? Does he mean
to suggest that in Elephantine, in the fifth century B.C.E., parties to
litigation, in quite modern fashion, would ordinarily be represented by attorneys,
but that in divorce proceedings they had to appear on their own behalf?

[12] On this significant formula see p. 130, below. This formula occurs
numerous times in the Bible and in the Aramaic papyri. So far as the writer
has been able to ascertain, there is nothing even remotely resembling it in
Babylonian or Assyrian deeds. The burden of proof clearly rests upon those
who would deny that the Jews of Elephantine brought some legal formulae
from their home country to show that the formula is also found in some ancient
documents outside of the Bible and the Aramaic papyri.

[13] See ch. 2, above. In deeds of gift from Susa, there occurs regularly in
the introductory part a recital that the gift was made *na na-ar-a-ma-ti-sa*,
which is rendered by Scheil as *en sa bienveillance*. See AJS, 329.2; 381.2, 382.3,
et passim. This corresponds to the word ברחמן which occurs a number of times
in the Aramaic papyri in connection with gifts and which is rendered by both
Cowley and Kraeling as "in affection". See Cowley 18.12; 25.11; Brooklyn 4.
4, 12; 7.41; 9. 5, 12, 17; 10.9.

("That the Most High ruleth in the kingdom of
men, And giveth it to whomsoever He will").

Note the complete parallelism between this verse and our
clause. In both the main indicium of ownership and control over
a thing, that of freedom to dispose of it at will, is used to
describe concretely the meaning of the same word—שליט. That
the verse was adopted by the author of the Book of Daniel
from the phraseology of the legal document which was current
in his day, becomes apparent from a modification thereof occurring in Dan. 5:21:

די שליט אלהא עליא במלכות אנשא ולמן די יצבא
יהקים עליה.

("That God Most High ruleth in the kingdom of
men, and that He setteth up over it whomsoever
He will").

The author apparently became aware that the stereotyped
phrase does not quite fit the subject matter for which he was
using it, the "kingdom of men" not being an object, like a
piece of property, which is "'given". He therefore changed the
word יתננה (giveth it) to יהקים עליה (appointeth over it).
In Ex. 21:8: לעם נכרי לא ימשל למכרה   (to a foreign people
he shall have no power to sell her), the Hebrew equivalent—
משל—of the Aramaic שלט (to rule, to have power) also seems to
have been adopted from the phraseology of the legal document,
so that this part of the clause seems to be much older than the
Book of Daniel.

Other parts of the *shallit*-clause also have significant parallels
in the Bible. The expression מעתה ועד עולם (from now and
forever) is found a number of times in the Bible.[14] The idea
of an everlasting covenant or conveyance also occurs very
frequently in the Bible. Note particularly the characteristic
phrase ובניך אחריך (and your children after you) in the *shallit*-
clause of Aramaic papyri. Again and again this phrase occurs
in the Bible in similar context. Indeed, it is more than likely

[14] See, *e. g.*, Is. 9:6; Mi. 4:7; Ps. 113:2.

that Genesis 13:15 and 17:7-8, and similar verses in the Bible
represent legal formulae of conveyance of property, or, to use
a term of the common law of the United States and England,
the *habendum* clause of the conveyance. Genesis 13:15 reads:

כי את כל הארץ אשר אתה ראה לך אתננה ולזרעך עד
עולם.

> ("For all the land which thou seest, to thee will
> I give it, and to thy seed for ever".)

Similar language is used in Genesis 17:7-8, which reads:

והקימתי את בריתי ביני ובינך ובין זרעך אחריך לדרתם
לברית עולם להיות לך לאלהים ולזרעך אחריך.
ונתתי לך ולזרעך אחריך את ארץ מגריך את כל ארץ
כנען לאחזת עולם.

> ("And I will establish My covenant between Me
> and thee and thy seed after thee throughout their
> generations for an everlasting covenant, to be a
> God unto thee and to thy seed after thee".
> "And I will give unto thee, and to thy seed after
> thee, the land of thy sojournings, all the land of
> Canaan, for an everlasting possession".)

That verse 15 of chapter 13 in Genesis represents a legal
formula is indicated by verse 17 of the same chapter which is a
command by God to Abraham to take formal possession of the
land.[15] Verse 17 reads:

---

[15] On this verse as a command to take formal possession, see BT, Baba
Bathra, 100a; PT, Kiddushin, 1:3,5. The order or authorization to take possession seems to be alluded to in Jer. 32:11: ואקח את ספר המקנה את החתום
המצוה והחקים ואת הגלוי (So I took the deed of the purchase, both that which
was sealed, containing the terms and conditions, and that which was open).
The word מצוה (order) seems to be a technical term for that part of the deed
in which it is recited that the grantor authorized the grantee to take possession
of the property conveyed. An authorization to take possession also occurs in
the story of the purchase of the Cave of Machpelah by Abraham, where
Ephron is reported to have said to Abraham: קבר מתך (bury thy dead) —
Gen. 23:11.
An interesting parallel to the authorization to take possession found in the
Bible, in the Aramaic papyri and in the Greco-Egyptian papyri is afforded by

קוּם הִתְהַלֵּךְ בָּאָרֶץ לְאָרְכָּהּ וּלְרָחְבָּהּ כִּי לְךָ אֶתְּנֶנָּה.

("Arise, walk through the land in the length of it
and in the breadth of it; for unto thee will I
give it".)

Verse 15 thus represents the 'terms' of the conveyance and
verse 17 represents the 'order' to take formal possession.

It seems that as time went on the *shallit*-clause underwent
considerable modification. When we first meet with it in 460
B.C.E. in Cowley 8.9-11,[16] it has two distinct parts, an affirmative
and a negative part. It reads there as follows:

אנתי שליטה בה מן יומא זנה ועד עלם ובניכי אחריכי
למן זי רחמתי תנתן לא איתי לי בר וברה אחרן אח
ואחה ואנתה ואיש אחרן שליט בארקא זך להן אנתי
ובניכי עד עלם.

("You have full rights over it from this day forever, and your children after you. To whom you
wish you may give it. There is no other son or
daughter of mine, brother or sister, or other woman
or man who has rights over this land, except you
and your children forever".)

Later on, the negative part in which it is stated that no
"other man or woman, son or daughter, brother or sister",
shall rule over the property was either altogether dropped as
in Brooklyn 3, 9, 10 and 12, or was compressed into the phrase

the *habere licere* (permission to take possession) clause of Roman documents
beginning about the middle of the 1st century C. E. See Girard, *Textes de
droit romain* (5th ed., 1923), p. 848f. Particularly striking is the parallel to
Gen. 23:11, afforded by a deed of gift of burial places in a sepulchre (2nd
century C. E.), which contains permission by the grantor to the grantee to take
possession by burying the dead and performing sacred rites ("...ossaque
inferre permisit, sacrumque quotiens facere vellit...permisit".) — *ibid,* 829f.
See also *ibid,* 830 (a document of the 2nd or 3rd century C. E.). In the last
document there is a provision that if the conditions of the gift are not
observed the gift is to be restored to the donor *sine ulla controversia* (without
any controversy), which is strongly reminiscent of the Hebrew בלי דין ודברים
or the Aramaic ולא דין ודבב Cf. p. 82, above.

[16] APC, 22f.

ולא איתי די ימחא בידך (and there is none that shall stay thy hand), or ואינש לא ימחא בידך (and no man shall stay thy hand). In the latter form the negative part of the *shallit*-clause appears in the Jewish deed of conveyance of the Middle Ages. The following is an example:

ושליט יהא פלוני דנן על זביני אילין דזבינית ליה למקנא
ולאקנויי ולאורותי ולאחסנא ולזובנא ולחלופא ולמידר
ולאוגורי ולמשכונא ולשנאה ולגמרה ולמיסתר ולמבנא
ולמעבד מחיצות ולמיהב במתנה לכל מאן דיצבי ואינש
לא ימחה בידיה ולא ביד ירתיה בתריה מן יומא דנן
ולעלם.[17]

("And the said N shall rule over this property (literally, these sales) that I have sold to him, to own and to convey to others, to leave to his heirs and to devise, to sell and to exchange, to dwell therein and to let or mortgage, to make alterations and completions, to pull down and to build and to make partitions, and to give away to whomsoever he will, and no man shall stay his hand or that of his heirs after him, from this day and forever".)

A close parallel to the phrase ואינש לא ימחא בידך (and no man shall stay thy hand) occurs in the Book of Daniel in a context—dealing with dominion and control—which makes it almost certain that it was borrowed there from the phraseology of the legal document. Dan. 4:31(34)-32(35) reads:

די שלטנה שלטן עלם ומלכותה עם דר ודר וכל דארי
ארעא כלה חשיבין וכמצביה עבד בחיל שמיא ודארי
ארעא ולא איתי די ימחא בידה.

("For His dominion is an everlasting dominion, and His kingdom from generation to generation; and all the inhabitants of the earth are reputed as nothing; and He doeth according to His will in the

[17] *Formulary of Rab Hai Gaon* (ed. Asaf), Supplement to *Tarbitz* I, 3, no. 5.

host of heaven, and among the inhabitants of the
earth; and none can stay His hand".)

These verses, together with the verses noted above, indicate
that when the Book of Daniel was written the negative part
of the *shallit*-clause of the Jewish deed of conveyance had already assumed substantially the same form as that found in the
Jewish deed of conveyance of the Middle Ages.

What has just been said about the negative part of the
shallit-clause brings us again to the *kyrieia*-clause of the Greco-
Egyptian papyri. In some of these papyri, of the first and
second century C.E., there occurs at the end of the *kyrieia*-
clause a formula of which the following is an example:

> καὶ μηδένα κωλύειν αὐτὸν καὶ τοὺς παρ' αὐτοῦ κυριεύον-
> τας τῆς αὐτῆς οἰκίας
> (and none shall hinder him or his representatives
> from exercising dominion over this house).[18]

This, it will readily be seen, is virtually identical with the formula
ולא איתי די ימחא בידיה of Dan. 4:32(35) and with ואינש
לא ימחא בידך of the *shallit*-clause of the Jewish deed of
conveyance of the Middle Ages. The phrase מחה ביד (literally,
to stay the hand), like the Greek κωλύειν, means *to hinder, to
interfere*.

As we have said above, the *kyrieia*-clause, like the *shallit*-
clause, is an authorization by the grantor to the grantee to take
possession of the property conveyed and become owner thereof.
The character of this clause as an authorization to take possession
appears most clearly in P. Oxy. 1205, a deed of sale of a
loom, dated 298 C. E. Hunt and Edgar's English translation of
the *kyrieia*-clause in this document reads:

> " . . . and this loom with its fittings you shall forth-
> with carry away from where it is kept and transfer
> it whither you wish without hindrance, and you
> with your descendants and successors shall possess

---

[18] P. BGU, 667.15. See also the similar clauses cited in PWB, 857, *s. v.*
κωλύω (all of them of between the first and third centuries C. E.).

and own it and have the right to use it or hire it
out or sell it as you choose . . . ".[19]

The phrase which is rendered by Hunt and Edgar as "you shall
forthwith carry away" reads in the original βαστάξεις ἐντεῦθεν
and should rather be rendered as *you shall henceforth lift up*.
As to ἐντεῦθεν it is clear from the Greek lexica that it means
henceforth, and not *forthwith*. It thus corresponds to מן תמה
(from now) of Brooklyn 12.22, to ἀπὸ τοῦ νῦν of the earlier Greco-
Egyptian papyri, and to מעכשיו (from now) of the Talmudic
formula, quoted above. As to βαστάζειν the choice between *lift up*
and *carry away* is not so clear. Liddell and Scott give both
meanings, with the former meaning as the basic one. However,
from the context in which the word occurs in the document it
appears that *lift up* is the correct rendering, for *to carry away
and transfer* would be tautologous. This is still more apparent in
P. Thead. 8.20 (306 C. E.), where in a similar context βαστάζειν
is followed by καὶ ἀποφέρειν (and carry away). Interestingly
enough, הגבהה (lifting up) is, according to the Talmud,[20] the
legal mode of taking possession of chattels for the purpose of
acquiring property in them, provided the chattels are such that
lifting them up does not entail undue difficulty.

Pringsheim,[21] who follows Hunt and Edgar in rendering the
term βαστάζειν as *carry away*, is nonetheless aware that the term
is a technical one implying an act of acquisition of ownership.
"The term" — he says — "does not mean transport only, but
appropriation by carrying off". His interpretation of the technical
meaning of the term is fully borne out by the Talmud which,
as we have seen above, furnishes in addition a clue to a more
precise definition of the legal significance of the act which it
implies.

The similarity between the *shallit*-clause and the *kyrieia*-
clause is so striking that it was precisely this similarity which

[19] SP, 107.
[20] See Mishnah, Kiddushin, 1:4; BT, Baba Bathra 82a.
[21] GLS, 331, n. 9.

misled C. B. Welles into believing that the essential formulae of
Dura Pg. 20 — a deed of sale of a woman slave, written in
Syriac in Edessa in the year 243 C.E. — are Greek. He went so
far as to say that "'there is little more Semitic in the document
than the language in which it is written".[22] Yet it is sufficient
to lay side by side the *shallit*-clause of Brooklyn 12, for example,
and the corresponding clause in Dura Pg. 20 for anyone to see
how little Greek and how much Semitic there is in this clause.
Lines 11-12 of Dura Pg. 20 [23] read:

דמן יומנא ולעלמא תהוא אנת תירו זבונא וירתיך שליט
באמתא הדא דזבנית לך למקנא ולמדברו ולמעבד בה כל
דתצבא.

(That from this day forever you, Tyro, the
purchaser and your heirs shall have power over
this woman slave that I have sold to you to acquire
and to lead away and to do with her all you
desire.).[24]

---

[22] C. Bradford Welles, *A Contract of Sale from Edessa*, Yale Classical
Studies V, 117.

[23] The document, together with an English translation and commentary,
was published by Torrey in *Zeitschrift für Semitistik*, 10 1935), 33ff. For technical reasons, our quotations from this document appear in Hebrew characters.

[24] This clause is to be compared with the *kyrieia*-clause in P. BGU. 316
(359 C. E.), a deed of sale of a slave from Ascalon, which reads:
κυρίως ἔχειν καὶ δεσποτικῶς κτᾶσθ[αι καὶ] πωλεῖν διοικεῖν ὅν ἂν αἱρῆτε
τρόπον, ἀπὸ τῆς σ[ήμερον] ἡμέρας καὶ εἰς ἀεί. (as master to have and as
lord to acquire and to sell, to manage in any manner that he may choose,
from this day and forever.). There can be no doubt that this clause is
an adaptation of an Aramaic original. Note particularly the expression
ἀπὸ τῆς σήμερον ἐμέρας καὶ εἰς ἀεί (from this day *and* forever). That
this is a literal translation of מיומא דנה ולעלם (from this day *and* forever),
which appears in the *shallit*-clause of Cowley 8 (460 B.C.E.) and of Dura
Pg. 20 and in the formula of the bill of divorce quoted in BT, Gittin, 85b,
is shown by the conjunction καὶ (and), which is clearly not Greek diction.
On the form מן...ועד (from... and to) in Biblical Hebrew, see GB 563b.
Note also the correspondence between שליט...למקנא (have power... to acquire)
in Dura Pg. 20 and δεσποτικῶς κτᾶσθαι (as master to acquire) in P. BGU
316.
It is generally held by papyrologists that the formulae in P. BGU 316 are

The two formulae, the one just quoted from Dura Pg. 20 and the one quoted above from Brooklyn 12, speak for themselves.

There remains for consideration the question of whether or not the *shallit*-clause of the Aramaic papyri was adopted from the style of Egyptian legal documents. Let it be stated at once that a clause very similar to the *shallit*-clause of the Aramaic papyri occurs frequently in Egyptian documents, although, so far as the writer has been able to ascertain, neither Egyptologists nor students of the Aramaic papyri have been aware of this. Before proceeding to an analysis and comparison of the respective clauses for the purpose of determining which is the original and which is the copy, we shall quote a significant passage from Griffith's Introduction to the *Catalogue of the Demotic Papyri in the John Rylands Library*:

> "Probably several causes contributed to make legal documents suddenly more abundant in the Twenty-Fifth Dynasty. The growth of trade by sea and land in the first millenium B. C. must have originated a new wealthy merchant class, causing property of all kinds to change hands rapidly, while contact with the crafty and business-like Phoenicians and other Semites opened the eyes of the Egyptians to the necessity of precision in their dealings. These influences would be felt most powerfully in lower Egypt, Upper Egypt receiving them only at second hand".[25]

To this the writer will only add that if the Egyptians learned from the "Phoenicians and other Semites" the use of legal document, it is not unreasonable to suppose that they also learned

---

"predominantly Roman". See E. Levy, *West Roman Vulgar Law* (1951), 65 and the authorities cited there. But surely the *kyrieia*-clause in this document is not Roman. The warranty clause there, too, in which the seller hypothecates all his property, that which he has and that which he may acquire in the future, for the obligation of the warranty (11.39-41), is not Roman. See p. 174, below.

[25] GCD, 10.

from them something about the style and form of legal documents.

The earliest occurrence of a clause corresponding to the *shallit*-clause of the Aramaic papyri, which the writer has been able to find among the Egyptian legal documents conveniently collected by Malinine and Pirenne, is in a deed of sale of three offices, and the revenues derived therefrom, in a certain temple, dated in the 21st year of Psametichus I (645-640 B. C. E.). This deed, in Griffith's English translation, reads, in part, as follows:

> "Thou hast caused my heart to agree to the silver (the price) of these three shares above (written). Neither children nor brethren, nor any man in the land or my own self likewise shall be able to control them without thee, beginning from year 21 of Pero-Psametik onward to any year; and including children, brethren, or any man in the land".[26]

This is to be compared with Cowley 8,[27] 11.9-11, which reads:

אנתי שליטה בה מן יומא זנה ועד עלם ובניכי אחריכי
למן זי רחמתי תנתן לא איתי לי בר וברה אחרן אח
ואחה ואנתה ואיש אחרן שליט בארקא זך להן אנתי
ובניכי עד עלם.

> ("You have full rights over it from this day forever, and your children after you. To whom you wish you may give it. There is no other son or daughter of mine, brother or sister, or other woman or man who has rights over this land, except you and your children forever".

It will be noted that the Aramaic formula states the proposition of the grantee's exclusive control of the property both affirmatively — that the grantee shall rule over the property — and negatively — that no other person shall rule over it. The Egyptian formula, on the other hand, states the same proposition only negatively — that no person other than the grantee shall be able to control the property. That the formula originally

[26] *Ibid.*, 44.
[27] APC, 22f

consisted of the negative part only and that the Aramaic scribes
adopted it from their Egyptian brethren and engrafted upon it
the affirmative part is, in itself, extremely unlikely. Besides,
and this is of decisive importance, the phrase למן זי רחמת תנתנן
(to whom you wish you may give it), contained in the affirmative
part of the Aramaic formula, is a very old one, going back to
the Susa documents of about 2000 B. C. E.[28] It seems therefore
that the Aramaic formula is the original and that the Egyptian
scribe who first used it was an imitator, and a poor one at that.
He began with the second, complementary, part of the formula
leaving out the first part which, logically, leads up to the second
one. In any event, the formula seems to be of Semitic origin,
and it is not unlikely that it was introduced by Jews, who, as
many scholars believe, began to settle in Egypt under Psa-
methichus I.[29]

Further support for the supposition that Egyptian legal
formulae, beginning with the 25th Dynasty, were influenced by
Semitic, possibly Jewish, models may be seen in a certain
characteristic phrase, rendered by Griffith [30] as "to-morrow or
the second morrow" which occurs in an Egyptian document of
about 631 B. C. E. and which, as will be shown below,[31] has
exact parallels in the Aramaic papyri (מחר או יום אחרן) and in
a document of about the 14th century B. C. E. from Ras-Shamra
(urram šêram). Apparently, no such phrase occurs either in
Babylonian or in Assyrian sources.

To return to Brooklyn 12. The interpretation of lines 22-24
of this document as an order to take possession and become
owner of the property affords a satisfactory explanation of a
peculiar feature of the document which, when properly understood, sheds considerable light on an important problem in legal
history. The document is in reality two documents — one up to

[28] See n. 13, above.
[29] See APK, 43f.
[30] See GCD, 58.
[31] See p. 159ff., below.

line 9, inclusive, and the other from line 10 to the end. The first one contains the date, the names of the parties, the price, a description of the property by metes and bounds and a recital to the effect that the price has been fully paid, no part thereof remaining outstanding. The second document, from line 10 to 21, contains again the date, the names of the parties, the price, a description of the property by metes and bounds (all of which are the same as in the first document) and a recital of the receipt of the price, and from line 22 on new matter appears as follows: 1. The order to take possession and become owner. 2. Renunciation of claim by the seller. 3. Provision for a penalty in case a claim is asserted against the buyer or his heirs and assigns by the seller or his heirs. 4. Attestation by witnesses. Kraeling, commenting on the two-in-one feature of the document, says:

> "This is an interesting and anomalous situation. Apparently the customers were dissatisfied about something the scribe had written, so that he had to begin with a new document, but after the new document — in which the scribe very naturally tended to go more briefly over the same ground — was completed, it was felt that some of the material first written was worth preserving, and so the new document was simply attached to the unfinished one and the whole thing was duly witnessed and sealed".[32]

This explanation sounds fairly plausible and at first the writer considered it acceptable, although he was unable to discover what precisely there was in the first document over and above the second one that "was worth preserving". However, upon further consideration and study it became clear to the writer that a far more satisfactory explanation may be had in terms of a legal practice abundant evidence of which is found in demotic documents of the Ptolemaic period. As has already

---

[32] APK, 268.

been mentioned in another connection,[33] two documents were used during this period to effect a sale of property — a document of sale, or a "document for silver", and a document of cession, or a "document of renunciation". Ryl. dem. 15 and 15b (163 B. C. E.) — a document of sale and a document of cession of the same property written on the same papyrus [34] are very much like Brooklyn 12, with this important difference: while in Brooklyn 12 there is only one attestation at the end of the second document, Ryl. dem. 15 and 15b have two attestations, one for each document. It may thus be readily seen that in Brooklyn 12 there is already discernible a tendency toward the amalgamation of the two documents — the "document for silver" and the "document of renunciation" — into one.

The problem of the purpose and significance of the "deed for silver" and the "deed of renunciation" has been extensively discussed by legal historians.[35] The view widely held by demotists has been summarized by Taubenschlag as follows:

> "According to the demotics the former resulted in the passing of the title, whereas the latter represented the cession of the claim to the property. Thus in spite of the "deed of silver" the grantor had the right to contest the sale, i. e. reclaim the property sold as long as the price had not been paid. Thence, the abandonment of the right of avoidance rendered the conveyance of the property a definite fact".[36]

This view is definitely refuted by Brooklyn 12. It is the first part of this document, which corresponds to the "deed for silver", that contains a recital of the receipt of the price in full, and the second part, wihch corresponds to the "deed of renunciation",

---

[33] See p. 22, n. 10, above.

[34] See GCD, 131, 134.

[35] See the literature cited by Taubenschlag, *The Law of Greco-Roman Egypt in the Light of the Papyri*, I, 240, n. 1.

[36] *Ibid.*, 241.

that contains the order to take possession and become owner, that is, to acquire title.

Referring to the Greco-Egyptian practice and alluding to the deeds of conveyance from Alexandria, Taubenschlag says:

> "Toward the end of the first century, a new formulary came into use, a combination of the συγγραφὴ πράσεως and the συγγραφὴ ἀποστασίου It adopted from the former the statement that land had been sold and the βεβαίωσις -clause, and from the latter, the right to abandon any claim. A new element was the clause relating to the receipt of the price and to the conveyance of κυριεία and κράτησις.[37]

But Brooklyn 12 shows that the "new formulary" came into use fully four centuries earlier, toward the end of the fifth century B. C. E., and that the clauses relating to the receipt of the price and the transfer of ownership and possession were not new elements in the Alexandrian papyri. The deed of conveyance as we find it emerging from the hands of Haggai b. Shemaiah, scirbe of Yeb, in the year 402 B. C. E. is strikingly similar to the deeds of conveyance of the last quarter of the first century B. C. E. from Alexandria.[38]

---

[37] *Ibid.*, 246. It is significant that *kyrieia* in the sense of ownership appears only in the legal language of Hellenistic Egypt. See OPU, 170, n. 3.

[38] An allusion to the two stages in the sale of property — payment of the price and transfer of possession — is already contained in Brooklyn 3, written by Haggai b. Shemaiah in 437 B. C. E. In line 3 it is stated אנחן זבן ויהבן, which Kraeling (APK, 155) very aptly renders as "we have sold and given (over)". In his comment on this line (*ibid.* 159), he says: "יהב means 'to give', but the text as a whole shows that no gift was involved, so here it must mean 'to transfer, give possession.'"

CHAPTER XII

THE WARRANTY CLAUSE IN BROOKLYN 3.

Brooklyn 3 is a deed of sale of a house, dated 437 B. C. E. The clause under consideration is a most elaborate warranty clause, in which the draftsman displays extraordinary ability to foresee all sorts of eventualities that may arise out of a sale of property and to make adequate provision for such eventualities.

A warranty clause, in which the vendor undertakes that in case an adverse claim is asserted by a third party against the property which forms the subject of the sale he will clear the property of such claim, is a very old institution. It occurs regularly in the Susa documents [1] mentioned above and in a large number of Old-Babylonian documents. [2] In all of the Susa documents and in many of the Old-Babylonian documents the key-word in the warranty clause is *izzaz*, [3] which literally means *he will stand up.* [4] Scheil translates this term, according to the general sense, as *se tiendra responsable,* [5] without attempting to explain how *nazâzu* (to stand up) came to have that meaning. According to San-Nicolo, the term means *einstehen* [6] and imports a guarantee by the vendor to the vendee against damages which the latter may sustain by reason of an eviction

---

[1] See AJS, nos. 42, 11.9-13; 44, 11.17-19, *et passim.*

[2] See M. San-Nicolo, *Die Schlussklauseln der altbabylonischen Kauf-und-Tauschverträge,* 138ff.

[3] See *ibid.,* 142.

[4] See *ibid.,* 146; C. Bezold, *Babylonisch-assyrisches Glossar,* 194a-b.

[5] See the documents cited in n. 1, above.

[6] San-Nicolo, *ibid.,* 142, 149. See also P. Koschaker, *Babylonisch-assyrisches Bürgschaftsrecht,* 174, n. 1.

by a third party.[7] In other words, the vendor's duty under the clause is to pay damages to the vendee after an eviction, but not to defend him in a lawsuit which may lead to an eviction.

In the writer's opinion, San-Nicolo's interpretation of the Old-Babylonian warranty clause rests on a misunderstanding of the precise sense in which the term *nazâzu* is used in this clause. One of the nuances of this term given by Bezold is *als Prozessgegner auftreten*[8] (to appear as an adversary in a lawsuit). It is in this sense that *izzaz* is used in the Old-Babylonian warranty clause, where it means: *he will stand up (in court)* for the purpose of defending the vendee against an adverse claimant. The clause therefore imports a duty to defend against eviction, and not, as San-Nicolo would have us believe, a duty to pay damages after eviction only. That this is so is shown by a number of non-cuneiform Oriental sources, among them Brooklyn 3.

The operative words in the warranty clause in Brooklyn 3 are נקום וננצל וננתן (we will stand up, save and give). The first word, it will readily be seen, corresponds exactly to *izzaz* of the Susa and Old-Babylonian documents. The two words that follow it show that קום (=*nazâzu*) is used here with the special nuance of standing up in court for the purpose of clearing property of an adverse claim. קום also seems to be used in the Bible[9] in this special sense of standing up in court as an adversary. The same word is used in the same sense in the warranty clause of the Bauer-Meissner papyrus[10] of 515 B. C. E. — אקם אנקה ואנתן (I will stand up, clear and give) — a clause which has been completely misunderstood by the editors of this papyrus. In Dura Pg. 20, referred to above,[11] the operative words of the warranty clause are אקום ... ואדון ואמרק ואדכא (I will stand up, litigate, clear and purge). Here there

<hr />

[7] *Ibid.*, 154.
[8] Bezold, *ibid.*
[9] See Mich. 6:1; Ps. 74:22.
[10] See n. 13 to ch. X, above.
[11] See n. 23 to ch. VII, above.

can be no doubt as to the sense in which אקום is used. Similarly, in P. Dura 101 [12] (227 C. E.) the operative words are διαδικήσει καὶ καθαροποιήσει (will litigate and clear), and in Pg. Dura 23 [13] (180 C. E.) — αὐτὸν ἀντικαταστάντα καθαροποιήσειν (to rise up against him and clear). In the warranty clause quoted in BT, Baba Metzia 15a, which we shall discuss more fully below, the operative words are אקום ואשפי ואדכי ואמריק (I will stand up, acquit, clear and purge). Finally, in the warranty clause of a number of Lombard documents,[14] which

[12] C. Bradford Welles, *Dura Papyrus 101*, AHDO, 1 (1937), 261ff. The warranty clause in this document represents a curious hybrid of the Roman and Oriental formulae. Under the Roman formula (See, e. g., Bruns, *Fontes iuris romani antiqui*, [3rd ed.] 185ff.) the seller undertakes that in case of eviction he is to pay to the buyer double the amount of the purchase price. Under the Oriental formula, on the other hand, the seller undertakes that in case an adverse claim is presented against the buyer, he, the seller, is to rise up in court and defend the buyer against such claim. In this document it is stated that if "anyone lays claim and recovers" the property the seller "will litigate and clear" (διαδικήσει καὶ καθαροποιήσει) the title for the buyer. The first part is from the Roman formula, while the second part is from the Oriental formula. The result of this combination is a legal monstrosity, for if the seller *will litigate and clear* there will be no eviction, and after an eviction, presumably by a party having a better title, there is no longer any occasion *to litigate and clear*.

[13] C. Bradford Welles, *Die zivilen Archive in Dura*, Münchener Beiträge Zur Papyrusforschung und antiken Rechtsgeschichte, Heft 19 (1934), 382f. In this document, as in the papyri from Gebelên discussed in ch. 8, above, the form "A has sold — B has purchased" is used.

[14] See *Codex Diplomaticus Cavensis* v. 1, nos. 2 (a. 798), 3 (a. 799), 4 (a. 801) *et passim*. In the light of the parallels quoted in the text there can hardly be any doubt that the term *antestare* is used in this clause in the sense of *to stand up in court against a party*, that is, as his adversary. The discussion of this term, and of the clause as a whole, by P. S. Leicht in his article entitled *Antestare et defendere* (Miscellanea Giovanni Mercati V, 635ff.) does not take into account the Oriental parallels. One is tempted to make the bold suggestion that *antestare* is used in the same sense in table I, section I, of the Twelve Tables: Si in ius vocat ni it antestator igitur em capito. Accordingly, this section should be rendered as follows: If when called to law the adversary does not go, then lay hold on him.

seem to have been influenced by an Oriental source, the operative words are *antestare et defendere.*

A warranty clause also appears in late-Babylonian deeds of the Persian period. The operative word in this clause is *marâqu,* which has been correctly recognized by Clay as the Aramaic מרק meaning *to clear.*[15] This clause is interpreted by San-Nicolo[16] as importing a duty on the part of the vendor to defend the vendee against adverse claims, but, following Koschaker,[17] he maintains that this type of warranty was introduced under Persian influence. Koschaker's theory of the Persian origin of the warranty clause in the Babylonian documents of the Persian period rests upon the fact that no warranty clause appears either in Assyrian deeds or in Neo-Babylonian deeds before the Persian period. However, the key-word — *marâqu* (=Aramaic מרק) — in the warranty clause points to a Semitic origin of the clause. Furthermore, a warranty clause with an operative word meaning *to clear* appears in Semitic sources long before the period of the Persian rule in Babylonia. In three of the Susa documents,[18] mentioned above, the word *nazâzu* (to stand up) is followed by the word *ebêbu* meaning *to clear.* In the Nuzi documents[19] of about the 14th century B. C. E. there appears a warranty clause with the key-word *zakú,* the meaning of which is similarly *to clear.* In the Bauer-Meissner papyrus[20] of 515 B. C. E., as we have seen above, the word קום (to stand up) is followed by נקה (to clear), exactly as in the three documents from Susa, which can hardly be a coincidence but, rather, points to a continuity of legal tradition from the Susa documents to the Aramaic papyri. All this tends to prove that the warranty clause in which the vendor undertakes to

[15] See UBBE, Series A, v. 8, 22; v. 9, 36-38; P. Koschaker, *ibid.*, 192f.

[16] San-Nicolo, *ibid.*, 194f.

[17] Koschaker, *ibid.*, 195.

[18] AJS, nos. 47.13; 49.12; 79.5.

[19] See Pfeiffer and Speiser, *One Hundred New Selected Nuzi Texts* (AASOR, XVI), nos. 15, 1.15; 16, 1.11; 18, 1.10, *et passim.*

[20] See note 13 to ch. X, above.

clear the property of adverse claims is much older than the
period of Persian rule in Babylonia.

As to the absence of a warranty clause from Assyrian and
Neo-Babylonian deeds of sale before the Persian period, it is
perhaps to be explained by a deterioration in legal draftsmanship
which set in in Babylonia after the period of the First Babylonian
Dynasty. While in Babylonia the warranty clause was forgotten during the dark period that set in after the First
Dynasty, it was preserved in some other area of the Near
East, whence it was reimported into Babylonia during the period
of the Persian rule there.

We shall now turn our attention to the Egyptian scene.
In Egyptian documents beginning from the 7th century B. C. E.
there occurs a warranty clause the key-word of which is rendered
by Griffith into English as *to clear*.[21] It would seem that this
clause was not brought to Egypt from Assyria during the
Assyrian domination of Egypt from 671 to 663 B. C. E., since,
as has been stated above, Assyrian documents of this period
do not contain such a clause. It is reasonable to suppose
therefore that the Egyptian scribes copied this clause from
the same legal tradition from which they copied the *shallit*-
clause. Be that as it may, the Egyptian documents, as we shall
presently see, shed considerable light upon the warranty clause
in Brooklyn 3.19-23a, which reads:

והן גבר אהרן יגרנך ויגרה לבר וברה לך אנחן נקום
וננצל וננתן לך בין יומן 30 והן לא ננצל אנחן ובנין ננתן
לך בית לדמות ביתך ומשחתה...ולא כהלן נצלן ננתן
לך כספך כרש 1 שקל 4 ובנינא זי תבנה בה וכל אשרן
זי יהכן על ביתא זך.

Kraeling's translation of this clause is inaccurate in some places.
We shall therefore add, in parentheses and in italics, our own
renderings in these places, and in the course of the discussion
will offer justification for these changes. The translation thus
modified reads:

[21] See GCD, 44-47, 59-60.

"And if another man sue thee or sue son or
daughter of thine, we will rise up and will recover(?)
(*save*) and will give (it) to thee within 30 days,
and if we do not recover(?) (*save*), we or our
children will give to thee a house in the likeness
of thy house and its measurements, ... (if) we
are not able to recover(?) (*save*), we will give
to thee thy money, 1 karsh, 4 shekels, and the
(value of the) building (improvements) which
thou didst build in it (*construction which thou
mayest construct thereon*), and all the lumber(?)
(*improvements*) which may go upon that house".
In some of the warranty clauses of Egyptian deeds of sale,[22]
where the subject of the sale is an animal, there is a provision
to the effect that in case the vendor cannot successfully defend
the vendee against an adverse claim by a third party, he is to
compensate the vendee not only for the animal, but also for
its offspring, if there be any in the meantime. In a deed of
sale of a cow, of about 560 B. C. E., the clause in question, in
Malinine's French translation, reads:

"Celui qui viendrait (pour faire une contestation)
contre toi a son sujet, avec l'intention de la reprendre de toi, disant — 'ce n'est pas ta vache',
je la libérerai pour toi. Si je ne la libère pas pour
toi, je te donnerai (alors) une (autre) vache de
sa race(?). Si je ne te donne pas une vache de sa
race(?), je te donnerai 1 (deben) 5/6 kedet
d'argent(?) en son échange; — sans compter tout
veau qu'elle aura produit: ton homme (— agent)
a droit de les reprendre par contrainte et je te les
donnerai. Si elle est reprise laissant derriere elle
un veau, je te donnerai un veau de sa race(?);
si elle est reprise, laissant une génisse derriere elle,
je te donnerai une génisse de sa race(?); si elle

[22] See AHDO, 5 (1950-1951), pp. 56-57, 57-59.

est reprise, laissant un (jeune?) boeuf(?), je te
donnerai un (jeune?) boeuf(?) de sa race(?) —
sans entrer en procès quelconque avec toi".[23]

It is quite obvious that the pattern of the warranty clause,
quoted above from the Egyptian deed, is the same as that of
Brooklyn 3. There are several eventualities envisaged in both
of these clauses and appropriate provision made for them,
namely: 1. If an adverse claim is asserted against the property
sold, the vendor is to clear the property of such claim. 2. If
he cannot clear it, he is to give the vendee another *res* like the
one which he sold him. 3. If he cannot give another *res*, he
is to give the equivalent in money. 4. Finally, if there be any
offspring in the meantime, in case the subject of the sale is an
animal, or if buildings be added and improvements occur, in
case of real property, the vendor is to compensate the vendee
also for these.

In Egyptian documents, the above pattern of the warranty
clause is found only in deeds of sale of animals. So far as the
writer has been able to ascertain, it is never found in Egyptian
deeds of sale of real property. It was quite natural that the
thought of an increase in the value of the *res* taking place
after the sale and before eviction and of the desirability of
making appropriate provision for such eventuality should first
occur to a notary in connection with a sale of an animal.
Egyptian notaries apparently never went further than that.
They did not generalize the idea so as to make it applicable
to real property as well. It was apparently left for some scribe

---

[23] *Ibid.*, p. 57. The rendering of the operative word in this warranty clause
— the pattern of which fully corresponds to that of Brooklyn 3 — by the
French *libérer* (to deliver, save) settles the question of the correct meaning of
the corresponding word in Brooklyn 3. This word, like its Egyptian counterpart, means *to deliver, save*. If the reading in Brooklyn 3 is פצל (Cf. APK, 162,
and my article in *Biblica*, 35 [1954], 201ff.), then it represents an interesting
amalgamation of the Hebrew נצל (to save) and the Aramaic פצא (to save).
This hybrid formation may have a bearing on the question of the language
that was spoken by the Jews of Elephantine.

in Yeb to do just that, and in doing so he made a distinction between an augmentation in the value of the property which comes as a result of expenditures and labor and one that comes of itself, including both types within the scope of the warranty. This is what is meant by ובנינא זי תבנה בה וכל אשרן זי יהכן על ביתא זך (and the building that thou mayest build in it and all the improvements that may go upon that house).

The word אשרן in the above formula is rendered by Kraeling as "lumber". This rendering is a pure guess, which has nothing to commend it either juristically or philologically. In his comments,[24] Kraeling mentions the suggestion the writer made to him, on the basis of the parallel שבחיהון (their improvements) in the Talmudic warranty clause, that the word be rendered as *improvements*. This is undoubtedly the correct rendering. It has ample support both from the juristic and the philological points of view. In the first place, the parallel clause in the Egyptian deed of sale of a cow, quoted above, suggests that the term has reference to an augmentation in value which comes of itself, similar to the birth of offspring in the case of a cow. Secondly, in the warranty clause quoted in BT, Baba Metzia 15a, two types of improvements are included within the scope of the warranty, namely improvements that come as a result of labor and those that come of themslves. The clause there reads:

אנא איקום ואשפי ואדכי ואמריק זביני אילין אינון
ועמליהון ושבחיהון ואוקים קדמך.

(I will stand up and acquit and clear and purge this sale, it and its labor and its improvements, and will set before thee).

The first type of improvements (עמליהון, literally, its toil, labor) corresponds to ובנינא זי תבנה בה (and the building that thou mayest build in it), and the second (שבחיהון — its improvements) apparently corresponds to אשרן. Finally, philo-

---

[24] See APK, 163.

logically אשר is a cognate of שבח. The *piel* of אשר is frequently used in the Bible [25] in the same sense as the *piel* of שבח is used there, namely that of *to laud, praise*. In Mishnaic Hebrew,[26] the noun שבח is used in the sense of *improvement of property* as well as in that of *praise*. There is perhaps some suggestion of the meaning *to augment* for אשר in Mal. 3:15: ועתה אנחנו מאשרים זדים גם נבנו עושי רשעה The apposition of אשר and בנה in this verse, exactly as in Brooklyn 3.22a-22b, is interesting and suggestive.

The correspondence between the warranty clause in the document under consideration and that quoted above from the Talmud is, in the writer's opinion, one of the most remarkable and significant features of this document. It testifies to a continuity of legal tradition between the Aramaic papyri and the Talmud with respect to an aspect of the law of warranty which, apparently, has no parallel in other legal systems of antiquity. The matter of the vendor's liability for improvements in case of an eviction of the vendee by a third party is already mentioned in the Mishnah,[27] where it seems to be predicated upon an undertaking by the vendee to that effect. Again, according to the Babylonian Talmud,[28] Mar Samuel instructed the scribe who was attached to his court not to include improvements (שבחא) within the scope of the warranty unless he was specifically authorized by the vendor to do so. This shows that the inclusion of improvements within the scope of the warranty had become so general that the scribes were wont to treat it as a matter of routine. On the other hand, there is apparently no trace of any such formula either in cuneiform tablets, or in demotic papyri, or in Greek papyri before the late Byzantine period. Only in the 6th century there appears in the Greco-Egyptian papyri a warranty clause

---

[25] See Gen. 30:13; Ps. 72:17; Pr. 31:28.

[26] See JDT, 1512a-b.

[27] See Mishnah, Gittin 5:3.

[28] BT, Baba Metzia, 15a.

in which the vendor assumes liability for improvements (βελτίωσις).[29] This is so obviously a literal translation of the Talmudic שבחא (improvement) that it is hardly necessary to adduce any other proof of the close relationship between the warranty clause in the Greco-Egyptian papyri of the late Byzantine period and the Talmudic warranty clause, though such proof is not lacking. The key-word in the former clause is καθαροποιεῖν (to clear),[30] which corresponds to the Talmudic מרק (to clear). In some documents [31] even the Talmudic idiom אמריק זביני אילין (I will clear this sale) is used, the formula there being: καθαροποιέσω ταύτην τὴν πρᾶσιν (I will clear this sale).

In the above quotation of the warranty clause in Brooklyn 3 we purposely left out a part thereof which requires separate treatment. This part, together with the words written above line, reads: בר מן בר זכר ונקבה זי אפולי או ברה לה יתה Kraeling failed to grasp the legal significance of this provision and was therefore unable to translate and interpret it correctly. He also failed to notice the significant fact, recited in line 4 of the document, that the house, which formed the subject of the sale, at one time belonged to 'pwly b. Misdai.

In order to understand the above provision, it is necessary to reconstruct the factual situation, and the legal consequences flowing therefrom, which led to its inclusion in the warranty clause. Bagazušt and his wife, the sellers, had bought the house from 'pwly, who was married and childless. The house had been settled upon 'pwly and his wife by the wife's father, upon condition that it descend to the common children of 'pwly and

---

[29] See, e. g., P. Cairo, Masp. 67097.69; P. Lond. 1735.18.

[30] See, e. g., P. Lond. 1722.44; P. Cairo, Masp. 67097.32, 68. See also the documents (all of them 6th-7th century C. E.), cited in PWB, 708, s. v. καθαροποιέω. For other points of similarity between the Byzantine deed of conveyance and Talmudic legal formulae see ch. 15, below.

[31] Journal of Philology XXII (1894), 268ff., documents nos. 1.55-56, 2.10-11, 3.38. See also P. Lond. 1735.16.

his wife.[32] The right of the children to receive the property
after their parents' death could not be defeated by conveyance
made jointly by their parents. When Bagazušt bought the
property from '*pwly* and his wife he expected that the sellers
were going to die childless. However, when he resold the
property and gave the buyer a warranty against all claimants
he specifically excepted from the scope of the warranty the
children of '*pwly*, if there be any, since he could have no
assurance that '*pwly* and his wife were not going to have children
at some future time. The above-quoted provision is therefore
to be rendered as follows: "except a child, male or female, or
daughter of '*pwly*, if there be (any)". The words לה יתה,
which have caused difficulty to Kraeling, are probably equal to
לו איתה and are to be rendered as "if there be (any)".

---

[32] A similar condition attached to a settlement of house property upon
husband and wife by the wife's father occurs in Cowley 9.9-10 (APC, 26f.).

CHAPTER XIII

DURA PG. 20 AND JEWISH NOTARIAL PRACTICE

Dura Pg. 20, the deed of conveyance to which reference has been made above,[1] exhibits a series of external characteristics all of which are part and parcel of the Jewish notarial practice. These characteristics are:

1. The document, when found, was rolled up and tied with a string.

2. The signatures of the witnesses appear on the *verso* of the document.

3. The witnesses' signature run transversely to the writing on the *recto*.[2]

These external characteristics most eloquently tell the story of the legal tradition to which D. Pg. 20 belongs. The first two are mentioned in the Mishnah and the third is mentioned in the Babylonian Talmud and the Yerushalmi.

In Mishnah, Baba Bathra 10:1-2 we read: גט פשוט עדיו מתוכו, ומקושר עדיו מאחוריו... גט פשוט עדיו בשנים ומקושר בשלשה. (A plain document has the signatures within; a tied-up document has the signatures behind... A plain document requires two witnesses; a tied-up one — three). In BT, Baba Bathra, 161a, it is stated that the witnesses to a *tied-up* document sign from bottom to top, and in PT, Baba Bathra 10:1 it is similarly stated that the witnesses to such a document sign lengthwise.

The above Mishnah proves beyond any peradventure of doubt that the *tied-up* document, with the signatures of three

---

[1] See p. 135, above.

[2] See Bellinger and Welles, *A Third-Century Contract of Sale from Edessa in Oshroene*, Yale Classical Studies, v. 5, pp. 95, 117.

witnesses on the *verso* thereof, was in common use among the Jews in the first century of the Christian era. Indeed, other evidence, no less convincing, shows that the use of the *tied-up* document among the Jews goes as far back as the 8th century B. C. E. Torczyner has correctly pointed out that Isa. 8:16 refers to the practice of tying up a legal document. In his Introduction to the Lachish Letters, he says:

> "Also the misunderstood passage in Isaiah VIII, 16 does not mean 'Bind up the testimony, seal the law among my disciples', but simply 'Bind up the testimony, seal the instruction (given here) upon the ties'. למודים is a well-known word for *ties* in the Mishnah".[3]

The verse is to be understood as referring to the binding up of the document and its sealing with the ties, exactly as was done with Dura Pg. 20.

Welles, when he first noticed that the signatures of the witnesses on Dura Pg. 20 appear on the *verso,* thought that this was a local custom in Edessa.[4] However, when he later discovered that in Dura P. 101, 74 and 90, all written in Greek in the years 227, 251, 254, respectively, the signatures also appear on the *verso,* he concluded that this was also the custom in Dura and that it was a Greek development.[5] Of the Jewish *tied-up* document he knew nothing at all. But his description of the Dura papyri just mentioned corresponds so closely to what is known from the Mishnah with regard to the *tied-up* document that there can hardly be any doubt as to the origin of the custom in Dura and Edessa. Says Welles: "At Dura, then, we find for all sorts of documents of a double character the practice existing, that witnesses sign their atteststions on the *verso,* each opposite a knot in the string tying closed the upper version of

---

[3] The *Lachish Letters,* The Wellcome Expedition to the Near East, Publications, v. 1, p. 16.

[4] See Bellinger and Welles, *ibid.*

[5] See C. Bradford Welles, *Dura Papyrus 101,* AHDO, 1, 279.

the text".[6] This is to be compared with Mishnah, Gittin 8:10:
ואיזהו גט קרח? כל שקשריו מרובין מעדיו (What is a bald [de-
fectively attested] bill of divorce? — One that has more knots
than witnesses).

We now come to a consideration of the third item listed
above, namely, the transverse position of the witnesses' signatures
on the *verso* with relation to the writing on the *recto*. From the
Talmud (BT, Baba Bathra, 161a) it appears that by this practice
it was sought to prevent forgery. The question arises, how and
what kind of forgery was it sought to prevent thereby? The
answer is to be found in the physical characteristics of the writing
medium which was used for the writing of legal documents.
The practice arose as a result of the use of papyrus for the
preparation of legal documents. In his discussion of the demotic
legal papyri, Griffith states:

> "A single leaf of prepared papyrus seldom measured
> more than 30cm, either way, and for all except small
> documents two or more leaves had to be pasted
> together. It would not be difficult to separate these
> leaves and substitute others".[7]

By having the witnesses sign their names on the *verso* transversely to the writing on the *recto* the possibility that one part
of the document will be detached and replaced by a forged part
was effectively forestalled, since by attempting such a forgery
the signatures would be chopped off in the middle and the forgery
would become patent.

This brings us to a consideration of the ספר המקנה (the
deed of the purchase) which is referred to several times in Jer. 32.
It seems that in this deed too, as in Dura Pg. 20, the witnesses'
names were written on the *verso*. In Jer. 32:10 we read:
ואכתב בספר ואחתם ואעד עדים (And I subscribed the deed, and
sealed it, and called witnesses). The sequence of writing, sealing
and attesting seems to indicate that the attestation by the

---

[6] *Ibid.*
[7] GCD, p. 32.

witnesses took place after the sealing of the document, which,
in turn, indicates that the witnesses' names were written on the
verso. Also, like Dura Pg. 20, Jeremiah's "deed of purchase" was
a double document, with a closed and an open part. Finally,
as in Dura Pg. 20, the open part was apparently an abbreviated version of the closed part. In Jer. 32:11 we read:
ואקח את ספר המקנה את החתום המצוה והחקים ואת הגלוי
(So I took the deed of the purchase, both that which was sealed,
containing the order and the terms, and that which was open).
The writer has suggested elsewhere [8] that the word מצוה (order)
is used here as a technical term meaning that part of the deed
in which it is recited that the grantor ordered the grantee to
take possession of the property conveyed by the deed, similar
to the order contained in the words קבר מתך (bury thy dead)
uttered by Ephron to Abraham in the case of the purchase of
the Cave of Machpelah (Gen. 23:11). Be that as it may, it is
quite obvious that "that which was open" contained less than
"that which was closed", that is, that it was an abbreviated
version thereof.

    A further indication that the Hebrew legal document of
antiquity had the signatures of the witnesses on the *verso* is
furnished by the Aramaic papyri. In most of the legal documents
in these papyri there appears the phrase ושהדיא בגו before the
signaturess of the witnesses, which are on the *recto*.[9] This phrase
has been misunderstood by all the commentators on the Aramaic
papyri. Cowley, for example, translates it as "and the witnesses
thereto". However, this translation is incorrect, the correct
meaning of the word בגו being *inside, within*. The phrase should
therefore be translated as "and the witnesses are within", that is,
the witnesses' signatures are on the *recto*. This would seem to
indicate that the signing by the witnesses on the *recto* constituted

---

[8] See the article בעלות in the Biblical Encyclopedia (Hebrew), v. 2, p. 296.
See also ch. 11, n. 15, above.

[9] See, *e. g.*, APC, 5.15, 8.28, 10.21; APK, 1.10, 2.14-15. See also Kraeling's
comment at p. 137.

a deviation from the old practice. In order to avoid misunderstanding, the scribe apparently thought it necessary to make special mention of the deviation.

Whether the practice of writing the witnesses' names on the *verso* of the document arose in Egypt or in Judea, is difficult to determine with certainty. However, the indications are that it was first introduced among the Jews. In Egypt this practice is found only towards the end of the 6th century B. C. E.,[10] while among the Jews it seems to have prevailed at an earlier period.

[10] See GCD, p. 20.

CHAPTER XIV

ON THE MEANING OF SOME PHRASES IN THE ARAMAIC PAPYRI.

1. בר ביתא

In Brooklyn 10.19; 11.14; 12.34, one of the attesting witnesses signs as רחום בר ביתא. Kraeling [1] correctly connects the term בר ביתא with the Babylonian *mar bîti* and points out that Arsham, the Persian satrap of Egypt, is called *mar bîti* in Babylonian texts and בר ביתא in the Borchard scrolls. He suggests that the term means perhaps "a house-born slave". He further calls attention to the similar Hebrew term בן בית, occurring in Gen. 15:3 and Eccles. 2:7, and suggests that "perhaps the added assumption is needed that the son of the house is adopted".

The writer believes that Kraeling's "added assumption" is the only one that is needed. The בן בית is a slave, not necessarily a house-born slave, who has been adopted by his master and thus given the status of a freedman who was under an obligation to serve and support his master "as a son supports his father". With regard to בן בית, this view was expressed by the writer in an article [2] published in 1951 and more recently in the article בן בית in the *Biblical Encyclopedia* (Hebrew). In the latter article, the writer cites O'Calahan, *Aram Naharaim*, p. 30, where Gen. 15:3 is compared with a deed of adoption from Nuzi in which it is stipulated that the adopted son is to succeed to the inheritance of his adoptive father, provided the latter leaves no natural child.

---

[1] See APK, 255f.

[2] See *Tarbitz* (Publication of the Hebrew University), 22, 194f.

There still remains the difficulty, noted by Kraeling,[3] that in the case of Rahum and of Arsham the individual, whose "son of the house" each of them, respectively, was, is not named, as he would usually be named in Babylonian texts. The solution of this difficulty seems to be that in these cases the adoptive father was the king, whom it was not necessary to name. The term "son of the house", without more, had apparently become a sort of nobility title meaning the adoptive son of the king. Incidentally, this will perhaps explain the fact that in the Lachish Letters one טביהו is referred to once (no. 3, 1.19) as עבד המלך (slave of the king) and another time (no. 5, 1.10) as זרע למלך (seed to the king), that is the adoptive son of the king.

2. מחר או יום אחרן

This phrase occurs very frequently in the Aramaic papyri.[4] Both Cowley and Kraeling render it into English as "tomorrow or another day".[5] However, from certain parallels in an Accadian document from Ras Shamra of about the fourteenth century B. C. E. and in a demotic document of the seventh century (ca. 631) B. C. E., respectively, it appears that the phrase should rather be rendered as "tomorrow, or the day after (tomorrow)"; that is, in the future. Thus understood, the phrase corresponds to the Biblical תמול שלשום ("yesterday, the day before yesterday"; that is, in the past).[6] The indefinite future in our phrase, like the indefinite past in the Biblical phrase, is expressed by the first two members in the unending series of days.

The document from Ras Shamra[7] referred to above, in Thureau-Dangin's transcription and French translation, reads in part as follows:

---

[3] APK, *ibid.*

[4] See, e. g., APC, 5.6, 8; 9.8, 13; APK, 2.7, 9, 10, 12, 13; 7.21.

[5] See, however, Professor Kraeling's note to 2.7, at p. 147, where he mentions the interpretation of the phrase proposed here, which I suggested to him on the basis of a similar phrase in Baba Metzia 17a.

[6] See, e. g., Gen. 31:2, 5; Exod. 5:7, 8, 14; 21:39, 36.

[7] F. Thureau-Dangin, *Trois contrats de Ras-Shamra*, Syria, XVIII (1937), 245ff.

ša-ni-tam šum-ma ur-ra-am
15 se-ra-am A-zi-ra-nu
ù Abdi-A-da-tum mâr Bu-ra-na
ù maru-šu-nu mâru mârî-šu-nu
i-tú[-ru]-nim a-na lib-bi-šu-nu
1 bilat kaspam ú-ma-lu-nim
20 a-na šarri
D'autre part, si demain,

15 après-demain A-zi-ra-nu
ou *Abdi-A-da-tum,* fils de Bu-ra-na
ou leurs enfants, (ou) les enfants de leurs
enfants
reviennent sur leur accord
1 talent d'argent ils paieront

20 au roi

In a note, Thureau-Dangin, after pointing out that the phrase
urram šeram occurs also in Accadian texts from Boghazkoi, says:

Il est probable que, de même que *umam urram*
signifie "aujourd' hui, demain", c'est-à-dire, "tous
les jours" ... urram šeram signifie "demain, après-
demain", c'est-à-dire "à l' avenir".[8]

The demotic document [9] mentioned above, in Griffith's
English translation, reads in part as follows:

"As Amûn liveth, as Pero liveth, as he is well
and as Amûn giveth him the victory, there belongeth
not to me, or to son, daughter, brother, sister, any
man in the whole land(?) that shall be able to ...
to-morrow or the second morrow(?)."

---

[8] *Ibid.,* p. 252, n. 1. The phrase occurs also in the tablets from Alalakh of
the 18th century B. C. E. See D. J. Wiseman, *The Alalakh Tablets,* no. 41,
and Speiser's comment thereon in Journal of the American Society 74, p. 23.

[9] GCD, 58. See also M. Malinine and J. Pirenne, *Documents juridiques
égyptiens,* AHDO, V (1950-51), 66. The phrase which is rendered by Griffith
as "to-morrow or the second morrow" is rendered by them into French as
"dorenavant", which, of course, conceals the idiomatic nature of the phrase.

The phrase מחר או יום אחרן occurs in the Aramaic papyri
precisely in the same context in which the corresponding phrases
occur in the document from Ras Shamra and in the demotic
document, namely, in the clause in which the maker of the
document declares that neither he nor his representatives shall
in the future contest the validity of the legal transaction evidenced by the document. In Cowley, No. 9 (460 B. C. E.), for
example, the clause in question, in English translation, reads:

> "If to-morrow or another day (הן מחר או יום אחרן)
> I should institute suit or process against you and
> say I did not give you this land to develop, and
> did not draw up this deed for you, I will pay you
> the sum of 10 *kerashim* by royal weight, at the
> rate of 2R to the ten, and no suit or process shall
> lie".[10]

A still closer approximation to the Ras Shamra document and to
the demotic document is found in Cowley, No. 1 (495 B. C. E.),
where the clause reads:

> "Hereafter, on a future day,[11] (למחר יום אחרן), we
> shall not be able to sue you in the matter of this
> your share, and say, We did not give it to you;
> nor shall a brother or sister (of ours), son or
> daughter, relative or alien be able to sue you; and
> whoever shall sue you in the matter of this your
> share which we have given you, shall pay to you
> the sum of 5 *karash* and the share is yours".[12]

It will be noted that in the document last quoted the word או
(or) does not occur in the phrase under discussion, which
makes it more nearly correspond to *urram šeram* of the Ras
Shamra document and to the Biblical תמול שלשום.

---

[10] APC, 27.

[11] This is Cowley's rather free translation of the phrase, which, in view of
the evidence discussed in the text, is inexact.

[12] APC, 2.

3. תתב על מוזנא

In Brooklyn 7.24f.[13] it is stated:

והן יה[וי]שמע תשנא לבעלה עניה ותאמר לה שני[ת]ך
לא אהוה לך אנתת כסף שנאה בראשה מהרה יאבד תתב
על מוזנא ותנתן ל[ב]עלה עניה כסף שקלן 2 ר 7

This is translated by Kraeling as follows:

> "And if Yehoyishma divorces her husband Ananiah
> and says to him, I divorce thee. I will not be to
> thee a wife the divorce money is on her head; his
> mohar is lost. She shall sit by the scales and shall
> give to Ananiah her husband silver shekels 7,2 R".[14]

In his comment on the phrase תתב על מוזנא Kraeling says:

> "The sentence differs only slightly from A. P.
> 15:23-4. We cannot agree with Cowley's rendering,
> 'she shall return to the scales', for על in the sense of
> אל is not to be expected here. Nöldeke rendered
> 'she shall sit *beside* the scales', which is probably
> correct. Personal presence is essential".[15]

The writer believes that the phrase in question means neither
"she shall sit by the scales" nor "she shall return to the scales"
but "she shall pay on the scales". The word תתב is the *hafel* of
תוב=Hebrew שוב, and, like the *hifil* of שוב in some passages
in the Bible, it is used here with the special nuance of *to pay*.
This nuance is especially pronounced in Ez. 18:7 חבולתו חוב ישיב,
which should be rendered as "his debt he pays". The word חבולתו
is apparently derived from the Accadian *ḫubullu* (debt) [16] and
ישיב corresponds to the Accadian *apâlu* (to answer, to return, to
pay).[17] A similar combination *ḫubullam apâlu* (to pay a debt)

---

[13] APK, 206.

[14] *Ibid.*, 207.

[15] *Ibid.*, 215.

[16] See C. Bezold, *Babylonisch-assyrisches Glossar*, 118b.

[17] See *ibid.*, 54b. For a discussion of the various shades of meaning of the
word in legal terminology, see p. 12f., above.

occurs in an old-Babylonian document cited by San-Nicolo.[18]
The *hifil* of שוב also occurs the sense of *to pay* in 2 Kings 3:4
והשיב למלך ישראל מאה אלף כרים ומאה אלף אלים and in 2 Chron.
27:5 זאת השיבו לו בני עמון.

4. פס שרת

The phrase occurs in Brooklyn 10.7, 9[19] and 12.9, 18.[20]
Brooklyn 10.7 reads:

זנה ביתא זי תחומוהי כתיבן בספרא זנה אנה ענני בר
עזריה יהבתה לך פס שרת. . . זי לא כתב על ספר אנתתכי.

This is rendered by Kraeling as follows:

> "This is the house of which the boundaries are
> written in this document. I, Anani son of Azariah,
> gave it to thee as remainder portion(?) which is
> not written in the document of thy marriage".

Credit is due to Kraeling [21] for having correctly rendered the
difficult word פס as "portion" and for having recognized the word
שרת as derived from the root שאר. With but a slight modification of his translation, the phrase becomes perfectly intelligible.
The phrase should be rendered as "additional portion", that is,
the portion that was given to Yehoyishma by her father in
addition to the dowry which was written in her document of
marriage. Accordingly, פס שרת על ספר אנתותכי in Brooklyn
10.9 should be rendered as "an additional portion above your
document of marriage".[22] The word על has this meaning of *above*
in Gen. 48:22: ואני נתתי לך שכם אחד על אחיך Cf. also יתר על
in Mishnah Kethuboth, 4:10. On שאר as *addition*, cf. שאר
רוח (addition of spirit) in Mal. 2:15.

---

[18] M. San-Nicolo, *Die Schlussklauseln der altbabylonischen Kauf-und
Tauschverträge*, 150, n. 32.

[19] APK, 248.

[20] *Ibid.*, 270.

[21] See his comments at p. 253.

[22] Cf. Gen. 31:14 יתען רחל ולאה ותאמרנה לו העוד לנו חלק ונחלה בבית אבינו
("And Rachel and Leah answered and said unto him: 'Is there yet any portion
or inheritance for us in our father's house?'").

CHAPTER XV

THE STYLE AND FORM OF THE BYZANTINE
LEGAL DOCUMENT.

Students of the Greco-Egyptian papyri have long since been aware that the style of the legal papyri of the late Byzantine period in Egypt is so different from that of the papyri of earlier periods that they may be regarded as in a class by themselves.[1] So far as the writer has been able to ascertain no explanation has been offered for this phenomenon. That an explanation is called for is obvious. The writer believes that the explanation is to be sought in the influence of the Jewish notarial style, that this influence was cumulative over a long period of time, and that it reached its culmination in the late Byzantine period. The result is that the Greek legal document of this period, in all of its essential features, is an almost exact counterpart of the Jewish legal document of the Middle Ages, which has a long history of many centuries behind it.

The lack of interest on the part of papyrologists in the Jewish medieval document and in the Talmud, despite the wealth of material that is obtainable from these sources for the eluci- dation of the Byzantine legal document, is amazing. It is sufficient to lay side by side a sixth century papyrus representing a deed of conveyance, for example, with a similar Jewish document from thirteenth century England for even the inexpert eye to see the close kinship between these two specimens.

The striking similarity between the form and style of the Hebrew legal document of the Middle Ages and that of the

[1] See J. Partsch, *Zur Geschichte des Wertpapieres*, Zeitschrift f. d. ges. Handelsrecht, 70, 442.

Byzantine legal document was noticed by Merx over sixty years ago. But, because of his failure to take into consideration the Talmudic sources upon which the Hebrew legal document is based, he arrived at the erroneous conclusion that it was patterned after its Byzantine counterpart, when exactly the reverse is true.

In view of the importance of Merx's early discovery of the similarity between the Hebrew and Byzantine legal forms, despite the erroneous conclusions he drew from this discovery, it will be interesting to quote him at some length.

After stating that he is limiting himself to the publication of certain documents in the original Hebrew and Arabic, together with a French translation, Merx continues:

> "There is, however, one point to which I allow myself to call attention because I flatter myself to have discovered, by studies which are foreign to Hebrew paleography, the true light in which the forms of contracts, as they appear in the specimens given here by me, are to be regarded. He who occupies himself for the first time with documents conceived in other languages and belonging to other lands, will be easily inclined to attribute to them a special character, whether Jewish, Arab or oriental, and, reflecting upon the origin of these formularies, detailed and prolix as they are, one might suppose that their form owes its origin to a certain disposition of the Semitic spirit; but this would be an error. The same forms are found in Coptic papyri, published by Father Ciasca, and in the collection of Greek and Arabic documents from Sicily, published by Mr. Casa. It follows, therefore, that in order to explain the style and phraseology of these documents, one need not have recourse to Moslem or Jewish jurisprudence, which will not explain the existence of similar forms among the Greeks; one must rather attribute the origin of these formularies to the practices of the Byzantine bureaus, whose

formularies were later accepted by the less civilized people who ravaged and occupied the provinces of this vast empire".[2]

In support of his conclusion that the Arab and Jewish legal forms were copied from Byzantine sources, Merx quotes A. von Kremer to the effect that long before the Arab invasion of the Eastern provinces of the Roman empire Roman law had so far penetrated the daily life of these provinces that, despite the "obstinate exclusiveness" of the Jews, its influence is even discernible in the Talmud.[3] The Arabs, according to von Kremer,[4] became acquainted with the institutions and practices of Roman law through two main avenues: 1. Daily contact with the sub- jugated peoples who practiced Roman law. 2. The legal literature of the Jews.

Merx apparently could not even conceive of the possibility that the Byzantine forms were copied from the Jews. He had it on the authority of von Kramer that the Jews were less civilized than the Byzantines and that the Talmud is replete with traces of Roman law influences.

As to the relative state of legal culture among the Jews and the Byzantines, the writer will not venture as dogmatic an evaluation as that made by von Kremer. But if copying by one system of law from another is any indication of the relative state of the systems concerned, it would seem that in some respects, at least, Jewish law was far superior to Roman law, as practiced in the Byzantine empire. As to the influence of Roman law on the Talmud, von Kremer's statement is without any foundation in fact. The writer has yet to be shown one clear instance of Roman law influence on the Talmud.

Talmudic influence on Byzantine legal practice is discernible, mainly, in legal forms and formulae. Our study will therefore

[2] A. Merx, *Documents de paléographie hebraique et arabe* (1894), 10-12. The English translation of the passage is the writer's.
[3] A. von Kremer, *Culturgeschichte des Orients unter den Chaliphen*, 1,534
[4] *Ibid.*, 535.

concern itself, for the most part, with a comparison of Hebrew and Byzantine legal documents. It should, however, be stated at the outset that a study of the medieval Jewish document alone is not sufficient for our purposes, since available Jewish forms are of a later period than the papyri. In order to establish the priority in point of time of the Jewish forms, a careful study must be made of portions of legal formulae found in the Talmud as well as of a variety of legal rules and doctrines found there and reflected in the Jewish forms of the Middle Ages.

The Deed of Conveyance.

For easy reference, we shall put our material in two parallel columns, placing in the left-hand column, with the letter G in front, portions from the Byzantine deed of conveyance, and in the right-hand column, with the letter J in front, portions from the Jewish deed of conveyance and from the Talmud.

G-1.

"We acknowledge that with free and fixed purpose and guileless intention and pure conscience . . . we have sold to you today and conveyed to you from now to all succeeding time the house belonging to us. . . " P. Lond. 1722 (a. 573) — Hunt and Edgar, *Select Papyri,* no. 30.

J-1.

" . . . acting with my own will, without compulsion, but with perfect heart and willing mind, I have delivered and sold. . . the aforesaid house. . . " — M. D. Davis, *Hebrew Deeds of English Jews,* no. 64 (a. 1280).

G-2.

". . . in its entirety from basement to house-top". — *Ibid.*

J-2.

". . . all of it, from the airspace to the ground" — An Aramaic deed of conveyance of a house found in the Dead Sea Region and dated in the third year of the freedom of Israel

(134 C. E.). Revue Biblique
61 (1954), 182ff.

G-3.

"and we have left nothing
unsold in the aforesaid house".
— *Ibid.*

J-3.

"... If a man sells property
to another, he should insert in
the deed of sale the words, 'I
have not reserved from this
transfer for myself anything' ".
— BT, Baba Bathra 62a.

G-4.

"... henceforth you the purchaser may own and be master
of the aforesaid house in its
entirety ... and administer and
manage it and build or sell or
give it away or bequeath it to
your children and descendants
or dispose of it in whatever
manner you choose without let
or hindrance ... " — *Ibid.*

J-4.

"And henceforth the said
William may go and take possession of the said house and
court, with all the appurtenances, and do therewith whatever he wills, and he shall rule
(שליט) — and his heirs after
him — over the house, court,
and all the appurtenances aforesaid, to build or pull down, and
to dig therein pits, ditches and
caves, from the depth of the
earth to the height of the sky,
to leave to heirs or to devise,
to sell and to pledge, or present
as a gift to whomsoever he
wills... and no man shall re-
strain him... " — M. D. Davis,
Hebrew Deeds, no. 64.

G-5.

"And if any person makes a
claim against you or disputes
the possession of the aforesaid

J-5.

"... will arise and acquit,
and purge and clear this sale".
— A portion of a warranty

house... we, the vendors, will repel him and make clear your title at our own expense". — *Ibid.*

"...on the security of all my property". — A portion of the warranty clause in P. Cairo, Masp. 67097.

clause quoted in BT, Baba Metzia, 15a.

"...on the surety of all my property...". — A portion of the warranty clause. — M. D. Davis, *Hebrew Deeds*, no. 64.

G-1 makes its appearance in the papyri of the Byzantine period only.[5] J-1 is found in virtually all Jewish legal documents of every description, whatever their provenience. As has been remarked above, there are no such documents or forms available for the early Middle Ages. However, the fact that a similar clause appears in all the available forms of the Jewish bill of divorce [6] is a strong indication that it is of great antiquity. The Jewish bill of divorce assumed a standard form at an early time. In fact, the Talmud [7] enjoins against making any changes in the form prescribed by the Sages.

G-2, which appears in Greco-Egyptian documents in the late Byzantine period only,[8] reads: ἀπὸ ἐδάφους ἕως ἀέρος. The Aramaic original of J-2 reads: כֹּל דִּי בה [מאוירא] לקרקעא. Abramson and Ginsberg, (BASOR 136, 17f.), have suggested מאיגרא (from the roof) for the missing word. On the basis of a Talmudic parallel (BT, *Baba Bathra* 63b), the writer (BASOR 136, 15f.) at one time suggested מרקיעא (from the sky), but upon reconsideration he believes מאוירא (from the air-space) more likely, since the former would have required לארעא (to the earth) as its antithesis, rather than לקרקעא (to the ground). Be that as it may, it is quite obvious that the missing term corresponds to ἕως ἀέρος of the Greco-Egyptian papyri. That the

---

[5] See PWB s. v. γνώμη.

[6] See, e. g., A. Gulak, *Ozar Hashtaroth*, nos. 67-70.

[7] See BT, Gittin 80a.

[8] See PWB s. v. ἀήρ.

Aramaic formula preceded the Greek by several centuries is no less obvious.

The no-reservation clause, quoted under G-3, is found only in late Byzantine papyri.[9] As may be gathered from J-3, a similar clause was considered a necessary part of every Jewish deed of conveyance as early as the beginning of the fourth century, Abaye, in whose name the proposition is quoted in the Talmud, having died in 338 C. E.

J-4 and G-4 are the *shallit* and the *kyrieia* clauses, respectively, fully developed and expanded to include virtually all possible indicia of ownership. It is unnecessary to repeat here what has already been said about these clauses.[10]

The warranty clause (G-5) with the characteristic term *to clear* (καθαραποιέω), that is to clear of encumbrances and of adverse claims, appears in the Greek papyri of the late Byzantine period only.[11] That it corresponds to the Talmudic clause quoted under J-5 can hardly be doubted. Indeed, in some of the 6th century papyri [12] even the Talmudic idiom is followed. The phrase about the clearing of the title reads there: καθαροποιήσω σοι ταύτην τὴν πρᾶσιν (I will clear for you this sale) which corresponds exactly to אמריק זביני אילין of the Talmudic clause. That this is not a coincidence is obvious, and that the Talmudic clause, which is quoted by Raba, an early 4th century authority, as being a form commonly in use among the Jews, preceded that of the Byzantine papyri is equally obvious.

Another indication of the close relationship between the Talmudic and Byzantine warranty clauses may be seen in the inclusion, in some of the papyri,[13] of the improvements (βελτίωσις) of the property within the scope of the warranty. The matter of improvements is mentioned already in Mishnah, Gittin 5:3.

---

[9] See PWB s. v. ὑπολείπω.

[10] See p. 125f., above.

[11] See PWB s. v. καθαροποιέω.

[12] See *Journal of Philology* 22 (1894), documents nos. 1.55-56, 2.10-11, 3.38. See also P. Lond. 1735.16.

[13] See PWB. s. v. βελτίωσις.

In a somewhat later Talmudic text [14] we are told that Master Samuel (180-257) enjoined the notary attached to his court not to incorporate in the warranty clause a provision regarding improvements unless told by the grantor to do so. It seems that such a provision had become so common that scribes were wont to incorporate it in deeds of conveyance, without previously consulting the grantor. Master Samuel warned his scribe against this practice. Indeed, in the portion of the warranty clause quoted in the Talmud [15] the grantor undertakes to warrant the improvements. On the other hand, in the Greco-Egyptians papyri the provision about improvements is found only in the warranty clauses of 6th and 7th century documents. It seems, therefore, that this feature of the warranty clause had been common among the Jews for several centuries before it made its appearance in the papyri.

Finally, the provision in the warranty clause in which the grantor pledges all his property for the performance of the obligation of the warranty had been a regular feature of the Jewish deed of conveyance at least since the second century, while in the papyri it is found only in deeds dating from the 6th and 7th centuries, and very occasionally at that. [16]

The Writing Obligatory in The Greco-Egyptian Papyri of The Late Byzantine Period and in The Documents from Dura-Europos.

In the Byzantine papyri of an obligatory nature, beginning with the latter part of the 5th century, there appears frequently a clause wherein the obligor pledges all his property, present and future, for the performance of his obligation.[17] From the Syro-

---

[14] BT, Baba Metzia 15a.

[15] See *ibid.*

[16] See, e. g., P. Lond. 1722, P. Mon. (both of them 6th century deeds of conveyance), where the pledging-of-property provision does not occur in the warranty clause.

[17] See A. B. Schwarz, *Hypothek und Hypallagma*, 49, n. 3.

Roman Law-Book, it appears that a similar clause was also common in Syria in the 5th century.[18]

[18] K. G. Bruns und E. Sachau, *Syrisch-Roemisches Rechtsbuch aus dem fünften Jahrhundert.* In section L. 111 it is stated that if a man borrows money from several individuals successively, giving each one of them a writing concerning the sum borrowed, and dies without having paid the debts, the creditor who is prior in time has a prior lien on the debtor's property. This, as Bruns (p. 280) remarks, is contrary to Roman law which puts all creditors, regardless of priority in time, on an equal footing with regard to execution against the debtor's property. Bruns therefore concludes that the writing referred to in this section is one containing a general hypothec on the debtor's property, and that hence the creditor who is prior in time is prior in lien. It seems that the clause providing for a general hypothec had become so common that the author of the Law-Book took it for granted that the writing contained such a clause. Again, in section L. 112 it is stated that if a man borrows money from another and gives him a bond in which he pledges the property which he has and which he will acquire, the debtor's oxen and cows are not covered by the pledge. Bruns (p. 281f.) notes the similarity between this section and C. 8, 16 (17), 7, which exempts plough cows and oxen from seizure by creditors, and remarks that the author of the Law-Book apparently confused the law of execution with the law of hypothec. It seems, however, that at the time of the writing of the Law-Book in Syria the distinction between the law of execution and the law of hypothec was no longer of much practical significance, since bonds generally contained a clause binding the debtor's property, present and future. The author merely wanted to say that a creditor may not seize the debtor's oxen and cows. But in his crude way he quoted the provision of the bond which was common in his day, although this had nothing to do with the proposition he was trying to state. Certainly, the inclusion of future acquisitions in the pledge would have no possible effect upon the creditor's right to seize a specific type of property, such as oxen and cows.

It should be noted that C. 8, 16 (17), 7, which was promulgated by Constantine in 315, has an interesting parallel in Mishnah, Baba Metzia 9:13, where it is stated that all implements used in the production of food are exempt from seizure by creditors. But while Constantine bases the exemption on the highly practical consideration that seizure of agricultural slaves, animals or implements might cause delay in the collection of taxes, the Mishnah bases its exemption on the humanitarian ground that the debtor would be deprived of the means of subsistence. The rule of the Mishnah is derived from Deut. 24:6: "No man shall take the nether or the upper millstone to pledge; for he taketh a man's life to pledge". This text readily lends itself to extension by analogy. Indeed, in another early Talmudic text (BT, Baba Metzia, 116a)

Among the Jews, a provision for a general lien upon the debtor's property had been a common feature of the writing obligatory at least five or six centuries before this provision began to appear regularly in the Greek papyri. Already at the beginning of the second century C. E. it was held by the Rabbis that this lien was implied in law, even where the clause providing for it was omitted from the bond.[19]

While in the Greek papyri stemming from Egypt the general hypothec clause makes its appearance toward the end of the fifth century only, it appears much earlier in Greek documents stemming from Dura-Europos and from Askalon. It is found in P. BGU 316=Mitteis Chrest. 271, a Greek papyrus from Askalon, dated in the year 359 C. E. Still earlier, in the year 121 C. E., the general hypothec is found in a parchment document from Dura-Europos, published by Rostovtzeff and Welles.[20]

Rostovtzeff calls attention to the fact that the document last mentioned does not contain the provision, usually found in the Greek special hypothec, whereby the debtor gives the creditor a guarantee against accident or damage to the hypothecated property.[21] He suggests, as a possible reason for this, that since under the terms of the document the debtor delivered himself into bondage to the creditor for the term of the loan, probably taking with him the hypothecated property into the creditor's possession, it was not necessary to have such a provision in the contract. However, it seems that a more plausible explanation is to be found in the essential difference between the special and the general hypothec. In the case of the special hypothec, where only specific property is pledged, a provision whereby the

plough cows are specifically mentioned as coming within the exempt class. Is it not possible that by the law of 315 Constantine merely gave legal sanction to a Biblical precept, and that he assigned a reason for the law which the provincial officials could more readily appreciate?

[19] See Mishnah, Baba Metzia 1:5.

[20] See Rostovtzeff and Welles, *A Parchment of Loan from Dura-Europos on the Euphrates,* Yale Classical Studies 2, 1ff.

[21] *Ibid.,* 14.

debtor is to bear the risk of accident or damage to the property affords added security to the creditor, in that it enables him, in case of damage or accident to the hypothecated property, to collect the debt from the debtor's remaining property. But in the case of a general hypothec, where all of the debtor's property, present and future, is pledged, such a provision would be entirely superfluous and meaningless. If an accident occurs to some part of the debtor's property, the remaining property continues to be bound for the payment of the debt, regardless of whether or not the loan agreement contains a guarantee against accident.

Rostovtzeff also calls attention to the fact that D. Pg. 10 does not contain the provision, generally found in the Greek hypothec, against alienation of the hypothecated property by the debtor.[22] Again, the difference between the special hypothec, which is a Greek institution, and the general hypothec of D. Pg. 10 and of the late Byzantine papyri, which was apparently borrowed from the Jews, fully accounts for the absence of the provision against alienation from D. Pg. 10. Where, as under the Jewish practice, every writing of an obligatory nature, regardless of the size and nature of the obligation, carries with it a general lien upon the obligor's property, it is not feasible that the obligor bind himself not to dispose of any of his property while the obligation remains undischarged. If a man, who owns property worth, say, ten thousand dollars, borrows a hundred dollars on a writing, he cannot be expected to forego his right to dispose of any of his property while the loan remains unpaid. Similarly, if a man, who owns several parcels of property, sells one of them with the usual warranty under which all the property remaining in his hands becomes bound for the performance of the obligation of the warranty, he cannot be expected to forego forever his right to dispose of his remaining property.

P. BGU 316, which was discovered in Egypt, is a deed of conveyance of a slave. It was drawn up in Askalon, where the transaction took place, and, apparently, brought to Egypt

---

[22] *Ibid.*

by the purchaser of the slave. The general hypothec is contained in the warranty clause, the seller pledging all his property, present and future, for the performance of his obligations under the warranty. This is in accord with Talmudic law under which every warranty invariably carries with it a pledge of the warrantor's property. Indeed, the same term, אחריות, is used in the Talmud to denote a warranty and a pledge of property.[23] In Egypt, on the other hand, the general hypothec in the warranty clause was by no means common even in the sixth century, when it had become there a regular feature of all writings obligatory.

One further detail of the Askalon papyrus, indicating that its form was influenced by that of similar Jewish forms, deserves to be noted. The document contains the familiar clause stating that the sale is made in perpetuity. What is peculiar, however, about this clause in the Askalon document is the phrase ἀπὸ τῆς σήμερον ἡμέρας καὶ εἰς ἀεί (from this day and forever). The word καὶ (and) is altogether out of place in this phrase unless the entire phrase is an exact literal translation of the Aramaic מיומא דנן ולעלם (from this day *and* forever), which, as we have seen above, is universally found in the *shallit*-clause of Jewish deeds as far back as the Aramaic papyri of the 5th century B. C. E. and is also mentioned in the Talmud.[24]

The gap, of over a century in the one case and of over three centuries in the other, between the Askalon and the Dura-Europos documents containing the general hypothec clause and the Greco-Egyptian documents containing the same clause is significant as indicating the direction whence this legal institution came. But more significant in this respect is the form which the general hypothec clause took in Egypt in the sixth century. A number of sixth century papyri [25] specify the property pledged by the obligor as *movable* and *immovable* κινητὸς καὶ ἀκινητός

---

[23] See BT, Baba Metzia 14a.
[24] See BT, Gittin 85b.
[25] See, e. g., P. Cairo Masp. 67127.18. See also PWB s. v. κινητός

Such a specification of property in the general lien clause is found in BT, Baba Bathra 44b, where it is stated in the name of Rabba (270-330 C. E.) that a clause containing it is valid. It also occurs in every available Hebrew form or document of an obligatory nature.

The most convincing proof, however, that the general hypothec clause in the documents of the late Byzantine period is of Jewish origin is to be found in the peculiar word κίνδυνος (risk or hazard) which is used in these documents in the sense of security or pledge.[26]

The Latin equivalent of κίνδυνος — *periculum* — is also used in the same sense in C. 8, 16 (17), 9 (a. 538), where it is stated that the formula *fide et periculo rerum ad me pertinentium* is sufficient to constitute a general hypothec upon the property which the obligor has as well as upon that which he may acquire in the future. It thus appears that by the year 538 this formula, without any further words of hypothecation or pledge, had come to be generally understood as constituting a general hypothec upon the obligor's property. The formula imported not only a right of execution against the obligor's property while he remained owner thereof, but also an *in rem* charge upon the property in the hands of the obligor's transferees.

The question arises: how did a word which in its original sense means *risk* or *hazard* come to mean *pledge* or *security?* The writer believes that in the answer to this question lies the key to the understanding of the origin of the general hypothec of the later Roman law.

The Hebrew word by which the general lien on the obligor's property, similar to the general hypothec of the later Roman law, is designated is אחריות.[27] This word is derived from אחר — after, behind or back of — and means a *standing back of, security*. From the original meaning of the word אחריות — *security, pledge* — there developed the secondary meaning of

---

[26] See, e. g., P. Grenf. II, 87; P. Oxy. 135, 138. See also PWB s. v. κίνδυνος.
[27] See JDT s. v.

responsibility for loss, or risk of loss. The Hebrew term אחריות
in the sense of security was translated into Greek as χίνδυνος
(risk or hazard), that is, by a Greek term which corresponds
to the secondary meaning of the Hebrew term. This Greek term
thus became assimilated with the Hebrew אחריות acquiring the
meaning of security which the latter term had in Hebrew.
Justinian's *periculo rerum ad me pertinentium* and its Greek
equivalent in the papyri are but literal translations of באחריות
כל נכסי (on the security of all my property) of the Hebrew
writing obligatory.

In addition to the word *periculum,* the word *fides* (surety
or guarantee) is used in the general hypothec formula in
Justinian's code. This makes the parallel with the Talmudic
general hypothec formula perfect, the Talmudic formula being
כל נכסי אחראין וערבאין — "all my property is gaurantee and
surety".[28]

A further indication of the Talmudic origin of the general
hypothec is furnished by a word which occurs in the general
hypothec clause of some sixth century papyri and which has
been generally misunderstood. The word is τίμημα which elsewhere
means *valuation.* Not knowing what valuation had to do with
the general hypothec formula, lexicographers invented for the word
a new meaning, namely, *cost,*[29] interpreting the word to import
an undertaking on the part of the obligor to bear the cost of
the procedure of execution against his property if it should become
necessary for the obligee to resort to such procedure. Thus the for-

---

[28] See Tosefta Kethuboth, 9:1; PT Shebuoth 5:1; BT, Gittin, 37a; Kethuboth, 82a. The combination אחר וערב also occurs in the warranty clause in
the Aramaic deed of conveyance from the Dead Sea Region cited above (See
the writer's comments thereon in BASOR 136, 15f. and cf. Milik in Revue
Biblique 62, 254). Gulak, in his *History of Jewish Law* (Hebrew), 51, has
already called attention to the similarity between χίνδυνος and *periculum* on the
one hand, and אחריות, on the other, but he failed to notice that the second
term in Justinian's formula — *fides* — also has an exact parallel in the
Talmudic formula.

[29] See PWB and Liddell-Scott-Jones, *A Greek English Lexicon,* s. v.

mula κινδύνῳ καὶ πόρῳ καὶ τιμήματι τῆς παντοίας μου ὑποστάσεως appearing in P. Strassb. 40.20 is explained by Preisigke as follows: "auf Gefahr und Preisgabe meines gesamten Vermögens, welches auch zur Bestreitung der Kosten des Verfahrens herhalten soll". The truth of the matter, however, is that τίμημα means here, as elsewhere, *valuation* and that the relationship of this term to the general hypothec can only be understood in the light of the Talmudic procedure of execution against the obligor's property. One of the steps in this procedure was *valuation* (שומא) by the court of so much of the obligor's property as was necessary to satisfy the obligation.[30]

The Byzantine Marriage Document.

In an article [31] on the history of the *Kethuba*, Kaufmann, after stating that the *Kethuba* of the Middle Ages exhibits "incontrovertible correspondence" to the Byzantine marriage document and that undobutedly one depends upon the other, says: "Since Merx has conclusively proved the influence of the Byzantine formulary upon Rabbinic legal forms we are inclined to recognize also here an imitation of the Greek form."[32] Merx' "conclusive proof" has already been discussed above. It remains to be said that this is a clear case of one error leading to another. All the evidence points to the conclusion that the Jewish *Kethuba* was the model, not the copy.

Kaufmann relies upon the correspondence between אוקיר ואפלה (I will cherish and worship) in the *Kethuba* and θάλπειν καὶ θεραπεύειν (cherish and worship) in P. CPR 30 II. 20, a 6th century marriage contract from Egypt. As to θεραπεύειν it is almost certainly a translation of פלח. This Aramaic word,

---

[30] See Mishnah Arakhin 2:1 and BT, Baba Metzia 35a.

[31] Kaufmann, *Zur Geschichte der Kethuba*, Monatschrift f. d. Geschichte und Wissenschaft des Judentums 41, 213ff.

[32] "Nach dem von Merx entschiedend nachgewiesenem Einflusse des Byzantinischen Urkundenwesens auf das Rabbinische werden wir auch hier geneigt sein, in der Aramäischen Formel die Nachbildung der Griechischen zu erkennen" — *Ibid*.

like the Hebrew עֲבַד, is used in the following senses: *to till, work;
to serve* (man or deity), *worship*.[33] According to the Greek
lexica the Greek word is similarly used. In the *Kethuba* פלח is
invariably used with בקושטא (in truth), which is an exact
parallel to לַעֲבַד בֶּאֱמֶת (to worship in truth) occurring a number
of times in the Bible [34] and which tends to show that the
formula is not of Greek origin. Furthermore, the Accadian *palaḫu,*
which is a cognate of פלח is used already in some Middle-
Assyrian marriage documents (c. 14th century B. C. E.) in the
same sense in which it is used in the *Kethuba.* In these
documents [35] there occurs a clause which, in David and Ebeling's
German translation, reads: "Solange sie (husband and wife)
leben, werden sie einander Ehrfurcht erweisen (*palaḫu*)." The
word אוקיר is also more likely the original than the copy. It has
a close parallel in BT, *Baba Metzia,* 59a, where Raba (early 4th
century) is reported to have said to the townspeople of Mahuza
אוקירו לנשייכו (cherish your wives).

In P. Cairo, Masp. 67006, another 6th century marriage contarct from Egypt, there occurs the combination
ϑάλπειν τρέφειν καὶ ἱματίζειν (to cherish, maintain and clothe).
The last two items are clearly derived from the Talmudic
tradition interpreting Ex. 21:10 as referring to the husband's
duties toward his wife.[36] It will be recalled that according
to the Talmud there is still a third item in the list of
these duties, namely intimacy between husband and wife.
Interestingly enough, in P. Lond. 1711 (6th century), the
husband after undertaking *to maintain and clothe* the wife (l. 27),
further undertakes not to refrain from intercourse with her —
καὶ μηδαμῶς ἀποστῆναι με τῆς σῆς κοίτης (l. 33). P. Lond. 1711
contains another provision which is of extreme importance in
determining the legal tradition from which the document stems.
The husband undertakes not to *hate* or *divorce* the wife

---

[33] See JDT s. v.
[34] See, e. g., 1 Sam. 12:24; 1 Kings 2:4; Jer. 32:41.
[35] E. Ebeling und M. David, *Assyrische Rectsurkunden,* No 1.
[36] See p. 45f., above.

execpt for *unchastity, ugly conduct and bodily irregularity*
καὶ ἐν μηδενὶ καταφρονῆσαι σου μήτε ἐκβαλεῖν σε ἐκ
τοῦ ἐμοῦ συνοικεσίι παρεκτὸς λόγου πορνείας καὶ
αἰσχρᾶς πράξεως καὶ σωματικῆς ἀταξίας. (ll. 29-31).

As has been stated above,[37] שנא (to hate) is used in Biblical
Hebrew and in the Aramaic papyri in the terminology of divorce.
Epstein [38] has called attention to the fact that the word is
similarly used in PT *Kethubot* 5:8 and *Baba Bathra* 8:8, where
it is stated in the name of R. Jose (3rd century): "Those who
write 'If he will hate (her), if she will hate (him)', it is a
condition with respect to matters pecuniary and is valid".
אילין דכתבין: אין שנא, אין שנאת, תניי ממון ותניין קיים.
It thus appears that in the 3rd century in Palestine the Jewish
marriage document contained a condition about divorce which
was couched in terms strikingly similar to those of P. Lond. 1711.

As to the grounds for divorce enumerated in the document,
it seems likely that in the first one — unchastity — there
is a reflection of Matt. 5:32 (παρεκτὸς λόγου πορνείας). However,
the last two items — ugly conduct and bodily irregularity —
point to the Jewish-Talmudic tradition as the origin of the
formula.

As to the second item, it seems to be derived from a certain
Talmudic text dealing with the subject of divorce. In BT,
Yebamoth 24b and in PT, *Kethubot* 7:6, there is an enumeration
of compromising circumstances, such as "the seller of perfumes
leaving (the house) and the woman fastening her petticoat",
warranting divorce by the husband, and in each case the
woman's conduct is characterized as דבר מכוער (an ugly thing).
It seems that R. Judah the Prince, the compiler of the Mishnah,
in whose name the proposition is reported in the Babylonian
Talmud, by characterizing the woman's conduct as "an ugly
thing", alluded to the phrase ערות דבר in Deut. 24:1, interpreting
it in this sense. This interpretation of the Biblical phrase is in

---

[37] See p. 40, above.
[38] J. N. Epstein in Jahrbuch d. jüd.-lit. Gesellschaft, 6 (1908), 368f.

remarkable agreement with that of the LXX who render it as
ἄσχημον πρᾶγμα (an ugly thing).[39]

The third item — bodily irregularity — points to Mishnah,
Kethubot 7:7 as its origin. In this text it is stated:

המקדש את האשה... על מנת שאין בה מומין, ונמצאו
בה מומין — אינה מקודשת. כנסה סתם ונמצאו בה
מומין — תצא שלא בכתובה.

("If a man betrothed a woman on the condition
that there were no defects in her, and defects were
found in her, her betrothal is not valid. If he
married her making no conditions and defects were
found in her, she may be put away without her
Kethubah").

The parallelism between this proposition and the provision
about bodily irregularity in P. Lond. 1711 is quite obvious.
It seems that in the matter of marriage and divorce Christianity
in 6th century Egypt was still not far removed from the Jewish-
Talmudic tradition.[40]

[39] The rendering of ערות דבר by the LXX in both Deut. 24:1 and 23:15
is perhaps also the basis of Rabbi Judah's dictum in מדרש תנאים to Deut.
23:15, interpreting the Biblical phrase as meaning *something shameful* (משום
בזיון). Perhaps, too, the School of Hillel's interpretation of this Biblical phrase
is in accord with the rendering of the LXX. See Albeck's incisive remarks in his
Commentary on the Mishnah, Nashim, 265.

[40] For further parallelisms between Jewish and Byzantine forms, see ch. 16,
n. 40, below.

CHAPTER XVI

JEWISH AND LOMBARD LAW

Law and legal institutions in medieval Europe are generally thought to be either Roman or Germanic in origin. Wherever a given legal institution of the Middle Ages cannot be traced to Roman law a Germanic origin is believed to be indicated.

The idea of a Germanic law which formed the basis of a considerable portion of medieval law has been so persistently propagated by German scholars that it is universally accepted without question. Yet, upon analysis, it is extremely doubtful whether there ever was any such thing as a "Germanic law" capable of developing into a legal system from which sprang such advanced legal institutions, for example, as the negotiable promissory note and the mortgage without delivery of possession. If the term "Germanic law" is to have any meaning at all, it must refer to that stock of legal ideas and institutions which the Germanic tribes who invaded the western part of the Roman empire possessed at the time of these invasions. That stock of ideas and institutions must have been very meager indeed, and it is unlikely that it bore within itself the seeds of an advanced legal system.

Only by a total disregard of common sense and by the wildest flight of imagination could Brunner, for example, arrive at the conclusion that an institution such as the *"juengere Satzung,"* the mortgage of the later Middle Ages, had its origin in Germanic law. Says Brunner:

> While comparative legal history may trace the Roman hypothec to Egyptian law, the tree of origin of the modern mortgage of real property takes us

to the primeval forests of Germany (*die germanischen Urwälder*), to the institution of outlawry.[1]

One cannot help observing the overtone of extreme nationalism, mixed with the mysticism of race, in which certain German scholars delight, implicit in the phrase "*"germanische Urwälder.*" Any sensible person would know that the *germanische Urwälder* had nothing to do with the "*juengere Satzung;*" that legal ideas do not grow in primeval forests, even when these forests are inhabited by supermen whose descendants are destined to rule the world; that the market place, the bank counter, the court and the academy are the media from which new constructive legal notions emerge. But logic and good sense are submerged when racism takes the ground.

Oddly enough, it so happens that whenever Brunner is particularly insistent upon the Germanic origin of a given legal institution the evidence is overwhelming that that institution owes its origin to the Jews. As the writer has shown elsewhere,[2] the "*juengere Satzung*," like the French "*engagement*" and the English "Jewish gage," was introduced by the Jews and was patterned after the Jewish writing obligatory—an old form going back to Talmudic times and earlier.

In the case of the Jews, no recourse to mysticism or exaggerated nationalistic claims is necessary in order to explain their influence on medieval legal institutions. The Jews are an ancient people with a long legal tradition behind them. Through the Talmud, which they studied with great zeal and religious fervor, this tradition remained unbroken among them and was further developed in the rabbinic literature. They also possessed a highly developed legal formulary, and frequently had occasion to adapt their legal formulae, written in Hebrew and Aramaic, to medieval Latin, especially in transactions with non-Jews. No wonder, then, that their legal ideas and formulae found imitators among

---

[1] Brunner, *Forschungen zur Geschichte des deutschen u. franzoesischen Rechts* (1894) p. 469.

[2] See ch. 23, below

non-Jews. A good legal fomula, like a good coin, somehow gains currency.

The writer will deal in the next chapter with the evidence of Jewish influence upon the development of Frankish law. In this chapter an attempt will be made to present the evidence of Jewish influence upon Lombard law.

One would naturally assume that if Jewish legal ideas exercised any influence upon the development of Lombard law such influence would be found in the realm of property law and of the law of obligations. The fact, however, is that through Jewish legal forms, which were copied by the Lombards, Jewish legal ideas found their way even into Lombard family law.

The Lombard Scriptum de Morgencap and The Jewish Ketuba.

The Lombard *morgencap,* as its name indicates, developed from the Germanic *Morgengabe,* which was a gift made by the husband to the wife on the morrow of the wedding. But, as Calisse [3] remarks, already in the period of the first written Lombard law the substance of the institution was no longer what its name implied. It was a settlement upon the wife of part of the husband's property in case he predeceased her. This settlement, like the Hebrew *ketuba,* was usually embodied in a writing —*scriptum.* But unlike the Hebrew *ketuba* [4] which provides for payment to the woman of a specified amount of money—a minimum of two hundred *zuz* to a maiden and of one hundred to a widow—the Lombard *morgencap* consisted of one-quarter or of one-eighth of the husband's property.

The Hebrew *ketuba* provides that all of the husband's property, movable and immovable, present and future, shall be bound for the payment of the woman's dower.[5] In the Lombard documents, we find that in the eighth century the husband endows the wife with a quarter of his property, without specifying

[3] Calisse, *History of Italian Law* (1928) p. 574-75.
[4] See Mishna, *Ketubot* 4, 7.
[5] See Maimonides, *Mishneh Torah,* Yibbum, 4, 33.

movable and immovable, present and future.[6] But after the eighth century the specification of movable and immovable, present and future, becomes general.[7]

With regard to the *quarta* (one-quarter) and *octaba* (one-eighth) of the Lombard *morgencap,* there is apparently no satisfactory reason given by historians of Italian law why in some cases the *morgencap* consisted of one-quarter of the husband's property and in others of one-eighth. Calisse [8] says that originally the *morgencap* consisted of one-quarter and that it was reduced to one-eighth by the Beneventine capitularies.

However, an examination of the available Lombard sources will reveal that this explanation is erroneous. There is in these sources reference to an *octaba* before the date (866) of the capitulary which suposedly reduced the *quarta* to an *octaba.*

Codex Diplomaticus Cavensis, I, 58 (a. 856), is particularly revealing in this respect. This is a deed of conveyance of land in which it is provided that if the grantor's wife and daughter-in-law shall claim their *octaba* and *quarta* in the land conveyed, the grantee may recover from the remainder of the grantor's land an equivalent of the land taken by the two women. It thus appears that the *quarta* and *octaba* coexisted side by side prior to the date of the Beneventine capitularies. Obviously, then, the *octaba* was not introduced by these capitularies.

Furthermore, the text of the capitulary in question shows that the *octaba* was not an innovation introduced by it. This capitulary provides in substance that the lack of a writing shall not prevent a woman, upon her husband's death, from recovering her *quarta* or *octaba.* It reads, in part, as follows:

> Si clarum manifestatumque fuerit qualibet foeminam consuete et legalier habuisset maritum, et quartam seu octabam habuisset ab eo sibi factam,

---

[6] See *Codex Diplomaticus Cavensis,* vol. I, p. 1 (a. 792).

[7] See, *e. g., ibid.* p. 75 (a. 860), 212 (a. 940); vol. ii, p. 21 (a. 965), 77 (a. 972)

[8] See Calisse, *op. et loc. cit. supra.*

> eamque perturbatione temporis perdidisse quomo-
> documque; vel si etiam, ut accidere solet multotiens,
> quartam eadem vel octaba non fuerit scripta, pro-
> pinquus mariti vel quilibet alter eandem quartam
> vel octaba, eidem mulieri rite conpetentem contrare
> minime praesumat.[9]

The phrase *quartam seu octabam habuisset ab eo sibi factam*
clearly implies that at the time the capitulary was issued both
the *quarta* and the *octaba* had the sanction of law.

Finally, in all of the marriage documents of the 10th and
11th centuries recorded in the *Codex Diplomaticus Cavensis* the
provision for the woman's dower is one *quarta*.[10]

The question, therefore, arises: under what circumstances
did law and custom require a provision for a *quarta,* and under
what circumstances was an *octaba* sufficient?

The wirter believes that the *octaba* was reserved for a widow
and that Lombard law followed Hebrew law in this respect. As we
have seen above, under Hebrew law the widow's *ketuba* called
for exactly one-half of that of the maiden. This was apparently
copied by the Lombards, so that in the case of a widow the
quarta became an *octaba.*

Some support for the hypothesis that the *octaba* was reserved
for a widow is furnished by the marriage documents recorded in
the *Codex Diplomaticus Cavensis.* In all af these documents,
save one, the provision is for a *quarta.* In the one document,
dated 882, in which provision is made for an *octaba* it is specifically stated that it was the woman's second marriage.[11]

The Lombard Betrothal Agreement of the 10th and 11th Centuries and the Jewish Ketuba.

In an appendix to his monumental volume of source material

---

[9] Adelchis, ch. 3, MGH, Leges, vol. iv (ed. Pertz, 1868) p. 211.

[10] See, *e. g., Codex Diplomaticus Cavensis,* vol. 1, p. 1, 75, 212; vol. ii, p. 21, 77.

[11] *Ibid.,* vol. i, p. 118.

on the history of the Jews in Spain, Baer advances the theory
that the legal forms which were used by the Jews in the Middle
Ages in Europe were strongly influenced by similar non-Jewish
forms.[12] This influence, he maintains, is discernible even in the
realm of family law, where one would least expect to find it.[13]
In support of his contention, he cites a Lombard betrothal agreement of the year 966, quoted by von Schwerin, which contains
provisions similar to those found in the form of a betrothal
agreement in the Formulary compiled by R. Jehudah Barzillai
of Barcelona about the end of the 11th century.[14] Like the
Lombard document of 966, the Barzillai form provides for a date
when the marriage is to take place and for the payment of a
penalty in case of non-performance.

The interesting thing about all this is that the *Codex
Diplomaticus Cavensis,* from which von Schwerin quotes the
Lombard betrothal agreement, contains ten such agreements,[15]
covering a period from 937 to 1059, and all of them, except the
one quoted by von Schwerin, contain several clauses which bear
unmistakable signs of having been copied from the Jewish *ketuba*
and betrothal document.

In the first place, all of these documents contain a clause in
which the groom undertakes to write for the bride, on the day
of the marriage, a *scriptum de morgencap,* "as now is the custom

---

[12] Baer, *Die Juden im christlichen Spanien,* vol. i (1929), p. 1044f.

[13] *Ibid.,* p. 1064f.

[14] *Ibid.,* p. 1065.

[15] *Codex Diplomaticus Cavensis.* vol. 1, p. 208 (a. 937); vol. ii, p. 31 (a.
966); vol. iv, p. 83 (a. 1006), 125 (a. 1008), 262 (a. 1016); vol. v, p. 131 (a.
1025); vol. vii, p. 17 a. 1046), 129 (a. 1050), 274 (a. 1056); vol. viii, p. 115
(a. 1059). The document dated 966, which is quoted by v. Schwerin, is unique
in that it contains only an undertaking on the part of the bride's father to give
his daughter in marriage to the groom on a certain date and provides for a
penalty in case of the father's failure to perform his undertaking. Simultaneously
with this document there was probably drawn up a second document embodying
the groom's obligations. But this second document, which must have been framed
in accordance with the formula which was in general use at the time in Salerno
and its vicinity, has not come down to us.

of Lombard men" (*sicut modo est consuetudo homini langobardi*).
Anyone who has the least familiarity with the form of the Jewish
ketuba will at once recognize that this is but a paraphrase of
כהלכות גוברין יהודאין ("as is the custom of Jewish men") of
the *ketuba*.[16] That this Aramaic phrase is Jewish in origin and
was not copied from a non-Jewish source, can hardly be doubted.
It occurs in every available form of the *ketuba,* whatever its
provenience, and a similar idiom, כהלכת בנת ישראל (as is the
custom with respect to Jewish women), is found already in the
Targum of *Exodus* XXI:9, the Biblical passage from which the
husband's obligations toward his wife are derived by the Talmud.[17]

Secondly, in the formula of the *ketuba* it is stated that the
groom said to the bride:

> Be thou my wife in accordance with the law
> of Moses and Israel and, with the help of Heaven,
> I will worship and cherish thee, provide for thee
> and supply food and clothing for thee, according to
> the custom of Jewish men who worship and cherish
> their wives, provide for them and supply food,
> maintenance and clothing for them in truth.

The Lombard documents also contain a promise on the part
of the groom to *cherish and worship his wife.* In *Codex Diplomaticus Cavensis,* IV, p. 262 (a. 1016), for example, it reads
as follows:

> . . . bene eam haberet atque coleret secundum
> suam possibilitatem, sicut et aliis bonis hominibus,
> pares sui, qui bene abent et colunt suis uxoribus
> (will cherish and worship her to the best of his
> ability, even as other good men, his peers, cherish
> and worship their wives).

Note the expression *bene eam haberet atque coleret,* which
is a literal translation of the Aramiac אוקיר ואפלח of the Jewish
ketuba. Note also the expression *sicut et aliis bonis hominibus,*

---

[16] See Gulak, *Ozar hashtarot,* p. 28f.
[17] See BT, *Ketubot,* 47b-48a.

pares sui, qui bene abent et colunt suis uxoribus, which corresponds to the expression "according to the custom of Jewish husbands, who cherish and worship their wives."

The most remarkable parallelism between the *ketuba* and the Lombard betrothal documents is found in a clause in some of the latter which provides that in case the wife is taken captive it shall be the husband's duty to redeem her.[18] Such a provision has been one of the terms of the Hebrew *ketuba* since time immemorial. So much so, that already in the time of the Mishna it became a condition implied in law of every marriage contract. Mishna, *Ketubot* 4, 8 reads:

> If he had not written her, "If thou art taken captive I will redeem thee and take thee again as my wife," [19] or, if she was the wife of a priest, "I will redeem thee and will bring thee back to thine own city," he is still liable to do so since that is a condition enjoined by the court.

The similarity between this Mishna and the clause in the Lombard betrothal contract mentioned above is obvious and needs no further comment. That such similarities do not occur by accident is no less obvious.

The only difference between the above Mishna and the provision in the Lombard documents concerning the husband's duty to redeem his wife is that in all of the latter, except one,

---

[18] *Cod. Dipl. Cav.,* vol. i, p. 208 (a. 937); vol. iv, p. 83 (a. 1006), p. 125 (a. 1008), p. 262 (1016); vol. v. p. 113 (a. 1025). In the first one of these documents, for example, the provision in question reads: *"Igitur alia wadia mihi ipse nominatus iohannes dedit tenorem quidem, ut, si quis heminentibus peccatum et ipsa prenominata filia mea aput illum foras civitatem aut castello depredata fuerit per qualecumque generatione et ista parte mare fuerit iubenta, tunc, de quantum pretium nos a nostris partibus dare boluerimus, una sorte quod est ad nostram partem, ille autem a sua parte dare due sortis de ipso pretium, ... et aput se eam reducad uxore abendum."*

[19] More precisely: "And will bring thee back to me as a wife." The quotation in the text is taken from Danby's translation of the Mishna (Oxford University Press, 1933).

the wife's family are to contribute one part of the ransom against
the husband's two parts, whereas under the rule of the Mishna
no contribution by the wife's family is required. But this is a
detail which does not change the substance of the provision.

Furthermore, if any doubt as to the Jewish origin of the
above provision in the Lombard documents should still be en-
tertained, it would be dispelled by an examination of a certain
phrase in the provisions in question in the Lombard documents.
This phrase is most peculiar. In most of these documents it
reads: "Si peccatis eminentibus ... depredata fuerit"[20] (If, by
reason of eminent sins, she should be taken captive). What are
those *eminent* sins, and who is the sinner? The answer is that
the phrase is an awkward translation of the Hebrew בעונותינו
הרבים (by reason of our many sins)—a phrase which occurs
most frequently in Jewish sources in similar context. It is a
pious recognition that the ways of the Lord are just and that any
calamities and misfortunes which may befall the Jewish people
are due to their "many sins." The Hebrew for *many* is רבים, but
the singular רב of this word means *great, eminent*,[21] hence, the
translation *eminent sins,* apparently, by one who was not too
familiar with the Hebrew idiom.

There is still another phrase in the redemption clause of
most of the Lombard documents, but not in all of them, which
betrays its Jewish origin. The groom undertakes to redeem the
wife and "to bring her back to himself, to have her as a wife"

---

[20] So in vol. iv, 262 (a. 1016). In vol. i, 208 (a. 937), the phrase reads:
"*Si quis heminentibus peccatum ... et depredata fuerit.*" In vol. iv, 83 (a. 1006)
and 125 (a. 1008), the phrase does not occur at all in the redemption-of-the-
wife clause. In vol. v, 113 (a. 1025) it occurs in the form of "*Si eminentibus
peccatum et ... depredata fuerit.*"

[21] See JDT, s.v. רב. The phrase also occurs, in similar context, in the *Edictus
Rothari,* c. 180 (MGH, *leges* 4, p.42). See the makeshift German translation of the
phrase by F. Beyerle in *Die Gesetze der Langobarden* (Weimar, 1947), p.65. When
a corrupt translation of a Hebrew or Aramaic phrase occurs in medieval text it
cannot but cause trouble to a modern translator. For an Aramaic version of the
phrase, see BT Yoma 66b — וחובי דרא סגיאין (and the sins of the generation
are many). See also BT Sanhedrin 97b.

(*et aput se eam reducad uxore abendum*).[22] This is an almost literal translation of ואותבינך לי לאינתו (and I will bring you back to me as a wife), which occurs in the Mishnaic clause, quoted above. It seems that when the Lombard notaries adopted a Jewish formula, they took it over lock, stock and barrel, together with the idiom characteristic of the Hebrew or Aramaic original. With the conservatism characteristic of the legal profession, the Lombard notaries continued to use these idiomatic phrases until some brave soul among them decided that there was no magic in them and dropped them from his forms.

We now come to another clause in the Lombard documents which betrays their Jewish origin. Beginning with the one dated 1016, four of these documents [23] contain a provision that in case the bride dies without children so much of the dowry, which she brought to her husband, as shall then remain intact is to revert back to him who has endowed her, or to his heirs. A similar provision in the *ketuba* is mentioned already in the Palestinian Talmud, where it is stated: "Those who write 'If she dies without children her dowry shall revert to her father's house,' it is a stipulation with respect to matters pecuniary and is valid." [24]

Assaf has correctly pointed out that such a provision was common in the Jewish *ketuba* in Italy and in southern France at an early time and that it was adopted in these countries from the Palestinian tradition which was very strong there.[25] Rabbi

---

[22] In vol. iv, 262 (a. 1016), and vol. v, 113 (a. 1025) this phrase is omitted.

[23] Vol. iv, 262 (a. 1016); vol v, 131 (a. 1025); vol vii, 17 (a. 1046); vol. viii, 115 (a. 1059). In the last one of these documents, for example, the provision in question reads: "*Si dei iudicio ebenerit et ipsa sorore mean antequam illum defunta fuerit et filium vel filiam non reliquerit, obligat se ipse alderisius, ut de omnes rebus et causa pertinente ipsius sorori mee stabilem et mobilem quod illis diebus abuerit, et quantum per eam beraciter datum aut iudicatum non fuerit, inclitum illut nobis nostrisque eredibus redat per iamdictam guadiam et pena obligata.*"

[24] Yerushalmi, *Ketubot*, 9, 1.

[25] Assaf, in מדעי היהדות, vol. i (Publications of The Hebrew University at Jerusalem, 1936), p. 82f.

Isaac b. Abba Mari of Marseilles, writing about the middle of
the 12th century, quotes his grandfather to the effect that "where
the woman died childless, her father is entitled to what he has
given to her husband except that what he has spent he has
spent, and what is left intact he [the father] collects from him
[the husband]." To this Rabbi Isaac adds:

> And it seems reasonable to suppose that it was
> customary to write so in the *ketuba,* as it is stated
> in the Yerushalmi 'If she dies without children the
> dowry shall revert to her father's estate, is a stipula-
> tion with regard to matters pecuniary and is valid.'
> But because the anticipation of misfortune is avoided,
> it has been said that even if they did not write so it
> is as though they had written so. And this custom
> is widespread among us, for the rule is well estab-
> lished that in matters relating to the *ketuba* the
> custom of the locality governs.[26]

Baer, who is not unaware of the above statement by Rabbi
Isaac, nevertheless maintains that the custom with regard to
the reversion of the dowry was adopted by the Jewish from their
non-Jewish neighbors.[27]   In support of his contention he cites
the fact that a municipal statute of Laon, dated 1128, as well
as several other municipal statutes in Northern France, enacted
at the end of the 12th century, contain a provision whereby if
a woman dies childless whatever remains of her dowry shall
revert back to him who has endowed her, or to his heirs. He
also cites Brunner to the effect that the principle of these French
municipal statutes has its origin in Germanic law.[28]   As to the
Yerushalmi, which Rabbi Isaac cites in support of the validity
of the reversion provision of the *ketuba,* Baer says that it is
nothing but an attempt to find Talmudic authority for a custom

---

[26] *Sefer Haittur* (ed. Lemberg), 43b.

[27] See Baer, *op. cit. supra,* p. 1067f.

[28] *Ibid.,* p. 1068, n. 1.

which arose independently of the Talmud.[29] He also says that
Assaf's statement about the Jews of Italy and southern France
having been under the influence of the Palestinian tradition is a
theory "which, in specific cases, should rather be tested than
assumed." [30] Well, let us test it in this case.

The close parallelism between the Lombard betrothal documents, which contain the redemption-of-the-wife provision along
with the reversion provision, on the one hand, and the passages
from the Mishna and the Yerushalmi quoted above, on the other,
even if there were no other evidence available, would be sufficient to warrant the conclusion that the formula of the Lombard
documents was adopted from a Jewish model. But there is other
evidence which fortifies this conclusion. It so happens that none
of the available forms of the Jewish *ketuba,* save one, contains
the redemption-of-the-wife provision, apparently because, as we
have seen above from the Mishna, this provision is implied in
law even if it is not mentioned in the *ketuba.* Neither Rab Hai
Gaon's formula of the *ketuba,* nor that of Rabbi Jehudah Barzillai
contains this provision. The one *ketuba* [31] which does contain it
stems from Jerusalem, which indicates that the Lombard betrothal
documents were copied from a Jewish specimen, or a translation
thereof, which followed the Jerusalem form.

It will perhaps be said that the presence of the reversion
custom is attested only for southern France and not for the
north and that it is therefore unlikely that the statutes of Laon
and other northern cities were influenced by the Jewish custom.
However, the absence of definite evidence of the existence of
such a custom in the Jewish communities of northern France early
in the 12th century does not mean that the custom did not then
exist in some of these communities.

Indeed, the famous statute adopted by the Assembly of

[29] *Ibid.,* p. 1068.
[30] *Ibid.*
[31] Gulak, *op. cit. supra,* p. 35.

Jewish delegates from Ile de France, Anjou, Poitou and Normandie and known as the statute of Rabbenu Tam (who was one of the signatories thereto) provides for the reversion of the remainder of the dowry if the woman dies childless within the first year of the marriage.[32] This statute refers to a previous statute of similar import adopted by the "Great Men of Narbonne and its environs." But whereas the Narbonne statute apparently did not contain the one year limitation, the Rabbenu Tam statute states in terms that the delegates saw fit to adopt such a limitation.

The exact date of Rabbenu Tam's statute is unknown, but it was probably adopted about the middle of the 12th century (Rabbenu Tam died c. 1171). It is therefore only the Laon statute, cited by Baer, that preceded it by some two or three decades, and there is no evidence whatsoever that the custom did not prevail among the Jews of Laon or its vicinity at the beginning of the 12th century. Indeed, bearing in mind the usual genesis of remedial legislation such as that involved in Rabbenu Tam's statute, it would seem likely that the adoption of that statute was preceded by a period of agitation which may have been due to differences in the customs of the communities represented in the Assembly. It is also possible that the purpose of the statute was to insure, by the threat of excommunication and divine punishment, the observance of an already existing custom. It requires strong measures to make a husband who is in possession of his wife's dowry part with it on her death. The one year limitation may also have been intended to insure the observance of the custom by limiting its scope. Be that as it may, it is fairly obvious from the Lombard documents, in which the reversion-of-the-dowry clause appears over a century before the Laon statute was adopted, that this provision did not originate in France and that it had as much to do with Germanic law as the redemption-of-the-wife clause had to do with it.

[32] See Finkelstein, *Jewish Self-Government in The Middle Ages* (1924) p. 163-65, where this statute is quoted in full.

The Death-Bed Gift.

Under Talmudic law there was a fundamental difference between a gift made by a person while enjoying good health and one made by a sick person in contemplation of death. In the former case, all the formalities of a valid transfer were required in order to make the gift irrevocable, while in the latter case these formalities were dispensed with, and an informal oral declaration by the donor in the presence of two witnesses was sufficient.[33] Also, a gift made by a person in his sick-bed was automatically revoked, if the donor recovered from his sickness.[34] As a result of these rules, special formulae were developed to indicate to which one of the two classes the gift belonged. In the case of a gift by a person in good health the deed would contain the phrase "while walking on his feet at market," and in the case of a gift by a person in his sick-bed the document drawn up by the witnesses to the donor's oral declaration would contain the formula: "As he was sick in his bed." [35]

In the formulary of Rab Hai Gaon (10th century) the preamble to the deed of gift in contemplation of death reads, in part, as follows:

> . . . And we came to him and found him sick and ailing and lying in his bed [but] possessing his consciousness and his understanding, and his speech [literally, his tongue] being right and correct in his mouth, and knowing how to transact business like other men who walk on their feet at market.[36]

The quaint concreteness with which the donor's physical and mental state is described in this formula is clearly traceable to the Talmudic formula quoted above, which goes back at least to the 3rd century. It is therefore very interesting and revealing

---

[33] See Mishna, *Baba Bathra, 9,7.*
[34] See *ibid., 9,6.*
[35] See BT, *Baba Bathra* 154a.
[36] *Formulary of Rab Hai Gaon,* ed. Assaf (Supplement of *Tarbiz,* vol. i, 3), no. 12.

to find that almost the same language occurs in chapter 6 of the Edict of Liutprand (a. 713). In this chapter it is provided that a Lombard "who is lying sick in bed but is able to speak correctly" may make a disposition of his property for the benefit of his soul. The text of the law reads:

> Si quis Langobardus, ut habens casus humanae fragilitatis egrotaverit, quamquam in lectolo reiaceat pro anima suo iudicandi vel dispensandi de rebus suis, quid aut cui voluerit; et quod iudicaverit, stabilem debeat permanere.

It is fairly obvious that this law was promulgated by the king under the influence of the Church, which was interested in obtaining royal sanction for death-bed gifts of which she was the principal beneficiary. It seems that the text of the law was framed in accordance with the formula of the death-bed gift which had been in use among the Lombards for some time before the law was promulgated. The law apparently gave legal force to an already existing custom inaugurated by the Church. That the formula upon which the law was based was a close copy of the corresponding Talmudic formula can hardly be doubted.

The formula of the death-bed gift in the Lombard documents of the 9th century follows closely the language of chapter 6 of the Edict of Liutprand and the corresponding Jewish formula. In *Codex Diplomaticus Cavensis*, vol. i, p. 93 (*a* 872), for example, it reads as follows: ". . . *dum iacere in lectu meum balidam infirmitates et recte loquero*" (while I am lying sick in my bed but speaking correctly).

While in the Jewish deed of gift in contemplation of death, which, like most other Jewish legal documents, is framed in the form of a deposition by the witnesses with respect to the words spoken in their presence by the donor, the latter is referred to in the preamble in the third person, in the Lombard deed of gift, in accordance with the usual form of Lombard documents, the maker speaks in the first person from the beginning to the end. The substance of the preamble, however, is the same in

the Lombard and in Jewish deeds. In both it is stated that the
donor was "lying in his bed but speaking correctly." In addition, the word for *bed* in the Lombard documents, as in the
corresponding phrase in the Talmud, appears with the personal
pronoun—*my bed*. Again, we have here a case of a Talmudic
idiom having been copied to its minutest detail.

It is interesting to note that as time went on the formula
was modified in the Lombard documents by dropping its quaint
concreteness and substituting therefor an abstraction about the
donor being "sick of body but sound of mind." In *Codex Diplomaticus Cavensis*, vol. vii, p. 60 (a. 1047), for example, the
formula reads: ". . . *quoniam a magna infirmitatem sum oppressa,
unde spero vitam finire. Sed tamen adhuc integram habeo mente
et recte loqui valeo*" (while oppressed by a great sickness, of
which I expect to die, but nevertheless having my mind whole
and being able to speak correctly).[37]

It should also be noted here that in the Middle Ages a
formula similar to the Talmudic "while lying sick in his bed"
was apparently common throughout Europe in deeds of gift
made in contemplation of death. With regard to the will in
medieval England, Pollock and Maitland state: "A common form
tells us that he is 'sick in body' though 'whole in mind'." [38]
In France, a still closer approximation to the Talmudic formula
is found in wills registered in the Parlement of Paris towards the
end of the 14th and at the beginning of the 15th century, where
the formula reads: ". . . *in lecto egritudinis jacens, sani tamen
intellectus, ac in ejus memoria et mente providus . . .*" (lying
in sick-bed, yet sane of intellect and provident in his memory
and mind).[39]

A similar formula is also met with some six centuries earlier

[37] See also *Cod. Dipl. Cavensis,* vol. iv, p. 236 (a. 1014); vol. vii, p. 214
(a. 1053).

[38] PMH, vol. ii, p. 340.

[39] *Mélanges historiques* (Collection de documents inédits sur l'histoire de
France, Paris, 1880) vol. iii, p. 346. See also *ibid.*, p. 268, 321.

in a document from Narbonne dated 821.[40] Interestingly enough, the testator in this document, who was apparently a Jewish

[40] Devic and Vaisette, *Histoire Générale de Languedoc*, vol. ii (Toulouse, 1876) p. 134-35. The writer has been unable to find in any European source a phrase similar to the Talmudic "while walking on his feet at market." However, a literal translation of this phrase into Greek ἐπὶ ποδῶν βαδίζοντες ἐπ' ἀγοραῖς occurs in P. Lond. 1727, lines 19-20 (a. 583-584). That this Greek phrase is of Jewish origin there can hardly be any doubt. The expression "walking at market" in the sense of being well is found already in the Mishna (*Gittin* 7,3). The further specification, "on his feet," is to be viewed in the light of Ex. XXI:19, which probably inspired it, and which reads as follows: "If he rise again, and walk abroad upon his staff, then shall he that smote him be quit; only he shall pay for the loss of his time, and shall cause him to be thoroughly healed." A person who is able to walk abroad *on his staff* (the word בחוץ — abroad — is rendered by the Targum as בשוקא at market) is only convalescing, while a person who is able to walk *on his feet* at market is presumably in perfect health.

A phrase which is apparently an adaptation of the Talmudic "walking on his feet at market" occurs in one of the Latin papyri from Ravenna, a testament dated 474 (Marini, *I papiri diplomatici*, Rome, 1805, no. 74, col. 4). The preamble to this document reads: "*Fl. Constantinus, v.h. Tinct. publicus, procedens sanus sana mente integroque consilio cogitans conditiones humanas...*" A curious mixture of a Jewish death-bed gift and a Roman testament occurs in the Ravenna papyri in a document, no. 74, cols. 6-7, dated 552. The preamble to this document reads: *Providae suae disponet arbitrium qui mentes sui corporis integritate consistens voluntatis suae arcana prodederit nam propter aegritudinem morbis mens solidum non potest habere judicium itaque ego Georgius v. d. Olosiricoprata civ. Rav. fil. v. d. Juliani de Civ. Anthiocia sanam habens mentem sed et linguam vel sensum gravi egritudine detentus agnoscens tam in omnibus introeuntes et exeuntes ad meam visitationem metuens emergentes casus humanos timens ne me inordinatom occupet mors hoc meae voluntatis condidi testamentum.*" Significantly enough, the testator apparently hailed from Antioch, in Syria.

A formula similar to that of P. Lond. 1727, discussed above, also occurs in P. Lond. 77.12 (8th century C. E.), the so-called will of Abraham, bishop of Hermonthis, which, like P. Lond. 1727, is, in its legal effect, not a will but an irrevocable gift to take effect after the donor's death. With respect to P. Lond. 77, H. Kreller (*Erbrechtliche Untersuchungen auf Grund der graeco-ägyptischen Papyrusurkunden*, 309f.) says that it represents an interesting exception to the rule that a will is revocable. He also cites (*ibid.*, n. 3) several Coptic wills which, by their terms, are irrevocable and concludes that in the late period

convert to Christianity, made a disposition of his property in favor of a monastery. The document is framed in the form of a deposition by witnesses with respect to the last will spoken by one Adelaldus, whose name was formerly Maimon. The witnesses state that they were present "when a man, named Adelaldus, who was formerly called Maimon, while lying sick in *his* bed within the walls of Narbonne, confined by a sickness of which he died, but possessed of his memory" (*quando homo, nomine Adelaldus, qui [fuit] Maimon vocatus jacebat in lectulo suo infra muros civitate Narbona ad egritudine reptemptus, unde et mortuus fuit, adhuc sua memoria in se abente*), made a certain disposition of his property. This document, in addition to its general form of a deposition by witnesses, which is the form invariably used in similar Jewish documents, contains certain details which leave not the slightest doubt that it was copied from the Talmudic formula. In the first place, *"jacebat in lectulo suo"* (was lying in his bed) is an exact translation of the Talmudic idiom רמי בערסיה. Secondly, the phrase *"unde et mortuus fuit"* (of which he died) is, according to the Talmud, a necessary part of the formula, since if the party recovered from his illness after he had made the disposition, even though he died later, the disposition is of no effect. In the Babylonian Talmud, *Baba Bathra*, 153a-153b, a case is reported of a deed of gift which con-

---

(*Spätzeit*) in Egypt there is noticeable a certain tendency toward the irrevocable disposition *mortis causa*. This tendency resulted from the assimilation of the will to the Talmudic irrevocable gift to take effect after the death of the donor. The characteristic formula "walking on his feet at market" is eloquent proof of that. It is interesting to note in this connection that in one Coptic document (E. Revillout, *Précis du droit égyptien*, 848ff.) the Talmudic phrase "walking on his feet" was changed to the Biblical phrase "walking on his staff" (Ex. 21:19). In Revillout's French translation: "... pendant que je vis encore et que je marche, appuyée sur mon baton, robuste dans mon corps...". The scribe who drew up the document was apparently well versed in the Bible, and he substituted the Biblical phrase for the Talmudic. But in doing so he got himself involved in an incongruity, for a person who needs the support of a staff for walking cannot be said to be "robust in body". Cf. A. Gulak, *Das Urkundenwesen im Talmud*, p. 136.

tained the recital "as he was lying sick in his bed," but did not contain the recital "and from his illness he passed away to his eternal abode." Abaye (280-328) ruled the deed defective, although there was proof that the donor had died, because it did not appear from the deed that the donor died from the illness during which he made the disposition.

The Donatio Post-Obitum

The *post-obit* gift (the gift which is to take effect after the donor's death), like the death-bed gift, was widely used in the Middle Ages throughout Europe. It is generally assumed that this type of gift is a product of Germanic law which, under the influence of the Church, developed it as a substitute for the Roman testament.[41]

While it is true that *post-obit* gift, like the death-bed gift, was developed under the influence of the Church, the assumption that this type of gift was a product of Germanic law rests upon an inadequate consideration of the pertinent sources on the part of historians of medieval law. They simply left out of account Jewish law and legal forms which are an important part of the legacy left by the ancient world to that of the Middle Ages.

In the Lombard documents evidencing *post-obit* gifts there occurs with regularity a most peculiar phrase in which the donor states that he is making the gift "from the present day, after my death." The following are examples from the *Codex Diplomaticus Langobardiae*: ". . . *a presenti die obitus mei*" (col. 74, a. 769): ". . . *ad presenti die obitus mei*" (col. 97, a. 774); ". . . *a presenti die obiti nostrorum*" (col. 131, a. 800); ". . . *a presenti dieae post meo discessum* (col. 1028, a. 952); ". . . *a presenti die et ora post meum decessum*" col. 1747, a. 1000). In *Memorie di Lucca*, V, 2, 317 (a. 836) the expression is *post*

---

[41] Huebner, R., *Die donationes post obitum und die Schenkungen mit Vorbehalt des Niessbrauchs im aelteren deutschen Recht* (Untersuchungen zur deutschen

obite meo a die presenti. A similar formula also occurs in *post-obit* gifts in the Frankish kingdom. *Marculfi Formularum Liber* II, no. 6, a form of a *post-obit* gift to a church, contains the phrase *post meum discessum de presentae*. In a *post-obit* gift, dated 719 and made by a woman to the monastery of Wissenburg (Pardessus, *Diplomata, Acta etc.*, II, 451) the phrase is *post discessum meum a die presenti*.

What is the origin and meaning of this peculiar phrase, which contains what at first sight is a contradiction in terms, the gift being made *from the present day* and *after the death* of the donor? The answer is that the phrase originated as a result of the highly technical legal reasoning of a Jewish jurist of about the middle of the second century. The *post-obit* gift is specifically mentioned in the Mishna, *Baba Bathra* 8, 7, where it is stated:

> If a man assigned his goods to his sons he must write, 'From today and after my death.' So R. Judah. R. Jose says:: He need not do so. If a man assigned his goods to his son to be his after his death, the father cannot sell them since they are assigned to his son, and the son cannot sell them since they are in the father's possession. If his father sold them, they are sold [only] until he dies; if the son sold them, the buyer has no claim until the father dies.

From the discussion following this Mishna in the Babylonian Talmud (*Baba Bathra* 136a) it appears that, according to Rabbi Judah, the deed must contain the recital "From to-day and after my death," because it must affirmatively appear therefrom that the donor made a present gift, though its enjoyment was postponed to a future time, for otherwise it would be construed as a promise to make a gift after death, which would be a nullity.

Rabbi Samuel b. Meir (Rashbam), in his commentary to *Baba Bathra* 136a, says: "We have found in the words of the Geonim that the custom in the Academy is in accordance with Rabbi Judah's opinion." This, then, is the explanation of the peculiar phrase *from this day, after my death* in the Lombard

and Frankish documents: it was copied from the Jewish form
of the *post-obit* gift, which follows the rule laid down by Rabbi
Judah in the Mishna.[42]

Staats und Rechtsgeschichte, no. 26) p. 1ff.

[42] It seems that the Talmudic *post obit* gift has a long history behind it
going back to the Aramaic papyri of the 5th century B.C.E. In Cowley 8. 3, 8
and Brooklyn 10. 11, 13, two deeds of gift of 460 and 402 B.C.E., respectively,
it is stated that the gift is made בחיי ובמותי (in my lifetime and after my
death). The plain inference from this formula is that some gifts were made
to take effect only after the donor's death. Fortunately, we need not rely
upon inference alone. The Brooklyn Museum collection contains a deed of gift
by father to daughter in which it is specifically stated that the gift is to take
effect after the donor's death. In Brooklyn 9.16-18 (404 B.C.E.) it is stated:

> זנא ביתא זי תחומוהי ומשחתה כתיבן ומלוהי כתיבן בספרא זנה אנה
> ענני יהבתה ליהוישמע ברתי במותי ברחמן לקבל זי סבלתני ואנה ימין
> סב לא כהל הוית בידי וסבלתני אף אנה יהבת לה במותי.

> "This house, whose boundaries and measurements are written
> and its words are written in this document, I, Anani, give it
> to Yehoyishma my daughter at my death in affection, because
> she did maintain me when I was old in days and was not able
> (to work) with my hands, and she did maintain me, so I,
> on my part, give (it) to her at my death". (Translation
> adopted from Kraeling, with slight modifications).

This, it will readily be seen, is a *post obit* gift like the one which is the subject
of the controversy between R. Judah and R. Jose in Mishnah Baba Bathra 8:7.

In addition to the similarity between Brooklyn 9.16-18 and Mishnah Baba
Bathra 8:7, there is further proof of continuity between the Aramaic papyri
and the Talmud with respect to the *post obit* gift. In BT. Baba Bathra 153a
there is reported a case of a deed of gift in which it was written בחיים ובמות
(in lifetime and after death), precisely as in Cowley 8 and Brooklyn 10,
referred to above, and the opinions of Rab and Samuel (early 3rd century)
were divided as to the legal effect of this formula (See J. N. Epstein,
Notizen zu den jüdisch-aramäischen Papyri von Assuan, Jahrbuch der jüdisch-
lit. Gesellschaft, 1908, 364f.).

In the Greco-Egyptian papyri, too, there are some deeds of gift which by
their terms are to take effect after the donor's death (See H. Kreller, *ibid,*
215ff.; R. Taubenschlag, *The Law of Greco-Roman Egypt in the Light of the
Papyri*, I, 153.). The earliest one of these deeds is P. BGU 993 (127 B.C.E.),
in which it is stated that the gift is to take effect μετὰ τὴν τελευτήν
(after the death) of the donor. In the writer's opinion, it is not without
significance that P. BGU 993 stems from Gebelên and belongs to a period

The foregoing discussion is as good an illustration as any of the value of legal formulae in tracing the origin and develop-

when the legal documents from this locality exhibit numerous other marks of influence of the legal tradition represented by the Aramaic papyri.

It is perhaps not without significance that in P. BGU 993 II. 13 the maker of the document states that he lives with his wife κατὰ νόμους (according to laws). This is not an isolated instance in the papyri from Gebelên. A similar statement occurs in P. Grenf. I 21.4, 13 (126 B. C. E.) and in Cairo 10388.5 (edited by Grenfell and Hunt in Archiv für Papyrusforschung I, 63ff.; 123 B. C. E.), both of which have been noted by Wolff (*Written and Unwritten Marriages in Hellenistic and Postclassical Roman Law*, pp. VI and 28, n. 96). These statements are strikingly similar to the formula כדת משה וישראל (according to the law of Moses and Israel) or כדת משה ויהודיא (according to the law of Moses and the Jews) in the Jewish marriage documents. According to Tosefta Kethubot 4:9 (ed. Zuckermandel 265.2) the first version, and according to PT Yebamoth 15:2 the second version, was part of the Jewish marriage document in Alexandria during the time of Hillel the Elder (the latter part of the 1st century B. C. E.). As has been noted by Epstein (Supplement to *Tarbitz* I, 13, n. 7), a similar formula —κατὰ τὸν νόμον Μωυσέως (in accordance with the law of Moses) — occurs already in the Book of Tobit 7:13, which is believed to have been written in Egypt towards the end of the third century B. C. E.

In some wills (P. Grenf. I, 12, 21, 24, Lond. 219) stemming from the Thebaid and belonging to the same group as the papyri from Gebelên it is stated that the testator was in health (ὑγιαίνων) at the time the will was made. Kreller (*ibid*, 309) states that this is obviously a temporary or local style peculiarity ("Es liegt hier offenbar eine zeitliche oder lokale Stileigentümlichkeit vor."). However, a reference to Mishnah Baba Bathra 9:6 makes one wonder whether there is not much more than just a matter of style involved here. This text, in Danby's translation (DM, 379), reads: "If one that lay sick assigned his goods to others [as a gift] and kept back any land soever, his gift remains valid; but if had kept back no land soever, his gift does not remain valid, if it was not written therein, 'while that he lay sick', but he said that he lay sick, whereas they said that he was in health, he must bring proof that he lay sick." From this Mishnaic proposition it appears that a recital in the instrument to the effect that the testator was in health at the time the instrument was made would serve as a protection to the beneficiary or beneficiaries against an attempt by the testator to revoke the will. Another characteristic feature of the wills from the Thebaid also seems to be explainable in terms of a Mishnaic proposition. The operative words in these wills are καταλείπω καὶ δίδωμι (I leave and give), instead of just καταλείπω (I leave).

ment of some important legal institutions. In discussing the
medieval will, Pollock and Maitland state:

> It is plain that the Church has succeeded in reduc-
> ing the testamentary formalities to a minimum. This
> has happened all the world over. The dread of in-
> testacy induces us to hear a nuncupative testament
> in a few hardly audible words uttered in the last
> agony, to see a testament in the feeble gesture
> which responds to the skillful question of the con-
> fessor, and that happy text about 'two or three
> witnesses' enables us to neglect the Institutes of
> Justinian.[43]

That the church was instrumental in spreading the institutions of the death-bed gift and the *post-obit* gift throughout
Europe is quite clear. She had an intense interest in these gifts,
of which she very often was the sole beneficiary. That in so doing

In Mishnah Baba Bathra 8:5 (DM, 377) it is stated: "If a man apportioned
his property to his sons by word of mouth, and gave much to one and little
to another, or made them equal with the firstborn, his words remain valid.
But if he had said that so it should be 'by inheritance', he has said nothing.
If he had written down, whether at the beginning or in the middle or at the
end [of his testament], that thus it should be "as a gift', his words remain
valid". If the testator had said only χαταλείπω (I leave), which is a technical
word of inheritance (Kreller, *ibid.*, 210), the division of the property would have
been void, as contrary to the laws of succession. But by adding the word δίδωμι
(I give), which is a word of gift, he rendered the division valid.

[43] PMH, vol. ii, p. 337. An interesting instance of what appears to be
Jewish influence upon the substantive provisions of a famous English will of
the 12th century is presented by the will of Henry II (a. 1182). Among
the bequests of sums of money to be used for various charitable purposes
are several ((parapraphs 19, 20, 21) to be expended in providing marriages
for poor women in the king's various dominions (see Rymer, *Foedera*, vol. i,
p. 57f). Paragraph 19, for example, reads: "*Ad maritandas pauperes et liberas
Foeminas Angliae, quae carent auxilio, 300 Marcas auri.*" With respect to the
Jewish will, Baron (*The Jewish Community*, vol. ii, p. 332) states: "The
rabbis classified facilitating the marriage of dowerless brides as among the
highest forms of charity, and philanthropists often left large bequests for
this purpose."

the church availed herself of formulae borrowed from the Talmud is, in the light of the evidence adduced above, equally clear. It is not unlikely that the Talmudic learning which some Jewish converts to Christianity brought to their new faith stood the church in good stead.

The Law of Obligations.

The Lombard law of obligations shows numerous traces of strong Jewish influence in its formative stage as well as in its later development. In the Lombard law of obligations the so-called *wadia* occupies a prominent place. By means of the *wadia* obligations were formally assumed. It consisted of some object, such as a glove, which was delivered by the party assuming the obligation to the party in whose favor the obligation was assumed.[44] In Jewish law, there is a procedure which is strikingly similar to the *wadia*. Virtually every legal transaction, whatever its nature, whether a transfer of property or an assumption of an obligation, is accompanied by a formality, called *kinyan*[45] (literally, acquisition), in which the party to whom the transfer is made, or in whose favor the obligation is assumed, hands to the party making the transfer, or assuming the obligation, some object, usually a scarf or a handkerchief, to make the transaction binding and enforceable. The Talmudists derived the formality of *kinyan* from *Ruth* IV:7, which reads: "Now this was the custom in former time in Israel concerning redeeming and concerning exchanging, to confirm all things: a man drew off his shoe, and gave it to his neighbour; and this was the attestation in Israel."

With respect to one aspect of *kinyan*, there is a difference of opinion between the Babylonian Amora, Rab, and the Palestinian Amora, Levi, the former holding that the object by means of which *kinyan* was performed had to be delivered by the

---

[44] See Brissaud, *A History of French Private Law* (1912) p. 484. See also Calisse, *op. cit. supra,* p. 759f.

[45] See BT, *Baba Metzia* 47a.

transferee, or by the obligee, to the transferor, or to the obligor, and the latter holding that the roles of the parties had to be cast in exactly the reverse order.[46]

It thus appears that the procedure of giving *kinyan*, according to the Palestinian Amora, Levi, was, in its main features, similar to that of giving *wadia* in Lombard law. But the most remarkable thing about *wadia* and *kinyan* is, that, according to the Targum on *Ruth* IV:7, the giving of *kinyan*, like the giving of *wadia*, was performed by means of a glove. The word נַעַל (a shoe) in *Ruth* IV:7 is rendered by the Targum as נַרְתֵּק יָד (a glove, a handshoe).

There is still a further detail which seems to indicate that the Lombard *wadia* was a copy of the Jewish *kinyan*. Under ch. 15 of the Edict of Liutprand (c. 720),[47] the giving of a

---

[46] See *ibid.*

[47] Ch. 15 of the Edict of Liutprand (*Monumenta Germaniae Historica, Leges*, 4, p. 113-114) reads as follows: *Quicumque homo sub regni nostri dicione cuicumque amodo wadia dederit et fideiussore posuerit presentia duorum vel trium testium, quorum fides amittitur, in omnibus complere debeat...*" The requirement of *two or three witnesses*, is traceable to Deut. XIX:15, which reads: "...at the mouth of two witnesses, or at the mouth of three witnesses, shall a matter be established." Some twenty six years after ch. 15 of the Edict of Liutprand was issued, namely, in the year 746, we find the Biblical "two or three witnesses" again in another connection. A certain Presbyter upon being appointed to office in Lucca, gives an undertaking to discharge the duties of his office faithfully and promises to pay a penalty for any act of malfeasance in office which shall be proved against him by the testimony of "two or three God-fearing men" (*et provata causa fuerit per duo vel tres homines Deum timentes*). *Memorie e documenti per servire all'istoria del Ducato di Lucca* (Lucca 1837) vol. v, pt. 2, p. 22.

It might be mentioned *en passant* that the requirement, generally prevailing in England and in the United States, that a will be attested by a minimum of two witnesses is also traceable to *Deuteronomy* XIX:15. Pollock and Maitland (*op. cit. supra*, vol. ii, p. 318-19) quote from a dialogue ascribed to Egbert, Archbishop of York (8th century), as follows: "Can a priest or deacon be witness of the *verba novissima* which dying men utter about their property?" — Let him take with him one or two, so that in the mouth of two or three witnesses every word may be established, for perchance the avarice of the kinsfolk of the dead would contradict what was said by the clergy, were there

wadia, if it takes place before *two or three witnesses*, makes the undertaking binding upon the party giving the *wadia*. Similarly, in Jewish law we find the rule stated in the Talmud that *kinyan* is binding when made before two witnesses.

We do not mean to imply that the rule laid down in the Edict of Liutprand was copied directly from the Talmud. Most likely, what happened was that under the influence of the Jews, who always had *kinyan* performed in the presence of two witnesses, a similar practice developed among the Lombards with respect to *wadiatio*, and that the Edict had reference to this practice. Again, the Targum on *Ruth* IV:7 is very instructive. The phrase בישראל התעודה וזאת (and this is the attestation in Israel) is rendered by the Targum as למקני נהגין והכין סהדיא קדם חבריה מן ישראל בית (and so it is customary among the sons of Israel to perform *kinyan* before *witnesses*).

The close relationship between the Talmudic *kinyan* and the Lombard *wadia* appears also from other Lombard sources. In the Edict of Ratchis (*c.* 746) ch. 5,[48] an agreement concluded by means of the delivery of a *wadia* in the presence of witnesses is referred to as a *stantia*. The exact meaning and derivation of the term *stantia* has never been satisfactorily explained. Wach is of the opinion that *stantia* merely means agreement, and that

but one priest or deacon present." In another place, as we have seen above, they refer to this text as "that happy text about 'two or three witnesses'." What Pollock and Maitland apparently did not know was that the "happy text" is in part a quotation from *Matthew* XVIII:16, which, in turn, is a paraphrase of *Deuteronomy* XIX:15.

[48] Ch. 5 of the Edict of Ratchis (*Monumenta Germaniae*, Leges 4, p. 187-88) reads as follows: "*Si quis amodo in presentia regis vel iudicis seu liberorum hominum qualecumque modo wadia dederit, et postea negare voluerit ille, qui wadia dedit, quod in tali tinore wadia non dedisset, sicut ille qui wadia suscepit queritur: si fuerit inter homines liberi, quorum fides amittitur, non habeat licentia iurare, quod in tali tinore wadia non dedisset: nisi qualiter iudex qui iudicavit rememoraverit, vel homines qui interfuerunt quando ipsa wadia dedit testificaverint, in tali conpleat, et in eorum testimonium credant. Quia si stantia, quam ante liberos hominis aliquis facit, stare debet...*"

stantia and *convenientia* are synonymous.[49] However, Wach's explanation can hardly be considered adequate, for the question still remains, how did *stantia* and *convenientia* come to mean the same thing. The answer is that *stantia* is a literal translation of the Aramaic קים, meaning that which is established, which stands fast, a *covenant*. The Hebrew ברית (a covenant), which occurs numerous times in the Bible, is always rendered by the Targum as קים. It seems that in the Jewish legal terminology of the early Middle Ages the term קיום was used in the technical sense of an obligation wherein no specific property is delivered by the obligor to the obligee by way of security. In the Formulary of Rabbi Jehudah Barzillai (11th century, Spain), which is based upon much earlier forms, it is stated by way of introduction to the form of the document of indebtedness as follows: "And the 34th document is a document of loan, that is a document of indebtedness which is called קיום and which is neither a mortgage with delivery of possession of the mortgaged property (משכנתא) nor a mortgage of specific property without delivery of possession (אפותיקי).[50] The term *stantia* was apparently used in Lombardy in the same technical sense in which קיום was used among the Jews.

The Form of The Writing Obligatory and Mortgage of the 8th and 9th Centuries

In a writing obligatory [51] dated 796 and executed in Milan, there is a provision that if the obligor should fail to pay the obligation on the due date, the obligee, or his messenger (*missus*), may make distraint upon the obligor's movable property, without the aid of the judge, and if such property be insufficient he may enter, without the court's messenger (*sine misso iudicis*), upon the obligor's real property, and seize therefrom the equivalent of the debt remaining unpaid.

[49] Wach, A., *Der Arrestprozess* (Leipzig 1868) p. 9-10.
[50] *Formulary of R. Jehudah Brazillai* (ed. Halberstam, Berlin 1898) no. 34.
[51] *Codex Diplomaticus Langobardiae*, col. 128.

These provisions are, on the whole, similar to the procedure of execution against defaulting debtors under Hebrew law. Under the latter procedure, as under the provisions of the above bond, resort would first be had to the debtor's movable property, and only in case the movable property was insufficient, the debtor's immovable property would be resorted to.[52] To be sure, this similarity, standing alone, would be insufficient to indicate any inluence of Jewish practice upon the terms of the above bond. However, the term *missus* which occurs twice in the instrument, once in the sense of the creditor's messenger and once in that of the court's bailiff, is significant. In the first place, there is a remarkable correspondence between the term *missus* and the Hebrew term for agent — שליח. The latter is derived from שלח (to send), and the former is similarly derived from *mittere* (to send). Secondly, a court's bailiff is called in Hebrew שליח בית דין, which corresponds to *missus iudicis*. Finally, the officer, who, under Jewish legal practice, would levy execution upon a defaulting debtor, was the שליח בית דין, the *missus iudicis* [53]

The obligee in the above bond apparently sought, by a specific provision to that effect in the bond, to do away with the requirement of the law that seizure of the debtor's property be effected by the court's representative. A similar provision in which the obligoi empowers the obligee, in case of default, to seize, without resort to the court, so much of his property as may be necessary to satisfy the debt is found in the Formulary of Rabbi Jehudah Barzillai,[54] which, as we have just said, is based upon much older forms.

---

[52] See *Shulhan Aruk, Hoshen Mishpat*, 101, 2.

[53] See BT, *Baba Metzia* 113a.

[54] No. 34. An authorization by the debtor to the creditor to seize his property, in case of default, and satisfy himself therefrom is also contained in a document from Amalfi of the year 1020. *Codice Diplomatico Amalfitano* (Naples 1917) p. 56. This document contains the following provision: "... *unde posumus vobis in pignus omnia nostra causa hereditates et substantias et inde vos pargiare debeatis...* " The word *pargiare*, which is obviously used here in

Further evidence of the influence of Jewish security forms upon those used by the Lombards is found in two mortgage instruments, dated 871 and 882, respectively and executed in Salerno. In these instruments there is a provision that if at any time during the term of the mortgage the mortgagor should wish to sell the mortgaged property he must sell it to the mortgagee for whatever it may be worth at the time.[55] The second one of these documents spells out the method by which the value of the property is to be determined, namely, by an appraisal to be made by experienced (*docti*) men. The usual number of appraisers under Lombard practice was three,[56] but in this document it is provided that the appraisal is to be made by six appraisers, three to be selected by the mortgagor and three by the mortgagee.

the sense of *to pay*, is peculiar. The Italian *pagare*, the French *payer* and the English *pay* are generally thought to be derived from the Latin *pacare* — to pacify (See Ducange, *Glossarium Mediae et Infimae Latinitatis*, s. v. *pacare*, and *Oxford Universal English Dictionary*, s. v. *pay*). Ducange cites a number of late medieval texts and documents, none of them earlier than the 12th century, in which either *pacare* or *pagare* is used in the sense of *to pay* a debt. It seems, however, that in the above Amalfi document we have a different form of the same verb, which casts considerable doubt upon the correctness of its generally accepted derivation. *Pargiare*, which seems to have been the original form of the verb, can hardly be said to be derived from *pacare*. That this is not a slip on the part of the scribe is indicated by the fact that in the same document the noun *pargiatura* is used in the sense of *payment*, whereas in some of the 12th and 13th century texts and documents cited by Ducange the same noun appears in the form of *pagamentum*. Furthermore, the word *pargiare* also occurs in an Amalfi document of the year 1158 (see *Codice Diplomatico Amalfitano*, p. 296). What, then, is the origin of this word? The writer believes that it is a latinized form of the Hebrew פרע to pay a debt — which was introduced by the Jews into the vernacular spoken by them and thence found its way into general use.

[55] In *Codex Dipl. Cav.* I, 92 (a. 871), the provision in question reads: "...*et si ipsa suprascripta terra datura abuerimus, bovis spondimus bindere ad iustos pretium quem baluerit.*" A similar provision is contained in vol. i, p. 121 (a. 882)

[56] Cf. *Cod. Dipl. Lang.*, col. 160 (c. 809), which contains a provision that in case of default, the land mortgaged shall be sold to the lender at a price to

Now a provision covering the contingency of a sale of the mortgaged property by the mortgagor, in all respects identical with the provision in the above-mentioned Lombard mortgages, is found in an early Talmudic text. In *Baba Metzia* 65b we read: "If a man mortgages a house or a field and he [the creditor] says to him, 'Should you wish to sell it, you must let me have it at this price [less than its value]'—that is forbidden; at its real value—that is permitted." A stipulation that the mortgagor sell the mortgaged property to the mortgagee for an amount equal to that of the loan is illegal, according to the Talmud, because it savors of usury, whereas a stipulation that he sell it at its true value is free of the taint of usury. That the Lombards, when they used the above provision in their mortgages, had in mind any such refinement of the usury laws as we find in the Talmud is unlikely. It seems that they just copied the provision from Jewish documents where it was framed in accordance with Talmudic law.

In addition to the similarity between the substance of the above provision in the Lombard mortgages and that quoted above from the Talmud, the method provided for in the Lombard documents for appraising the property is also strikingly similar to that used by the Jews since Talmudic times. Appraisal by *three experienced men* שלשה בקיאים is the usual method found in the Mishna and Gemara.[57]

In Lucca, too, several mortgage instruments of the early 9th century reveal definite marks of Jewish influence. In these documents,[58] the amount of the loan is payable in *"Solidi, boni,*

---

be determined by three just men (*"quanto tres justi hominis exstimaverit"*). This provision is strikingly similar to the procedure used under Jewish law in execution against a defaulting debtor's property. See authorities cited below n. 57.

[57] See Mishna, *Sanhedrin* 1, 3; BT, *Baba Bathra* 107a; Maimonides, *Mishneh Torah, Malveh* 22, 9.

[58] See *Memorie e documenti per servire all'istoria del Ducato di Lucca,* vol. v, pt. 2, p. 235 (c. 813), 254 (c. 819), 257 (c. 819). The description of the purchase money in several Ravenna papyri of the 6th century representing

mundi, grossi et expendibiles" (good, pure, full-weight and expendable). This description of the money in which the loan is
payable is identical with that found in medieval Jewish documents of similar import.[59] Two of the adjectives, "'good and
full-weight," are found in the Babylonian Talmud, *Baba Metzia*
44b, quoted in a passage in the name of Rab, an early third
century authority. The third one, "expendable," is traceable to a
rule of law with regard to which the Babylonian Talmud reports
a difference of opinion between Rab and his contemporary Mar
Samuel. In *Baba Kama* 97a-97b, it is stated:

> If a man lends his fellow something on condition that
> it should be repaid in a certain coin, and the coin
> became obsolete, Rab said that the debtor would
> have to pay the creditor with the coin that had
> currency at that time, whereas Samuel said that

deeds of conveyance also follows closely the Jewish formula. In Marini, no. 114,
1.41 (c. 539-546), it is *"auri solid. dominicos probitos obriziacos optimos
pensantes;"* in no. 115, 1.2 (c. 540) — *"optimos pensantes;"* in no. 120, 1.?ᴼ
(c. 572) — *"probitos obriziatos integri ponderis;"* in no. 121, 1.10 (c. end of
6th century) — *"probatos obriziatos optimos pensantes integri ponderis;"* and
in no. 122, 1.30 (c. 591) — *obriziacos optimos pensantes."* The words *optimos*
and *pensantes* are obviously the equivalents of the Talmudic טבין and
תקילין respectively. Some of the notaries apparently deemed it necessary to
substitute the words *integri ponderis* for *pensantes,* or to use both, because
pensantes alone, which is a literal translation of תקילין — weighing — did not
convey the same meaning in Latin as it did in Aramaic.

It seems that the Lucca documents represent a tradition which is independent of that of Ravenna, although in both cases the description is ultimately
traceable to the same source. Instead of *pensantes* of the Ravenna documents,
the Lucca documents use *grossi,* instead of *optimi* — *boni,* and instead of
obriziati — *mundi* (see Harper's *Latin Dictionary,* s. v.obryzum). Also, the word
expendibiles, which occurs in the Lucca documents, but does not occur in any
of the Ravenna documents, indicates that the former were based upon a Jewish
model of considerably later date than that from which the latter were copied.
For, as may be gathered from *Baba Kama* 97a-98b quoted in the text,
the equivalent of *expendibiles* came into the Jewish formulary later than טבין
ותקילין.

[59] See Gulak, *Ozar Hashtaroth,* p. 31, 205, 207, 209, 230, 233.

the debtor could say to the creditor 'Go forth and spend it in Meshan.'

The specification "expendable" was designed to provide for the contingency of the coin becoming obsolete, contemplated by Rab and Mar Samuel.

The Mortgage in The Form of A Conveyance

In the 11th century there appears in Lombardy a form of a mortgage similar to the one that was used in England in the 13th and 14th centuries. Under this form, the debtor would deliver to the creditor an instrument of conveyance of the mortgaged property, and the creditor, on his part, would undertake, by a separate instrument, to return to the debtor the instrument of conveyance cancelled, if the latter should pay the mortgage debt on the due date.[60]

The writer has shown elsewhere [61] that this form of mortgage was in use among the Jews since Talmudic times, and that it was introduced by them in England. That in Lombardy too it was introduced by the Jews is quite likely, in view of the continuous influence of Jewish forms upon the development of security devices in Lombardy.

The probability that the above form of mortgage is of Jewish origin is enhanced by the provision, which is generally found in these mortgages, that upon payment of the mortgage debt the creditor is to return to the debtor the instrument of con-

---

[60] The nature of this mortgage appears most clearly from the following form in the *Cartularium Langobardorum* (*Monumenta Germaniae Historica, Leges* 4, 597): "*Martine, modo promitte et sponde te et tuos heredes Petro et suis heredibus, quod si Petrus aut sui heredes tibi aut tuis heredibus dederint aut sanationem fecerint de 100 solidos ab hac die usque ad kalendas tales in civitate Papia in domo habittationis tuae, reddatis ei cartam illam venditionis quam in vobis emisit de petia una de terra quae jacet in tali loco quae habet coherentias tales capsatan et taliatam ut in se nullum obineat robur.*" For documents evidencing such mortgages, see Ficker, *Forschungen z. Reichs- und Rechtsgeschichte Italiens*, vol. iv (1874) p. 76 (a. 1035), 140 (a. 1113).

[61] See ch. 20, below.

veyance *incisum, capsatum,* or *taliatum,*[62] that is, cancelled. Incision, cutting or tearing is the standard method prescribed by the Talmud, *Baba Bathra* 168b, for the cancellation of legal instruments.

Another indication that the form is of Jewish origin may be seen in the provision that the debt is to be paid at the creditor's residence.[63] Upon the surface, this provision seems to be without much significance. However, when viewed in the light of certain rules of Hebrew law and of the practice which grew out of these rules, it is not as insignificant as it appears.

Under Jewish law, a debtor who, with the consent of the creditor, sends the money he owes through a messenger, is discharged from his obligation as soon as he hands the money to the messenger.[64] The risk of loss of the money in transit falls upon the creditor. In order to forestall a plea by the debtor that the money was sent through a messenger with the creditor's consent and to prevent the risk of loss in transit from falling upon creditor, a provision was usually inserted in the bond that the money was to reach the creditor at his place of residence. The purpose of this provision appears most clearly in the Hebrew form of a bond quoted by Mordecai b. Hillel in the name of Rabbi Jacob of Orleans (died in 1189), in which the debtor undertakes, at his risk, to cause the money to reach the creditor's hand in the town of X. This form reads, in part, as follows:

> I, the undersigned, acknowledge a true acknowledgment that I owe to X so much, by reason of a loan he made to me in the month of . . . and I am bound to pay him the money within fifteen days of demand made by him and to cause it to reach his hand in the town of . . . at my risk.[65]

---

[62] See documents cited above, n. 60.

[63] See *ibid.*

[64] See *Shulhan Aruk, Hoshen Mishpat,* 121, 1.

[65] *Haggahoth Mordecai, Baba Kama,* ch. 5, sec. 455.

The Deed of Conveyance

The Lombard deed of conveyance of the 8th century contains two important clauses [66] which do not occur anywhere else in Europe at that period. They are: (1) The no-reservation clause in which the grantor states that he has reserved nothing for himself in the property conveyed. (2) The warranty clause in which the grantor undertakes to defend the property *against all men.* The writer has shown elsewhere [67] that both of these clauses are mentioned in the Talmud and are also found in the late Byzantine papyri from Egypt. That these two clauses did not come into the Lombard deed from a late Roman source is indicated by the fact that neither of them is found in the Latin papyri of the 6th and 7th centuries from Ravenna.[68] There is, to be sure, in the Ravenna papyri a clause providing for the contingency of the grantee's eviction by a third party. But this clause is fundamentally different from the warranty clause of the Lombard deed. Whereas under the latter the grantor undertakes the duty of defending the grantee's title in court against attack by third parties, and to pay double the value of the property as improved in case of his failure to defend successfully, in the former he only undertakes to pay the grantee, in case of his eviction, double the value of the property as improved, and undertakes no duty to defend the grantee's title.

The difference between Roman and Lombard law in this respect was summarized in the 11th century in the rule that a

[66] The following is a typical example: "...*Nihil mihi in suprascripta loca aliquid reservassem sum professus. Sed dico me meosque omnis exinde a presenti die foris exissent. Quidem et spondeo ego suprascriptus Rotaris abba cum meis successoribus suprascriptis omnibus in integrum ab omni homine defensare vobis Ansilperge abbatisse seu successorum vestorum. Quod si defendere minime potuero ego aut meis successoribus, tunc dupla suprascripta res in integrum sicuti in tempore meliorata fuerit, in subscripta loca et in ipso monasterio vestro restituamus et nihil mihi ex pretium rei suprascripte aliquid redere dixi.*" *Cod. Dipl. Lang.*, col. 70 (c. 768).

[67] See ch. 15, above.

[68] See Marini, *I papiri diplomatici* (Rome 1805) no. 114 *et seq.*

Lombard, in case his title to property is disputed, always presents his grantor in court for the purpose of defending his title, while a Roman stands in the grantor's place (*"Langobardus semper dat auctorem et numquam stat loco auctoris; Romanus semper stat loco auctoris, et numquam dat auctorem"*).[69] It has been supposed [70] that this rule is a reflection of the difference between the Roman and the Germanic law of procedure. It is more likely, however, that the Lombard warranty clause, as a result of its continuous use, gave rise to the rule rather than the reverse, and that this clause, like the no-reservation clause, owes its origin to the Jews. In any event, the Lombard warranty clause had nothing to do with the Germanic law of procedure, just as the similar warranty clause in the Greco-Egyptian papyri of the 6th and 7th centuries had nothing to do with Germanic law.

It seems that under the rule of the Roman law, as it stood in the 6th century, the grantor of property, in case his grantee's title was challenged by a third party, could not defend the title in court because the suit was between the grantee and the challenger, and the grantor could not intervene in a suit to which he was not a party. The form of the warranty clause in the Ravenna papyri apparently follows Roman law in this respect, and therefore the grantor does not undertake to defend the grantee's title. In the Greco-Egyptian papyri of the late Byzantine period and in the Lombard deeds, on the other hand, which follow the form of the Jewish warranty clause, the grantor undertakes the duty of defending the grantee's title in court, and the possible objection by the challenger to the grantor's intervention in a suit against the grantee is disregarded, just as it was disregarded under Talmudic law. In a rule reported in the Babylonian Talmud, *Ketubot* 92b, in the name of Abaye (280-328) it is stated that if A conveys property to B with warranty, and C, who holds a mortgage on the property, later

---

[69] Walter, F., *Corpus iuris germanici antiqui* (1824) vol. i, p. 726.

[70] See Calisse, *op. cit. supra*, p. 714. See also Holmes, *The Common Law*, p 372.

comes and claims the property from B, A may appear in court and defend (מצצי) B's title against C. C will not be heard to say to A, "You are not my adversary," because A may retort to him, "If you evict him he will have recourse against me."

Traditio per Cartam

Brunner has convincingly shown that under Lombard law title to real property could be validly transferred by delivery of the deed of conveyance without delivery of the property itself.[71] He is of the opinion that this important innovation, which made the transfer of property easy and convenient, was copied by the Lombards from what he calls *"roemisches Vulgarrecht,"* that is the vulgar Roman law of the provinces, whose relationship to the written Roman law, he maintains, was similar to that of the vulgar Latin spoken by the provincials to the literary Latin of Rome.[72] The well known proposition of the Roman law *traditionibus et usucapionibus dominia rerum, non nudis pactis, transferuntur* (by delivery and usucaption, and not by naked agreements, is title to things transferred) was, according to Brunner,[73] modified by the provincials to the extent that transfer of title could be effected by *delivery* of the deed of conveyance.

Like all other historians of the law of the early Middle Ages, Brunner failed to take account of the "people scattered abroad and dispersed among the peoples" who had a highly developed legal system and a formulary of a high degree of perfection, which, in the sixth century, had already a long history of at least over a thousand years behind it. What he calls "roemisches Vulgarrecht" is nothing but good Jewish law.

As every student of the Talmud knows, acquisition by deed (שטר) is one of the modes of acquiring title to real property.[74]

---

[71] Brunner, *Zur Rechtsgeschichte der roemischen und germanischen Urkunde* (1880) p. 130f.

[72] *Ibid.*, p. 113f.

[73] *Ibid.*

[74] See Mishnah, *Kiddushin*, 1, 5.

When this method is used, it is through the delivery of the deed that the transfer of title is effected. In connection with the procedure of transferring title by deed, there are under Talmudic law two formal acts: [75] (1) The signing (חתימה) of the document by two witnesses. (2) The delivery (מסירה) of the deed by the transferor to the transferee in the presence of two witnesses. According to Rabbi Eleazar (2nd century C.E.), whose opinion is the prevailing one,[76] it is the witnesses to the delivery that are indispensable to the validity of the transfer.

It seems that with respect to the use of the written document in connection with the transfer of property, the later Roman law, like Lombard law, was strongly influenced by Jewish practices. A law promulgated by Justinian [77] in 528 requires, in case a document is drawn up by a *tabellio* (notary) that there be a *completio* and *absolutio* of the document. The precise meaning of *completio* and *absolutio* in this connection is obscure, and these terms have given rise to considerable speculation among Romanists.[78] But Brunner has shown that *absolutio* refers to the delivery of the deed by the transferor to the transferee.[79] As to *completio*, he states that it refers to *Vollziehung* (execution) by the notary.[80]

It will readily be seen that *absolutio*, as interpreted by Brunner, corresponds to the Hebrew מסירה (delivery). But more significant is the correspondence between חתימה and *completio*. The Hebrew term is used in the Mishna [81] in the sense of a *subscription* and also in the sense of a *closing, completion, conclusion* (not necessarily of a document but sometimes of a prayer). *Completio* therefore seems to be a Hebraism

---

[75] See Mishnah, *Gittin* 9, 4 and Babylonian Talmud, *ibid.* 22b.

[76] See *ibid.*

[77] Cod. IV, 21, 17.

[78] See Brunner, *op. cit. supra*, n. 71, at p. 73 and authorities cited there.

[79] *Ibid.*, p. 75.

[80] *Ibid.*, p. 73f.

[81] See, *e. g.*, Mishnah, *Berakot* 1, 4 and *Pesahim* 10, 6. See also JDT, s. v. חתם.

for subscription. That this is so is indicated by the fact that *complere* and *subscribere* are used interchangeably in some 6th century Latin documents from Ravenna. The phrase *subscripta atque signata a testibus* is used in these documents as the equivalent of *completa atque signata a testibus*.[82]

Conclusion

The law reflected in the Lombard documents relating to family law, the law of wills, the law of property and the law of obligations bears unmistakable signs of Jewish influence in important respects. This influence was exercised mainly by means of what the Germans call *Formularjurisprudenz*—the jurisprudence of the legal formulary. At least since Talmudic times, and probably much earlier, the Jews possessed a legal formulary of a high degree of perfection. Many of the Jewish legal forms, and with them the law which they contained, found their way into the Lombard formulary and, through it, into Lombard law.

[82] See Marini, no. 74, col. 2, 1.8, col. 4, 1.9 col. 5, 1.13.

CHAPTER XVII

JEWISH AND FRANKISH LAW

Rachimburgs

In a number of places in the *Lex Salica* and in other early Frankish sources mention is made of a group of officials called *Rachimburgs*.[1] These officials were seven in number. They acted as judges or jurymen and as appraisers in an execution against the property of a defaulting debtor. Also, agreements of every kind were often made in the presence of the *Rachimburgs,* apparently for the purpose of imparting to these agreements greater force and validity.

The derivation of the designation *Rachimburgs* is obscure. Cheruel,[2] in his *Dictionnaire Historique*, says that it is of an uncertain etymology. Some scholars derive the word from *Recht* and *Bürger*.[3] Savigny thinks that it is derived from the old Germanic word *rek* — meaning great or mighty — and *Bürger*.[4]

A group of officials similar to the *Rachimburgs* is found among the Jews at an early time. These officials are referred to in the Talmud as *shiva tove ha-ir* — *the seven good men of the town*.[5] In post-Talmudic sources, the seven good men are sometimes referred to as *rashe ha-ir* — *the heads of the town*.[6]

---

[1] *Lex Salica*, 50, 3; 57,1; *MGH, Legum Sectio* II, p. 9; *Legum Sectio* V pp. 211, 251.

[2] *Dictionnaire Historique des Institutions*, s. v. Rachimburgs.

[3] *See ibid*

[4] *See ibid.*

[5] BT, *Megillah* 26a. See also Baron, *The Jewish Community,* v. 1, p. 133; vol. II, p. 55; v. III, p. 120.

[6] See *Teshuboth Maimonyoth,* Shoftim, no. 10. See also Baron ibid, v. II, p. 55.

The functions of the *good men of the town* were apparently similar to those of the *Rachimburgs,* and their number — seven — was the same as that of the *Rachimburgs.* What is more, the *Rachimburgs* are often called in the sources *boni homines,*[7] which is, of course, the exact equivalent of the Hebrew designation.

In view of the striking similarities, in number, function and name, between the two groups of officials, it is perhaps not far-fetched to suggest that the word *Rachimburgs* itself is partly of Jewish origin, consisting of the Hebrew word *rachim* — heads — and the German word *burg* town.

The Title De Migrantibus of the Lex Salica

Title 45, *De Migrantibus,* of The *Lex Salica* is the most debated [8] and probably the least understood part of the law of the Salian Franks. Chapter 1 of this title provides:

> 'Si quis super alterum in villa migrare voluerit, si unus vel aliqui de ipsis qui in villa consistunt eum suscipere voluerit, si vel unus exeterit qui contradicat, migrandi ibidem licentiam non habebit.'

Chapter 2 prescribes the procedure whereby the objector may enforce his right to have the migrant expelled. Chapter 3 provides:

> 'Si vero quis migraverit et infra xii menses nullus testatus fuerit, securus sicut et alii vicini maneat.'

In an article in the *Revue historique de droit français et étranger*[9] Mr. Thibault discusses the various theories which have been offered in explanation of the Title 45 and, after concluding that none of these theories is satisfactory, he offers one of his own.

Mr Thibault is particularly outspoken against the theory, which for a long time prevailed among German scholars, that Title 45 reflects a form of communal organization of the village among the Salian Franks. 'For many years,' he says, 'this text

---

[7] See Pardessus, *Loi Salique,* p. 576.

[8] Geffcken, *Lex Salica,* p. 178.

[9] Vol. 45 (1921), p. 449 f.

has served to construct a theory according to which every village
formed a rural association or community. . . . The community of
the Germanic village is a legend in which no one believes any
longer'.[10]

Thibault's own theory may be summarized as follows: The
Roman system of levying taxes upon the owners of land was
still in force at the time of the adoption of Title 45. There were
certain classes of persons, such as Frankish warriors, in whose
hands land was exempt from taxation. In order to avoid the
payment of land taxes, landowners belonging to the non-exempt
classes would invite persons of the exempt classes to come and
settle upon their land, under some arrangement which was to
their mutual advantage, thus freeing the land from the burden
of taxation. This burden would be shifted by the tax-collecors,
who had been accustomed to collect a certain total amount from
all the inhabitants of the village, to those landowners of the village
who did not resort to this ruse. As a result, these landowners
would suffer a loss in the form of increased taxation. The law,
by giving each inhabitant of the village the right to bar the
stranger, afforded him an effective means of protecting himself
against this type of fraudulent practices.

The difficulty with this view is that the law, by its terms, is
of general application, and makes no distinction between a migrant who belongs to the exempt classes and one who belongs to
the tax-paying classes. If, as Thibault supposes, the law has
reference to some sort of transfer of land, either as a *precarium*
or in some other form, by an inhabitant of the village to the
migrant, it would have been sufficient to bar such transfers by an
individual belonging to the tax-paying class to one belonging to
the exempt class.

Oddly enough, a veritable flood of light is shed upon Title 45
of the *Lex Salica* by Jewish medieval sources of which the historians of Germanic law were totally unaware. An institution
which was almost identical with Title 45 of the *Lex Salica* pre-

[10] *Ibid.*, p. 450.

vailed among the Jews of Germany and France in the Middle Ages, and was known as *hezkath hayishub* (the possessory right of settlement) or *herem hayishub* (ban against settlement) [11] Under the *hezkath hayishub*, as under Title 45 of the *Lex Salica*, the consent of the entire community was necessary in order that a newcomer might settle in the community.[12] The objection of but a single inhabitant was sufficient to bar the stranger from settling in the community. But if the newcomer remained in the town unmolested for a period of twelve months he acquired the right of settlement and could no longer be ejected.[13]

About the origin of the *hezkath hayishub* there are conflicting views. Some fifteenth century authorities[14] ascribe it to Rabbenu Gershom b. Jehuda (960-1028), while twelfth and thirteenth century authorities speak of it as having originated with the *Rishonim* or *Kadmonim*,[15] that is with the 'ancients,' without even mentioning Rabbenu Gershom's name in connection with it.

As to the legal basis of the *heren hayishub* the views are equally divided. Rabbi Solomon Ytzchaki (1040-1105), known under the name of Rashi, was of the opinion that it was based upon Talmudic authority [16] and that, therefore, it had the force of *din* (law), rather than *minhag* (custom) or *takkana* (ordinance or special enactment of the later sages). Rabbenu Tam (twelfth century), on the other hand, spoke out rather vigorously against the restrictions of the *hezkath hayishub*, denied its Talmudic basis, and asserted that it had been introduced by later sages only for the

[11] See L. Rabinowitz, *The Herem Hayyishub* (London, 1945); L. Finkelstein, *Jewish Self-Government in the Middle Ages* (New York, 1924), pp. 10-15.

[12] Responsum of Rabbi Meir b. Baruch (thirteenth century), quoted in Gloss to Maimonides' Yad-hazakah, Shkenim, 6.

[13] See p. 225f., below. See also Rabinowitz, *ibid.*, p. 21.

[14] See Gloss to Asheri on *Baba Bathra*, II, 12. See also Rabinowitz, *ibid.*, p. 25.

[15] See p. 226, below. See also Rabinowitz, *ibid.*, p. 23f.

[16] See *Or Zarua*, I, 115. See also Responsa of Rabbi Joseph Colon, no. 172 and Gloss to Asheri, *Baba Bathra*, II, 12.

purpose of barring informers and other undesirable individuals from freely widening the scope of their activities.[17]

Among modern writers, Finkelstein [18] asserts that the *hezkath. hayishub* antedates Rabbenu Gershom, and Rabinowitz [19] argues for its Talmudic basis. The writer believes that the similarity between the *hezkath hayishub* and Title 45 of the *Lex Salica* furnishes conclusive proof of the correctness of the views of these writers.

When one places the provisions of the Title 45 of the *Lex Salica* side by side with those of the *hezkath hayishub* it becomes obvious that we have before us an original and a copy, though it may not be apparent at first sight which is the original and which is the copy. In either event, whether the Jews furnished the model for Title 45 of the *Lex Salica* or copied from the latter, the Jewish counterpart of Title 45 must have preceded Rabbenu Gershom. For, by the year 819 Title 45 had become so completely misinterpreted and misunderstood in the Frankish kingdom that nothing remained of its original meaning.[20] The drafters of the capitulary of that year interpreted the provisions of Title 45 as having reference to property owners who were dispossessed by strangers. The capitulary abolished the twelve months' limitation period, which was considered unjust to the dispossessed owners, and decreed instead that the party in possession must prove rightful ownership or vacate the land. Chapter 9 of this capitulary reads:

> 'De xlii capitulo, de eo qui villam alterius occupaverit. De hoc capitulo iudicaverunt, ut nullus villam aut res alterius migrandi gratia per annos tenere vel possidere possit; sed in quacumque die invasor illarum rerum interpellatus fuerit, aut easdem res querenti reddat aut eas, si potest, iuxta legem se defendeno sibi vindicet.[21]

---

[17] See Responsum of Rabbi Moses Taku, quoted by Rabinowitz at p. 23.
[18] *Ibid.*, p. 14.
[19] *Ibid.*, ch. IV.
[20] See Geffcken, *ibid.*, 282.
[21] MGH, *Legum Sectio* II, vol. I, p. 293.

The time when the copying, either on the part of the Jews or on the part of the Franks, occurred must therefore be fixed prior to 819, that is long before Rabbenu Gershom.

With regard to the question of whether or not the *hezkath hayishub* was based upon Talmudic authority a comparison with Title 45 of the *Lex Salica* is also very illuminating. It focuses attention on one of the features of the *hezkath hayishub,* which, so far as the writer knows, has received little attention from modern writers on the subject and about which considerable confusion prevailed among Jewish authorities of the later Middle Ages. The writer is referring to the rule that residence in a community for a period of twelve months gave the newcomer the right to remain there permanently.

The Talmudic passage upon which the *hezkath hayishub* is said to be based reads as follows:

'R Huna the son of R. Joshua said, "Assuredly the resident of one town can prevent the resident of another town (from engaging in a competing trade or business), but if he (the newcomer) belongs to the same *krage,*[22] he cannot prevent him."[23]

There is no mention in this passage of any period of time after which the resident of the town cannot object to the newcomer. The twelve-month period is mentioned only by the medieval authorities.

Rabbi Israel Krems [24] (beginning of the fifteenth century) states that residence for a period of twelve months gives rise to a presumption of right, similar to the presumption arising under Jewish law from undisturbed possession of real property for a period of three years, and not to a right. But one is at a loss to understand how the period came to be fixed at twelve months, when the usual period of undisturbed possession giving rise under

---

[22] Capitation tax. See JDT, p. 664.

[23] BT, *Baba Bathra,* fol. 21b.

[24] Gloss to Asheri on *Baba Bathra,* II, 12. See also Gloss to *Shulhan Aruk, Hoshen Mishpat,* ch. 156, 7.

Hebrew law to a presumption of rightful ownership, is three years and not twelve months.[25]

The solution of the difficulty is to be found in the fact that the word *hazakah* (possessory right, possession, presumption) in *hezkath hayishub* misled Rabbi Israel and the authorities upon whom he relied. The truth of the matter is that the twelve-month period had nothing to do with *hazakah* in the sense of a presumption, and that it gave rise to a right and not to a presumption of a right only. This clearly appears from a passage in a book called *Zaphnath-paaneah* by Ravan (Rabbi Eliezer b. Nathan, early twelfth century), quoted in the responsa of Rabbi Joseph Colon [26] (fifteenth century).

This passage reads, in part, as follows:

> 'And therefore the ancients (Rishonim) followed the custom that when a man absented himself from his community for a period of twelve months he lost his right, for just as he acquires it in twelve months so does he lose it in twelve months, when he leaves the community and settles in another place.'

The above passage shows conclusively that residence for a period of twelve months gave rise to a right and not to a presumption of a right, and that non-residence for a similar period resulted in a loss of the right. It also seems to show that while the rule about the loss of the right was established by custom as a corollary of the rule about the acquisition of the right, the latter rule was considered based not on custom but on positive law.

Where, then, is this rule of positive law to be found? The answer is that the rule is based on Mishnah, Baba Bathra, 1, 5, where we read:

> '. . . How long must a man be in a town to count as one of the men of the town? Twelve months . . .[27]

---

[25] Mishna, *Baba Bathra*, 3, 1.
[26] No. 191.
[27] Danby, The Mishnah, *Baba Bathra* 1, 5, at p. 366 (Oxford, 1933).

This Mishnah is interpreted [28] as meaning that after twelve months of residence the newcomer is obliged to bear his share of the taxes together with the other inhabitants of the town. It follows, as a matter of logic and natural justice, that he who shares the burdens of residence in a town is also entitled to share the benefits of such residence. Indeed, the above-quoted passage in the Talmud relating to objections to strangers by inhabitants of a town makes the payment by an individual, together with the other inhabitants of the town, of the capitation tax the test of the individual's right to become a permanent resident of the town.

We now come to a consideration of the relationship between the *hezkath hayishub* and Title 45. Did the Jews borrow their *hezkath hayishub* from the Franks, or did the Franks follow a pattern set by the Jews? The writer believes that the latter was the case.

First, the apparently Talmudic origin of the *hezkath hayishub* virtually precludes the possibility of the Jews having borrowed from the Franks.

Secondly, it seems that Title 45 of the *Lex Salica* was not an indigenous product, but rather a foreign importation, for, as has been stated above, it was completely misunderstood by the Franks within a comparatively short time after its incorporation in the body of their own law.

One may well see in Title 45 an attempt on the part of Jewish merchants of the early Middle Ages to limit competition. It was precisely because the law was of limited application, and was introduced into the *Lex Salica* to answer the needs of but a small group of the population that its true import and meaning were completely forgotten after the lapse of a comparatively short period of time.

Finally, the term 'twelve months,' after which the newcomer could not be ejected, is indicative of the Jewish origin of the rule. It was probably derived from Mishnah Baba Bathra, 1, 5, quoted

[28] Commentary of Rabbi Solomon Itzchaki (Rashi) *ad locum*.

above. The writer can see no reason why a non-Jewish source should have used the term 'twelve months,' instead of 'one year,' unless it was influenced by some Jewish source.[29] In the case of the Mishnah it is easy to see why the term *twelve months* was used. A period of twelve months is a measure of time which is not variable, while the period of one year is variable. The Jewish year, as is well known, sometimes has an intercalated month and consists of thirteen months, instead of twelve. Indeed, the term twelve months is used very frequently in the Mishnah and Talmud as a measure of time.[30] The difficulties which may arise from using the term 'one year,' instead of the term 'twelve months,' are illustrated by the following passage from the Mishnah:

> 'If a man let a house to his fellow by the year and the year was made a leap-year, the advantage falls to the tenant. If he let it by the month and the year was made a leap-year, the advantage falls to the owner. It once happened in Sepphoris that a person hired a bath-house from his fellow at "twelve golden denars a year, one denar a month," and the case came before Rabban Simeon b. Gamliel and before R. Jose. They said: Let them share the advantage of the added month'.[31]

It is true that Title 46 of the *Lex Salica,* which deals with the procedure of appointing an heir, also mentions a twelve months' period. It seems, however, that this is merely a carry-over from the title that precedes it.

To summarize: The rules laid down in chapters 1 and 3 of Title 45 of the *Lex Salica* are virtually identical with the Jewish *hezkath hayishub* of the Middle Ages which is apparently based upon the Talmud. There seems to be no explanation for the

[29] In the other Barbarian laws the term "annus" rather than 'XII menses' is used. See *e. g.* Rotharis, 74, 112, 127, 361, and Liutprand, 24, 96, 100.

[30] See *e. g.* Mishnah, *Yebamoth,* 13, 12; *Gittin,* 7, 8; 7, 9; *Baba Metzia,* 8, 6; *Baba Bathra,* 3, 1; *Erakin,* 9, 3; 9, 7.

[31] Danby, The Mishnah, *Baba Metzia,* 8, 8 at p. 362.

period of twelve months mentioned in Title 45 of the *Lex Salica,* other than that it is of Jewish origin.

Title 50 of the Lex Salica

There is a remarkable correspondence between the procedure described in Title 50 of the *Lex Salica* and the Jewish procedure of execution against defaulting debtors. Under the *Lex Salica,* the creditor summons the debtor three times (per tres nondenas) to pay the debt. If the debtor does not pay after the third summons he is *iactivus* (a term which we shall presently explain), and the creditor may proceed, with the aid of the seven *Rachimburgs,* to distrain upon his property.

The term *tres nondenas* has been interpreted to mean three market or court days,[32] the custom apparently having been to hold court on days set aside as market days.

As to the term *iactivus,* which occurs quite frequently in early Frankish documents,[33] there is nothing but conjecture. Brunner's explanation may be summarized as follows: Formal agreements were made by the Franks through the throwing by the obligor upon the ground, or into the bosom of the obligee, of a *festuca* (wand). When the obligor failed to perform the obligation, the obligee would come to court to declare the obligee *iactivus.* He would produce the *festuca* which constituted proof of his adversary's assumption of the obligation, and throw it upon the ground. Hence, says Brunner, the term *iactivus.*[34]

The above explanation can hardly be considered adequate. In the first place, there is not the slightest reference to the throwing of a *festuca* in any of the documents in which the term *iactivus* occurs. Secondly, there seems to be no reason why the obligee, when he appears in court to declare the obligor *iactivus,* should throw the *festuca.* The act of throwing the *festuca* was, as

[32] See Herman, *Die Grundelemente der altgermanischen Mobiliarvindication,* Gierke's Untersuchungen zur deutschen Staats-und Rechtsgeschichte, no. 20, p. 162f.

[33] See Brunner, *Deutsche Rechtsgeschichte,* v. II, pp. 368-369.

[34] *Ibid.*

we are told,[35] a symbol of giving up certain rights to, or assuming an obligation toward, the party to whom it was thrown. Throwing the *festuca* to the judges would threfore seem to be out of place, and without any possible meaning.

The writer believes that the key to the meaning of the term *iactivus*, is to be sought in certain Jewish legal procedures which were apparently copied by the Franks.

Under Jewish legal procedure, a waiting period of three court days (which were also market days) must elapse before the court may take action against a defaulting debtor.[36] After the lapse of this period the debtor is declared by the court to be *m'nudeh*, that is excommunicated. The word *m'nudeh* is derived from *n'de*, meaning to throw,[37] and corresponds to *iactivus*. Both of these terms are probably to be rendered as cast out of the community, or, briefly, an *outcast*.

There was still another occasion, besides default in the payment of a debt, when a person could be declared *iactivus* under Frankish law. A contumacious party, who failed to appear in court after having been duly summoned, could be declared *iactivus*.[38] In some of the documents it is stated that the plaintiff appeared in court and waited three days — *triduum* — for the defendant's appearance. Other documents speak about the plaintiff's having waited till sunset — *solsatire*.[39] Sometimes a document *notitia de iactivus* [40] — stating that the defendant failed to appear in court would be drawn up by the *boni homines* and given to the plaintiff.

Under Hebrew law, a similar procedure prevailed. A contumacious party, who failed to appear in court when summoned,

---

[35] See Brissaud, *A History of French Private Law*, p. 482.

[36] BT, *Baba Kama*, 112b; *Hoshen Mishpat*, 98, 5. Monday and Thursday, which were Market days, were also set aside for holding court. See *Mishnah Megillah* 1, 1-2 and *Kethuboth* 1,1.

[37] See JDT, *s. v.* נדי.

[38] See *e. g.*, form quoted at p. 240, below.

[39] See MGH, *Legum Sectio* V, pp. 8-9.

[40] See form cited in note 38 above.

was declared *m'nudeh* — excommunicated — after the lapse of three court days from the day appointed for his appearance.[41]

As under the Frankish procedure, a document—called *ptiḥa*—stating the fact of the defendant's failure to appear would be drawn up by the court and given to the plaintiff.

Cartam Levare in Frankish Deeds

In a large number of Frankish deeds, beginning with the latter part of the 8th century, reference is made to a procedure which is called *cartam levare* — lifting up the charter.[42] This procedure may be described as follows: Before the writing of an instrument of conveyance, the grantor would lift up the blank parchment, together with the inkwell and quill, from the ground, and would deliver them to the notary. The latter would then proceed to fill out the parchment in accordance with the instructions given to him by the grantor.[43]

Brunner[44] offers the following explanation of this procedure. Originally, a conveyance of land was not considered valid among the Germanic peoples without a real investiture. Grantor and grantee, together with their witnesses, would appear on the land to be conveyed, and the grantor would deliver to the grantee some object, such as a twig, or a sod of turf, closely associated with the land. The delivery of the twig constituted a symbolic delivery of the land. Later on, when written instruments were introduced among the Germanic peoples, and conveyances came to be made by written charters, the symbolism of the delivery of the land was extended from the twig to the charter. The charter represented, so to speak, the land in miniature. The twig or turf continued to be delivered even after written charters

---

[41] BT, *Baba Kama,* 113a.

[42] See Brunner, *Zur Rechtsgeschichte der roemischen und germanischen Urkunde,* p. 104f. See also Zeitschrift der Savigny-Stiftung fuer Rechtsgeschichte v. IV, germ. Abt., p. 115.

[43] *Ibid.*

[44] *Ibid.,* n. 19 at pp. 303-304.

had been introduced, and since these had to be lifted from the ground, the parchment was also placed on the ground to be lifted together with them.

Brunner's explanation is followed by leading historians of German law, such as Gierke,[45] Von Amira [46] and Zeumer,[47] although it presents a number of difficulties. In the first place, it does not quite adequately account for the lifting up and delivery of the quill and inkwell. Secondly, it would seem that the elaborate ceremonial should have accompanied the delivery of the written charter to the grantee, rather than the delivery of the blank parchment to the scribe. Finally, there are documents representing transactions other than conveyances of land where *levatio cartae* was used. It is true that Brunner attempts to explain the difficulty last mentioned by saying that the procedure was first used in connection with conveyances of land and was later extended to other transactions. However, this amounts to saying that the significance of the symbolism was lost sight of almost as soon as it was introduced, only to be rediscovered by Brunner in the 19th century.

In a study under the title *Cartam Levare*,[48] Goldmann subjects Brunner's theory to a thorough analysis, and arrives at the conclusion that it is totally untenable. He then proceeds, in a long discourse, to describe the magic effect commonly attributed, in various places throughout the world and through the ages, to contact with the earth, and concludes that the placing of the parchment, inkwell and pen upon the earth is one of the manifestations of this popular belief.

Goldmann's theory of the significance of *cartam levare* will best be stated in his own words:

"The magic power of the earth is to flow into the

[45] Gierke, *Privaterecht*, v. II, p. 272.

[46] Von Amira, *Grundriss des germanischen Rechts* (3rd ed., 1913), p. 227.

[47] Zeumer, *Cartam Levare in Sankt Gallen Urkunden*, Zeitschrift d. Savigny-Stiftung fuer Rechtgechichte, IV, germ. Abt., p. 113ff.

[48] Mitteilungen des Instituts fuer Oesterreichische Geschichtsforschung, v. 35, p. 1ff.

parchment, ink and quill, imparting durability and indestructibility to the relationship which is to be written down on the parchment".[49]

It is difficult to argue, on logical grounds, against a theory such as the one advanced by Goldmann. This type of reasoning by free association knows no logic. However, one or two simple questions may not be out of place. Why, it may be asked, was it necessary for the grantor himself to lift up the parchment etc. from the ground? Why could not the quality of indestructibility be imparted to these objects by having the notary lift them up from the ground? Again, why do the documents stress the lifting up from the ground — *de terra levavi* — rather than the placing upon the ground, which, as Goldmann would have us believe, was the operative act believed to produce the desired magic effect?

It is to be noted that Goldmann, with commendable frankness, states that he is offering his theory only as a hypothesis, that there is no direct proof for it in the sources, and that it is to stand only so long as no better solution is forthcoming.

The writer proposes to show that those who grappled with the problem of the origin and meaning of the supposedly Germanic *cartam levare* were engaged in a thankless task, since the only sources in which the correct solution of this problem is to be found were to them *terra incognita*.

Strangely enough, *levatio cartae*, in all of its details, is found among the Jews to this very day. In divorce proceedings, conducted in accordance with Jewish law, the husband lifts up the paper on which the *get* — bill of divorce — is to be written, together with the inkwell and pen, and delivers them to the scribe, before the *get* is written. The lifting up of the paper, inkwell and pen by the husband, and their delivery by him to the scribe, are mentioned by a number of medieval Jewish authorities, notably Rabbenu Tam, Mordecai and Rabbi Asher b. Yechiel.[50]

---

[49] *Ibid.*, p. 33.
[50] See *Tur Even Ha-Ezer*, 154 and Gloss to Asheri *Gittin* 2,20.

Fortunately, there is no mystery about the reason for this procedure in the Jewish *get*, as there is in the case of the Frankish deeds. There is no need for far-fetched theories which are as untrue as they are ingenious. The reason is simple and is clearly stated in the Hebrew authorities on the subject. It is this: The instrument by means of which a conveyance is effected, — and a divorce in Hebrew law is looked upon as a conveyance in the nature of a release, — must be the property of the party making the conveyance, that is, of the grantor. The Talmud [51] bases this upon the words *"sefer ha-miqnah* — the deed of purchase"* (Jeremiah 32:11), reading these words as *sefer ha-maqneh* — the deed of the seller — and interpreting them as meaning that the deed must belong to the grantor. Under ordinary circumstances, the paper, inkwell and pen belong to the scribe, and not to the grantor. It is therefore necessary that the grantor acquire property in these so that the instrument when written may belong to him. Under Hebrew law, *hagbaha* — lifting up — is the only valid mode of acquiring property in chattels capable of being lifted up.[52] Hence, the lifting up by the husband of the paper, inkwell and pen before the writing of the *get*.

The possibility that the Jews of the Middle Ages borrowed this procedure from the Germanic peoples hardly needs to be discussed. As I have stated, the procedure is based upon Talmudic authorities which preceded in point of time any extended contacts between Jews and Germanic peoples. Furthermore, lifting up is a peculiarly Jewish mode of acquiring title to chattels.

Nor is it likely that the similarity between the Jewish and Frankish procedure is the result of mere chance. The points of similarity are too many to be accounted for by chance. Also, the several rules of Hebrew law, which are reflected in the procedure, preclude the possibility of a chance similarity. Complicated legal patterns of a technical nature are not duplicated by mere coincidence.

[51] See BT, Gittin 20b.
[52] See *Hoshen Mishpat,* 198, 1.

There remains the only possibility that the Franks adopted the procedure from the Jews who were probably in no small measure responsible for the dissemination of the use of written instruments in medieval Europe.

Traditio Per Cartam

In the Frankish sources reference is often made to *traditio per cartam* — delivery by deed — by which is meant a form of conveyance of land wherein, instead of a real investiture through delivery by the grantor to the grantee of a symbol of the land to be conveyed, the grantor delivers to the grantee a charter of conveyance. Brissaud,[53] following Brunner and others, states that while among the Romans, from whom the Germans adopted the use of the written instrument, the instrument served only as evidence of title, "the Germans gave it a new bearing and character; they saw a delivery *per cartam* where there was only a *traditio cartae* for the Romans".[54]

However, in view of what has been said above about the origin of the Frankish *levatio cartae,* the writer believes that it is more likely that the *traditio per cartam* was borrowed by the Franks from the Jews. Conveyance by deed is, as we shall presently see, one of the oldest methods of transferring land under Hebrew law. Where this method of conveyance is used, it is by the delivery of the deed that the transfer is effected, according to Jewish law.

Comparison of Handwriting

A capitulary ascribed to Carl The Great provides that where the authenticity of a charter of emancipation of a slave is disputed, and the *boni homines,* in whose presence the slave claims to have been set free, are absent, he who holds the charter and

[53] See Brissand, *A History of French Private Law,* p. 374 and authorities cited there.

[54] *Ibid.*

claims his liberty under it must prove its authenticity by producing, for the purpose of comparison of the handwriting, two
other charters written by the same *cancellarius*.

> "Si quis per cartam ingenuus dimissus fuerit et a
> quolibet homine ad servitium interpellatus fuerit,
> primo legitimum auctorem suae libertatis proferat
> et in sua libertate perseveret. Si vero legitimus auc-
> tor defuerit, testimonium bonorum hominum, qui
> tunc aderant quando liber dimissus fuit, se de-
> fendere permittatur. Si vero testes defuerint, cum
> duabus allis cartis, quae eiusdem cancellarii manu
> firmatae sunt vel subscriptae, suam cartam quae
> tertia est veracem et legitimam esse confirmet".[55]

Brunner [56] asserts that the above method of proving the authenticity of documents was borrowed by the Franks from
Roman legal practice. He cites Code Theod. II, 27, 1, 1 and
Justinian, Nov. 73, 7, 2, where mention is made of comparison
of handwriting as a method of proving the authenticity of documents.

However, the texts cited by Brunner, as he was well aware,
indicate that both, Theodosius and Justinian, viewed this method
of proof with great suspicion. The former required "many other
proofs" in addition to a comparison of handwriting, while the
latter allowed it to be used only as a last resort, and even then
required that the party producing the document solemnly swear
to its authenticity.

Furthermore, there is no mention anywhere in the Roman
law sources of the requirement, contained in the capitualry
quoted above, that the proof be conducted with two other
documents.

Is it a coincidence that under Talmudic law, as under Frankish law, comparison with two other documents was required to
prove the authenticity of documents? In the Babylonian Talmud,
Kethuboth 20a, we read:

---

[55] MGH, *Legum Sectio* II, p. 215. See also *ibid.* 430 and Lex Riburia 59, 5.
[56] Brunner, *Deutsche Rechtsgechichte,* v. I, p. 564, n. 20.

"... The Nehardeans said: A document is confirmed only from two kethuboth or from two fields, and only when their owners were in quiet possession for three years".

To this R. Shimi b. Ashi adds that the two documents by which the authenticity of the third one is to be established must belong to a person or persons other than the party seeking to prove the authenticity of the disputed document.

It is obvious that all these elaborate precautions were designed to prevent forgery and the use of forged documents in court. The Franks apparently became acquainted with the rule about *two* documents through their contacts with Jews. The additional requirements as to the nature of the documents and as to their source were such as could not be expected to be copied by people who had only a superficial and indirect acquaintance with the legal system in which they arose.

Further evidence to the effect that the procedure of authenticating written instruments was copied by the Franks from the Jews may be seen in the fact that the term *firmatio chartarum*, which was used in the Frankish kingdom to denote this procedure,[57] is an exact translation of the Hebrew term *kiyum shetaroth*, used in the Talmud [58] to denote the same procedure.

Carta and Notitia

Legal documents evidencing conveyances and other transactions in the Frankish period are designated either as *carta* or as *notitia*. The latter form is also called *memoratorium*.[59] The difference, in form as well as in substance, between *carta* and *notitia* has been the subject of a now famous article by Brunner.[60]

---

[57] See Brunner, *Die Entstehung der Schwurgerichte*, p. 64.

[58] See BT, *Gittin* 3a.

[59] See *Cod. Dipl. Cavensis*, v. II, pp. 2, 6, 8, 14, 16.

[60] Brunner, *"Carta und Notitia"* in *Commentationes philologicae in honorem Th. Mommseni*, pp. 570-589. Reprinted in Brunner, *Abhandlungen zur Rechtsgeschichte*, v. I, pp. 458-486.

The difference in form between the *carta* and the *notitia* is apparent upon the face of the documents. In the *carta* the grantor speaks in the first person, while the *notitia* is framed in the third person, and represents an attestation by the court or by witnesses of a transaction already completed.

As to the difference in substance between the two forms, Brunner maintains that while the *carta* was a dispositive or constitutive instrument the *notitia* was a mere evidentiary instrument — *Beweisurkunde*.[61]

In Jewish law similar two forms co-existed at least from the 3rd century. These two forms were called *shtar haqnaah*[62] — charter of conveyance — and *dukhram pithgama*[63] — memorandum, respectively.

In Baba Bathra, 136a, the Talmud deals with the question of the validity of a conveyance of a future estate to take effect after the grantor's death. It is there stated that, according to Rabbi Judah, where the conveyance is made by means of a *shtar haqnaah* — charter of conveyance — it is not necessary to specify that it is made in the present to take effect in the future, since the charter speaks as of its date; but that when the conveyance is evidenced by a *dukhran pithgama* — memorandum — it is necessary to state that it is made "from this day and after the death" of the grantor.

It will readily be seen that the above technical difference between the two Jewish forms is an outgrowth of the difference in their nature, similar to the one suggested by Brunner for the *carta* and *notitia*, the *shtar haqnaah* being a dispositive instrument and the *dukhran pithgama* being an evidentiary instrument. In the case of a dispositive instrument the instrument speaks as of its date, since it is through the instrument itself that the conveyance is effected. But in the case of an evidentiary instrument, which only records a past transaction, it is necessary to state

---

[61] *Abbandlungen zur Rechtsgeschichte*, v. I, p. 463.
[62] See *e. g., Baba Metzia* 16b and *Baba Bathra* 172a.
[63] See *Baba Bathra* 136a and *Sandhedrin* 29b.

that the transaction was not one purporting to be a conveyance
in the future after the grantor's death.

The distinction between a dispositive and an evidentiary
document is clearly stated in the following passages of the Mishnah and Gemara:

> "Property for which there is security [64] can be ac-
> quired by money or by deed or by usucaption; and
> that for which there is no security [65] can be acquired
> only by the act of drawing. Property for which there
> is no security in conjunction with property for which
> there is security can be acquired by money, by
> deed, or by usucaption, and imposes the need for an
> oath also on property for which there is security".[66]

This Mishnah is followed in the Gemara by a discussion
which reads, in part, as follows:

> "By money: Whence do we know it? — Said Heze-
> kiah: Scripture saith, *men shall acquire fields with
> money.* (Jeremiah, 32, 44). Yet perhaps the pur-
> chase is invalid unless there is a deed too, since it
> continues, and *subscribe the deeds, and attest them?*
> — Were 'acquire' written at the end, it would be
> as you say; now, however, that 'acquire' is written
> at the beginning, money gives a title, while the deed
> is merely evidence... "And by deed. How do we
> know it? Shall we say, because it is written *and
> subscribe the deeds, and attest them and call wit-
> nesses* — but you have said that the deed is merely
> evidence? — But from this verse, *so I took the deed
> of purchase*".[67]

From a certain passage in the Talmud it appears that the
dukhran pithgama — memorandum — form, was especially

---

[64] Immovable property.
[65] Movable property.
[66] *Mishnah, Kiddushin* 1, 5
[67] BT, Kiddushin 26a.

adapted to transactions attestted by a court. In Sanhedrin 29b, we read:

ההיא אודיתא דהוה כתב ביה דוכרן פיתגמי וכל לישני דבי דינא

(A certain recognizance contained the phrase *dukhran pith-gama* and the rest of the phraseology of judicial documents).

The *notitia* too, it seems, was especially adapted to the style of judicial documents, as will appear from the following examples:

"Noticia, qualiter veniens illi Andecavis civetate ante venerabile vir illo abbati vel reliquis quam plures bonis hominibus, qui cum ipsi aderunt, cuius nomina vel scripcionibus adque signaculum subter teniuntur inserta, interpellavit alicus hominis his nominibus illus et illus, dum dicerit, quasi vinia sua in loco noncupante illo male ordine persvasissit. Quia ipse illi et illi taliter in respunso (dederunt), quod autore habebant legitimo nomen illo maiore, quia ipsa vinia ad eos dedissi, sic ab ipsis viris fuit denonciatum, ut die illo Andecavis civetate ipso illo in autericio presentare; se hoc non facebat, cum legis beneficio ipso illo de ipsa vinia revestire deberet".[68]

"Noticia, qualiter et quibus presentibus veniens homo alicus nomen ille in pago illo, in loco que dicitur ille, in mallo publico ante vir illo comite vel reliquis quam plures bonis hominibus, qui illo ante ipso comite aframitum habuisset. A co placitum venit ipse ille, placito suo custodebat. Et nec ipse ille eum placitum venit nec misso in vicem suam direxit, qui ulla sonia nuntiasset; et placito suo neglexit et iactivos exinde remansit".[69]

In addition to the general form, there is another mark of Jewish influence on the style of the *notitia*. The reader will have noticed that the *notitia* begins with the word *qualiter* (as). This is apparently a mere introductory word. Its sole function is that

[68] MGH *Legum Sectio* V, p. 21.
[69] *Ibid*, p. 189.

of introducing the preamble or recital of the document. A similar word — אִיךְ (as) — with like meaning and like function, is used in two judicial documents quoted in the Talmud [70] and in numerous Jewish documents of the Middle Ages.[71] The similarity goes even further. In Jewish documents the word אִיךְ is usually followed by a statement to the effect that a certain party *came before* the court (אִיךְ בָּא לְפָנֵינוּ פְּלוֹנִי בֶּן פְּלוֹנִי). The same is true of the word *qualiter* in the Frankish *notitia*.

Non Fraude Sed in Publico

In some Frankish forms of conveyance of property it is stated that the conveyance was made *non fraude sed in publico* [72] — not fraudulently but publicly. Sometimes this formula is more elaborate and reads as follows:

> "Non occulte sed publicae non privatum sed palam",[73] " . . . Non absconse sed publice, non private sed palam".[74]

A similar formula is found almost universally in Jewish forms of conveyance,[75] and is based upon the following passage of the Talmud:

> "Rab Judah said: A deed of a gift drawn up in secret is not enforceable. What is meant by a deed of gift drawn up in secret? R. Joseph said: If the donor said to the witnesses. 'Go and write in some hidden place'. Others report that what R. Joseph said was: If the donor did not say to the witnesses 'Find a place in the street or in some public place and write it there' . . ."[76]

In medieval Jewish documents the formula usually reads:

> "And he (the grantor) said to us thus: This deed

---

[70] BT, *Gittin* 35a, *Yebamoth* 39b.

[71] See, *e. g.,* Gulak, *Ozar Hashtaroth,* nos. 179-181.

[72] MGH, *Legum Sectio* V, p. 189.

[73] Roziére, Recueil Général des Formules, v. I, p. 232.

[74] *Cod. Dipl. Lang. col.* 754.

[75] See, *e. g.,* Gulak *ibid., nos.* 198-200.

[76] *BT, Baba Bathra* 40b.

of sale (or gift) ye shall write at the market and
sign in the open, so that it shall not be a secret sale
(or gift) but one that is open and notorious".

The similarity between the above Jewish and Frankish formulae requires no comment, and the obviously Talmudic origin
of the Jewish formula precludes the possibility of the Jewish
formula being a copy of its Frankish counterpart.

Super Fluvio Illo

In some Frankish forms the locality in which the document
was drawn up is identified, in addition to its name, by the name
of the river on which it is situated.[77] A similar place description
is universally found in the Jewiseh *get* [78] — bill of divorce —,
where formalities are strictly observed, and, occasionally, in the
kethuba [79] — instrument of endowment. In no other legal forms,
besides the Jewish and Frankish, has the writer been able to
find such place description.

Cassatura

When the debt evidenced by a bond was paid or otherwise
discharged, the bond would be cut or a notation of the fact of
payment or discharge would be made thereon.[80] This notation
was called *cassatura* (a breaker), the term evidently having reference to the effect of the notation upon the instrument.

It is quite obvious that "breaking" is not a very appropriate
term to describe the discharge or cancellation of a written instrument. How, then, did the term *cassatura* originate? The answer
is that it is an exact translation of the Hebrew "shover" (a

---

[77] See MGH, *Legum Secio* V, pp. 188, 266-284.

[78] See Gulak, *ibid.*, nos. 68, 69. See also BT, *Gittin* 27a.

[79] *Ibid.*, nos. 26, 28, 29.

[80] Bei der Rueckgabe pflegte die cautio durch Zerschneiden oder durch einen
schriftlichen Vermerk (cassatura) entkraeftet zu werden". — Brunner, *Grund-
zuege der Deutschen Rechtsgechichte* (7th ed., Leipzig, 1923), p. 209. See also
Brissaud, *A History of French Private Law* (The Continental Legal History
Series), p. 507, n. 1.

breaker), which is used in the Mishnah [81] and Talmud in the same sense, in which *cassatura* is used in the Frankish sources, namely, that of acquittance or release. The Hebrew term probably goes back to the times when legal instruments were written on clay tablets and the discharge of an obligation was accompanied by the breaking of the tablet evidencing it.[82] Indeed, in an Assyrian instrument of acquittance there occurs a phrase which is translated by Ungnad as *seine Urkunde wird zerbrochen werden.*[83]

As to the *cutting* of the instrument, it seems that this too was borrowed from the Jews. Cutting or incision has been, since Tamudic times, the standard method of cancelling legal instruments under Jewish practice. Indeed, the Talmud [84] prescribes the exact manner in which the incision is to be made, namely, lengthwise and crosswise, or in the place where the witnesses' signatures appear.

As will be shown in ch. 23, below, incision of documents appears in some non-Jewish documents of the later Middle Ages in a context which leaves no doubt of its Jewish origin.

The Form of The Deed of Conveyance

The deed of conveyance in the Frankish formularies generally consists of two main clauses: 1. The *habendum* clause, in which the grantor authorizes the grantee to exercise, "from the present day", the rights of ownership over the property being conveyed. 2. The penal clause providing for the payment of a penalty by the grantor or other enumerated persons in case the validity of the conveyance is contested by any one of them. Both of these clauses exhibit unmistakable marks of Jewish influence.

In the *Formulae Andecavenses,* the *habendum* clause in one of the forms of a deed of conveyance (of a slave) reads as follows:

---

[81] See *e. g., Mishna, Kethuboth* 9:9.

[82] See Gulak, *Das Urkundenwesen im Talmud im Lichte d. griechisch-aegyptischen Papyri und d. griechischen und roemischen Rechts,* p. 148, n. 1.

[83] Kohler und Ungnad, *Assyrische Rechtsurkunden,* no. 234, pp. 174-175.

[84] See BT, *Baba Bathra* 168b.

"... ut, quicquid ab odierna diae ipso vernaculo
facere volueritis, abendi, tenende, donande, vendende
seu communtandi, quomodo et de reliqua mancipia
vestra obnoxia exinde facere volueritis, liberam ha-
beatis protestatem". (... so that whatever, from the
present day, you may wish to do with this slave,
having, holding, giving away, selling or exchanging,
in the same manner as you may henceforth wish to
do with your other slaves, you shall have free power
to do).[85]

Freundt,[86] who has noted that the *habendum* clause in the
Frankish formularies and deeds bears a striking resemblance to the
kyrieia clause of the deed of conveyance in the Greek papyri, has
concluded that the former was influenced by the latter. About
the *shallit* clause of the Aramaic papyri of the 5th century
B. C. E. and of the medieval Jewish deed of conveyance he
apparently knew nothing at all. As has been shown above, the
kyrieia clause itself was copied from the *shallit* clause.[87] It is
therefore virtually certain that the *habendum* clause of the Frankish deed of conveyance is either directly or indirectly traceable
to the *shallit* clause of the Jewish deed of conveyance.

The penal clause of the Frankish formularies also reveals
signs of Jewish influence, and in the case of this clause there are
definite indications that the influence was direct. In no. 1(c) of
the *Formulae Andecavenses* the penal clause reads:

"Et si fuerit ullumquam tempore, qui contra hanc
cessione ista, quem ego in te bona voluntate con-
scribere rogavi, aut ego ipsi, aut ullus de heredibus
meis vel propinquis meis, aut qualibet homo vel
extranea aut emissa persona, venire voluerit, aut
agere vel repetire presumpserit, ante lite ingressus

---

[85] MGH, *Legum Sectio* V, p. 7.

[86] K. Freundt, *Wertpapiere im antiken u. frühmittelalterlichem Rechte* v. I,
p. 116.

[87] See p. 125ff., above.

duplet tibi tantum et alio tantum, quantum cessio
ista contenit, aut eo tempore meliorata valuerit et
repeticione sua non optineat effectum, et haec cessio
ista adque voluntas nostra omni tempore firma per-
maneat."

(And if at any time there will be anyone, either I
myself or one of my heirs or relatives or any man,
or stranger or person sent(?),[88] who against this
cession, which I, of my good-will, ordered to be
written for you, will wish to come, or will presume
to assail it or demand its return, he shall, before
commencement of suit, pay you double, as much and
again as much as this cession contains or will at
that time be worth as improved, and his demand shall
have no effect and this cession and our will shall for
all time remain firm.)[89]

This clause is to be compared with the warranty clause of
the Jewish deed of conveyance of the Middle Ages and with the
penal clause of the deed of conveyance in the Aramaic papyri of
the 5th century B. C. E. The warranty clause in Jewish deeds of
conveyance reads, with some minor variations, as follows:

"And whoever shall come from the four winds of
the world, man or woman, Jew or Gentile, son or
daughter, heir or legatee, relative or stranger, who
shall arise and contrive and make any claim or
demand whatsoever on the said William, or his heirs
or representatives, regarding the said house with the
court and appurtenances, it will be obligatory upon
me, my heirs and representatives, to free them and

---

[88] In some forms the phrase reads *submissa persona*, that is, a person who
is subordinated to the grantor, under his authority. This is in striking agreement
with the phrase ואיש לי occurring in similar context in Brooklyn 8.5 (416
B. C. E.), with regard to which Kraeling (APK, 229), quite correctly, comments:
"איש לי 'anyone of mine' — a person under his authority." Cf. also Cowley
25.10 (416 B. C. E.), and the comment thereon (APC, 81).

[89] MGH, *Legum Sectio* V, p. 5.

protect them against those claimants, and to maintain them in quiet and peaceful possession of the
house, court and appurtenances aforesaid, on the
surety of all my property, landed or movable, which
I now possess or may in future acquire".[90]

The penal clause in the Aramaic papyri reads:

"I shall have no power to institute suit or process
against you, I and my son and my daughter, brother
and sister of mine, relative and stranger, concerning
this land, (against) you and your son and your
daughter, brother and sister of yours, relative and
stranger. Whoever sues you in my name concerning
this land shall pay you the sum of 20 kerashim
royal weight, and this land shall also be yours".[91]

It will readily be seen that the general pattern of the formulae just quoted from the Jewish sources, with the rather
detailed enumeration of the possible contestants, is strikingly
similar to that of the Frankish penal clause. The similarity becomes still more striking when some of the phrases in the Jewish
and in the Frankish formulae are analyzed and compared. The
phrase "relative or stranger" in the Jewish formulae corresponds
to "ullus de *propinquis* meis... vel *extranea persona*" of the
Frankish formula. The phrase *ante lite ingressus* (before commencement of suit) corresponds to the phrase ולא דין ולא דבב
(without lawsuit or complaint) in the penal clause of some of the
Aramaic papyri.[92] Both of these phrases mean that the penalty
is to be paid without controversy, before the grantee shall have
instituted suit for its recovery.

In addition to the penal and *habendum* clauses, there is in
some Frankish forms of a deed of gift a clause in which all "prior

---

[90] Abrahams, Stokes and Loewe, *Starrs and Jewish Charters in the British Museum*, v. I, p. 109.

[91] Cowley 6.12ff. (456 B. C. E.).

[92] See, *e. g., Cowley* 8.21f. (460 B. C. E.); 9.15 (460 B. C. E.). Cowley's rendering of the phrase as "and no suit or process (shall lie)" is inaccurate. In Cowley 15.25f., 29, he renders the same phrase as we have rendered it.

and subsequent" deeds made by the grantor with respect to the same property are declared void, and which, as has been shown above, are traceable to Jewish sources.[93]

Further evidence of Jewish influence upon the form of the Frankish deed is found in the form of the deed of exchange of property in the Frankish formularies. The penal clause of this form in *Marculf* II, No. 24, for example, reads:

> "Si quis vero aliquis ex ipsis aut heredes eorum vel quicumque hoc emutare voluerit, rem quam accepit pare suo amittat et insuper inferat pare suo cum cogenti fisco auri uncia una, et quod repetit vindicare non valeat".
>
> (If either one of them, or their heirs, or anyone else should wish to breach (literally: change) this, he shall lose to his fellow the property he has received and in addition he shall pay to his fellow, and to the fiscus compelling payment, one ounce of gold, and his claim shall not be valid.[94]

The phrase *pare suo* (to his fellow), used here in the sense of *to the other party*, is a Hebraism, *par* (fellow) being a literal translation of the word חבר (fellow). This word is often used in Mishnaic Hebrew,[95] as the word רע (fellow) is used in Biblical Hebrew,[96] in the sense of "another person with whom one stands in reciprocal relation".

Another Hebraism or Aramaism in this clause is the word *emutare* (to change) which is used here in the sense of breaching an agreement. This is a literal translation of שנה (to change) which is used in Mishnaic Hebrew in the same sense of breaching an agreement.

In Mishnah Baba Metzia 6:2 it is stated:

כל המשנה ידו על התחתונה וכל החוזר בו ידו על התחתונה.

---

[93] See p. 116f., above.
[94] MGH, *Legum Sectio* V, p. 91.
[95] See, JDT, 421f.
[96] GB, 764bf.

(Whosoever breaches [literally, changes] is at a disadvantage, and whosoever retracts [literally, turns] is at a disadvantage". In their Aramaic form the words for *changing* and *turning* are invariably found in the deed of gift of the Jewish formularies in the phrase דלא להשנאה בה ודלא למיהדד מינה (not to be breached and not to be retracted).[97]

The word שנה (change) in the sense of breaching a covenant also seems to occur in Mal. 3:6 כי אני ה' לא שניתי ואתם בני יעקב לא כליתם. which is to be translated as follows: *For I the Lord have not breached my covenant and ye, the sons of Jacob, have not perished.* There is here, apparently, an allusion to Lev. 26:44: "And yet for all that, when they are in the land of their enemies, I will not reject them, neither will I abhor them, to destroy them utterly, and to break My covenant with them; for I am the Lord their God". The term שנה (to change) in the sense of breaching an agreement has thus a long history in Hebrew.

A significant phrase showing that *emutare* in the sense of breaching an agreement came into use in the legal Latin of the early Middle Ages by way of the Jewish formulary occurs in the Visigothic Code. In Lex Visigothorum, II, 5, 5 it is stated:

> "Pactum vero vel placitum convenienter hac iustissime inter partes conscriptum, si eitiam penam in eis inserta non fuerit, revolvi aut inmutari nulla ratione permittimus" (And any contract or agreement, properly and justly drawn up between the parties, even if it contains no penalty, we shall under no circumstances suffer to be retracted from or breached).

We have here a combination of both terms, *inmutare* (to change) and *revolvere* (to turn), used, exactly as their equivalents are used in the Mishnah and in the Jewish formularies, in the sense of breaching an agreement or retracting therefrom. That this combination is not the result of a coincidence is quite obvious.

---

[97] See, *e. g.*, Gulak, *ibid*, nos. 174, 178, 180, 196.

Absque Iudicio et Contradictione

In the Frankish formularies, beginning with that of Marculf, there is a form in which the former owner of property, who had conveyed it to a church, is granted a usufruct for life, or for the joint lives of himself and his wife, with a provision that upon his, or their death, the church shall recall back the property into its ownership, *absque ullius iudicis aut heredum nostrorum expectata traditione* (without an awaited delivery by any judge or by our heirs).[98] There are also variations in this formula. In some forms it reads: *absque ullius iudicis contradictione* (without contradiction on the part of any judge.)[99] In others: *absque ulla contrarietate heredum neorum vel ullius iudicis adsignatione vel contradictione* (without any objection on the part of my heirs or assignment or contradiction by any judge).[100]

Upon a close scrutiny of the above formula it appears that the reference to the *iudex* (judge), which occurs in all of the variations quoted above, is quite incongruous. Why should any objection be raised on the part of any judge to the recall of the property by the church, or why should *delivery* by a judge be necessary? The writer believes that the incongruity will be fully accounted for if it is assumed that originally the formula read *absque iudicio et contradictione* (without judgment and contradiction) and that it was a literal translation of the Hebrew בלי דין ודברים (without lawsuit or controversy). As has been shown above,[101] this Hebrew phrase occurs frequently in the Talmud and in Jewish sources of the Middle Ages, and its equivalent in Aramaic is also found in the Aramaic papyri. In the course of time, notaries who did not understand the import of the formula tried to make it sound more plausible by introducing some changes therein. The *iudicium* was changed into *iudex* and the word *contradictio* into *traditio*, and as a result the formula assumed the form in which it appears in the Formulary of Marculf.

[98] MGH, *Legum Sectio* V, p. 77f.
[99] *Ibid.*, 235f.
[100] *Ibid.*, 242f.
[101] See p. 82f., above.

CHAPTER XVIII

THE JEWISH GAGE, THE GENERAL RELEASE, THE RECOGNIZANCE AND REPRESENTATION BY ATTORNEY IN ENGLISH LAW

1. *Introduction*

The Jews came to England in considerable numbers after the Norman conquest.[1] They were able to establish themselves under the protection of the king, who welcomed them as a source of income and ready cash. Their financial transactions were numerous and involved large amounts of money. For some time they had a virtual monopoly of the moneylending business, because the taking of interest was prohibited to Christians by the Church.[2] Many a castle was built with funds advanced by Jews to the nobleman who built it, and even some monasteries were built with money borrowed from the Jews.[3] When Aaron of Lincoln—probably the richest Jew in their midst—died, a special branch of the Exchequer was required to handle his financial affairs, so that the king's share of the estate might be collected.[4]

Justice in civil matters between Jew and Jew was adminstered by the Chapters of the Jews, that is, by Rabbinical courts, in acordance with Jewish law.[5] A special court, the Exchequer of the Jews, which at one time consisted of Jews and Gentiles, had

---

[1] PMH, I, 468; J. M. Rigg, *Select Pleas, Starrs & Other Records from the Rolls of Exchequer of the Jews. A.D. 1220-1284.* Selden Society Publications, XV, p. x.

[2] PMH, I, 473.

[3] J. Jacobs, *The Jews in Angevin England,* p. xiv.

[4] *Ibid.,* p. xvii.

[5] Rigg *op. cit.,* p. xii. n. 1.

jurisdiction over disputes arising between Jew and Gentile.[6]

For many centuries before their settlement in England Jews had cultivated the study of law with great devotion and religious fervor. *Dine mamonot, i.e.,* that branch of the law which deals with matters relating to property, contract, and torts, as distinguished from ritual law, was particularly favored by men of acute intellect among them. "He who wishes to acquire wisdom should study *dine mamonot,*" reads an early Talmudic text.[7] Throughout the lands of their dispersion justice was administered among them by Rabbinical courts in accordance with Talmudic law as interpreted by leading Rabbis.[8] As a result of centuries of study and practice there developed among them a body of law, and with it a large number of legal forms and devices, far more mature and complex than anything that was known to English lawyers of the twelfth century. Under these circumstances it would be very strange indeed if the Jews did not use the legal forms with which they were familiar, and which were elaborately discussed in their legal literature.

That so little attention has been given to the possible influence of Jews upon the development of the law of the creditor-debtor relationship, a field where their influence should have made itself felt more effectively than in any other legal field, is probably due to the fact that most sources of Jewish law are not available in English. Even where available, it takes years of study to master their iniricacies.

Pollock and Maitland have this to say about the possible influence of Jewish law upon English law:

> Whether the sojourn of the Jews in England left any permanent marks upon the body of our law is a question that we dare not debate, though we may raise it. We can hardly suppose that from *Lex Judaica,* the Hebrew Law which the Jews adminis-

[6] *Ibid.,* p. xx.
[7] Mishna, Baba Batra, end.
[8] See Finkelstein, *Jewish Self-Government in the Middle Ages,* pp. 6-7.

tered among themselves, anything passed into the code of the contemptuous Christians. But that the international *Lex Judaismi* perished in 1290 without leaving any memorial of itself, is by no means so certain.[9]

While it may be conceded that cases of deliberate and conscious adoption by English lawyers of rules and doctrines from the Hebrew law were rare—although this is by no means certain—the adoption of security devices used by the Jews falls into an entirely different classification. Their origin is extrajudicial, they are born of the exigencies and necessities of trade and commerce, where Jew meets Gentile on more or less equal terms, and where religious prejudices are thrust into the background. The judiciary but passes on their effect and validity and is in a limited sense only a party to their creation.

The researches conducted by the present writer have revealed that the *lex judaismi* did leave some important memorials of itself in English law, but that these had come to be so integrated in the English legal system that their origin was completely forgotten.

2. The Jewish Gage

The form of security most frequently used by the Jews in England was known as the "Jewish gage." The nature of this gage has never been fully understood by historians of English law,[10] for the simple reason that its roots are to be found in Hebrew law, with which these historians were totally unfamiliar. The form of security represented by the "Jewish gage" was, as Pollock and Maitland[11] point out, a completely novel institution in England, in that it gave rights in land to a creditor who was not in possession of the land. It was introduced by the Jews and patterned by them after devices which they had used

[9] PMH, I, 475.
[10] *Ibid.*, p. 473.
[11] *Ibid.*, p. 469

for many centuries prior to their settlement in England. Only a reference to Hebrew law can give us a clue to its understanding.

The Hebrew device that gave rise to the Jewish gage is not a mortgage in the sense of a pledge of specific property as security for the payment of a debt. It does not form part of the Hebrew law of mortgages, but is rather an integral part of the Hebrew law of execution.[12] It is a general lien in favor of the creditor upon all the real property owned by the debtor at the time the debt is incurred. By virtue of this lien the creditor may follow the property into the hands of a transferee who acquired the property after the lien had attached to it.[13] The lien is implied in law as an incident of every debt evidenced by a *shtar* bond, signed at the instance of the debtor by two witnesses and accompanied by sufficient publicity,[14] and of every judgment of a court of competent jurisdiction.[15] Although a stipulation to the effect that the debtor binds his property for the payment of the debt is usually incorporated in the bond, its omission has no legal effect. In the language of the Talmud,[16] the omission is presumed to be an error of the scrivener.

There is, however, one important limitation upon the right of the creditor to follow the debtor's property into the hands of a transferee. As long as the debtor has free assets sufficient to satisfy the debt in full, the creditor cannot proceed against the property in the hands of a transferee.[17] This limitation of the creditor's right under the lien of the Hebrew *shtar* is an important characteristic of this lien and distinguishes it from a mortgage. The debtor's land, according to Hebrew law, stands surety for the payment of his debts, and just as the surety's liability, under ordinary circumstances, is secondary—that is, he

---

[12] Shulhan Aruk, Hoshen Mishpat, ch. 111, sec. 1.

[13] Mishna Baba Batra 10:8; Hoshen Mishpat, ch. 39, sec. 1, and ch. 111, sec. I.

[14] *Ibid.*

[15] *Ibid.*, ch. 372, sec. 8.

[16] Baba Mezia 15b.

[17] Mishna Gittin 5:2; Hoshen Mishpat, ch. 111, sec. 8.

is liable only in case the principal debtor does not possess sufficient assets to satisfy the debt—so the liability of the debtor's land is only secondary.

Originally, the creditor's lien attached only to the debtor's immovable property.[18] At a later period it was held that by inserting a special provision to that effect in the *shtar,* the lien could be extended to the debtor's movable property.[19] At an earlier period the question was raised by the Babylonian scholar, "Master Samuel," as to whether or not the debtor could subject his future acquisitions to the lien of the creditor.[20] By analogy with conveyance of property, some argued that a lien on property to be acquired in the future by the debtor should be ineffective, just as a sale of such property would be ineffective. The conclusion of the Talmud, however, is that the creation of a lien is not to be likened to a conveyance.

In the post-Talmudic period the practice became almost universal to incorporate in every *shtar* a lien on the maker's property *movable and immovable, present and future.*[21] This standardized lien clause was introduced by the Jews in England into the bonds they used when advancing money to Gentiles, and was apparently given full force and effect by the English courts. The Latin formula used was *obligo omnia bona mea, mobilia et immobilia.*[22] The legal effect given to this formula by the Exchequer of the Jews was substantially the same as that given to it by Jewish law. The lien of the creditor upon the debtor's land was enforced by the Exchequer of the Jews not only against the debtor himself, but also against a transferee.[23] Similarly, the rule of Jewish law that the lien is enforceable against the transferee only where the debtor does not possess free

---

[18] Baba Batra, 44b; Hoshen Mishpat, ch. 113,, sec. I.

[19] *Ibid*

[20] Baba Batra, 157 a-b; Hoshen Mishpat, ch. 112, sec. 1.

[21] See *e.g.,* Sefer Hashtarot (Formulary) of Rabbi Judah Barzillai, No. 34.

[22] Rigg, *op. cit.,* pp. 33, 93, 94, n. 1.

[23] *Ibid.,* pp. 18, 53, 63.

assets sufficient to satisfy the debt was followed by the Exchequer.[24]

From the Jewish bonds the lien clause found its way into general use; in the thirteenth and fourteenth centuries we find that almost every bond made in England contains the formula: *Obligo omnia bona mea, mobilia et immobilia.*[25] The provision for the binding of the debtor's future acquisition occurs less frequently, but it, too, is found in several bonds in Madox's *Formulare,*[26] and elsewhere,[27] where the lien clause reads: *Obligo omnia bona mea, mobilia et immobilia, presentia et futura.*

The Jewish gage, which, as we have seen, is part of the Hebrew law of execution, the fundamental idea of which is that the entire property of the debtor, movable and immovable, is bound for the payment of his debts, had a profound influence upon the development of English economic life and English law. It was this idea, which gradually gained a foothold in feudal England with its fixity of ownership of land, that resulted, on the economic side, in broadening the base of credit by making land, the principal source of wealth, readily available as security, and, on the legal side, in making land in possession of the debtor liable for the payment of his debts. As Pollock and Maitland have already noted,[28] the statute creating the *writ of elegit,* enacted in 1285, was patterned after the Jewish gage. This writ gave a judgment creditor, or a creditor upon a recognizance, the right to collect his debt from the debtor's real property, to the extent of one-half thereof, by seizing the property through judicial process and holding it until the debt had been paid by the debtor, or until the creditor had satisfied himself out of the rents and profits. The limitation of the creditor's right to one-

---

[24] *Ibid.,* p. 65; *Calendar of the Plea Rolls of the Exchequer of the Jews,* I, p. 73; *Calendar of the Close Rolls,* Edw. I, I, p. 389.

[25] PMH, II, 2, n. 2 & 225, n. 6; Madox, *Formulare Anglicanum,* Nos. 159, 640, 644

[26] *Madox, op. cit.,* Nos. 119, 643, 645.

[27] *Calendar of the Close Rolls,* 1268-1272, pp. 243, 258, 300, 410-411.

[28] PMH, I, 475, n. 1.

half of the debtor's property followed an earlier enactment, during the reign of Edward I, which put a similar limitation upon the Jewish creditor.

The idea of the Jewish gage gradually gained a foothold in England, for, contrary to the view of Pollock and Maitland, the *statute of elegit* was not altogether an innovation. According to Pollock and Maitland, prior to 1285 the only remedies available to a creditor against a defaulting debtor were the writs of *fieri facias* and *fieri levare,* the former directing the sheriff to seize the debtor's chattels and make the debt therefrom, and the latter directing him to make the debt from the fruit of the debtor's land.[29] It was only in 1285, these writers assert, that the creditor was given a right in the debtor's land. However, it appears from certain bonds made some twenty-five years before the enactment of the *statue of elegit* that provision was already made then for seizure of the debtor's land by the creditor upon default. Thus in a bond [30] executed about 1260 we find the formula *obligo omnia bona mea, mobilia et immobilia* followed by the clause giving the obligee the right, upon default by the obligor, to seize the latter's land and receive the profits therefrom until the obligation had been fully satisfied, a procedure which was invariably followed in the case of the Jewish gage in which the formula *obligo omnia bona mea, etc.* originated. A similar provision is found in several other bonds [31] enrolled upon the Close Rolls during the reign of Henry III. In still another bond [32] of about the same time we find a specific provision to the effect that the obligation shall constitute a charge upon the obligor's land even in the hands of a transferee. Obviously, then, the creditor's right in the debtor's land was not unknown in England before 1285. What was new in the *statute of elegit* was the extension of this right to all judgment creditors. It may therefore be said that

---

[29] *Ibid,* II, p. 596.

[30] Madox, *op. cit.,* n. 25, No. 635.

[31] *Calendar of the Close Rolls,* 1259-1261, pp. 463-464; 1264-1268, pp. 395, 504.

[32] *Ibid.,* 1264-1268, p. 521.

this statute and the practices preceding it, which are the basis
of the modern law of execution in England and the United States,
are an outgrowth of the *Jewish gage*.

3. *The Hebrew Odaita and the English Recognizance*

Although under Hebrew law a bond attested by two witnesses gave the creditor a lien on the entire property of the
debtor, good against the whole world except prior lienors, creditors
very often sought further means to facilitate collection of their
debts and to overcome procedural difficulties in their enforcement. One of these was the so-called *Odaita*, literally, confession
or recognizance. It consisted of a formal declaration by the
debtor, before a court of competent jurisdiction, acknowledging
the existence of the debt. The declaration was embodied by the
court in a document attested by it, and had the force of a
judgment.[33]

According to the Talmud, the principle upon which the
validity of this device is based is this: an admission against
interest is as good as the testimony of "a hundred witnesses." [34]
A rule of evidence was thus converted into a means of effecting
and initiating jural relationships between the parties, instead of
merely proving the existence of such relationships.

The debtor's declaration was sometimes made before two
witnesses, rather than before a court, and in such case it was
necessary either for the creditor or the debtor to address the
witnesses and ask them to bear witness to the declaration about
to be made.[35] This safeguard was intended to remove the possibility of the declaration having been made in a jocular manner.

In the twelfth century Maimonides, the great Hebrew phi-
losopher and codifier of Hebrew law, introduced an innovation into the Hebrew law of recognizances or, perhaps, codified
an innovation introduced earlier. He maintained that the re-

[33] Sanhedrin, 29b; Hoshen Mishpat, ch. 39, sec. 7, and ch. 250, sec. 3.
[34] Gittin, 40b.
[35] Hoshen Mishpat, ch. 81, sec. 6.

quirement for the debtor to address the witnesses with the words
"ye be my witnesses, etc." applies only to cases where the declaration is made in the course of a casual conversation. Where the
debtor, on the other hand, makes a true or genuine recognizance
—*hodaah gemurah,* in Hebrew—this requirement may be dispensed with.[36] As a result of this innovation the phrase "make
a true or genuine recognizance" was incorporated in almost every
Hebrew recognizance document.

From a certain passage in the Talmud it appears that
Odaita was in frequent use among Jews during the Talmudic
period.[37] In the post-Talmudic period this form of security became
still more frequent, because, according to some authorities,[38]
when the debt was evidenced by an *Odaita* the consideration for
it could not be inquired into by the court. A totally gratuitous
promise, when made in the form of a declaration of a debt, is
valid and enforceable, according to these authorities; by his
declaration the debtor has precluded himself from attacking the
validity of the debt on any ground. Although the prevailing
opinion [39] is that a gratuitous promise is valid when accompanied by sufficient formality and solemnity, whether made in
the form of a declaration of debt or in the form of an assumption of
an obligation, practical draftsmen sought to remove all doubt by
drafting most of their documents in the form of a declaration. Only
where the declaration form was not feasible, as in the case of a conditional obligation, or of an obligation which could not be reduced to

---

[36] Hoshen Mishpat, ch. 81, sec. 8; Yad Hahazakah, ch. 7. The phrase
"*Hodaah Gemurah*" does not appear in the printed editions of Maimonides's
Code. It appears in Tur's quotation of the passage from Maimonides. A comparison of a large number of quotations from Maimonides's Code, as found in
Tur, has led the writer to believe that the author of Tur had before him a revised
and corrected version of the code. Certain evidence recently found by the writer
points to the conclusion that the phrase *Hodaah Gemurah* did not originate
with Maimonides and that it is of considerably earlier date than his Code.

[37] Baba Kamma, 84b.

[38] Ketubot, 101b, Rashi's commentary *ad loc.;* see also the commentary of
Rabbi Asher b. Yehiel *ad loc.*

[39] Hoshen Mishpat, ch. 40, sec. 1.

a certain sum (such as the promise to support a child for five years) was the form of an assumption of an obligation used.[40]

The Jews of medieval England used the *Odaita*—recognizance form—in practically all documents written in Hebrew and evidencing transactions between Jew and Jew or Jew and Christian.[41] The Hebrew starrs of acquittance, which are the most numerous of all available Hebrew documents of medieval England, and which the writer will discuss later in more detail, all take the form of a recognizance. The introductory phrase in these documents usually reads: "X recognizes a true recognizance"—a phrase which, as we have seen, is characteristic of the Hebrew *Odaita* and is directly traceable to the rule about the formal requisites for the validity of a recognizance. In the Calendar of the Plea Rolls of the Exchequer of the Jews there are virtually hundreds of entries of starrs of acquittance, and in all of these the recognizance form is used. One of the earliest extant documents evidencing a debt by a Christian to a Jew takes the form of a recognizance.[42] In the thirteenth century all the documents evidencing debts owed by Chritians to Jews, take the form of a recognizance. These are found either in full or in abbreviated form in the published records of the Exchequer of the Jews. In a British Museum collection of Hebrew documents, published by the Jewish Historical Society of England, we find a document containing two parallel texts, one in Hebrew and the other in Latin, where the Hebrew phrase *Mode Hodaah Gemurah* is translated *recognosco veram recognicionem*.[43] The Norman-French equivalent of this phrase *reconnusse verreye reconusaunce* is found in Madox's *Formulare Anglicanum*[44] in a document of recognizance, made by a Jew and dated 1275, and

---

[40] See Hoshen Mishpat, ch. 60, sec. 2.

[41] See *e.g.*, Meyer D. Davis, ed., *Hebrew Deeds of English Jews*, Nos. 1, 7, 8, 9.

[42] John H Round, ed., *Ancient Charters*, Pipe Roll Society Publ., X, p. 82.

[43] Abrahams, Stokes and Loewe, *Starrs & Jewish Charters in the British Museum*, pp. 4-5 (1234).

[44] N., 689.

in several documents in the Calendar, etc. In the Madox document the introductory phrase reads: *Jeo ke suy ensele de suz reconnusse verreye reconusanuce et testemoine.* The word *testemoine*—testify—is indicative of the procedural origin of the recognizance. As has already been remarked, the recognizance takes the place of testimony by witnesses, on the principle that an admission against interest is as good as the testimony of a hundred witnesses.

On the origin of the Hebrew recognizance, a document found in the Public Records Office in London and published in Meyer D. Davis's collection of Hebrew documents is particularly illuminating. The document reads: "I, the undersigned, recognize a true recognizance that what is written above in the Latin tongue is true and that I made this starr of acquittance to Prioı Alexander so that it may be in his hands and in the hands of his assigns as proof of their rights even as a hundred witnesses. And what I have acknowledged I have signed, Jacob, son of Samuel."[45] The phrase "even as a hundred witnesses" is clearly an allusion to the Talmudic dictum that an admission against interest is as good as the testimony of a hundred witnesses. From this the recognizance derives its force and validity.

The close resemblance between the form of the Hebrew *Odaita* and that of the recognizance of English law is quite obvious. But the resemblance is not only one of form; it extends to the most fundamental feature of these devices. In the earliest reported cases of recognizances the debtor not only confesses the debt, but also binds his property as security for its payment, a feature which is characteristic of the Hebrew *Odaita,* as well as of other forms of obligation in Hebrew law. Thus in Select Civil Pleas[46] pl. 25 (Hilary Term, 1201), we fiind: "Miles de Hastings owes to Brian, son of Ralph twenty marks; to wit, ten marks on the Octave of Easter and ten marks at the Nativity of St. Mary the Virgin; and thereof [Miles] places in pledge to

---

[45] Davis, *op. cit.,* n. 41, No. 193.
[46] Selden Society Publications, III.

him his land of Hokinton, which he holds of the fee of William de Hastings.' And again in pl. 174 (Octave of Michaelmas, 1202), it is recorded: "John the vintner demands against Ralph the priest of Elmham thirty-six shillings and four pence; and they make a concord to the effect that Ralph shall give (John) two marks of silver (now), and shall pay him one mark within the octave of S. Edmond, and another within the Octave of Mid-lent; and in case he shall not have paid (them) he has put in pledge to (John) all the lands which he holds as of lay fee in Suffolk."

Further, more direct evidence of the Jewish origin of the recognizance and of its effect in giving the creditor a right in the debtor's land, is found in an entry in the Close Rolls [47] which contains the full text of the instrument executed by the obligor, not just a notation of its tenor and import. Both, the obligor and obligee, were Christians, yet the instrument is a perfect specimen of a Jewish bond, giving the creditor the fullest protection possible under Hebrew law and practice. In the first place, it contains the clause *obligo omnia bona mea, mobilia et immobilia, presentia et futura* which, as we have seen, is characteristic of every kind of Hebrew obligation. Secondly, it contains a provision that in case of default by the debtor the creditor shall have the right to seize the debtor's land and hold it until he had been fully paid, a right which was in all respects identical with that of the Jewish creditor under the "Jewish gage." Thirdly, the provision contained in the instrument, that the surety who guaranteed performance be bound as a principal debtor, is one which is found in Jewish bonds in England, and which goes back to early Talmudic times. In an early Talmudic text (*c.* second century) we read: "If a man lent his fellow money on a guarantor's security, he may not exact payment from the guarantor [in the first instance]; but if he said, 'on the condition that I may exact payment from whom I will,' he may exact payment from the guarantor [in the first instance]." [48]

[47] *Calendar of Close Rolls* 1256-1259, p. 493.
[48] Mishna Baba Batra, 10:7.

Later on the two types of undertaking to answer for another's
debt, the one imposing upon the accommodating party a primary
liability and the other imposing upon him a secondary liability,
became so far standardized that they were referred to by two
different names, the former being called *Kabblanut* and the
latter *Arabut,* very much as these same types of undertaking
later came to be called in English and American law by two
different names, *suretyship* and *guarantee.* When the Jews came
to England they applied this distinction, which had become
elementary in Hebrew law, to their transactions with Christians,
and wherever possible they made provision that the accommodating party be primarily liable.[49] This provision, which is
very convenient from the creditor's point of view, was adopted
by Christian creditors, together with the other features of the
Jewish bond, when they entered the business of moneylending.

That Jewish security devices should have been adopted by
the English is not at all surprising. It must be borne in mind
that when the Jews came to England they did not find fixed and
established forms of security which they could use. Moneylending
on a large scale was unknown in England before the arrival of
the Jews. It was the Jew who developed this business, and with
it the instruments through which it was carried on. Under these
circumstances it was almost inevitable that he use forms of
security with which he was familiar, and that these should later
be adopted by moneylenders generally.

In this connection it is interesting to note Pollock and
Maitland's observations on the nature and origin of the recognizance: "The parties go into the chancery or the exchequer and
procure the making of an entry upon the close roll or some other
roll. The borrower confesses that he owes a certain sum which
is to be paid upon a certain day, and grants that, if default be
made, the money may be levied by the sheriff. This practice,

---

[49] Davis, *op. cit.,* n. 41, No. 54. This is an assignment of a debt in which it
is recited that William de Huneworth is the debtor and Roger Michael of Holt
Market is the *kabblan,* i.e., the surety with primary liability.

which is of some importance in the history of the chancery may have its origin in the fact (for fact it is) that some of its officers were moneylenders on a great scale." [50] The close connection between the Exchequer and the Jews is well known. It was a special branch of the Exchequer, the Scaccarium Judeorum, that had jurisdiction over the financial affairs of Jews and over disputes arising between Jew and Gentile. The moneylending barons of the Exchequer apparently adopted the convenient device of the recognizance from their Jewish wards whose business affairs they were charged with supervising. For convenient it certainly was, since it afforded the easiest way of proving the debt and at the same time bound the debtor's property for its payment.

4. *The General Release and the Hebrew Starr of Acquittance*

The General Release is a legal form used by lawyers throughout the United States and England whenever a settlement between the contending parties to a controversy is effected out of court. It is one of the most widely used legal forms.

This form contains some very peculiar language to which hardly anyone pays attention. It states, for instance, that the party giving the release releases and discharges the party to whom the release is given from all claims, demands, etc., "from the beginning of the world" to the day when the release is executed; an obvious exaggeration which calls for explanation. Yet no one, as far as the writer is aware, has ever attempted to trace the origin of this form or to account for its peculiarities. It has become part of the daily routine of office practice, and is taken for granted by those using it without arousing their curiosity.

It can be shown that the General Release is an adaptation of an old Hebrew form, introduced by the Jews of medieval England into their dealings with their Christian neighbors; and this accounts for some of its quaint phraseology.

One of the forms most frequently used by the Jews in

[50] *Op. cit.*, II, p. 204, n. 1.

England was the so-called Starr of Acquittance, the word "starr" being an Anglicized form of the Hebrew word *shtar*. The starr would be executed by the Jewish creditor and delivered by him to his Christian debtor upon payment of the debt owed by the latter to the former.

A large number of such starrs is found in the collection of Hebrew *Shtarot* published by M. D. Davis. Most of these starrs were written in Hebrew, and even when written in Latin or Norman-French they were endorsed in Hebrew by the Jewish creditor, to prevent forgery by the debtor or a plea of forgery by the creditor. In these starrs the creditor, after specifying the debt or claim to which the starr related, would proceed to release the debtor from all other debts "from the creation of the world" to the date of the execution of the instrument, or, sometimes, "to the end of the world." The following is a translation from the Hebrew original of a typical starr of acquittance: "I, the undersigned, recognize a true recognizance that Roger fil. Godward de Sewenington and his heirs are quit from me and my heirs of ten marks and one measure of wheat and of all debts, pledges and challenges from the creation of the world until Pentecost in the 43rd year of the reign of our Lord the King Henry fil. John, and what I have recognized I have signed." [51] The pattern of this starr is exactly like that of the General Release found in fourteenth century documents written in Latin, and in our own time may be found in every formbook used by lawyers through the length and breadth of the United States and England. Both have this outstanding characteristic in common: in

---

[51] Davis, No. 118. It may well be that the General Release is a very old form which, through the Jews, was transmitted from antiquity to modern times. P. Hib. 96 (259 B.C.E.), referred to above (p. 99), is a mutual General Release of all claims "of former times" by two parties to one another. In Tosefta, Kethubot 4:11 (ed. Zuckermandel 265.8f.) there is reference to a form of a release containing the phrase מן קדמת דנה (from before this [time]), which points to the generality of the release. Cf. קודם היום (before this day) in form no. 40 of the Formulary of Rabbi Judah Barzillai, which is probably a translation into Hebrew of the Aramaic מן קדמת דנה.

addition to specifying the claim or debt immediately preceding the execution of the instrument they include all debts, claims, etc., from the beginning or the creation of the world.

The question naturally arises, who copied from whom? Did the Jewish creditors follow a pattern set for them by English draftsmen, translating it into Hebrew, or did the latter copy from the Jews?

Were there no other evidence as to the origin of the starr of acquittance, the fact that Jews for a long time occupied the position of principal financiers in England, and that they had a highly developed system of law and legal forms of their own, would make it reasonable to suppose that, at least in documents written in Hebrew, they used their own forms rather than adaptations of English forms. But one need not rely solely on this circumstancial evidence. The internal evidence from documents used in England, and the evidence from Hebrew sources outside England, is so abundant and convincing as to leave no doubt of the Hebrew origin of the Starr of Acquittance and its counterpart, the General Release.

To begin with, the phrase "from the beginning of the world" suggests a Jewish origin. It is well known that the Jews count the years of their calendar from the creation of the world. The present year, [1955-1956] for example, is 5716, according to Jewish tradition. When the Jewish draftsman wanted to set down a date as far back as possible, it was natural for him to go back to the beginning of the calendar. The exaggeration implict in this phrase was apparently overlooked because of the absolute certainty it afforded in removing all possible future controversies as to the debts and claims to which the acquittance related, including possible claims against the releasee's predecessors in interest.

Secondly, the starrs, as has already been remarked, were usually written in Hebrew, and even when written in Latin they were endorsed by the creditor in Hebrew. The Hebrew equivalent of the phrase, "from the beginning of the world" found in the modern General Release, is *"mibriat ha-olam,"* literally, from the creation of the world. This phrase occurs uniformly in all the Hebrew starrs, while in the Latin releases there are variations. Along with a *creatione seculi,*[52] which is the exact equivalent of the above Hebrew phrase, we find a *principio seculi,*[53] *ab initio seculi,*[54] *a principio mundi*[55] and *ab origine mundi.*[56] The uniformity of the Hebrew phrase, on the one hand, and the variation in the Latin versions, on the other, suggest that the former was the model and the latter were the copies.

Finally, the essential characteristics of the General Release are found in a Hebrew form occurring in a whole series of Hebrew formbooks and responsa of leading Rabbis, beginning with the tenth century—that is, long before the Jews came to England—down through the centuries almost to our own day. In the earlier sources this form is called *Shtar Abizarya*—the word *abizarya* meaning acquittance—and a distinction is drawn between it and the *Shtar Mehila,* the latter being a release of a specific claim or debt. In the later sources it is called *Mehila Kolelet,* which is the exact Hebrew equivalent of the English term "General Release." Under its former name it is found in a recently published fragment of the formbook of Rab Saadia Gaon,[57] where the creditor releases the debtor from all claims and demands *"from the days of the world until now."* Under the same name it appears in the formbook Rab Hai Gaon,[58] where it is very elaborate and very nearly approaches our modern General Release. It also appears, still under the name of *Shtar Abizarya,* in the formbook of Rabbi Judah Barzillai,[59]

[52] Rigg, *Select Pleas,* p. 42.

[53] *ibid.,* p. 72.

[54] *Madox, op. cit.,* No. 142.

[55] *Ibid.,* No. 702.

[56] *Ibid.,* No. 703.

[57] Supplement to *Tarbiz,* publication of the Hebrew University of Jerusalem, I, No. 3, p. 70.

[58] *Tarbiz, ibid.,* p. 22.

[59] No. 4.

and in the *Sefer Haittur* of Rabbi Isaac b. Abba Mari of
Marseilles.[60]

In a thirteenth century case in the responsa of Rabbi Solomon
b. Adreth a similar form was apparently used, but it is no longer
referred to as *Shtar Abizarya*. From the responsum it is evident
that the form under discussion was in general use, and that it
was very comprehensive in scope. Indeed, in the table of contents it is called *Mehila Kolelet*—general release. The responsum
reads, in part, as follows: "Question: R sold a field to S with
warranty. Many years thereafter R and S had again dealings
between them, and S released R from everything and every
obligation, as is customary, and he did not remember the obligation of the warranty at the time when he executed the release.
Is the obligation of the warranty included in the release?" [61]

A little later in the thirteenth century, in the responsa of
Rabbi Asher b. Yehiel,[62] we find reference to a form, the substance of which is that the creditor releases the debtor "from
all demands he had against him to this day" the form itself
not being quoted by the Rabbi, but only its import stated. In
the fourteenth century, in the responsa of Rabbi Nissim Gerondi [63]
and in those of Rabbi Isaac b. Sheshet [64] there is reference in
the text itself to a release which is called *Mehila Kolelet*.

Finally, in a sixteenth-century formbook, compiled by Rabbi
Solomon Jaffe [65] in accordance with the usages prevailing in the
Jewish communities of Constantinople and Salonica, we find a
most polished specimen of this form under the name *Shtar Mehila*.

In order to show concretely the close resemblance between
the form of the General Release now in use in England and in
the United States, and the Hebrew forms that have just been

[60] S. v. Mehilah. See *Tarbiz, ibid.*
[61] Responsa of R. Solomon b. Adret, *sub nomine* Toledot Adam, No. 217.
[62] Ch. 76, sec. 3 & 4.
[63] No. 22.
[64] No. 404.
[65] Tikkun Soferim, No. 50.

mentioned, the writer will quote the material portions from the former and from some of the latter.

The General Release reads, in part, as follows:

> Know all men by these presents, that I . . . . have remised, released and forever discharged, and by these presents do for myself and my heirs, distributees, executors and administrators, remise, release and forever discharge the said . . . his heirs, distributees, executors and administrators, of and from all manner of action and actions, cause and causes of action, suits, debts, dues, sums of money, accounts, reckonings, bonds, bills, specialties, covenants, contracts, controversies, agreements, promises, variances, trespasses, damages, judgments, extents, executions, claims and demands whatsoever, in law and in equity, which against the said . . . I ever had, now have, or which I or my heirs . . . hereafter can, shall or may have for, upon or by reason of any matter cause or thing whatsoever *from the beginning of the world* to the date of these presents, and more particularly . . .

The *Shtar Abizarya* in the formbook of Rab Hai Gaon reads, in part, as follows:

> X son of Y said to us: Ye be my witnesses and accept *"Kinyan"* [a symbolical delivery of some object, ordinarily a kerchief, which confirms the transaction and imparts to it binding legal force] and hand over [the document attesting the transaction] to A son of B, that of my own free will, without duress, [I have made this declaration] that I have received and accepted and have been fully paid everything he owed me, growing out of all there was between us *from the days of the world* until now. . . . And in accordance with what preceded between them, whether partnership or a loan, business transactions or purchase and sale, inheritance or things other than these, one is to

specify accordingly, and then generalize and write of everything that transpires among men: of partnership, of joint venture, of business transactions, of inheritance, of purchase and sale, of deficit and surplus, of profit and loss, of loan and bailment, of pledge and of suretyship, of trespass and of fraud and of all manner and fashion of things in the world. And I cleared and acquitted the above named and his heirs, for myself and my heirs for all generations, of all *claims, challenges* and demands which men may demand of one another.

The introductory paragraph of the *Shtar Mehila* contained in the formbook of Rabbi Samuel Jaffe reads as follows:

Before us, the undersigned witnesses, X, of his own free will, without duress, but wholeheartedly and willingly, made a true, valid and effective recognizance that he has received total and complete satisfaction of all the demands, rights and complaints that he had, or might have had, against Y and his representatives, *from the day the world was created* to the present day, and particularly of such and such a debt, and such and such a demand.

The similarity between the pattern of the General Release, on the one hand, and that of the two Hebrew forms quoted above, on the other, is obvious and needs no further elaboration. But the similarity is not only one of pattern; it extends to some of the most significant terms and clauses of these forms. In his chapter on Releases, sec. 508, Littleton says: "Also, if a man release to another all manner of demands, this is the best release to him to whom the release is made, that he can have, and shall enure most to his advantage." To this Coke, fol. 291b, adds: "Demand, *demandum*, is a word of art, and in the understanding of the common law is of so large an extent, as no other one word in the law is, unless it be *clameum*, whereof Littleton maketh mention, sect. 445."

A mere glance at the Calendar of the Plea Rolls of the Exchequer of the Jews will reveal that both of these terms, *claims* and *demands,* occur in starrs found on almost everyone of its pages, while the Hebrew equivalents of these terms may be found in numerous documents in M. D. Davis's collection of Hebrew *Shtarot.* As in the case of the form itself, and perhaps more convincingly, the question as to which was the model and which the copy, the Hebrew terms or their equivalents in Latin and Norman-French, is answered by a reference to the Rab Hai Gaon form quoted above which dates back to the tenth century, and in which the same Hebrew terms signifying claims and demands, as those found in the Hebrew *Shtarot* in England, occur.

5. *Representation by Attorney in English Law*

In their account of the nature and origin of the legal profession in early English law, Pollock and Maitland, after discussing the pleader, whose plea could be disavowed by the party on whose behalf it was made, state with respect to the attorney as follows:

> "It is otherwise with the attorney, for the attorney represents his principal: he has been appointed, attorned (that is, turned to the business in hand), and for good and ill, for gain and loss (ad lucrandum et perdendum) he stands in his principal's stead. In England and in other countries the right to appoint an attorney is no outcome of ancient folk-law; it is a royal privilege. The King, as is often the case, has put himself outside of the old law: he appoints representatives to carry on his multitudinous lawsuits, and the privilege that he asserts on his own behalf he can concede to others. Already in Glanvill's day everyone who is engaged in civil litigation in the King's court enjoys this right of appointing an attorney. . . ."[66]

The writer believes that in this account of the origin of the

[66] PMH, I, 212-213.

legal profession in England an important element has been left
out of consideration, namely, Jewish law, which prevailed among
the Jews in England prior to their expulsion in 1290, and under
which the appointment of an attorney for the enforcement and
collection of claims is permitted. He has been led to this belief
by the quaint formula *ad lucrandum vel perdendum* by which the
attorney's authority is described. An exact counterpart of this
formula — בין לזכות בין לחובה (whether for gain or for loss) —
occurs in almost every available Jewish form for the appointment
of an attorney [67] and is also mentioned in the Yerushalmi (Palestinian Talmud) in the name of Rabbi Jose b. Hanina (third
century).[68]

In the Jewish form for the appointment of an attorney the
above formula is certainly not due to the vagaries of the legal
draftsman's style. It is not mere surplusage or style embellishment.
There is reflected in it a combination of two rules of Jewish law,
namely, that the attorney is but an agent שליח of the party who
appointed him,[69] and that an agent's authority, unless it is otherwise specifically provided in his authorisation, is limited to acts
which are beneficial to the principal.[70]

It will hardly be maintained that the "for gain or for loss"
formula appearing in a Talmudic source as early as the third century, and reflecting as it does two specific rules of Jewish law,
suddenly reappeared in England in the twelfth century as a result
of mere chance. It seems therefore that we have here an instance
of a Jewish legal formula having been adopted by the English
in the Middle Ages.

In addition to the *ad lucrandum vel perdendum* formula,
there is, in some cases, a further similarity between the Jewish
form for the appointment of an attorney and that which was

---

[67] See, *e.g.*, A. Gulak, *Ozar Hashtaroth*, Nos. 292, 294-299.

[68] PT, Gittin, 5:4. See also Rabinowitz, מדרש לשון הדיום in *Tarbitz*, 22,
194.

[69] BT, Baba Kama 70a; *Mishneh Torah, Sheluhin Veshutafin*, 3, 1.

[70] See BT, Kethubot 99b, Baba Bathra 169b.

used by non-Jews in medieval England. The Jewish form often contains a clause in which it is provided that the attorney shall have the power to appoint another attorney in his place.[71] This provision is in accordance with the rule of Jewish law under which an attorney may not appoint another attorney in his place unless he is specifically authorised to do so.[72] A similar clause is found in some entries upon the Close Rolls during the reign of Henry II, recording the appointment of attorneys *ad lucrandum vel perdendum.*[73]

[71] See Gulak, *ibid.,* Nos. 296, 298.
[72] Mishneh Torah, *ibid.* 3, 8.
[73] See *Calendar of the Close Rolls,* 1268-1272, pp. 281-282, 542.

CHAPTER XIX

WARRANTY OF REAL PROPERTY AND
THE INCHOATE RIGHT OF DOWER

I. *Origin and Purpose of the English Warranty Clause*

In his article *The Gage of Land in Medieval England*,[1] Hazeltine includes warranty of real property among the obligations which, in medieval England, gave the obligee an *in rem* charge upon the obligor's property. When a parcel of real property was conveyed with warranty, all other real property remaining in the hands of the grantor became bound for the "acquittance, defence and warranty" of the grantee, and this charge was not affected by a transfer of the property to a third party. How this came about, that is, how the grantor's personal obligation to "warrant, defend and acquit" the grantee became a charge upon his property, even in the hands of an alienee, is not quite clear.

Nor is this the only feature of the early law of warranty which remains unexplained. In fact, the origin of the English warranty clause itself has never been satisfactorily explained. Pollock and Maitland are in accord with the opinion expressed by Blackstone that warranty was introduced for the purpose of barring the heir of the grantor from denying the validity of his ancestor's grant, made without his, the heir's, consent. They believe that this occurred about the year 1200 when we find that the heir's consent was no longer considered necessary to a valid transfer. To quote from their *History of English Law*:[2] "Blackstone, Comment. ii, 301 says that express warranties were introduced in order to evade the strictness of the feodal doctrine of non-

---

[1] Hazeltine, *The Gage of Land in Medieval England*. Harv. L. Rev., 18, 36.
[2] PMH, 2, 313, n.l.

273

alienation without the consent of the heir.' This, though the word 'feodal' is out of place, we believe to be true. The clause of warranty becomes a normal part of the charter of feoffment about the year 1200."

There are, however, several difficulties in this explanation. In the first place, an examination of a large number of twelfth century charters will reveal that, more often than not, these charters, too, contain warranty clauses.[3] Secondly, a warranty clause is contained in numerous twelfth-century conveyances by religious houses [4] in which there could be no objection raised by an heir. Finally, if the purpose of the warranty clause had been to bar the heir, it would not have taken the form it took. It would have followed the old clauses in the deeds of the Frankish period on the continent [5] and of the Anglo-Saxon period in England.[6] These clauses would have been most fitting for the purpose of barring the heir from contesting the validity of a transfer by his

---

[3] See *e. g., Records of the Templars in England in the 12th Century.* (British Academy, Records of Social and Economic History, 9), 168-9, 245, 257, 259, 275; *Ramsey Cartulary* (Public Records Office, Chronicles and Memorials, no. 79), pp. 30, 150; *Pipe Roll Society* Publ., 17 (1195), 26, 47, 50, 62. Furthermore, in *Pipe Roll Society Publ.,* 17, 157-8 reference is made to the action of *warantia cartae,* which was an action for the enforcement of a warranty, in connection with the levying of fines in court. The fines are dated 1196, and the fact that at that early date there was already a well-established remedy for the enforcement of a warranty, and that this remedy was used in a fictitious action for the purpose of levying a fine, clearly indicates that warranty of real property had been general in England for quite some time before the beginning of the thirteenth century.

[4] See *e.g., Ramsey Cartulary,* 150 (a conveyance by the Abbot of Ramsey, made between the years 1133 and 1160; *Records of the Templars* 245 (an exchange of land between the Templars and Kirkstead Abbey, made in 1162).

[5] See Roziere *Recueil Général des Formules,* 1,71f. The following is a typical clause: "Et si quis vero, aut ego ipsi, aut aliquis de propinquis meis vel qualibet extranea persona, qui contra hanc vindicionem quem ego bona voluntate fieri rogavi, agere conaverit, inferit inter tibi et fisco soledus tantus coactus exsolvat, et quod repetit vindecare non valeat et haec vindicio atque volontas mea perenni tempore firma permaniat."

[6] See Kemble, *Codex Diplomaticus,* Introd. lxiii ff.

ancestor. They attack the problem directly and say, in so many words, that the heir shall not impugn the transfer, whereas the English warranty clause of the thirteenth century accomplishes this purpose by indirection, by imposing upon the heir the positive duty of warranting his ancestor's grant, from which the negative duty of refraining from attack upon it flows.

The writer proposes to show that the classical English warranty clause was copied by the English from the Jews, and that it answered a pressing need which arose when the Jews introduced new security devices into England.

Necessity for the Warranty Device.

The form of security which was most frequently used by the Jews in England was known as the "Jewish gage."[7] This form of security was, as Pollock and Maitland point out,[8] a completely novel institution in England, in that it gave rights in land to a creditor who was not in possession of the land. It was a general lien in favor of the creditor upon all the real property owned by the debtor at the time the debt was incurred. By virtue of this lien the creditor could follow the property into the hands of an alienee who acquired the property after the lien attached to it.[9] Land in England thus became burdened with invisible liens and charges.[10] This situation called for some such device as a warranty when property was transferred by one party to another. For, if the land may be burdened with invisible charges while it remains in the grantor's possession, the grantee will inevitably demand

[7] PMH, 1, 473; 2, 123; Hazeltine, *loc. cit. supra* note 1, See also ch. 18, above.

[8] PMH, 1, 115.

[9] *Select Pleas, Charters and Other Records from the Exchequer of the Jews* (Selden Society Publ, 15) 18, 53, 63.

[10] "Very early in the thirteenth century we may see an abbot searching the register, or rather the chest, of Jewish mortgages at York in quite modern fashion. A little later an abbot of the same house, when buying land, has to buy up many encumbrances that have been given to Jews, but has difficulty in doing so because some of them have been transferred." PMH, 1, 124.

some sort of protection against the risk of being evicted by one
of the grantor's creditors. The Jews, who brought about this situation, had a remedy ready for it in the form of an all-embracing
warranty clause which, as we shall see later, had been known to
them for many centuries prior to their settlement in England, and
was used by them in England, as elsewhere, in every transaction
involving a sale of real property.

The English and the Jewish Warranty Formulae.

The standard formula of the medieval English warranty
clause reads: "Ego et heredes et assignati mei warrantizabimus
acquietabimus et defendemus predicto . . . et heredibus et assig-
natis suit contra omnes homines."[11] Sometimes the words "et
foeminas"[12] are added, and at other times the words "Christianos
et Judeos" are further added, so that the last phrase in the clause
reads: . . . "Contra omnes homines et foeminas, Christianos et
Judeos."[13]

The warranty clause in the Hebrew documents of the Middle
Ages reads, with some minor variations, as follows:

> "And whoever shall come from the four winds of
> the world, man or woman, Jew or Gentile, son or
> daughter, heir or legatee, near or far, who shall
> arise and contrive and make any claim or requisition
> whatsoever on the said William, or his heirs or
> representatives, regarding the said house with the
> court and appurtenances, it will be obligatory upon
> me, my heirs and representatives, to free them and
> protect them against those claimants and to maintain
> their possession of the house, court and appurtenances
> aforesaid, in peace and comfort (peaceably and

---

[11] Madox, *Formulare Anglicanum*, No. 331; *Pipe Roll Society Publ.*, 17,
26, 36, 158, 159, 173, 189.

[12] *Pipe Roll Society Publ.*, V. 10, 93-94; Madox, *ibid.*, No. 315; *Pipe Roll
Society Publ.*, 23, 122-123; 24, 212-213.

[13] Madox, *ibid.*, No. 326; Close Rolls (1268-1272) 262, 301-2, 413.

quietly), on the surety of all my property, landed
or moveable, which I now possess or may in future
acquire."[14]

It is fairly obvious that there is a close similarity between
these two formulae with respect to the enumeration of the possible
contestants. In this respect the Jewish formula, which is considerably longer than the English, has a long history behind it going
back, at least, to the Aramaic papyri of the 5th century B.C.E.,
as will appear from the following example:

> "I shall have no power, I Y, or any sons or female
> or male dependent of mine shall have no power to sue
> son or daughter of yours, brother or sister, female or
> male dependent of yours, or any man to whom you
> may sell this house or to whom you may give it as a
> gift."[15]

The opening phrase of the Jewish formula is traceable to a
certain analysis of warranty found in the Talmud.[16] According to
the Talmud, there are three kinds of warranty: 1) Warranty
against the acts of the grantor himself; 2) warranty against those
claiming through the grantor, such as his heirs or creditors;
3) warranty against "the whole world." A famous tenth century

---

[14] Abrahams, Stokes and Loewe, *Starrs and Jewish Charters in the Brtish
Museum* (1280) 109. For similar clauses see Davis, Hebrew Deeds (Shtaroth)
Nos. 3, 11, 26, 29, 33, 35, 39, 44, 45, 46 (a conveyance by a Jew to a
non-Jew), 48. Substantially the same formula is found in the Formulary of
Rabbi Judah Barzillai (11th century, Spain) No. 26, pp. 45-46. In a deed
of conveyance made at Léon in the year 1053 and published in 4 Révue des
Etudes Juives, 227-229, the warranty clause, in French translation, reads as
follows: 'Et vienne, d'un des quarte coins du monde, fils, fille, frère, soeur,
parent, étranger, successeur ou héritier, Juif ou non-Juif, verbalement ou par
écrit et soulève au sujet de cette vente une contestation quelconque, ses paroles
seront nulles et considérés comme un tesson brisé, qui n'a point de valeur,
á charge pour moi de répousser et rendre vaine toute contestation et réclamation de façon a la maintenir dans son droit d'un maintien complet et d'une
conservation complete."

[15] APC. 25. 9-11.

[16] BT, *Kethubot*, 91b-92a.

Hebrew authority [17]arranges these types of warranty in an ascending order, the lowest on the scale being warranty against the acts of the grantor and the highest being warranty against the whole world. He adds that each type of warranty includes the one or the ones below it on the scale and excludes the one or the ones above it. Thus where a deed contains an express warranty against the acts of the grantor, the other two types of warranty are excluded. Where it contains a warranty against those claiming through the grantor, warranty against the grantor's own acts is included and warranty against the whole world is excluded. Where it contains warranty against the whole world, the other two types are included. The phrase "If anyone should come from the four winds of the world" was apparently intended to convey the idea of a warranty against the whole world. Although this all-inclusive phrase made the specific enumeration of possible contestants superfluous, if not confusing and ambiguous, draftsmen, with the conservatism characteristic of the legal profession, continued to include the enumeration in their formulae.

Influence of the Jewish Formula upon the Structure of the English Warranty Clause

In the light of the above discussion, the phrase "Contra omnes homines et foeminas, Christianos et Judeos" in the medieval English warranty clause becomes intelligible. It was borrowed verbatim from the Jewish warranty clause, and the "omnes homines et foeminas" part of it is, as we have seen above, traceable as far back as the Aramaic papyri of the fifth century B.C.E. This is what the writer had in mind when he said that the English warranty clause bears unmistakable signs of its Jewish origin. For, while it may be difficult to prove that the idea of warranty and the rules flowing out of the warranty clause were borrowed by one system of law from another, since in such matters it is almost impossible to eliminate the possibility of parallel development, the use of such quaint phrases as the one referred to above falls into a differ-

---

[17] Rab Hai Gaon, *Mekah Umimkar*, c. 28.

ent classification. Here this possibility is so remote that it may safely be disregarded.

Having thus shown that at least part of the medieval English warranty clause was borrowed from the Jews, we shall now consider the three operative words of the medieval English warranty clause, "warrantizare, defendere et acquietare," which are to this day found in our deeds in their English form "warrant, defend and acquit." Of these the first one was probably borrowed from the procedure in the action of theft, the *actio furti*, where the common defence was the voucher of a warrantor.[18] "Defendere" and "acquietare," on the other hand, are translations of equivalent Hebrew terms. The term לשפות which corresponds to "acquietare" is found in almost every one of the available Hebrew deeds from Angevin England,[19] and was certainly not borrowed by the Jews from the English, since it is also found in the portion of the warranty clause quoted in the Talmud and referred to above. The equivalent of the term "defendere," להדיח, occurs in several Hebrew deeds from England [20] and in the Formulary of Rabbi Judah Barzillai.[21] Here again, as in the case of the phrase "Contra omnes homines" etc., it is fairly obvious that the English adopted these terms from the Jews.

It should be borne in mind that the warranty clause was not the only legal form which the English adopted from the Jews. The position of the Jews in England during the twelfth and a good part of the thirteenth century was such that it was almost inevitable that they should have exercised an important influence upon the development of English legal forms and devices, which were then in their formative stage. The Jews were the principal financiers and money-lenders in England during that period, and their financial transactions were numerous and involved large amounts of money.[22] They brought with them to England a high-

---

[18] See PMH, II, 663.
[19] See note 14, above.
[20] Davis, *op. cit. supra* note 14, Nos. 3, 5, 11, 26, 29, 33, 35, 39, 52.
[21] See *ibid.*, No. 26.
[22] See PMH, I, 469; II *ibid.*, 118-119.

ly developed system of law and a large number of legal forms and
devices. The idea of warranty was particularly well developed
among them. The analysis of warranty quoted above from the
Talmud is as valid today as it was in the fourth century. In
England there was hardly a transaction among the Jews to which
there was not attached some kind of warranty. To what point of
refinement the Jews of medieval England carried the idea of warranty is illustrated by the following example. Long before the
common law laboriously worked out an adequate method of dealing with an assignment of a chose in action, the Jews of England
were dealing in bonds and recognizances pretty much in the same
way in which banks today deal in commercial paper. Among the
available Hebrew documents from England there are quite a few
assignments of debts. Since the Jewish bond carried with it a
general lien on the real property of the debtor, and therein lay
its main value, the assignor would warrant that there were no
other bonds outstanding against the debtor.[23] This is, of course,
an exact counterpart of a warranty against prior encumbrances
in our modern mortgage.

An interesting bit of evidence of the Jewish origin of the
medieval English warranty clause is found in Y.B. 30 Edw. I
where there is almost contemporary testimony to that effect. At
page 190 Brumpton, J. says: "The word 'defend' was used when
the Jews were in the land, and was first provided to meet their
case." What is true of "defend" is also true of "acquit" and of
warranty in general, although at the end of the thirteenth century
warranty had become so much a part of English law that its
origin had been entirely forgotten. What Brumpton, J. says about
"defend" having been first provided to meet the case of the Jews,
that is, of Jewish debts outstanding against the property being
conveyed, is, of course, entirely in line with what the writer has
said at the beginning of this chapter about the Jews having created
a situation which called for some such device as a warranty.

[23] See e.g., *Calendar of the Plea Rolls of the Exchequer of the Jews*
(published by the Jewish Historical Society of England), III, 206, 207, 208.

Jewish Derivation of the Rules Governing Warranty

Together with the warranty clause some of the important rules governing warranty of real property were borrowed by the English from the Jews. One of these is the rule giving the remote grantee a right to enforce the warranty against the original grantor. Mr. Justice Holmes in his book *The Common Law* devotes a whole chapter of profound learning to the origin of this rule.[24] He traces it to the identification of the heir with his ancestor, which is found in early Roman law as well as in Germanic law, and to the notion that the assign is a quasi-heir. However, the solution of this problem seems to be much simpler than that. The right is traceable to the inclusion of the assign within the scope of the warranty which, as we have seen above, is found in the standard Hebrew warranty clause and goes as far back as the Aramaic papyri of the fifth century B.C.E. English conveyancers simply borrowed this feature of the warranty clause together with the rest of the clause.

Furthermore, the inclusion of assigns within the scope of the warranty was rendered necessary by the introduction of the "Jewish gage" which, as we have seen above, constituted a general lien upon the debtor's real property. If an owner of real property could be divested of his property through the enforcement of a lien created by a party other than his immediate grantor, it was natural to provide him with a remedy over against that party.

It is true, as Mr. Justice Holmes has pointed out, that Bracton speaks in several places of the assign as "quasi-heres," and explains his right to enforce the warranty on this ground. But this is probably a bit of medieval scholasticism attempting to find a formal ground for a rule dictated by practical considerations.[25]

---

[24] Holmes, *The Common Law* (1881), 371-409.

[25] *Ibid.,* 373-374. Holmes quotes Bracton, fol. 176, to the effect that assigns had the right to sue the original grantor on the warranty only where they were named in the warranty clause, that is, where the warranty ran to the grantee, his heirs and assigns. This would seem to indicate that the practice of including assigns within the scope of the warranty preceded the rule

It seems to the writer that the assign's right to sue the original grantor on his warranty was, at least in Hebrew law, based upon the same principle as that of the remote holder of negotiable paper to sue the maker. Warranty of real property is a perfectly natural intermediate step between the strictly personal nonassignable obligation and the impersonal freely transferable negotiable instrument. When negotiable instruments came into vogue among the Jews, the difficulty which Jewish jurists saw in their enforcement was that the obligation seemingly ran to an unknown person. It was argued that the instrument should be invalid for lack of definiteness, which is a necessary requisite of every enforceable obligation. However, a great thirteenth century Jewish jurist held that where the obligee is ascertainable in the future, although he is unknown at the time the instrument is drawn, the requirement of definiteness is fully satisfied.[26] In support of his opinion, interestingly enough, the learned Rabbi cited the Biblical case of Saul offering a reward to whomsoever will defeat Goliath. In the case of a warranty running to the grantee and his assigns, Jewish jurists apparently saw no difficulty because the warranty could be enforced only by one who was the owner of the property, and this was considered a sufficient description of the obligee to satisfy the requirement of definiteness.

That some such notion also prevailed among Englishmen may be seen from the warranty clause in a certain charter dated 1202. This warranty clause reads: "I, the aforesaid Roger and my heirs, will finally warrant to the aforesaid Peter and his heirs, or to

giving them a right to sue the original grantor, and that the courts only recognized the validity of a device which had been introduced by conveyancers.

It seems that at the time when warranty of real property was introduced in England in the twelfth century, the civil law maxim of *Alteri nemo stipulari potest* had not yet been adopted in England. Conveyancers therefore saw no difficulty in making the warranty run to assigns who were not parties to the transaction between the grantor and the grantee. Bracton's theory of the assign being a quasi-heir may have been prompted by a desire on his part to reconcile the assign's right to sue on the warranty with the above maxim of the Roman law.

[26] Responsa of Rabbi Asher ben Yehiel, 68, 9.

whomever they give, sell or assign them, against all men and women; and this my charter becomes for them a warranty even as to the aforesaid Peter".[27] The assigns are thus put on a par with the grantee with regard to the warranty. Their right, like his, is based upon the charter, that is, upon the promise running to them directly, and not upon the promise to the grantee by representation.

We shall now return to a consideration of the rule that the obligation of the warranty constitutes an *in rem* charge upon the property of the warrantor. This rule is easily explainable if we assume the Hebrew origin of the English warranty. It is a cardinal principle of the Hebrew law of obligations that every obligation, whether originating in a loan of money [28] or in a warranty incidental to the conveyance of real property [29] or in the endowment of the wife by the husband, when embodied in a writing executed in the presence of at least two witnesses, carries with it a general lien upon all of the obligor's property. This principle is known in Hebrew law as "ahrayut," a word which denotes what is probably the most fertile concept in Hebrew law. Freely rendered, it means that all of the obligor's property stands surety for the discharge of the obligation assumed by him.

[27] See Adler, *Jews in Medieval England* 263-266, where the original is copied in full and translated from a manuscript preserved in the Library of St. Paul's Cathedral.

The writer's attention has been called to the English practice whereby the granttee of land received the accumulation of deeds which his grantor had received from his predecessors; and it has been suggested that this practice strengthens the analogy between the right of the holder of a negotiable instrument to sue on the instrument and that of the assign to sue on the warranty.

The writer wishes to add that the language of the warranty clause quoted in the text seems to bear out the above suggestion. It was apparently contemplated by the parties that if the grantee should transfer the property to another, the assign would receive the original deed, and that his right to sue the original grantor on the warranty would be predicated upon his holding of that deed.

[28] Mishnah, Baba Bathra, 10:8.

[29] BT, Baba Metzia, 15b.

There is not a single Hebrew writing of an obligatory nature which does not have "ahrayut" attached to it. What is more, "ahrayut" is implied in law even when it is omitted from the writing. In the language of the Talmud [30] the omission is presumed to be an error of the scrivener. In all of the available Hebrew deeds of conveyance from England there is not a single one which does not carry a warranty, and there is not a single warranty which does not carry with it a charge on the warrantor's property, movable and immovable, present and future. It was this idea of "ahrayut," borrowed by the English from the Jews together with the warranty clause, which was responsible for the rule that a warranty creates an *in rem* charge upon the property of the warrantor.[31]

II. *Origin of the Inchoate Right of Dower*

This brings us to consideration of the inchoate right of dower. Briefly stated, it is the contingent right which a woman has, during her husband's lifetime, to have a life estate in one-third of the real property which her husband owned during coverture set off to her, if she should survive him. Hazeltine, with a great deal of insight, puts this right of the married woman in the same class with the right of the grantee to enforce a warranty, as constituting an *in rem* charge upon land in medieval England. But he was unaware of the fact that these apparently disconnected rules of law are traceable to one common source and spring from one root-idea, namely, that of "ahrayut."

A comparison of English medieval law and practice with

---

[30] *Ibid.*

[31] An interesting document, showing the close relationship between the English warranty clause and its Hebrew equivalent, is found in Madox, *op. cit. supra note* 11, No. 119 (1287). The grantor, after stating that he is bound to warrant, defend and acquit the grantee, proceeds to state that in case of failure on his part to do so, all his property, *movable and immovable, present and future,* shall be bound for the payment of the damages the grantee may sustain by reason of such failure. This, it will readily be seen is an almost perfect specimen of a Hebrew warranty clause with 'ahrayut.' Cf. documents cited in note 14 above.

Hebrew law and practice, ancient and medieval, on the same subject will, the writer believes, make this abundantly clear. Pollock
and Maitland have this to say about the wife's rights during
marriage in the twelfth and thirteenth centuries:

> The unspecified dower is therefore treated as a charge
> on all the husband's lands, a charge that ought to be
> satisfied primarily out of those lands which descend
> to the heir, but yet one that can be enforced, if need
> be, against the husband's feoffees. If, however, we go
> back to Glanvill, we shall apparently find him doubt-
> ing whether, even in the case of a specified dower,
> a widow ought ever to attack her husband's feoffees,
> at all events if the heir has land out of which her
> claim can be satisfied.

> Some hesitation about this matter was not unnatural,
> for our law was but slowly coming to a decision of
> the question whether and how the land burdened
> with dower can be effectually alienated during the
> marriage. The abundant charters of the twelfth cen-
> tury seem to show that, according to common opinion,
> the husband could not as a general rule bar the
> wife's right without her consent, that he could bar it
> with her consent, and that (though this may be less
> certain) her consent might be valid though not given
> in court.[32]

It appears from the above quotation that the rule giving the
wife a charge upon her husband's property for the enforcement
of her dower developed slowly in England, and that the common
opinion in the twelfth century was in advance of that of the
judges in this respect. While Glanvill was still hesitating about
the widow's right to claim dower in lands conveyed by her
husband during his lifetime, the practice of obtaining the wife's
consent to a grant by her husband, for the purpose of barring
her right of dower, had become general.

[32] PMH II, 423-424.

As for the Jews, this practice prevailed among them for at least a thousand years prior to their settlement in England. A rule ascribed by the Talmud [33] to Simeon B. Shatech (first century B.C.E.) subjects all of the husband's property to a charge in favor of the wife for the enforcement of her dower rights. As a result of this rule the practice developed to have the wife release her dower rights in the property which the husband was about to convey. Such a release is mentioned already in the Mishna.[34]

Among the Jews of medieval England the practice continued in pretty much the same way as in Talmudic times. Among the available Hebrew deeds of conveyance in England, from Jew to Jew and from Jew to non-Jew, there are hardly any which are not accompanied by a release by the grantor's wife.[35] The adoption by the English of the above practice would have been sufficient to give rise to the rule that where there was no release by the wife the property conveyed by the husband during his lifetime remained subject to dower. There is also strong evidence to the effect that the formula of the Jewish "Kethuba," or endowment document, binding all of the husband's property for the payment of the dower, was similarly adopted by the English. In Blackstone, v. II, p. 134, note p, we read: "When the wife was endowed generally . . . the husband seems to have said, 'with all my lands and tenements I thee endow,' and then they all became liable to her dower. When he endowed her with personality only, he used to say, 'with all my worldly goods' (or, as the Salisbury ritual has it, 'with all my worldly chattel') 'I thee endow'." These formulae, which were used for the purpose of creating a charge upon the husband's property in favor of the woman, are strikingly similar to that part of the

---

[33] BT, *Kethuboth*, 82b. See also p. 42, above.

[34] Mishnah, *Kethuboth* 10:6. A release by the seller's wife is also contained in an Aramaic deed of conveyance from the Region of the Dead Sea, dated in "the third year of the freedom of Israel". See Revue Biblique 61 (1954), 182ff., and the writer's comments thereon in BASOR 136, 15f.

[35] See e.g., Davis, *op. cit. supra note* 14, Nos. 29, 44, 50, 100.

Hebrew "Kethuba," which was used for the same purpose and which reads as follows: "I take upon myself and my heirs the responsibility of this marriage contract, . . . so that all this shall be paid from the best part of my property, real and personal, that I now possess or may hereafter acquire." [36]

It is true that while this similarity is very suggestive, it is not conclusive of the Hebrew origin of the English formulae. There is, however, one bit of evidence, again in the form of a quaint phrase no one has hitherto thought necessary to explain, which tells the story most eloquently. In his chapter on Dower, sections 48 and 49, Littleton describes a certain kind of dower, which he calls "*Dowment de la pluis beale*" and which, he says, would arise under the following circumstances: A man died seised of certain land, part of which he held of one lord by knight's service and the other part of another in socage. He left a widow and a son under age. The lord under whom the deceased held by knight's service entered upon the land, held under him, as guardian in chivalry, and the widow entered upon the other land as guardian in socage. If the widow brought a writ of dower against the guardian in chivalry he could plead the above matter, "and pray that it may be adjudged by the court that the wife may endow her selfe de la pluis beale, i. e. of the most faire of the tenements which she hath as guardian in socage."

Why, it may be asked, was the widow to endow herself of the fairest part of the land? Was this an act of chivalry toward the lady on the part of the guardian in chivalry? This might have been so had he offered her part of what he himself held in guardianship, but not when he insisted that she obtain her dower from the land which was held by her husband in socage, and of which she herself was the guardian.

The writer believes that only a reference to the Hebrew

[36] Jewish Encyclopedia, 7, 472. See also, Maimonides, *Yad Ha-chazaka, Yibbum Ve-chaliza*, 4, 33, for the full text of the Jewish "Kethuba," and McClintock & Strong, *Cyclopedia of Biblical, Theological and Ecclesiastical Literature*, 5, 776, for an English translation.

"Kethuba" formula quoted above will furnish the answer. It will be recalled that this formula states that the woman is to be paid from "the best part" of her husband's property, a phrase which is almost identical with Littleton's "de la pluis beale." Littleton's phrase is aparently a relic of the old English endowment formula which was copied from the Jewish "Kethuba." It did not come into existence by accident, just as the equivalent Hebrew phrase did not find its way into the "Kethuba" by accident. The Hebrew phrase has a long history behind it, and the reason for its insertion in the "Kethuba" is to be found in a certain rule of the Hebrew law of execution going back to the time of the Mishna, that is, at least to the second century. In Mishna Gittin, 5, 1 we read: "Compensation for damage is paid out of property of the best quality, a creditor out of land of medium quality, and a woman's kethubah out of land of the poorest quality."

It should be added by way of explanation that the term "n'zikin" in the original, which the translator renders by the English term "damage," means damage resulting from a tortious act. The rule of the above Mishna, therefore, is that a judgment creditor of a tortfeasor is to collect from property of the best quality; a lender, who became a creditor voluntarily, is to collect from property of medium quality; and the woman is to collect her dower from the poorest quality, since, in the words of the Talmud, she is more anxious to get married than the husband is.

In order to overcome this rule of the Mishna, placing the woman in an inferior position, it became customary among the Jews to insert in the "Kethuba" a definite provision to the effect that the woman is to collect her dower from the best part of her husband's property. The English apparently copied this provision from the Jews together with other provisions of the Hebrew "Kethuba."

III Conclusion

The warranty clause in the conveyance of real property was introduced in England by the Jews in substantially the same form in which it had been used by them for many centuries prior to their settlement in England. Some of the elements of this clause are of great antiquity.

The rule of Anglo-American law giving the remote grantee a remedy against the original grantor for the enforcement of the warranty is traceable to the inclusion of assigns within the scope of the warranty, a feature which is characteristic of the Hebrew warranty clause as well as of the warranty clause in the Aramaic papyri of the fifth century B.C.E. Similarly, the rule that gave the grantee an *in rem* charge upon the property of the grantor for the enforcement of the warranty is traceable to a rule of the Hebrew law of obligations which provides for such a charge in favor of the obligee, as an incident of every obligation embodied in a written document and executed with certain required formalities.

The inchoate right of dower, which gives the widow a charge upon all the real property owned by her husband during coverture, is of similar origin. The endowment document was treated in Hebrew law, as well as in Egyptian law of the Ptolemaic period, like any other obligation, so that it gave rise to a charge upon the husband's property in favor of the wife, and the Hebrew "Kethuba" states so specifically. The English adopted this feature of the Hebrew "Kethuba" together with some of its other provisions. The most definite trace of Hebrew influence upon the development of the English endowment document is found in the medieval English dower *de la plus beale,* which originated in a provision in the Hebrew "Kethuba" giving the wife the right to collect her dower from the best part of her husband's property.

CHAPTER XX

THE COMMON LAW MORTGAGE AND THE CONDITIONAL BOND

The classical mortgage of the common law takes the form of an absolute conveyance of the mortgaged property, with a defeasance clause providing that upon payment of the mortgage debt on the due date the property is to revert back to the mortgagor.[1] This form of mortgage goes back, at least, to the 12th century, and contrary to the prevailing view, was certainly in general use by the middle of the 13th century.[2] Originally,

[1] PMH, v. 2, 122-123.

[2] Hazeltine has traced it only as far back as 1230, to pl. 458 in Bracton's Note Book. See his *Gage of Land in Medieval England* (1904) 17 Harv. L. Rev. 549, 557, n. 1. Pollock and Maitland, *loc cit. supra* note 1, apparently place its beginning after the 13th century, although in a note they say: "It is very possible that this form of gage, the conditional feoffment, had been in use from an early time, but that text-writers found little to say of it, because it fell under the general doctrine of conditional gifts." But these great historians of English law apparently overlooked the fact that this type of mortgage underwent two distinct stages of development, and that the first stage, in which two instruments were used, reaches as far back as the time of Henry II. No. 509 in Madox, Formulare Anglicanum (temp. Henry II) clearly represents a transaction of this type. It is an agreement between mortgagor and mortgagee that within 2½ years from the date of the instrument the mortgagor or his brothers or nephew may redeem the property, and that upon their failure to do so the property is to remain to the mortgagee *in accordance with his charter*. "Et nisi poterimus ad istud terminum terram illam emere, teneat praedictus Toma... sicut carta sua testatur..." Obviously, two instruments, a charter of feoffment and an agreement of repurchase, were used in this transaction. What the writer cannot understand is that Pollock and Maitland cite this instrument as an instance of what they call the "Bractonian mortgage," under which a term of years was turned into a fee upon the mortgagor's failure to

the transaction would take the form of two separate instruments, one an absolute charter of feoffment, and the other providing for a defeasance of the conveyance upon payment of the mortgage debt.[3] Later on it became customary to include both, conveyance and defeasance, in the same instrument.[4] In the earlier stage of the development of this form of mortgage the charter of feoffment and the instrument of defeasance were usually delivered to a third party, "in equal hand," to be turned over to the lender in case of non-payment of the mortgage debt on the due date, or to be returned to the borrower in case of payment. This last feature of the early development of the classical English mortgage has been entirely overlooked by writers on the subject, although it appears quite frequently in entries on the Close Rolls

pay the mortgage debt. The above quotation from the instrument shows beyond any doubt that a charter of feoffment was delivered to the mortgagee, or perhaps to a third party, simultaneously with, or prior to, the execution of that instrument.

Holdsworth, *A History of English Law* (3rd ed. 1923) V. 3, 130, referring to the classical English mortgage, says: "It gained in popularity from the 14th century onwards." And in note 3 he adds: "This fact can be illustrated from the forms of conveyance printed in Madox Form. In 1255 (No. 230) we have a mortgage of the older type made by a lease for fifteen years. In Edw. III's reign the custom seems to have been to employ two deeds... In 1401 only one deed is used, and the condition is indorsed on the deed... 19 Hy. VI we get a mortgage in modern form." But the cases cited in note 3 *infra,* show that this type of mortgage was prevalent in the 13th century, and that the custom of employing two deeds goes well beyond the reign of Edw. III. Indeed, there is almost contemporary testimony to the prevalence of the classical English mortgage in the 13th century. In Rye v. Tumby, 8 Edw. II, 36, 38, which was a case involving a mortgage in the form of two separate instruments, there is the following statement: "In past times men were often wont to make such covenants and conditions."

[3] Madox, *Formulare* (ca. 1248) No. 631; *Calendar of The Close Rolls,* 1261-1264, pp. 310-311; 1264-1268, pp. 105, 385-386, 391-392, 525; 1272-1279, pp. 332, 413, 415, 421, 428.

[4] Madox, *Formulare* (1401) No. 579. The defeasance is indorsed on the back of the charter of feoffment. In (1448) No. 589 the defeasance clause is on the face of the charter, as in our modern mortgage.

during the latter part of the reign of Henry III and during the
reign of Edward I.[5]

The origin of this obviously artificial device, which does not
correspond either to the true economic significance of the transaction or to the intention of the parties has never been satisfactorily explained. Nor is the reason for it quite apparent. Why
should a mortgage, given to secure a debt, take the form of an
immediate and absolute conveyance of the mortgaged property,
when what is intended is a forfeiture of the property to take
effect in the future in the case of non-payment of the mortgage
debt?

[5] In all of the entries cited in note 3 *supra,* from Close Rolls, 1261-1264
and 1264-1268, as well as in those at pp. 421 and 428 of 1272-1279, the "equal
hand" is specifically mentioned. In the three other entries there is no mention of
a deposit with a third party, but this does not necessarily mean that there was
no such deposit in these cases. See also Y. B. 21 & 22 Edw. I, p. 222, and
Rye v. Tumby, note 2 *supra.* In the former case, which was an action of novel
disseisin, the defendant's answer is recorded as follows: "B came and said that
he (Adam) could not have an action; for the reason that Adam had pledged
the said tenements to him for 40£ to be paid on two certain days, viz., 20£
on such a day, and the other 20£ at such a day; and that, if he failed in
payment at the days fixed, the land should remain to B and his heirs in fee;
and that in pursuance thereof he made a charter of feoffment, which was
deposited with an umpire, to be delivered to him to whom it ought to be
delivered after the days were passed..."

Reference to a conditional conveyance, probably by way of security for
a loan, in which the instruments were delivered to a third party, is also contained
in the following entry on the Pipe Rolls: Prior de Kenillewurda debet c. s. pro
habendo judicio de Flechamsteda secundum cartas suas quas Templarii tenent."
Pipe Roll Society Publ. v. 2 (n. s.), p. 128 (1191). The treasury of the
Templars was often used as the depositary, the "equal hand," in such conditional
conveyances by way of security for loans. In the document cited above from
Close Rolls, 1264-1268, pp. 385-386, 391-392, there is the following recital:
"Carta vero feoffamenti quam idem ... habet de dicto ... super dictis maneriis
in equali manu de consensu partium ad Novum Templum Lond' liberetur." A
similar recital is also contained in Close Rolls, 1261-1264, pp. 310-311. See also
Calendar of the Charter Rolls, v. 1 pp. 72, (1228), 73 (1228), 438 (1255), and
Calendar of The Plea Rolls of the Exchequer of The Jews, v. 3, pp. 283-284,
for references to deposits with the Templars of cash and documents in conditional transactions of various kinds.

This strange form of the common law mortgage becomes still more puzzling when we compare its pattern with that of the conditional or penal bond and find a striking similarity between them. The conditional bond contains in itself the same logical twist as that involved in the common law mortgage. Instead of the conditional obligation it is intended to be, with the obligation emerging upon the happening of a certain contingency, it takes the form of an absolute obligation which is to become void in case of the non-occurrence of the contingency upon which the obligation is made to depend.[6]

As far as the writer is aware no one has ever called attention to this similarity of pattern between the mortgage and the conditional bond. Yet it is exactly this similarity which has led the writer to what he believes to be the clue to the whole situation. For, upon investigation, it appears that not only is the conditional bond, in the form in which it has come down to us, similar in pattern to the mortgage, but that its course of development has also been the same as that of the mortgage.

In order to trace the origin of the two devices under discussion it will be necessary for the writer to make a little excursus into Talmudic law. There is in Talmudic law a certain doctrine, very vaguely stated, which has given rise to a whole literature in post-Talmudic Hebrew lore. This doctrine is known as "asmakhta" and relates to conditional conveyances and obligations. In a terse phrase, characteristic of the Talmud, the rule is laid down that "asmakhta" is not valid. But what "asmakhta" is, that is, wherein its flaw consists, is a matter of lively dispute among post-Talmudic Hebrew authorities. Various theories have been offered as to the nature of "asmakhta," and as to the reason for its ineffectiveness. These will be discussed later. But in order to introduce the reader to the subject several concrete cases in which the doctrine is said to be applicable will be cited here from the Talmud.

A and *B* enter into a purchase and sale agreement, and *A*,

---

[6] See Blackstone, *Commentaries upon the Laws of England,* v. 2, 340.

the buyer, hands *B*, the seller, earnest money. They stipulate that in case of a breach by *A* his earnest money shall be forfeited, and in case of a breach by *B* he is to return to *A* double the amount of the earnest money. Rabbi Jose says: the agreement is binding. Rabbi Judah says: the agreement is not binding. Such is the substance of an early text, quoted in the Babylonian Talmud. In discussing this text the Talmud classifies the transaction as an "asmakhta," and says that Rabbi Jose holds that "asmakhta" is valid, while Rabbi Judah holds that it is not valid.[7]

A loans money to *B* on the security of a field, and *A* says to *B*: "If you do not repay the loan within 3 years, the field shall be mine." The field is *A*'s, if the loan is not repaid within the time agreed upon. This, again, is the substance of an early text, which is followed by an elaborate discussion in the Babylonian Talmud.[8] The conclusion of the Talmud is that *B*'s stipulation, upon its face, is an "asmakhta," and that therefore it ought not to be binding. In order to reconcile this text with their view of "asmakhta" the Talmudists assert that the text has reference to a case where *B* said to *A* "kni meakhshav," that is, acquire from now. As to the exact meaning of the cryptic phrase "kni meakhshav" opinions vary among post-Talmudic authorities. Rashi, the famous 11th century commentator of the Talmud, holds that the phrase means an actual present sale of the property with an option to repurchase, while others hold that the mere inclusion of the phrase "from now" in the forfeiture formula saves the transaction from the infirmity of "asmakhta."

A, the owner of a field, leased the field to *B* under a crop-sharing agreement, and *B* let the field lie fallow. *B* must pay to *A* the value of his share of the crops which the field would have produced had it been cultivated. To this the Talmud adds that if *B* had stipulated to pay a thousand "zuz" in case of his failure to cultivate, that is an amount in excess of the actual loss

---

[7] *Baba Metzia,* fol. 48b.
[8] *Ibid.,* 65b *et seq.*

to *A,* the stipulation would not have been binding because of "asmakhta."[9]

A paid part of a debt he owed to *B.* They deposited the bond with a third party under an agreement by the terms of which the third party was to return the bond to *B,* enabling him to recover the full amount named therein, if *A* should fail to pay the balance of the debt within a specified time. Rabbi Jose says: the agreement is valid. Rabbi Judah says: it is not valid. Here again the reason given by the Talmud for Rabbi Judah's holding is "asmakhta."[10]

Finally, *A* deposited with the court the documents upon which his case rested, agreeing that if he did not appear again within a certain time, these should be null and void. This agreement is binding, although it is an "asmakhta," but only when made before a prominent court, and where *A*'s failure to appear is not due to unavoidable circumstances.[11] It should be added here that there is an important body of opinion holding that the rule in this case is one of procedure, and that it applies only to stipulations made in court in connection with the conduct of a trial.[12]

These are the main cases, dealing with "asmakhta," which are mentioned in the Talmud. Among post-Talmudic Hebrew authorities two major trends of thought are discernible with regard to this doctrine. One, represented by Rav Hai Gaon[13] and Maimonides,[14] is that the flaw of "asmakhta" consists in the futurity of the conveyance or of the emergence of the obligation. According to these authorities a conveyance or an obligation in order to be valid must take effect immediately upon the performance of the act in law which is to give rise to it. If a conveyance is made or an obligation assumed to take effect in

[9] *Ibid.,* 104a-104b.
[10] *Baba Bathra,* 168a.
[11] *Nedarim,* 27a-27b.
[12] Rif (Rabbi Isaac Alfassi) on Baba Bathra, ch. 10.
[13] *Mekach Umemkar,* ch. 17 (Vienna, 1810).
[14] *Yad Hachazakah* (Code of Hebrew Law), *Mekhirah,* ch. 11, sec. 18.

the future upon the happening of a contingency which is to occur after the act in law is performed, the conveyance or the obligation is not valid. In other words, a conditional transaction is valid only when the condition is subsequent, and not when it is precedent.

The other trend of thought, represented by Rashi,[15] Ri,[16] and Rabbi Solomon ben Adreth,[17] is that the flaw of "asmakhta" consists in the fact that the conveyance is made, or the obligation assumed, as a penalty for the non-compliance with an undertaking to which it is collateral. There is lacking, according to these authorities, that finality of determination which is requisite for the validity of an act in law, since the intention of the party purporting to make the conveyance, or to assume the obligation, is to fulfill his main undertaking, and not to effect a transfer of his property, or an assumption of an obligation, other than his main obligation. In the case of a mortgage with a forfeiture

---

[15] *Commentary on Baba Metzia,* 48b, s.v. *Asmakhta kanya.*

[16] *Tosaphoth on Baba Metzia,* 66a, s.v. *Uminyomi.*

[17] *Responsa of Rabbi Solomon ben Adreth,* no. 933 (Lemberg, 1811). This theory of the nature of "asmakhta" finds confirmation in the light of modern research, which has revealed that throughout the ancient Orient penalty clauses were generally incorporated in agreements of every kind and description. See Blau, *Monatsschrift für die Wissenschaft des Judentums,* v. 69, p. 139f. Blau was first to call attention to the connection between the doctrine of "asmakhta" and the penalty clauses in Assyro-Babylonian deeds. But his assertion that the doctrine is confined to the Babylonian Talmud, and that it was unknown among the Jews of Palestine is obviously incorrect, since it is definitely mentioned in the Palestinian Talmud under the name "izzumim". See Lieberman, *Greek in Jewish Palestine* (1942) 4, and authorities there cited. See also Palestinian Talmud, Baba Bathra, c. 10. sec. 5.

Viewed in this light the cryptic statement in the Babylonian Talmud, Baba Metzia, 66b, that "every if is not valid" becomes intelligible. The word "if" in this statement is used as a *terminus technicus,* and the statement should be rendered in English as follows: "Every 'If' clause is not valid," that is every clause providing for a penalty, if the main undertaking is not fulfilled, is not valid. See Beth Joseph on Tur Choshen Mishpat, c. 207, sec. 18, for a discussion of the difficulty involved in this statement when the word "if" is understood in its literal non-technical sense.

clause, for example, the intention of the mortgagor is to undertake to pay the mortgage debt, and not to effect a conveyance of his property. The forfeiture clause is intended as a penalty for the non-payment of the debt, and therefore it is not valid. Only where there is a present sale of the property with an option of repurchase is the transaction valid. The test for distinguishing between a true conditional sale and a mortgage is, according to Rashi,[18] the existence of a debt. If the party receiving the money is bound to repay it, at the option of the party parting with it, even after the time fixed by the agreement has expired, so that the risk of destruction and depreciation of the property falls upon the former, the transaction is a mortgage, and not a conveyance. But where the repayment of the money is optional with the party receiving it, and the party parting with it bears the risk of loss and depreciation, the transaction is a true conditional sale. Such, in broad outline, is the doctrine of "asmakhta," as expounded by the leading authorities in Hebrew law.

Let us now see how all this bears upon our problem of the origin of the English mortgage and the conditional bond. Maimonides in his Code of Hebrew Law [19] cites the following device which was used by the "sages of Spain" for the purpose of removing the flaw of "asmakhta" from conditional obligations. The obligor would undertake an immediate and absolute obligation, and the obligee, on his part, would undertake to release the obligor upon the non-occurrence of the contingency upon which the obligation was to depend. The doctrine of "asmakhta" not being applicable to releases and defeasances, this device accomplished the purpose of a conditional obligation in a legally valid manner by inverting the condition and attaching it to the release instead of the obligation. This device, in a slightly different form,

---

[18] *Commentary on Baba Metzia*, 66b, *s. v. Meakhshav kni.*

[19] *Loc. cit. supra* note 14. See Sma on Choshen Mishpat, ch. 207, sec. 45, where it is said that two separate undertakings, embodied in two separate instruments, are necessary in order to remove from the transaction all appearance of "asmakhta."

is also mentioned in a responsum by Rabbi Joseph Ibn Miggash,[20] Maimonides' master.

From Maimonides' language it appears that the device described by him had been in common use among the Spanish Jews long before he wrote his code. Considering the leading position of the Spanish rabbis of the time among the Jews of Europe, it is quite likely that this device was adopted by the Jews of England and used by them in their dealings among themselves and with their Christian neighbors. Indeed, there is direct proof that this device was used by the Jews of England as early as the latter part of the 12th century. A deed, dated 1183, recites that William of Tottenham acknowledges that he owes a hundred marks of silver to Avigaia, the Jewess of London, and Abraham, her son, at Martinmas, for which he undertook to pay them 13½ per cent interest. If at Christmas following he pays them 40 marks, the remainedr of the debt is to be reckoned at only 40 marks, on which he is to pay them 25 per cent. And if he fails to pay the 40 marks at Christmas, the debt is to remain a hundred marks.[21] Apparently, the amount of money actually loaned was 80 marks, and the additional amount of 20 marks was intended as a penalty for non-payment of the install-ment of 40 marks on the due date. This, it may readily be seen, is the Maimonides device, adapted to the special circumstances of the transaction. The essential characteristic of that device, namely that what is intended as a penalty for the non-per-formance of an undertaking appears as an absolute obligation with a condition subsequent, is obviously present in this trans-action.

At a somewhat later period, in the middle of the 13th century, we find reference to this device in the responsa of Rabbi Solomon ben Adreth, a leading authority of Barcelona, Spain. In one of these responsa [22] he discusses a case in which 2 bonds

---

[20] Responsa of Rabbi Joseph Ibn Miggash, No. 97 (Warsaw, 1870).

[21] Round, *Ancient Charters* (Pipe Roll Society Publ. v. 10) 82.

[22] Responsa of Rabbi Solomon ben Adreth *sub nomine* Toldoth Adam, No. 242.

of 1000 denarim each, were deposited, one by each of 2 parties, with a third party, to be delivered by the depositary to one of the parties in case of a breach of certain conditions by the other. The question was raised whether or not the transaction suffered from the flaw of "asmakhta." The rabbi decided that it was entirely free from "asmakhta," adding that such transactions were everyday occurrences, and that "the sages of past generations did not refrain from holding such transactions valid." In another responsum [23] by the same rabbi we find a case in which an instrument containing an absolute obligation, "without any condition or reservation," together with a release containing a condition, was delivered to a depositary, and again the question of "asmakhta" was raised with similar result. A case similar in all respects to the case first above cited from the responsa of Rabbi Solomon ben Adreth is also discussed in the responsa of Rabbi Asher ben Yachiel [24] (1250-1328) with like result. Here, too, the remark is made by the rabbi that "such transactions are everyday occurrences."

Turning to England again we find in the collection of Hebrew Shtaroth (deeds),[25] published by the Jewish Historical Society of England, a Norwich document dated 1251 and embodying a transaction between two Jews, in which it is stated that a bond, together with a release, was delivered to a depositary, and that the depositary was to deliver both instruments to one of the parties in case the other failed to perform certain conditions.

In the 13th century this device was also used extensively by the Jews of England in their transactions with non-Jews. There are numerous entries on the rolls of The Exchequer of The Jews showing the use of this device. The following is a typical example: "Gilbert de Pelham attached to answer to William de S. in a plea of detention of a starr. The said William complains that whereas a starr, in which it was contained that if he paid to

---

[23] *Id.* at No. 33.

[24] Responsa of Rabbi Asher ben Yechiel, ch. 72, sec. 2.

[25] Davis, *Hebrew Deeds* (Shataroth) No. 22.

Abraham son of Ben', a Jew, at the feast of All Saints last past 10 marks, then he should be quit of a debt of 20 in which he was bound to the said Jew, was handed over, under his seal to Gilbert to be kept, the aforesaid Gilbert delivered it to the said Jew fraudulently and maliciously, to Williams' damage of £20".[26] It is to be noted here that in this case, as in most others of this kind, the starr of acquittance was delivered to a third party, 'in equal hand,' a procedure which, as we have seen above, was characteristic of such transactions among the Jews as well as of the classical English mortgage in the earlier stage of its development.

As to transactions between non-Jews, we find in the 13th century an occasional entry in the Close Rolls of a conditional obligation in the form of two separate instruments, a recognizance and a defeasance thereof.[27] But alongside with these, and much

---

[26] Calendar of The Plea Rolls of The Exchequer of The Jews, v. 3, p. 83 (1276). See also v. 1, p. 149 (1268) — an acknowledgment by a Jewess that upon payment of 12 marks 2 chirographs, one of 20 marks and another of 2 marks, are to be quit; pp. 162-163 — a starr to the effect that upon payment of 28s the debtor is to be quit of a chirograph in the sum of 100s, was placed in "equal hand"; p. 168 — "Defence, that it was agreed between them that if Henry should pay Diai 18s at the Purification of Blessed Mary in the 46th year, he should be quit of the chirograph of 40s", p. 209 — an acknowledgment by a Jew that upon payment of £10 is to be quit; pp. 300-301 — an agreement for the sale of timber: "And for the faithful performance of the said agreement, ... he, Michael, made the said Jew a charter for £20 and caused it to be placed in the Cambridge Chirograph Chest, on condition, nevertheless, that if he, Michael, should deliver the said timber to the said Jew at the terms aforesaid, then he should be quit of the said charter of £20." For similar transactions see v. 1, pp. 10, 58, 161, 162-63, 189, 242, 306; v. 2, pp. 2, 4, 8, 30, 225, 293; v. 3, pp. 283-84, 297-99.

[27] Alan grants to John the wardship of certain manors. Alan agrees that if John should be deprived of the wardship he would pay him £50 for every year he is so deprived. In another instrument John grants that if he should be deprived of the wardship, and Alan should pay him, "without plea or dispute," £24, together with damages and expenses, he would release Alan of the remainder. Calendar of The Close Rolls, 1271-1279, pp. 123-24 (1274).

It is to be noted that the phrase "without plea or dispute" seems to be a literal translation of the Hebrew בלי דין ודברים. See p. 82f., above.

more often, we find provisions for penalties,[28] entirely undisguised, as well as provisions that in case of default the obligor is to pay to the obligee his damages and expenses, as to the amount of which the obligee is to be believed on his simple word or, sometimes, on his oath.[29] At the beginning of the 14th century,[30] however, the conditional obligation in the form of two separate instruments becomes more frequent, and by the middle of that century[31] it becomes the regular, and, apparently, the only method of effecting a conditional obligation. As in the case of the conveyance with the condition subsequent, the conditional obligation continues for a long time to be incorporated in two separate instruments. The single instrument, containing both the obligation and the defeasance, makes its appearance only at the beginning of the 15th century,[32] about the same time that the

[28] *Id.*, 1268-72, pp. 292, 557-58.

[29] *Id.*, 1254-56, pp. 378--79; 1268-72, pp. 243, 292, 300, 410-11; 1272-79, pp. 254, 344, 355; Madox, *Formulare*, No. 159 (1257). Professor Maitland was apparently unaware of the Hebrew origin of this device. He thought it curious, and grouped it together with the device of making penal stipulations in favor of some charity, a device which, as will be shown in note 33 *infra* also originated with the Jews, and which is of an entirely different nature than the damages and expenses device. In his article, *A Conveyancer in the 13th Century* (1891) 7 L. Q. Rev. 63, 68, Prof. Maitland says: "Very curious too are the manifold devices by which the sin of usury is evaded, penal stipulations in favor of the relief of the Holy Land, or in favor of the building of Westminster Abbey, and agreements to accept the creditor's unsworn estimate of the 'damages and costs' that he has been put to by being kept out of his money." Now, while it is true that the damages and costs device was used for the purpose of evading the usury laws, the same cannot be said of the stipulations in favor of some charity, since the creditor would never obtain the penalty stipulated for, it being payable, in most cases, to the King for the use of the charity.

[30] *Calendar of The Close Rolls,* 1302-1307, pp. 317, 450; 1307-13, p. 334; 1318-23, pp. 339, 343, 359, 715, 724.

[31] *Id.*, 1341-43, pp. 244, 277, 696; 1349-54, pp. 238 239, 244-45, 246-47, 392, 405, 477, 481; 1354-60, pp. 67, 70, 80.

[32] The transition from two separate instruments to one single instrument may be seen in the volume of the Calendar of The Close Rolls covering the years 1399-1402. At page 419 the transaction appears in two separate entries, a recognizance and a condition, and at pages 507, 586, recognizance and con-

mortgage in the form of a conveyance with a condition subsequent begins to be incorporated in one single instrument.

The reason for the adoption by Englishmen of the two instrument device in the case of conditional obligations was the same as that which, as we have seen above, prompted the Jews to develop it, namely the rule against penalties. Whether directly influenced by the Hebrew doctrine of "asmakhta" or not,[33] the

dition appear in the same entry. The practice of incorporating the obligation and the defeasance in two separate instruments continued for some time, even after the single instrument became the usual form. No. 181 in *Madox*, for example, which is dated 1433, is a defeasance of a writing obligatory, made under the "Statute Merchant" to secure the performance of certain covenants in a marriage contract. It is quite likely that during this transitional period the single instrument came to be known as the "single bond," and that this name clung to it for a long time after the two-instrument form became obsolete. This may well be the explanation of the term "single bond" in Act 1, Scene 3, of The Merchant of Venice. Pollock and Maitland interpret this term as meaning a bond without a condition or penalty. In vol. 2 at 225, n. 2, they say: "Not one of the commentators, so far as we know, has rightly understood this term in the place where Shakespeare has made it classical... Shylock first offers to take a bond without a penalty, and then adds the fantastic penalty of the pound of flesh as a jesting afterthought." Why Shylock should have first offered to take a bond without any penalty at all, when the usual practice in those days was to name an amount equal to the amount of the principal obligation as a penalty in case of default, is not quite clear. It would seem therefore that the writer's explanation of the term is more in accord with the Shakespearean text. Shylock first offered to take the standard bond with the usual penalty, and then changed the penalty to a pound of flesh.

[33] The influence of the Hebrew doctrine of "asmakhta" upon the development of the rule against penalties in English law may have been indirect. It may have been exercised through the devices which the Jews used in their transactions among themselves for the purpose of overcoming the difficulty of "asmakhta," and which were adopted by Englishmen. In all of the available Hebrew documents, evidencing transactions between Jew and Jew in 13th century England, there is not a single one in which provision is made for a penalty payable to the obligee. Instead, these documents contain provisions for penalties in favor of the King, the Queen, and at least in one document, there is even a provision for a penalty payable to Earl Richard, the King's brother. See Davis, *Hebrew Deeds,* Nos. 23, 54, 65, 69, 87, 105, 128, 129; see also Calendar of The Plea Rolls of The Exchequer of The Jews, v. 2, p. 237,

rule against penalties in English law seems to have been first
extensively invoked against Jewish creditors. In the Close Rolls

and v. 3, pp. 31, 53, 307. Occasionally, too, there is provision for a penalty
payable to some charity, such as a synagogue or a Jewish cemetery. Davis, Nos.
47, 67. This device, like many others used in connection with writings obligatory, was apparently copied by Englishmen from the Jews. There are
numerous instances of the use of this device by Englishmen in the 13th century.
See e. g., Calendar of The Close Rolls, 1256-59, p. 493; 1259-61, pp. 474-75;
1272-79, pp. 254, 343-344, 413.

That this device originated with the Jews can hardly be doubted, for
with them it filled a definite need, namely, that of overcoming the difficulty
of the doctrine of "asmakhta," which rendered all penalties payable to the
obligee invalid. The Jewish obligee, who could not have the full benefit of a
penalty payable to himself, endeavored to have at least a provision which
would serve to deter the obligor from defaulting. He therefore made the penalty
payable to the King, who could be relied on to collect it, or to a charity to
which the doctrine of "asmakhta" is not applicable. It should be borne in mind
that this doctrine has nothing to do with laws of usury. These laws deal with
what is permissible and what is not, while the doctrine of "asmakhta" deals
with what is valid and enforceable and what is not. Usury is a sin; a provision
for a penalty, under Hebrew law, is not. It just is unenforceable. The penalty
clause in the Hebrew documents cited in this note was thus designed to
remedy a difficulty created by a doctrine which was peculiarly Hebrew in
origin and development, and just as the difficulty was of the Jews' own making,
so was the remedy. The provision for a penalty payable to the King is also
found among the Jews of Spain at a much earlier time than the 13th century.
In a Hebrew deed of conveyance, made at Leon, Spain, and dated 1053, there
is a provision in the warranty clause to the effect that if the grantor fails to
warrant, he is to pay 100 denarim to the King. The French translation of this
provision given in Revue des Études Juives 4, 227-229, where the document
was first published, reads as follows: "Et si je suis empêché de repousser et
rendre vaine une contestation et réclamation quelconque concernant cette vente,
je payerai en cette ville la valeur de cette vigne sans aucun retard, et s'il avait
retard, je payerai au roi cent deniers." See also Sefer Hashtaroth (Formbook)
of Rabbi Judah Barzillai (11th century, Spain), form No. 72, where a similar
provision is found. In this form there is also a provision that the payment
of the penalty shall not discharge the obligor of his principal obligation. The
last provision is also found in all of the above Hebrew documents from Angevin
England, in which there is a penalty clause.

Through the frequent use of this device by Englishmen the notion may
have gradually gained ground among them that a provision for a penalty

of Henry III and Edw. I we find a number of cases in which royal equity is exercised in favor of Christian debtors, relieving them from "penalties and usuries" to Jewish creditors.[34] The terms "usuries" and "penalties" always go together in these royal mandates.

The Jewish creditor could not even always take shelter under the form of an absolute obligation with a conditional release. Form readily yielded to substance where the Jew was involved. Thus in the Close Rolls of Edw. I [35] we find that by royal mandate to the Justices of the Jews the Convent of St. Mary is to be acquitted from "pains and usuries" to the Jews. In the same mandate the King orders the Justices to cause an inquest to be made as to how much money was received by the Convent from the Jews. Apparently, the penalties were disguised in the form of an absolute obligation, and the King ordered to disregard the form and ascertain the true amount of the loan. Some interesting entries bearing on this point are found in the Calendar of The Plea Rolls of The Exchequer of The Jews. "At the suit of Th. comes Deudoné Cryspin with Chirographs etc., to account, and demands of Th., by two charters which are in the King's treasury for his talliage, £22 with £20 interest. Defence, that the claim is unlawful, for that one of the charters was only by way of penalty, and is quit by the other, pursuant to a starr which is in the hands of J., clerk of the Chirograph chest of York."[36] In another case [37] the Christian debtor alleged that the Jew, by his starr, granted that he, the debtor, be quit of a charter of £40

payable to the obligee is not valid, and that it savors of usury. The device may thus have preceded the rule among Englishmen, and may have contributed to its adoption by them. Some support for this supposition may be seen in the fact that for some time there seems to have been hesitation among Englishmen as to whether or not penalties were enforceable. See documents cited note 28 *supra.*

[34] See *Calendar of The Close Rolls,* 1264-68, pp. 265-66, 305, 403; 1268-72, pp. 346, 370, 583-84; 1272-79, pp. 170, 177, 271, 286.

[35] *Id.,* 1272-79, p. 177.

[36] *Calendar of The Plea Rolls of The Exchequer of The Jews,* v. 2, p. 295.

[37] *Id.,* v. 3, pp. 167-68.

upon payment of £24 on or before a certain date, and of a charter for £30 upon payment of £15. And since the King granted that all penalties and usuries should cease, "he is not bound to answer touching the sum contained in the said charters which is, *as it were*, penalty."

It thus appears that already during the reign of Henry III penalties were thought to be akin to usuries and to belong to the same class. It is true that for some time it was apparently thought that only penalties growing out of a loan of money partook of the nature of usury, and that clauses providing for what we might call "liquidated damages" in case of breach, in contracts arising out of transactions other than a loan of money, did not come within the prohibition of usury. Thus we find during the reign of Edw. I a number of recognizances in the nature of liquidated damages in case of failure on the part of the obligor to perform certain undertakings, as, for example, in case the obligor fails to enfeoff the obligee of certain land,[38] or in case the obligor's son, a minor, upon reaching maturity disaffirms his marriage to the obligee's daughter.[39] However, towards the close of the same reign conveyancers seem to have begun to doubt the validity of such clauses, and the conditional obligation in the form of an absolute recognizance and a defeasance thereof begins to take the place of the provision for liquidated damages. By the middle of the 14th century, as we have seen above, this becomes the universal method of effecting a conditional obligation.[40]

It should be noted here that the employment of a third party, the "equal hand," as a depositary, is a prominent feature in the 14th century transactions between Christian and Christian, just as it is in the numerous 13th century transactions between Jew and Jew and Jew and Christian. In a case decided in 1313 the headnote reads as follows:

"Debt, where the original bond was unconditional,

[38] *Calendar of The Close Rolls,* 1272-79, p. 430.
[39] *Id.,* at 41 see also Eyre of Kent, 6 & 7 Edw. II, v. 2, p. 27.
[40] See note 31 *supra.*

and there was an indented conditioned penalty bond
[un endenture condicionnel de couste], both of which
were delivered to one G. The condition was satisfied
and G died. The bond came into the hands of his
executors, one of whom was one of the parties to
whom the bond was made; and because the defendant could not deny the unconditional bond the
court gave judgment that the executor should recover the debt, though he had only obtained possession of the bond as executor, and notwithstanding
the fact that the defendant had a bill of detinue
claiming the same bond and others pending against
him in the same eyre."[41]

To return to the conveyance with the condition subsequent.
The evidence is quite abundant that this device was used extensively by the Jews during the middle ages in exactly the
same manner and for the same reason as the absolute obligation
with the conditional release were used by them. Conveyance
and defeasance were usually incorporated in two separate instruments and both instruments were delivered to a third party, to
be returned to the mortgagor in case of payment of the debt
on or before the due date, or turned over to the mortgagee in
case of non-payment. A case involving two such documents is
discussed in a responsum by Nachmanides.[42] The two documents
were delivered to a third party, to be held by him for a period
of four years, the term of the mortgage. The argument was
advanced by the mortgagor-grantor that the deed was not valid,

[41] Eyre of Kent, 6 & 7 Edw. II, v. 2, 19.

[42] Responsa of Rabbi Solomon ben Adreth (Rashba), attributed to Rabbi
Moses ben Nachman (Ramban), No. 11. This is a collection of responsa which
were erroneously thought to have been written by Ramban. It was later
discovered that their author, for the most part, was not Ramban, but Rashba.
There are, however, some responsa in this collection which were penned by the
former, and the responsum cited in the text is one of them. Rashba himself
in one of his signed responsa refers to this one as having emanated from
Ramban. See Responsa of Rabbi Solomon ben Adreth, No. 916 (Lemberg, 1811).

since it represented an attempt to convey the property in futuro. This argument was dismissed by the rabbi on the ground that the deed effected an immediate conveyance, subject to defeasance within the time specified in the defeasance instrument, and was not a conveyance in futuro. Another case involving two such documents delivered to a third party, is discussed in a responsum of about the same time, written by Rabbi Solomon ben Adreth [43] (1235-1310).

Earlier, in the 12th century, an interesting question arose in connection with such conditional conveyances by way of security in a case decided by Rabbi Abraham ben David.[44] In this case, as in the cases just cited, the deed of conveyance was delivered to a third party to be held by him during the term of the mortgage. Before the end of the term the grantee-mortgagee conveyed his interest in the property to another. When, after the expiration of the term, the mortgagee's grantee asserted his claim to the property, the mortgagor resisted this claim, contending that the conveyance by the mortgagee was void. He supported his contention by the argument that at the time of the attempted conveyance the mortgagee had no interest in the property which he could validly convey, since his interest was not to become absolute before the term of the mortgage was over. The conveyance by the mortgagee, he argued, was in the nature of an attempted transfer of future acquisitions which, according to Hebrew law, is not valid. The rabbi decided in favor of the mortgagee's grantee, holding that at the time of the delivery of the deed to the third party the mortgagee acquired an immediate and present interest in the property, subject only to defeasance upon repayment by the mortgagor of the money advanced to him by the mortgagee within the period agreed on, and that therefore the conveyance by the mortgagee within that period was valid, although subject to the same defeasance.

[43] *Responsa of Rabbi Solomon ben Adreth sub nomine* Toldoth Adam, No. 188; see also No. 299 for a similar case.

[44] Cited in Tur, Choshen Mishpat, ch. 54, sec. 13.

Still earlier, in the 11th century, the conditional conveyance by way of security is mentioned in the responsa of Rabbi Isaac Alfassi.[45] Finally, it should be borne in mind that the doctrine of "asmakhta" is discussed in the Talmud in connection with a mortgage, and that the rule is laid down there that a forfeiture clause is not valid, and that only a present absolute conveyance with a provision for repurchase or defeasance is valid. So much for conditional conveyances by way of security used by the Jews in countries other than England.

As for England, the evidence is rather indirect, but no less convincing, nevertheless. In a 13th century Hebrew document,[46] evidencing a sale of a house by one Jew to another, we find the grantor making a representation under oath that he had made neither a deed of mortgage of the property, nor a deed of conveyance by way of security for a debt, previously to the conveyance attested by the document. Again, there are some entries on the Close Rolls [47] to the effect that a charter of feoffment was delivered by a Christian to the Chirographers to be kept in the "Jewish Chest". In these cases the charter was apparently delivered by way of security for a loan. Also, in a schedule of chattels which belonged to two deceased Jews, and which were found in the London Chest we find the following item: "Hamo and Ursell have 10 charters of feoffment of land."[48] These charters, too, were apparently kept in the chest as security for loans. Finally, in the Mandate of The King Touching Lands and Fees of The Jews in England,[49] dated 1271, by which the Jews were deprived of the right of holding freeholds "in manors, lands, tenements, fees, rents or tenures of any kind whatsoever by charter, grant, feoffment, confirmation, or any other kind of obligation," it is stated that "touching lands and tenures, however,

---

[45] No. 286 (Leghorn, 1781).

[46] Davis, *op. cit. supra* note 33, No. 58.

[47] *Calendar of The Close Rolls,* 1247-51, p. 308; 1254-56, pp. 424-25.

[48] V. 1, p. 68 (1244).

[49] *Select Pleas, etc., from The Exchequer of The Jew* (1901) 15 Selden Society Publ. LI-LIV.

of which Jews were enfeoffed before the present statute and which they now hold, it is our pleasure that such infeudations be altogether annulled, and that those lands and tenements remain to the Christians who demised them to the Jews; so nevertheless that the Christians discharge what is due to the Jews on account of the money or chattels contained in their charters or chirographs, and given to them by the Jews for such grant of feoffment, without interest [sine usura]." The whole tenor of the above mandate or statute, and particularly the provision that the Christian grantors are to "discharge what is due to the Jews ... without interest," clearly indicates that these transactions originated in loans, that the charters of feoffment were given to the Jews by way of security, and that they became absolute upon default by the Christian debtors. With regard to the above statute it might be added parenthetically that had the royal sense of justice been equally outraged at the oppression of the debtor class by the creditor class when the latter were Christians as when they were Jews, it might not have taken English courts several centuries before they evolved the doctrine of the equity of redemption.

To sum up. The conditional conveyance by way of security had been in use by the Jews for a long time prior to their settlement in England, and was used by them in England in their transactions with Christians. The technical device by which the conditional conveyance was effected was, in evry detail, identical with the classical English mortgage in its original form, namely, two separate instruments were used and a third party was employed as a depositary. A device similar in conception and design to the conditional conveyance was used by the Jews during the middle ages in England and elsewhere for the purpose of effecting conditional obligations. This device, too, was in every respect identical with the common law conditional bond in the earlier stage of its development. Both of these devices were developed by the Jews for the purpose of evading a certain rule of Hebrew law which is similar to the rule against penalties in English law.

The Jews introduced the business of money-lending on a large scale in England, and with it the means by which this business was carried on. When Englishmen learned the business of money-lending from the Jew they adopted his methods and devices, outstanding examples of which are the conditional conveyance by way of security and the conditional bond which have survived to our own day.

CHAPTER XXI

THE MORTGAGE WITH DELIVERY OF POSSESSION IN MEDIEVAL ENGLAND

In their History of English Law, Pollock and Maitland speak of the "Glanvillian and Bractonian mortgages" as representing two distinct stages in the development of the English law of mortgages.[1] On the basis of an obscure passage in Glanvill they concluded that, at the time when Glanvill's treatise was written, a forfeiture of gaged land by the gagor, in case of failure on his part to pay the mortgage debt on the due date, could be validly effected by an appropriate provision to that effect in the mortgage agreement, and that in the absence of such a provision the gagee could enforce a forfeiture by a proceeding in court. The Glanvillian mortgage was, according to Pollock and Maitland, one in which a forfeiture was either expressed or implied, and in the latter case the gagee had to have recourse to what we might call a foreclosure proceeding in order to enforce a forfeiture. The "Bractonian mortgage," they assert, took the form of a lease for a definite period of time, with a provision that upon failure on the part of the gagor to pay the debt at the end of the period fixed in the mortgage instrument the land was to become the property of the gagee absolutely.

As to the "classical English mortgage" in the form of an absolute conveyance with a condition subsequent, Pollock and Maitland are apparently of the opinion that it came to the fore in the fourteenth century only, by reason of the fact that the lawyers of that time found it difficult to square the notion of a term of years swelling into a fee with their ideas of seisin.[2]

[1] PMH, v. 2., 119-122.
[2] *Ibid.*, 122-3

311

The writer proposes to show that neither in the twelfth nor in the thirteenth century could a forfeiture be effected either by agreement between the parties or by a proceeding in court, as in the so-called "Glanvillian mortgage;" that a term of years could not be converted into a fee by nonpayment of the mortgage debt, as in the so-called "Bractonian mortgage;" that Pollock and Maitland failed to take fully into account a very potent influence upon the development of English law during the period under discussion, namely the influence of Hebrew law and legal forms; and that English mortgages of the twelfth and thirteenth centuries were patterned after similar Jewish forms and devices.

The writer has examined the various forms of mortgages which prevailed in England during the twelfth and thirteenth centuries, on the one hand, and the corresponding Hebrew forms, on the other, and has found a remarkable similarity between them. But before discussing this similarity it may be well to consider the Pollock and Maitland classification of the medieval English mortgages.

The passages in which Glanvill speaks about the forfeiture of gaged property occur in Chapters 6, 7, and 8 of Book 10 of his treatise. In Chapter 6, he says:

> "Praeterea cum ad certum terminum res aliqua ponitur in vadium aut ita convenit inter creditorem et debitoren quod si ad terminum illum vadium suum non acquietaverit debitor ipse, tunc vadium ipsum remaneat ipsi creditori, ita quod negotium suum sicut de suo inde faciat aut nihil tale convenit inter eos. In primo casu stabitur conventioni. In secundo, existente termino si fuerit debitor in mora solvendi debitum, poterit se inde conqueri et institiabitur quod ad curiam veniat et inde respondeat, et per hoc breve."

> "In addition — when a thing is pledged for a definite period, it is either agreed between the Creditor and Debtor, that if, at the time appointed, the Debtor should not redeem his pledge, it should then

belong to the Creditor so that he might dispose of it as his own; or no such agreement is entered into between them. In the former case, the agreement must be adhered to; in the latter, the term being unexpired, without the Debtor's discharging the Debt, the Creditor may complain of him, and the Debtor shall be compelled to appear in Court, and answer by the following Writ."[3]

In Chapter 7 he gives the form of a writ by which the debtor is called upon to acquit the gage, and in Chapter 8 he states that if the debtor comes to court and acknowledges the gage, he is given a reasonable time within which he is to acquit the gage, and upon his failure to do so "dabitur licentia ipsi creditori de cetero negotium suum de vadio ipso sicut de re propria facere quo modo voluerit."[4] That is, "Liberty shall be given to the Creditor, from that time, to treat the pledge as his own property and do whatever he chuses with it."

The above passages occur in Glanvill's discussion of gages of personal property. The sentence introducing the subject begins: "Cum itaque res mobilis ponitur in vadium."[5] But Pollock and Maitland apparently base their conclusion as to the applicability of the same rules to gages of land upon another passage in which Glanvill, after defining a ""mortuum vadium" as a gage of land in which the profits from the land are not applied by the gagee to the reduction of the debt, states: "Cetera serventur ut prius de vadiis in rebus mobilibus consistentibus dictum est."[6]

While on its face the sentence last quoted seems to support the Pollock and Maitland conclusion, a close examination of the entire Glanvillian text dealing with gages [7] will reveal that the

---

[3] "*Existente termino.* This is palpably false reading — it should be *elapso termino,* the term being expired." Note *ad locum* in Beames' translation of Glanvill, *De Legibus* (1812).

[4] Glanvill, *De Legibus,* bk. 10, ch. 8.

[5] *Ibid.,* ch. 6.

[6] *Ibid.,* ch. 8.

[7] *Ibid.,* ch. 6.

above sentence is not to be taken at its face value. There are in this text several rules which are obviously not applicable to gages of land. The rule that the gagee is to keep the gage safely is one, that he is not to use it is another, and that in case it is necessary to incur expenses the agreement of the parties is to govern is still another. The general statement that the rules applicable to gages of chattels are also applicable to gages of land is therefore obviously inaccurate, and one cannot draw from it any conclusions as to whether or not the rules with regard to the forfeiture of gaged property were applicable to gages of land.

If the passages in Glanvill dealing directly with the subject do not give us any definite indication as to the applicability of the forfeiture rules to gages of land, there are other passages which, though not dealing directly with the subject, seem to point to the conclusion that these rules were not applicable to gages of land.[8] The mortgagee's seisin was, according to Glanvill, a seisin "ut de vadio" and not a seisin "ut de feodo."[9] In the case of a disseisin of the mortgagee by a stranger, the former could not have a writ of novel disseisin. The mortgagor was the only one to whom this writ was available in such a case. Similarly, in the case of a disseisin of the mortgagee by the mortgagor, the former could not have this writ, but was relegated to his remedy in an action of debt. Now, if a forfeiture of gaged land was possible either by agreement or by the order of the court, as Pollock and Maitland would have us believe, a whole series of questions arises: Was the nature of the seisin changed upon forfeiture from one "ut de vadio" to one "ut de feodo"? Where a forfeiture was provided for by express agreement was the gagee entitled to a writ of novel disseisin in case he was disseised, either by the gagee or by a stranger, after the term of payment of the mortgage debt had expired? And where a forfeiture was effected by judgment of the court, did the court order an enfeoffment of the gagee by the gagor? On what terms? How were the

---

[8] *Ibid.*, bk. 13, ch. 26.
[9] *Ibid.*

services to be performed by the feoffee to the feoffor to be determined? Glanvill would hardly have remained silent on these matters, if he meant to include land in his statement of the rule about a forfeiture of gaged property.[10]

[10] At this point the writer wishes to call attention to another misunderstanding which arose from the vagueness of the Glanvillian text dealing with the mortgage. Pollock and Maitland are of the opinion that under the "Glanvillian mortgage," when the gagee was disseised of his gage either by the gagor himself or by a stranger, he had no remedy whereby he could repossess himself of the gaged land, the writ of novel disseisin not being available to him. All he could do was to bring an action of debt against the gagor, in which action he could only recover a money judgment. This anomalous position of the "Glanvillian gagee" was, according to Pollock and Maitland, the reason for the disappearance of the "Glanvillian gage." To quote from their *History of English Law* (2nd ed. 1898) 120-1:

> "But of the practice described by Glanvill we know exceedingly little; it is not the root of our classical law of mortgage, which starts from the conditional feoffment. It seems to have soon become antiquated and the cause of its obsolescence is not far to seek. The gagee of Glanvill's day is put into possession of the land. Unless the gagor has put the gagee into possession, the king's court will pay no heed to the would-be gage. It will be one of those 'private conventions' which that court does not enforce. So the gagee must be put in possession. His possession is called a seisin, a *seisina ut de vadio*. For all this, however, it is unprotected. If a stranger casts the gagee out, it is the gagor who has the assize. But more; if the gagor casts the gagee out, the gagee cannot recover the land. The reason given for this is very strange: — What the creditor is really entitled to is the debt, not the land. If he comes into court he must come to ask for that to which he is entitled. If he obtains a judgment for his debt, he has obtained the only judgment to which he has any right.
>
> "Now, if a court of law could always compel a debtor to pay his debt, there would be sound sense in this argument. Why should a court give a man security for money when it could give him the money? But a court cannot always compel a debtor to pay his debt, and the only means of compulsion that a court of the twelfth century could use for such a purpose were feeble and defective. Thus the debtor of Glanvill's day could to all appearance reduce his gagee from the position

Furthermore, if the gagee of land had a right to a forfeiture, it must have depended upon his continuing in possession of the gaged land, for if he was disseised, either by the gagee or by a stranger, he was, as we have seen above, relegated to his remedy in an action of debt. It follows, therefore, that in every case where a gagee of land sought to enforce a forfeiture the preliminary question of who was in possession of the land at the time the writ issued would have had to be decided before the court could have given a judgment of forfeiture. Yet when Glanvill

> of a secured to that of an unsecured creditor by the simple process of ejecting him from the gaged land. Such a state of things can have been but temporary."

The writer believes that the assumption that in his action of debt the gagee could only recover a money judgment is unwarranted. There are several entries in the Pipe Rolls which clearly indicate that about Glanvill's time, that is at the beginning of the reign of Richard I, the gagee was given a remedy for the recovery of his gage. To quote some of these entries: "Herueus de Weston debet iii m. pro habendo recto de ix m. vel de vadio suo." Pipe Roll Society Publ. v. 1 (n. s.), p. 116. Hugo f. Lefivin et Willelmus de Buggeden r. c. de x m. pro habenda villa de Corneburc usque ad terminum cruisiatorum sicut vadium suum. Pipe Roll Society Publ. v. 2 (n. s.), p. 76. Liulfus homo ducis Saxonie debet Lx m. ut habeat vadium suum de terra de Stebbinge." Pipe Roll Society Publ. v. 1 (n. s.), p. 108. Some ten years later we find the following entry on the Pipe Rolls: "Willelmus de Keuil" et Nicolaus frater eius debent x. li. pro habenda saisina maneriorum de Camel' et Hunesspil que Willelmus de Mariscis eis invadiavit que eis adjudicata fuerunt esse vadia eorum." Pipe Roll Society Publ. v. 12 (n. s.), p. 99.

In these cases the gagees obtained possession of the gaged land by judicial process, and in one case at least the gagee demanded that either the debt be paid or that posssession of the gaged property be delivered to him. This being so, the rule stated by Glanvill that the gagor cannot have a writ of novel disseisin is not at all unreasonable and technical. The writ of novel disseisin was available only to a party who claimed the land absolutely, and claimed nothing else, while a gagor's claim was primarily for money, and not for possession of the land. He claimed the land only as an alternative to the claim for money, and not absolutely at that, but only for as long as the debt remained unpaid. It was only reasonable therefore that the disseised mortgagee should be given his remedy in an action of debt, and not by writ of novel disseisin. We still say to this day that a mortgage is incidental to the debt which it secures.

speaks in detail about the possible issues that may arise between the gagor and gagee when both appear in court, he says nothing about the case in which the gagor acknowledges the gage, but denies that the gagee remains in possession.[11]

So much for the internal evidence from the Glanvillian text itself. Let us now turn to the evidence outside of the text. Pollock and Maitland state that they could not find the writ calling upon the debtor to acquit the debt — that is the writ by which a forfeiture was enforced — even in the earliest Registers.[12] Now if the writ was applicable to land, its absence from the Registers would be rather peculiar. But if we should assume that it was applicable to chattels only, this absence could be easily accounted for inasmuch as recourse to this writ must have been very rare, since a loan on the security of chattels did not ordinarily involve a large amount of money, and a royal writ was quite an expensive commodity in those days.

Another indication that a provision for a forfeiture was not valid may be seen in the fact that Pollock and Maitland were apparently unable to find a single document of the twelfth century, or of a later date for that matter, in which there is a provision for a forfeiture. On the contrary, some of the available twelfth century mortgages would seem to indicate that a provision for a forfeiture was not considered valid in the twelfth century. No. 509 in Madox, Formulare, for example, is an agreement between mortgagor and mortgagee that within a period of two and one-half years from the date of the instrument the mortgagor or his brothers or nephew may redeem the property, and that if they do not redeem within that period, the property is to remain to the mortgagee *in accordance with his charter*. Obviously, we have here a case of the "classical English mortgage" in which an absolute charter of feoffment was delivered by the mortgagor to the mortgagee, and an instrument of defeasance or of the right of repurchase was executed by the latter and delivered

---

[11] Glanvill, *De Legibus,* bk. 10, ch. 8.
[12] PHM, v. 1, 120, n. 2.

to the former. Again, in Pipe Roll 3 Ri. 1 we find the following entry: "Prior de Kenillewurda debet c. s. pro habendo judicio de Flechamsteda secundum cartas suas quas Templarii tenent."[13] Apparently, what happened here was that the owner of Flecham- steda had mortgaged his property to the Prior and delivered a charter of feoffment to the Templars, to be returned to him upon payment of the mortgage debt, or turned over to the Prior upon default in payment. The writer has shown elsewhere [14] that such a delivery of the instrument of conveyance to a third party was the regular procedure employed in what Pollock and Maitland call "the classical English mortgage" during the early stage of its development, and that the treasury of the Templars was often used by the parties as the depositary in such conditional conveyances. If a provision for a forfeiture was valid in the twelfth century, it is difficult to see why the parties should have gone to the trouble of executing two instruments and, at least in one case, delivering it to a third party, when they could have provided for a forfeiture in a single instrument.

Further evidence to the effect that a provision for a forfeiture was considered invalid in England at a very early time is found in a document, dated 1127, and contained in the Cartulary of the Monastery of Ramsey.[15] This document, if the writer's inter- pretation of it is correct, represents a mortgage in which a most ingenious method was used for the purpose of effecting a for- feiture — a method which would do honor to the most astute corporation lawyer in our own time. The instrument recites that as a dispute had arisen with regard to certain land between one William Wilard and the Abbot of Ramsey, the latter gave to the former 100 s. upon condition that if Wilard will repay the 100 s. at the end of three years his claim to the land shall be as good as, "and better not worse," as on the day when suit was com- menced. If at the end of the three years Wilard failed to repay

---

[13] *Pipe Roll Society Publ.* v. 2 (n. s.), 128 (1191).
[14] See ch. 20, above.
[15] *Ramsey Cartulary,* (Chronicles and Memorials no. 79), 144, no. LXXI.

the money, the Abbot was to hold the land for another three years, and if at the end of the second three-year period Wilard again failed to repay the money, he was to lose his claim to the land.

In all probability this was just an ordinary mortgage, and the dispute was nothing but a fiction intended to cover up a provision for a forfeiture which would otherwise have been invalid. The circumstances of the transaction definitely point in this direction. The sum of 100 s., which was paid by the Abbot to Wilard, was quite a substantial amount in the early part of the twelfth century. Money was scarce, and he who had it could dictate terms pretty much his own way to the one who needed it. If, then, this had been a settlement of a real controversy, it is hardly likely that the Abbot would have given Wilard the option of repaying the money and reasserting his claim after the lapse of three years, and a further option at the end of a second three-year period. Furthermore, parties to a settlement, especially the one that has to part with money, usually wish to make the settlement final, and do not wish to leave the issue of the controversy in doubt.

The most amazing thing, however, about this transaction is that it conforms with a certain rule of Hebrew law concerning forfeitures, as stated in an early Talmudic text of the second century. This text reads as follows:

> "Where two parties entered into a penal sti-
> pulation [for the appearance in court], and one
> said to the other: 'If I do not come from now until
> such a day, you shall have in my hands so much',
> and the other demanded that much, R. Jose says:
> 'the condition shall stand', and R. Judah says: 'how
> does he become entitled to that which has not come
> into his hands, let him summon him'. Where
> one delivered his house or his field to another in
> pledge for a loan of money, and said to him: 'If
> I do not repay you from now until such a day, I
> shall have nothing in your hands', and the time

arrived and he did not pay, R. Jose says: 'The
condition shall stand'. R. Judah says: 'How does
he become entitled to that which is not his, let
him summon him'. R. Judah admits, however, that
in the case where two individuals were contending
over a house or over a field, and one of them said
to the other: 'If I do not come from now until
such a day, I shall have nothing in your hands,'
and the time arrived and he did not come, he has
lost his claim."[16]

---

[16] Tosefta Baba Metzia 1:16-17 (ed. Zuckermandel, 372). The Hebrew
text, according to the version of Nahmanides (Novellae to Baba Metzia 48b,
cited by Lieberman in תוספת ראשונים, 2, 107), reads:

שנים שנתעצמו זה בזה ואמר אחד מהן לחבירו אם לא באתי מיכן ועד
יום פלוני יהא לך בידי כך וכך תבע פירש (פלוני) הגיע זמן ולא בא
יתקיים תנאו דברי ר' יוסי אמ' ר' יהודה היאך זוכה זה בדבר שלא בא
לתוך ידו אלא ינתחנו. מישכן לו בית ומישכן לו שדה ואמ' לו אם לא
נתתי לך מיכן ועד יום פלוני אין לי בידך כלום היגיע זמן ולא נתן
יתקיים תנאו דברי ר' יוסי אמר ר' יהודה היאך זוכה זה בדבר שאינו
שלו אלא ינתחנו מודה ר' יוסי בשנים שהיו עוררין על הבית ועל השדה
ואמ' אחד מהם לחבירו אם לא באתי מיכן ועד יום פלוני אין לי בידך
כלום הגיע זמן ולא בא בידוע שאיבד את זכותו.

The word פירש is apparently an error of some copyist who had before him the
abbreviation 'פ and he expanded it to פירש, instead to to פלוני as he should
have done.

The procedure of entering into a penal stipulation for an appearance in
court is similar to the procedure of *vadimonium facere adversario* of the Roman
law. See A. Berger *Encyclopedic Dictionary of Roman Law*, 757f. For a similar
procedure in Egypt, with a thirty-day period for appearance in court, see R.
Taubenschlag, *The Law of Greco-Roman Egypt in the Light of the Papyri*, I,
383. The word ינתחנו, which literally means *let him lay hold on him*, alludes
to the method of summoning a party to court by laying hold on him, similar
to *in ius vocatio* of the Roman law. The verb נתח is similarly used in
BT Baba Metzia 113a: אמר שמואל שליח בית דין מנתח נתוחי אין, אבל משכוני לא
which is to be rendered as follows: Said Samuel: the court's messenger may
lay hold [on a defendant], but may not take pledges [from him]. Cf. also התוקף
שנים שנתעצמו בדין and את חברו בדין in BT Sanhedrin 31b. The former
refers to a procedure similar to *in ius vocatio* and the latter to one similar to
vadimonium. On *laying hold on* as a method of summoning to law, cf. ותפשו
בו אביו ואמו ("then shall his father and his mother lay hold on him") in
Deut. 21:19.

It thus appears from the above text that according to R. Judah a provision for a forfeiture is not valid, unless the ownership of the property to be forfeited is in dispute, and one of the parties to the dispute stipulates for a foreiture in favor of the other. It should be added here that R. Judah's opinion is the one that prevails according to the Talmudists.

It will readily be seen that the method of providing for a forfeiture, which was used in the English mortgage discussed above, corresponds exactly to the hypothetical case put by R. Judah, in which, he admits, a provision for a forfeiture is valid. Indeed, there is a very close, and to the writer's mind very significant, similarity between the phraseology of the condition as stated by R. Judah, and that of the English mortgage. Nowhere is a word denoting payment, such as "solvere" or "persolvere" mentioned in the English instrument. "Si non venerit, afferens quae supradicta sunt, sciat se perdidisse omnem calumniam," reads the forfeiture clause in that instrument. Willard is to "come and bring" the money, exactly as in the Talmudic text, "If I do not come." Furthermore, the entire form of the instrument is rather peculiar. It does not speak in the first person, as English documents of the Middle Ages usually do. It is not a grant or demise by Wilard, but is rather an attestation by the court of a stipulation entered into before it by the parties to a suit. It speaks in the third person, "in hoc breviculo ostendit ... sciat se perdidisse." This feature of the instrument, too, is in remarkable agreement with Hebrew law on the subject of forfeitures. There is an important body of opinion among post-Talmudic authorities holding that R. Judah's statement about the validity of a forfeiture provision where the property to be forfeited is in dispute has reference to a case in which the provision was embodied in a stipulation made before a prominent court in connection with the conduct of a trial.[17]

The writer believes that the parallelism between the above English mortgage and the rules of Hebrew law with regard to

---

[17] See Rabbi Isaac Alfasi on *Baba Bathra,* ch. 10, sec. 941.

forfeitures is so close that it is hardly possible to explain it away as a mere coincidence. We seem to be dealing here with a pattern shaped on the basis of a whole series of rules, exceptions to the rules, and modifications of these exceptions. Such patterns do not come into existence by accident. It is quite likely that the Abbot followed an example set by the Jews, or that he obtained the advice of a Jewish expert in the money-lending business before he advanced the money. Be that as it may, the fact that the parties had to resort to an elaborate fiction in order to provide for a forfeiture in a legally valid manner shows that ordinarily a provision for a forfeiture was not considered valid.

What has been said above about the invalidity of a forfeiture provision in Glanvill's time applies with equal force to what Pollock and Maitland call the "Bractonian mortgage." The law was not changed in this respect between the time of Glanvill and that of Bracton. But a few words must be added about the documents which Pollock and Maitland cite as examples of the "Bractonian mortgage." An examination of these documents will reveal that they do not quite represent what these great historians of English law claim they represent. No. 509 in Madox has already been discussed by the writer. It is an example of the "classical English mortgage" in its earlier stage of development, in which two documents, a charter of feoffment and an instrument of defeasance, were used. No. 230 in Madox is a lease by the mortgagor to the mortgagee for a period of fifteen years at a rental of sixpence a year. The instrument provides that if at the end of the fifteen-year period the mortgagor fails to pay the debt, the mortgagee is to hold the property from year to year at the original rental. The land was not to become the property of the mortgagee absolutely upon default by the mortgagor. He was only to hold it from year to year until the debt was paid. The mortgagor's right to redeem the property at the end of any year continued indefinitely. This, if anything, tends to show that a forfeiture clause was not considered valid, and that a term of years could not be changed into a fee by the mortgagor's default.

The same is true of the document cited by Pollock and Maitland from Chron. de Melsa I.[18] Upon default by the mortgagor at the end of a period of thirty years the mortgagee was to hold the property from year to year at a fixed rental.

The Yearbook case cited by them [19] may have been one of a "classical English mortgage," with an absolute charter of feoffment and an instrument setting forth the exact terms of the mortgage. The defendant in his answer in that case probably referred to the latter instrument, which usually recited that if the debt was not paid at the end of the term fixed by the parties, the property was to remain to the mortgagee, but that if it was paid, the property was to revert back to the mortgagor.

The same is true of the document cited by them from Guisborough Cartulary.[20] This document was probably accompanied by a charter of feoffment. At any rate, the document does not represent a "Bractonian mortgage" in the form of a lease for a term of years, with a provision that upon failure on the part of the mortgagor to pay the mortgage debt at the end of the term the property is to belong to the mortgagee absolutely. For, in the first place, it appears that the property was not demised to the mortgagee for a term of years. There are no words of demise anywhere in the document. The operative words used are "obligavi et impignoravi." Also, there is a provision in the document that the mortgagor should not sell the property to anyone, except the mortgagee, in case he should not wish "to hold it in his hand," which seems to indicate that the mortgagor remained in possession. Again, the fact that there is no provision for a deduction from the principal amount of the loan for the use of the property indicates that the mortgagee was not in possession, for if he had been, the transaction would have been a "mortuum vadium," a species of usury according to Glanvill.

It is true that the texts dealing with the subject in Bracton's

---

[18] Page 303.
[19] PMH, v. 2, 122. The case is found in Y. B. 21-2 Edw. I, 125 (1294).
[20] Page 144.

treatise [21] do seem to support the Pollock and Maitland conclusion. But it is likely that Bracton left out of account the absolute charter of feoffment, which was part of every mortgage in which the mortgagee was to become the owner of the mortgaged property in case of default by the mortgagor. He had in mind only the document setting forth the terms of the mortgage, and this document, standing alone, does seem to have the effect of turning a term of years into a fee. He may have been prompted to overlook the charter of feoffment by a desire for logical symmetry, for in the same passage in which he speaks of a term of years being turned into a fee by a condition he also speaks of a fee being turned into a term of years by a condition.

A very strong indication that Bracton's text is not to be taken at its face value may be found in the fact that in all of the entries in the printed Close Rolls, recording mortgages during the latter part of the reign of Henry III, the transaction takes the form of two separate instruments: an absolute charter of feoffment, and a document setting forth the terms of the mortgage.[22] A diligent search of these rolls by the writer has failed to uncover a single case in which a term of years was to be turned into a fee without the aid of an absolute charter of feoffment, executed by the mortgagor simultaneously with the execution of the document setting forth the terms of the mortgage.

We now come to a consideration of the various types of mortgages found in the Talmud and other Hebrew sources, and their English counterparts. The outstanding feature of the Talmudic law of mortgages is that a provision for a forfeiture of the mortgaged property upon default by the mortgagor is not valid. There were, however, ways of evading this rule against forfeitures. The usual method by which what amounts to a forfeiture was effected under Hebrew law was as follows: the mortgagor would convey the property to the mortgagee absolutely, and the

[21] Bracton, fol. 20, 268-9.
[22] See, e. g., *Calendar of the Close Rolls*, 1261-1264, 310-311; 1264-1268, 105, 385-386, 391-392, 525.

mortgagee, on his part, would undertake to return the property to the mortgagor upon repayment, within a specified period, of the money advanced by him to the mortgagor. The mortgagor's conveyance and the mortgagee's undertaking would be embodied in two separate instruments, and both instruments would be delivered to a third party, to be turned over to the mortgagee or returned to the mortgagor, as the case may be, at the end of the period specified in the agreement between them.

It has been shown above [23] that this type of mortgage, in all of its essential features, such as the use of two separate instruments and the delivery of these instruments to a third party, was adopted by the English from the Jews, and that it gave rise to what Pollock and Maitland call the "classical English mortgage," which is still in use throughout England and the United States. In this chapter the writer will discuss several types of mortgages, other than the one just mentioned.

The pledge of land with delivery of possession to the creditor was in common use among the Jews at a very early time. A wide variety of gages of land with delivery of possession to the gagee is discussed in the Talmud, tractate Baba Metzia,[24] in the chapter dealing with the laws of usury. The connection between these gages and the usury laws is to be found in the fact that in many cases the gaging device was used for the purpose of evading these laws. The principal types of gage mentioned in the Talmud are:

(1) A gage for a specified term, during which the gagor is precluded from paying the debt and redeeming the property.

(2) A gage of indefinite duration, under the terms of which the gagor may at any time pay the debt and redeem the property.

(3) A gage with deduction, under the terms of which the gagee deducts from the principal a certain amount, usually smaller than the normal rental or income from the property, for the use of the property.

[23] See ch. 20, above.
[24] 67a-68a.

(4) A gage without deduction, in which no deduction is made from the principal for the use of the property.

(5) "Kitzutha," a gage in which for a specified period of time the gagee is to deduct a certain amount from the principal, after which period the entire income from the property is to be deducted from the principal.

(6) "Mashkantha of Sura," a gage under the terms of which the entire debt is to be extinguished at the end of a specified period of time in exchange for the gagee's use of the land.

From the point of view of the usury laws there is a difference of opinion among post-Talmudic authorities as to the effect of these various types of gage. According to the French school represented by Rashi [25] and Rabbenu Tam,[26] types (3), and (6) are wholly free from the taint of usury, while (4) is only quasi-usury — "abak ribbith," literally the dust of usury and is prohibited only by Rabbinical law, and not by Pentateuchal law. Others hold that type (3) is also usurious, and that only (5) and (6) are not; and still others are of the opinion that the only type of gage which is wholly free from usury is (6), under which the debt is entirely extinguished at the end of a specified period.[27]

With regard to quasi-usury, the rule is that although the lender commits a moral transgression, the temporal courts will, nevertheless, not intervene to invalidate the transaction and compel the lender to return to the borrower what he has received from him by way of usury.

A comparison of these Talmudic gages with the Glanvillian "vadium" will reveal a close correspondence between them. Glanvill speaks of the "vadium ad terminum," the gage of land for a term, and the "vadium sine termino," the gage without a term.[28] Pollock and Maitland apparently interpret the text in Glanvill

---

[25] *Baba Metzia,* 67b, s. v. *Beathra.*
[26] Tosaphoth on Baba Metzia, 67b, s. v. *Rvina.*
[27] See Rabbi Asher b. Yechiel on Baba Metzia, 67a.-68a.
[28] Glanvill, *De Legibus,* bk. 10, ch. 6.

to mean that under the "vadium ad terminum" the lender may not demand the repayment of the loan before the expiration of the term, while under the "vadium sine termino" he may do so at any time.[29] However, the plain meaning of the text is that the term has reference to the mortgage and not to the loan. The difference between a mortgage with a term and one without a term, therefore, consists in the fact that under the former the mortgagor may not redeem the land by paying the mortgage debt before the expiration of the term, while under the latter he may do so at any time. It may readily be seen, by a reference to the Talmudic gages enumerated above, that Glanvill's "vadium ad terminum" and "vadium sine termino" are the exact counterparts of types (1) and (2), respectively, of these gages.

Again, in the same book, Glanvill speaks of the "mortuum vadium," and explains the same as a gage under the terms of which no deduction from the principal is made by the lender in favor of the borrower for the use of the land by the former during the term of the gage.[30] This is obviously type (4) of the Talmudic gage. Type (3) is not specifically mentioned by Glanvill, but is clearly implied in his definition of the "mortuum vadium." "Mortuum vadium dicitur illud cujus fructus vel redditus interim percepti *in nullo se acquietant.*" From this it follows that where a deduction is made, even though it is less than the full value of the income from the land, the transaction is not a "mortuum vadium."

The above interpretation of the Glanvillian text is borne out by a passage in the Dialogus de Scaccario (probably written in 1176 by Richard Fitz-Neale, Bishop of London and the king's treasurer), which reads as follows:

> "Publicas igitur et usitatas usuras dicimus quando, more Iudeorum, in eadem specie ex conuentione quis amplius percepturus est, quam commodauit, sicut libram pro marca vel pro libra argentii ii. denarios

---

[29] PMH, v. 2, 120.
[30] Glanvill, *De Legibus,* bk. 10, ch. 8.

in septimanam de lucro preter sortem. Non publicas autem set tamen dampnabiles cum quis fundum aliquem vel ecclesiam pro commodato suscipit et, manente sortis integritate, fructus eius, donec sors ipsa soluta fuerit, sibi percipit. Hoc genus propter laborem et sumptum qui in agriculturis solent impendi, licentius visum est; set proculdubio sordidum est et inter usuras merito computandum".[31] (We speak of usuries as public and ordinary when, in the manner of the Jews, one is by agreement to receive more of the same species than what he lent, as a pound for a mark, or twopence per pound per week as interest besides the principal. As non-public, but also damnable, when one receives a field or a church for a loan and, while the principal remains intact, he receives its fruit until the principal is paid. This kind, by reason of [the threat of the loss of] labor and expenditures which usually hangs over agriculture, is looked upon as more permissible; but it is without doubt sordid, and I hold that it should be counted among usuries.).

What is here defined as *usura non publica* is clearly the same thing as Glanvill's *mortuum vadium*. The phrase *manente sortis integritate* implies, as does Glanvill's *in nullo se acquietant*, that where some deduction is made the transaction is not usurious.

It is interesting to note that the implied distinction, made by Fitz-Neale, between agricultural land and other property is one that is made by Rabbi Chananel [32] (early 11th century), Rashi [33] (late 11th century) and Maimonides (12th century). In his Code, Book 13, Creditor and Debtor Law, ch. 6, sec. 7, Maimonides states:

"My masters taught: Where one loans money to

---

[31] *Dialogus de Scaccario*, ed. Hughes, Crump and Johnson, 138.

[32] See *Maggid Mishneh* to Maimonides' *Yad-Hazakah, Malveh* 6, 7.

[33] See Rashi to *Baba Metzia*, 64b, s. v. *Qa mashma lan.*

another who delivers to him a field as a gage, with the understanding that he (the creditor) is to enjoy the fruit of the land during the term of the gage, though no deduction is to be made from the principal of the loan, it is only quasi-usury (abbaq ribbith), and is not recoverable in a court of law. For a gage of a field is unlike a gage of a house, since there is no fruit in the field at the time the loan is made, and (as to the future) while it is possible that there will be fruit, resulting in gain, it is also possible that seed and labor will go to naught, resulting in loss. Therefore, it is only quasi-usury".

It will readily be seen from the above that the distinction made in Jewish law between directly stipulated usury (*ribbith q'zuzzah*) and quasi-usury (*abaq ribbith*) corresponds to Fitz-Neale's distinction between *usura publica* and *usura non publica,* and that the further distinction made in Jewish law between agricultural land and other property is also made by Fitz-Neale, and for the same reason as that given by Maimonides. That all this is the result of chance is hardly likely. If, then, as seems likely, Richard Fitz-Neale and Glanvill borrowed some ideas about the legal aspects of usury from the Jews, it may be inferred that in the 12th century there was some traffic in ideas, at least about things legal, between Jewish scholars in England and high English officials.

Pollock and Maitland apparently did not give the proper weight to the words "in nullo" in Glanvill's definition of the "mortuum vadium." They are therefore of the opinion that, according to Glanvill, the only type of gage which was wholly free from the taint of usury was the one in which the entire income from the property was deducted from the principal of the loan. Having failed to find instances of such gages in the twelfth and thirteenth centuries they concluded that the sin of usury involved in the "mortuum vadium" was disregarded by money-lenders. To quote from their History of English Law:

"The specific mark of the mortgage is that the

profits of the land received by the creditor are not
to reduce the debt. Such a bargain is a kind of
usury; but apparently it is a valid bargain even
though the creditor be a Christian. He sins by
making it, and, if he dies in his sin, his chattels will
be forfeited to the king; but to all seeming the
debtor is bound by his contract... Even the Christian, if we are not much mistaken, was very willing
to run such risk of sin and punishment as was
involved in the covert usury of the mortgage. The
plea rolls of the 13th century often show us a
Christian gagee in possession of the gaged land,
but we have come upon no instance in which he was
called upon to account for the profits that he had
receievd."[34]

However, a close examination of some of the available
thirteenth century mortgage instruments will reveal that in form
at least money-lenders did not disregard the sin and risk involved
in the "mortuum vadium." There is a provision in these instruments for some deduction, however small and nominal, for the
use of the property. In No. 230, Madox, Formulare Anglicanum,
which has already been mentioned, the gagee was to deduct sixpence per year, and in Chronicles de Melsa, the deduction was
one of one shilling per year.[35] These mortgages were therefore
similar to type (4) above of the Talmudic gage.

A comparison between No. 230 in Madox and the standard
Hebrew gage with deduction, given in the formbook of Rabbi
Jehudah Barzillai [36] (11th century, Spain) is particularly illuminating in this respect. There is an almost complete identity of
pattern between the two. In the Madox instrument the land
was delivered to the gagee for a period of fifteen years at a rental
of sixpence per year, with a provision that upon failure on the

[34] PMH, v. 2, 119.
[35] V. 1, 303.
[36] Form no. 42.

part of the gagor to pay the debt at the end of the period the gagee was to hold the property from year to year at the same rental until he was paid in full. In the Barzillai form the gage is similarly given for a definite period of time, with a fixed annual deduction by way of rent, and with a provision that in case of default the gagee is to hold the property from year to year at the original rental until he is fully paid.

A truly remarkable parallelism between the Talmudic law of mortgages and the English law on the same subject, as laid down by Glanvill, is to be found in the passage in which the latter speaks of the usurious character of the "mortuum vadium," where he says that although the "mortuum vadium" is a species of usury it is not prohibited by the king's court.[37] This is obviously in complete agreement with the view of the Talmud, as interpreted by the French school of commentators, on a mortgage without deduction. The transaction, according to the Talmud, is quasi-usurious and involves a sin, but does not involve a legal wrong which would warrant the intervention of a temporal court.

An interesting variation of type (5) of the Talmudic gage is found in an English mortgage, dated 1190.[38] According to the terms of this mortgage a certain sum was to be deducted from the principal annually until the twenty-fifth year, that is, during the first half of the term of the mortgage, which was made for a period of fifty years. After the twenty-fifth year the mortgagor was to get the benefit of one-half the income from the land, together with one-half of the original rental. The similarity between this elaborate scheme and the gage konwn in the Talmud as "Kitzutha," type (5) above, is more than suggestive. It will be recalled that according to most authorities this type of gage is wholly free from the taint of usury and does not even involve moral sanctions. The term of fifty years may have been suggested to the parties by the Biblical law of the Jubilee year. Indeed,

---

[37] Glanvill, *De Legibus,* bk. 10, ch. 8.

[38] Round, *Ancient Charters, Pipe Roll Society Publ.,* v. 10, 93.

the Talmud likens a mortgage with deduction to the sale of land
under the laws of the Jubilee year.

Type (6) of the Talmudic gage, the so-called "mashkanta of
Sura" under which the debt was entirely extinguished at the end
of a specified term was similarly used in England at a very early
period. Pollock and Maitland, in discussing the gage for years,
state:

> "Now in our records it is not always easy to mark
> off the gage for years from those beneficial leases of
> which we have spoken above. Both of them will
> serve much the same purpose, that of restoring to a
> man a sum of money which he has placed at the
> disposal of another, though in the case of the benefi-
> cial lease there is nothing that could be called a debt.
> As already said the beneficial lease was common. It
> was particularly useful because it avoided the scandal
> of usury." [39]

It will readily be seen from the above that the gage for years
was the exact counterpart of the 'mashkanta of Sura," and that
both were used for the same purpose, namely, that of evading
the prohibition of usury.

Finally, an interesting reflection of Talmudic law is found
in a mortgage cited by Madox in his introduction to the Formulare Anglicanum.[40] A Jewish mortgagee leased the mortgaged
property to the mortgagor's wife. Madox calls this transaction
singular, and singular it certainly is to anyone not familiar with
Hebrew law. But a reference to the chapter in the Talmud
dealing with usury will at once reveal the reason for this peculiar,
and apparently fictitious set-up.

In this chapter [41] mention is made of a certain method of
evading the usury laws which the Talmudists condemn. This
method consisted in the mortgagee's leasing the property to the

[39] PMH, v. 2, 121-2.
[40] P. XXII.
[41] *Baba Metzia,* 68a.

mortgagor at a fixed annual rental. The instrument would recite that the borrower mortgaged the property to the lender, and that the latter leased it to the former. When the objection was raised to this form of instrument that the lender could not at the same time and by the same instrument become mortgagee and lessor, the formula was changed to read: The borrower mortgaged the property to the lender and, after the lender had remained in possession for some time, he leased it to the borrower. Still the Talmudists condemned this type of transaction as savoring of usury, because payments were made directly by the borrower to the lender. In the Madox mortgage the mortgagor's wife was brought into the picture in order to avoid direct payments by the borrower to the lender.[42]

The writer has attempted to show that every type of gage which was used by the Jews since the days of the Talmud was known and used in medieval England. This complete parallelism, together with the fact that there is hardly a phase of English medieval law, connected with the creditor-debtor relationship, which has not been influenced by the Jews, leads to the conclusion that the English copied these devices from the Jews.

[42] See *ibid.*, 69b, where it is said that the usury laws apply only to direct payments to the lender.

CHAPTER XXII

THE ORIGIN OF THE NEGOTIABLE PROMISSORY NOTE

The subject of the origin of the negotiable promissory note has been widely discussed by legal historians. Brunner, who has devoted a number of articles[1] to the subject, maintains that the principles underlying the negotiable promisory note are traceable to Germanic law and that the main elements of the negotiability clause are discernible in Lombard documents of the 8th, 9th and 10th centuries.[2] Under the Germanic law of procedure, Brunner asserts, the emphasis was upon the vadility or invalidity of the defendant's defence, and not upon the vadility of the plaintiff's claim. In other words, it was incumbent upon the defendant to show why he was not liable to the plaintiff. Therefore, he says, when the promise ran to the person in whose hands the instrument will appear, the defendant had no valid defence against the holder of the instrument, who was not required to show how the defendant became liable to him.[3]

---

[1] See the following articles by Brunner: *Die fraenkisch-romanische Urkunde,* Zeitschrift f. d. ges. Handelsrecht, vol. 22, pp. 59ff, 105ff, 505ff. ; *Zur Geschichte des Inhaberpapiers in Deutschland,* ibid, vol. 23, p. 225ff. ; *Carta und Notitia, Commentationes philologicae in honorem Th. Mommseni,* p. 570ff. (reprinted in his *Abhandlungen zur Rechtsgeschichte,* vol. 1, p. 458ff.); *Das franzoesische Inhaberpapier des Mittelalters, Festschrift fuer H. Thoel,* p. 7ff. (reprinted in *Abhandlungen,* vol. 1, p. 487ff.).

[2] Brunner, *Die fraenkisch-romanische Urkunde,* Zeitschrift f. d. ges. Handelsrecht, vol. 22, pp. 105ff. Brunner's theory of the origin of negotiable instruments is followed by Jenks (*The Early History of Negotiable Instruments, Select Essays in Anglo-American Legal History,* vol. 3, p. 51ff.) and by Holdsworth (*The Origin and Early History of Negotiable Instruments,* Law Quarterly Review, vol. 31, p. 12ff.).

[3] Brunner, *Abhandlungen,* vol. 1, p. 539f. See also Holdsworth, *op. cit.,* p. 20.

It seems, however, that Brunner's so-called "principle of the Germanic law of procedure," which supposedly lays stress upon the validity of the defendant's defence—a most peculiar principle indeed—is but a product of his own imagination. He cites no evidence whatsoever for this principle, except the facts which he seeks to explain by it. Furthermore, Brunner would apparently have us believe that the spirit of the Germanic law of procedure, having asserted itself through the Lombard notaries of the 8th, 9th and 10th centuries, lay dormant for about three centuries until it came back to life again in the French bearer instruments of the early 14th century.

The theory of the Germanic origin of the negotiable promissory note has been effectively refuted by Freundt.[4] He has shown that the clauses in the Lombard documents, mostly deeds of conveyance, which Brunner considered the prototypes of the negotiable promissory note, have nothing to do with negotiability. Of late it has been recognized by historians of English law that at least in England in the 13th century the Jews played an important part in the development of the negotiable promissory note.[5] But the full story of the origin of this legal device still remains to be told.

---

[4] K. Freundt, *Wertpapiere im antiken und fruemittelalterlichen Rechte,* vol. 2, p. 76ff.

[5] Beutel, *The Development of Negotiable Instruments in Early English Law,* Harvard Law Review, vol. 51, p. 813ff. See also Bailey, *Assignment of Debts in England from the Twelfth to the Twentieth Century,* Law Quarterly Review, vol. 47, pp. 516, 534. The theory that the negotiable instrument is of Jewish origin was first advanced by Auerbach. See his *Das juedische Obligationsrecht* (1871), pp. 250ff, 270ff. He was, however, unable to draw upon the documentary material, particularly from Anglo-Jewish and Spanish-Jewish sources, which has since become available. Also, his assertion that the negotiable instrument was known and used by the Jews in Talmudic times seems to be without support in the Talmud. While it is true that the legal principle upon which Jewish authorities of the later Middle Ages based the validity of negotiable instruments is found in the Talmud, it does not seem that this principle was made use of until the later Middle Ages.

The Negotiable Promissory Note With the Order Clause

The forerunner of order paper, in the form of a promise to pay to a named individual or to "your messenger" (*vel certo nuncio* or *misso tuo*), begins to appear regularly in Genoa about the middle of the 12th century.[6] Brunner correctly points out that the term *nuncius* in these documents does not mean just a messenger (*Bote*).[7] The *nuncius* was a true agent vested with authority to settle or compromise the claim on behalf of the principal. The appointment of a *nuncius* was a formal act requiring the preparation of a notarial document. Brunner cites such a document from Italy, dated 1156, which reads in part as follows: *Ego Solimanus facio te Ogerius de Ripa nuncium meum ad recuperandum tarenos 1255 . . . quos mihi debet Jordanus de Molino.*[8] (I, Soliman, make you, Ogerius de Ripa, my agent to collect the 1255 *tarenos* which Jordanus de Molino owes me).

The *vel certo nuncio tuo* clause also occurs in 12th century documents from Constantinople [9] and from Venice.[10] In Marseilles [11] it is found in the first half of the 13th century, and in England [12] it appears in the second half of the same century. The term *nuncius* is also found used in England in the 13th century in connection with several transactions involving the assignment of bonds by Jews, where the assignee is referred to as the Jew's *nuncius*.[13]

---

[6] See, e. g., *Il Cartolare di Giovanni Scriba*, vol. 1 (*Documenti e Studi per la Storia del Commercio e del diritto Commerciale Italiano*, no. 1), pp. 3, 10 (1155), 34, 62 (1156), 411, 414 (1160).

[7] "Der nuncius, message, ist in diesen Urkunden nicht als ein blosser Bote, sondern gleich dem procureur als ein Befollmaechtiger aufzufassen, der quittieren und klagen darf". — Brunner, *Abhandlungen*, v. 1, p. 554.

[8] *Il Cartolare di Giovanni Scriba*, vol. 1, p. 59 (1156).

[9] *Archivio Veneto*, vol. 7 (1874), p. 97f. (1148).

[10] *Ibid.*, vol. 8, p. 149f. (1168).

[11] See, e. g., L. Blancard, *Documents inédits sur le Commerce de Marseilles*, vol. 1, pp. 12, 38, 48, 52.

[12] PMH, vol. 2, p. 227.

[13] See *Calendar of The Plea Rolls of the Exchequer of the Jews*, vol. 1, p. 223; vol. 2, p. 255.

The question arises: how did the word *nuncius*, which in its original sense denotes a mere messenger, come to mean an agent vested with authority to act on behalf of the principal, or even an assignee who acts in his own behalf? This question becomes still more pointed when we bear in mind that the Latin term most approximating that of agent for the collection of a debt is *procurator*. Indeed, in 13th century instruments for the appointment of agents we find that while the term *nuncius* is still retained, the term *procurator* is added.[14]

The answer to the above question is that the origin of the documents using the term *nuncius* in the sense of agent is Jewish. There is only one word in Hebrew for both messenger and agent. The word is שׁלִיחַ, which is derived from the verb שׁלח (to send). The difference beween the noun שׁלִיחַ in the sense of messenger and the same noun in the sense of agent can only be gathered from the verb which is used in connection with this noun. A שׁלִיחַ—messenger is sent (שׁלח שׁלִיחַ); a שׁלִיחַ—agent is made (עָשָׂה שׁלִיחַ). In the legal literature of the Jews the term שׁלִיחַ usually means an agent. Thus, the part of Maimonides' Code which deals with agency and partnership is called הלכות שׁלוחין ושׁותפין.

The messenger (שׁלִיחַ) or the representative (בא כּח) of the creditor is referred to in some of the forms in the formularly of R. Judah Barzillai (11th century, Spain).[15] In a Hebrew bond from Barcelona, dated 1112 and made by a Jew to a non-Jew, the debtor undertakes to pay to the creditor or to his representative (בא כּח).[16]

The Jews, who had occasion to use Latin documents in their dealings with Christians, simply translated the word שׁלִיחַ, which in its original sense means messenger, by the Latin word

---

[14] See, e. g., *Historiae Patriae Monumenta*, vol. 6, col. 1356 (1228) and col. 1479 (1248); Blancard, *op. cit.* p. 60 (1234).

[15] ספר השׁטרות (Formulary) of R. Judah Barzillai (ed. Halberstam, Berlin, 1898), nos 7, 34, 42.

[16] J. Millas i Vallicosa, *Documents hebraics de jueus catalans* (Institut d'Estudis catalans, Memories, vol. 1, fasc. 3), no. 21.

nuncius or *missus* having the same meaning. Christians followed the example set by the Jews. So much so, that in the 12th century they used the phrase *facio nuncium*—I make an agent— which corresponds to the Hebrew עושה שליח. Even in the 13th century, when Italian and French notaries had become familiar with Roman legal terms, those arch-conservatives still retained the terms *facio* and *nuncius,* though they added the words *constituto* and *ordino* to the former and the word *procurator* to the latter.[17]

In addition to the term *nuncius* or *missus,* the documents containing the *vel certo nuncio tuo* clause reveal other marks of Jewish influence. We shall list these seriatim.

1. The documents from Genoa [18] and those from Marseilles [19] are framed in the form of an acknowledgment (recognizance) of the debt by the debtor. In the Genoa documents it is the word *profiteor* or *confiteor* (I profess or confess) that is used; in most of the Marseilles documents it is the phrase *profiteor et recognosco* (I profess and acknowledge); and in some of the latter it is *profiteor et in veritate recognosco* [20] (I profess and in truth acknowledge). It is the last phrase which betrays the Jewish origin of the form. This phrase is an adaptation of the Hebrew *modeh hodaah gemurah* (acknowledge a true acknowledgment). As the writer has shown elsewhere,[21] the Hebrew phrase, which is translated in a 13th century document

---

[17] See documents cited in n. 14, above.

[18] See documents cited in n. 6, above.

[19] See documents cited in n. 11, above.

[20] See Blancard, *ibid.,* pp. 62-74. In a Spanish document of 1226 (F. Baer, *Die Juden im Christlichen Spanien,* vol. 1, p. 85f.), representing an acquittance made by a Jew, the same phrase occurs. In a number of 12th century acquittances from Montpelier the following variations of this phrase occur: "Scio et vere cognosco" — *Liber Instrumentorum Memorialium, Cartulaire des Guillemo de Montpelier,* p. 329 (1165); "Scio et in veritate cognosco et assero" — *Ibid.,* p. 332f. (1196-1197); "Scio et in veritate cum hac carta cognosco" — *Ibid.,* p. 344 (1200); "Scimus et in veritate cum hac carta cognoscimus et profitemur" — *Ibid.,* p. 156 (1149).

[21] See p. 258f., above.

from England as *recognosco veram recognitionem*,[22] grew out of certain rules of Jewish law with regard to the validity of recognizances.

2. The Genoa, Constantinople, Venice and Marseilles documents contain a provision for a general lien upon the obligor's property in favor of the obligee, which has been a regular feature of the Jewish writing obligatory since Talmudic times and possibly earlier.

In the Constantinople and Venice documents the clause providing for a general lien on the obligor's property contains a quaint phrase which betrays the Jewish origin of the clause. The obligor binds "all his lands and houses and all his property *in this world*" for the performance of his obligation. In the Constantinople document, dated 1148, the clause in question reads:

> "hec que supprascripta sunt si tibi non observavero tunc emendare debeam cum meis heredibus, tibi et tuis herebidus omnia tua suprascripta in duplum de terris et casis meis, et de omnibus que habere visus fuero in hoc seculo."
>
> (If I do not observe that which is written above, I and my heirs shall be obligated to pay to you and to your heirs double of all that is written above out of my lands and houses and out of everything that I shall be seen to own in this world).

In the document from Venice, dated 1168, the obligor's after-acquired property is included within the scope of the lien, the clause reading: "...de omnibus que nunc habeo vel in antea habere debeo in hoc seculo." In another document from Venice, dated 1173, the clause in question reads "...que nunc habemus aut in antea habituri sumus in hoc seculo." [23] (...of all that I now have, or shall in the future have in this world). In the Jewish form of the writing obligatory, in the formulary of Rab Hai Gaon (ca. 1000), for example, the obligor binds all his

---

[22] Abrahams, Stokes and Loewe, *Starrs and Jewish Charters in the British Museum,* vol. 1, pp. 4-5 (1234).

[23] *Archivio Veneto,* vol. 9(1875), p. 101.

property, which he has and which he may acquire in the future, *under heaven.*[24]

3. The documents from Genoa contain a provision in which the creditor is empowered, in case of default by the debtor, to enter upon the debtor's property and obtain satisfaction of the debt therefrom. This provision, too, is a regular feature of the Jewish writing obligatory of the Middle Ages.[25]

4. The documents from Marseilles[26] contain a clause in which the debtor undertakes that in case of default in payment he is to pay to the creditor the damages he may have suffered and the expenses he may have incurred by reason of such default, and that as to the extent of such damages and expenses the creditor shall be believed on his simple word. As the writer has shown elsewhere,[27] a similar clause is found in Jewish documents considerably earlier and is based upon a principle of Jewish law going back to Talmudic times.

5. In some of the documents containing the *vel tuo certo nuncio* clause the coin in which the debt is payable is described as *boni et justi ponderis*—good and of correct weight.[28] This description of the coin, as the writer has shown elsewhere,[29] is a regular feature of Jewish bonds throughout the Middle Ages and is also found in the Babylonian Talmud[30] in the name of a third century authority.

---

[24] ספר השטרות (Formulary) of Rab Hai Gaon, ed. Asaf, no. 4, Supplement to *Tarbitz* (publication of the Hebrew University of Jerusalem), vol. 1. See also ספר השטרות of Rab Saadiah Gaon (882-942), published by Asaf in the Saadiah volume, edited by Fishman (Jerusalem, 1942), p. 77. It is interesting to note that the phrase *all things under heaven* also occurs in some Constantinople and Venice releases, where the party executing the release states: "Et nichil inde remansit de ulla re de sub celo" — *Arch. Veneto,* v. 7, p. 95 (Constantinople, 1147); v. 8, p. 138f. (Venice, 1161).

[25] See p. 209, above.

[26] See e. g., Blancard, *ibid.,* pp. 38, 48, 52, 75.

[27] See p. 358ff., below.

[28] See documents quoted by Goldschmidt in his *Universal-geschichte des Handelsrects,* pp. 421-426.

[29] See p. 212, above.

[30] *Baba Metzia,* 44b.

All of the above, in its cumulative effect, leads to the conclusion that the *vel certo nuncio* clause is of Jewish origin. We shall now turn our attention to the alternative bearer clause.

The Promissory Note with The Alternative Bearer Clause

The *vel tuo certo nuncio* clause was undoubtedly an important step towards achieving negotiability. The debtor, who bound himself in advance to pay the creditor's agent, could not refuse to recognize the right of the holder of the note, who was the creditor's agent, to demand payment. But this clause did not achieve true negotiability, the essence of which is that the holder of the instrument may demand payment in his own right. True negotiablility was only achieved by the clause in which the maker bound himself to a named individual or to the bearer of the note. Under this clause, the holder of the note was just as much entitled to demand payment in his own right as the party named therein.

The earliest French note with an alternative bearer clause-- *à N. ou à qui cette lettre portera*—cited by Brunner, is dated 1291.[31] But evidence of the use of the alternative bearer clause by Jews in notes written in Hebrew is found considerably earlier. As already noted by Beutel,[32] the records of the Exchequer of The Jews in England contain a Latin translation of a Hebrew note with an alternative bearer clause made by one Jew to another as early as 1252. The translation reads as follows:

> "Diei le Evesk', Judeus, recognovit per starrum suum, quod tenetur Abrahe, filio Joscei, de Eboraco, in xiiL sterlingorum, reddendis ei, vel cuicunque presens starrum deferenti, ad . . . et si dictum terminum transierit, dicto Abrahe licebit mutuo accipere dictos denarios per manum alicuius Christiani ad usuram, videlicet, pro una libra II denarios in septimana; et pro toto predicto debito et lucro

[31] Brunner, *Abhandlungen,* p. 508.
[32] Beutel, *ibid.,* p. 821.

dictus Diei obligavit dicto Abrahe unam domum . . .
dum dictus Abraham vel aliqui assignatorum suorum
habeant dictum starrum dictus Diei non possit
alienare (allegare?) aliquam acquietanciam de predicto debito nisi aliquod starrum de acquietancia
inde facta per predictum Abraham." [33]

("Diaia le Eveske, Jew, acknowledged by his starr,
that he is bound to Abraham, son of Joce, of York
in L 12 sterling, payable to him, or bearer of the
present starr, at . . . and should he miss the said
term, it shall be lawful for the said Abraham to
borrow the said money by a Christian hand at
usury, to wit, 2d. a pound a week; and for all the
said debt and interest the said Diaia has engaged
to the said Abraham a house . . . and so long
as the said Abraham or any of his assigns hold
the said starr, the said Diaia may not alienate
(allege?) any acquittance of the said debt except
a starr of acquittance thereof made by the said
Abraham.")

A promissory note with an alternative bearer clause, written
in Hebrew and dated 1249, is also found in the collection of
Hebrew *shtaroth* published by Davis.[34]

Evidence of the use of the promissory note with the alternative bearer clause by the Jews in the 13th century is still
more abundant for Spain than for England. This evidence is
all the more important, since it comprises a detailed discussion
by some of the leading Jewish jurists of Spain of the principles
underlying the validity of the promissory note with the alternative bearer clause.

The question of the validity and legal effect of a promissory
note with an alternative bearer clause came before Rabbi Meir

---

[33] Rigg, ed., *Select pleas, Starrs and Other Records from The Rolls of The Exchequer of The Jews* (Selden Society Publications, vol. 15), p. 65.

[34] M. D. Davis, ed., *Hebrew Deeds of English Jews before 1290*, no. 207.

Abulafia of Toledo, Spain (died in 1244). The portion of the instrument which is quoted by Rabbi Meir reads as follows:

"Reuben and Simeon have constituted us witnesses, with complete *kinyan* [35] from now, to the effect that there rests upon them a true obligation by reason of a loan, with credence, to pay eighty gold denars to R. Nassai Jacob, or to him who produces this writing, Jew or Gentile, from this day to March of this year, without dispute and without asking for the judicial extension of time. And if Reuben and Simeon, the aforementioned borrowers, fail to pay the said amount to the said lender, or to him who produces this writing, Jew or Gentile, they shall pay all the expenditures that the said R. Jacob may incur in collecting the debt from them, or from one of them, up to five gold denars per hundred for each month that shall have passed after the said term; and the said borrowers, for themselves and for their heirs after them, have given to the said R. Jacob, with regard to every matter that may arise out of this transaction, with regard to these expenditures and with regard to all possible pleas that they might plead against this debt and these expenditures, the credence accorded to two lawful witnesses. . .".[36]

There can be not the slightest doubt that the above document represents a true negotiable instrument of the alternative

---

[35] "Kinyan (literally: acquisition) — a formality, simulating an exchange, wherein the party to whom a transfer of property is made, or toward whom an obligation is assumed (or the witnesses to the transaction on his behalf), delivers to the party making the transfer, or assuming the obligation, some object such as a scarf or a handkerchief, to make the transaction binding and enforceable". Rabinowitz, tr., *The Code of Maimonides, Book XIII, The Book of Civil Laws* (Yale Judaica Series, vol. 2), p. 332 (Glossary).

[36] *Responsa of R. Meir Abulafia* (in ספר אור לצדיקים, [Saloniki, 1799], no. 922).

bearer type, which may be enforced by the bearer in his own right and not just as an agent or representative of the payee named in the instrument. That it was so understood by all concerned becomes obvious from Rabbi Meir's discussion of the instrument.

In the course of his discussion, Rabbi Meir states that there was advanced against the validity of the above instrument an argument based on the following two rules of Jewish law: 1. A conveyance made, or an obligation assumed, in favor of a person yet unborn is invalid, the unborn person lacking capacity to acquire any rights. 2. If an obligation is assumed toward several obligees one of whom lacks capacity to acquire any rights under the obligation, the obligation is void as to all of the obligees. The description of the obligee in the instrument as "he who produces this instrument," being general, includes within its scope persons yet unborn at the time of the making of the instrument. As to these persons the instrument is invalid under the first rule. Therefore, it was argued, the instrument is void as to all others by virtue of the second rule. Rabbi Meir, however, held the note valid. As to the above argument advanced against its validity, his answer was that the note, being ambiguous, should be so construed as to uphold its validity, and that therefore the phrase "he who produces the instrument" should be construed as referring only to those persons who were in being at the time of the making of the note. It thus appears that the bearer's right to enforce payment was considered to be entirely independent of that of the named payee, and that the bearer was in no way considered the payee's representative.

The question of the legal effect of an alternative bearer clause came also before Rabbi Solomon b. Adreth (1245-1310) who decided that the holder was entitled to demand payment without producing an instrument of assignment.[37] The holder, Rabbi Solomon held, is on a *par* with the named obligee. He

---

[37] *Responsa of R. Solomon ben Adreth* (Lemberg, 1812), no. 921. See also no. 922.

does not derive his right from the named obligee. The obligation runs to the one as well as to the other. All that is necessary for the holder to qualify as an obligee under the terms of the note is to produce the note.

As a necessary logical consequence of the rationale of the holder's right to sue, Rabbi Solomon, like Rabbi Meir before him, added that where the holder of the note was not yet born at the time the note was made to the original obligee he would be unable to sue on it in his own name. The rule being that one cannot validly bind himself to a person yet unborn, the holder who was born after the note was made could not have been comprehended within the terms of the obligation clause.

It is interesting to contrast the rule stated by Rabbi Meir and Rabbi Solomon relative to the holder who was unborn at the time the note was made with the rule found in 14th century French sources that "homme mort n'a porteur de lettres" [38] (a dead man has no bearer of letters). The one rule stands for the proposition that the holder of the note is a principal, and as such he must be in being at the time the obligation is incurred, whereas the other rule stands for the proposition that the holder is an agent of the obligee named in the note and that the death of his principal terminates the agency.

It will be noted that the notes discussed by Rabbi Meir and Rabbi Solomon were of the so-called alternative bearer type, that is, they were payable to a named payee or to the bearer of the instrument. Such a note, while it is in principle freely transferable and does not require an instrument of assignment in order to enable the holder to sue on it, was, in some Jewish communities, not given the full effect its terms implied. In Toledo, for instance, it was customary to require that the holder produce an instrument of assignment executed by the named obligee. Rabbi Asher b. Jechiel (1250-1327), in one of his responsa, states that the custom is to be respected and followed by the courts.[39] And so custom imposed upon the negotiability

---

[38] See Brunner, *Abhandlungen,* vol. 1, p. 517.
[39] *Responsa of R. Asher b. Yechiel,* ch. 68, sec. 7.

of these instruments a restriction which was opposed to principle. But the ingenuity of creditors was quite a match to the conservatism of the courts. Soon the instrument with the pure bearer clause, without a named payee, made its appearance. The courts could not require from the holder an instrument of assignment, executed by the original obligee, since the latter's name did not even appear in the note. They had no choice but to recognize the holder's right to sue on the note without producing an instrument of assignment. A case involving such a note with a pure bearer clause is discussed in another responsum by Rabbi Asher b. Jechiel,[40] who divides his argument in favor of the holder's right to sue into two parts. In the first part he says that an obligor may enter into an obligation to a person who is not present at the transaction, either personally or through an appointed agent, by virtue of the principle of *zekhiah*, which is to the effect that a right may be validly conferred upon a party through the mediation of another, even in the absence of the party upon whom the right is conferred and without his knowledge. In the second part he says that one may validly bind himself to an unknown person, if that person is ascertainable in the future, and cites the case of king Saul, who bound himself to reward the person who would defeat Goliath.

It seems that the true negotiable note which was introduced by the Jews before the middle of the 13th century and which was based on the principle of *zekhiah* mentioned above had a long struggle for recognition against opposition by non-Jewish jurists. It was alien to the principles of the Romanized jurisprudence of the time which adhered to the maxim "alteri nemo stipulari potest". In France in the 14th century, as we have seen above, the bearer was looked upon as the agent of the named payee and the death of the payee terminated his agency.[41]

---

[40] *Ibid.*, ch. 68, sec. 9. See also sec. 11.

[41] Brunner (*Abhandlungen*, vol. 1, p. 540) states that from the beginning of the 13th century French jurisprudence was under the strong influence of

In Spain, under the *Las Siete Partidas,* completed about 1263, a promise in the form of "I promise to give you, or so and so, such-and-such a thing" could not be enforced by the third party.[42]

However, some twenty odd years after the completion of the *Las Siete Partidas* we find several notes with an alternative bearer clause, written in Spanish and made by non-Jews to Jewish creditors. One of these notes, dated 1285, reads in part as follows:

> "Sepan quantos esta carta vieren, commo yo P. A. et yo M. J., su muger, anbos a voz de uno et cada uno por lo todo, por todos nuestros bienes muebles et rayces.... conozcemos et otorgamos, que devemos dar a vos Cahadia judio..., o a *quien esta carta mostrare,* 900 mr.. alf".[43]

These notes, in addition to the alternative bearer clause, contain another clause which indicates that they were patterned after the form of the Jewish promissory note. We are referring to the clause in which the obligor binds all his property, *movable and landed (bienes muebles et rayces),* for the performance of his obligation. The phrase *bienes muebles et rayces* is most peculiar. One would expect instead bienes *muebles et immuebles,* movable and immovable being almost a natural dichotomy. How then did it happen that in these documents the phrase *bienes muebles et rayces* is used? The answer is that this phrase is an exact translation of the Talmudic *metaltelin um-*

Roman law and that it was by reason of this influence that in the 14th century the question arose whether the bearer of a promissory note with an alternative bearer clause had an independent right of action against the maker. Bearing in mind that the promissory note with the alternative bearer clause appears in France only towards the end of the 13th century, it is difficult to reconcile Brunner's statement with his view that this type of note was an indigenous French product based upon the principles of Germanic law.

[42] *Las Siete Partidas,* V, II, 7 (English translation by S. P. Scott, p. 1095).

[43] *Anuario de historia del derecho espanõl,* vol. 1, p. 394. This document is quoted by Baer, *op. cit.,* p. 1058.

karkein [44] (movable and landed property) universally found in all Jewish documents of an obligatory nature, in which the debtor binds his property, *movable and landed,* for the performance of his obligation.[45]

The close dependence of the alternative bearer clause, both in Spain and in France, upon a Jewish model may also be seen in the wording of this clause. In France, it is *ou à qui cette lettre portera* or *apportera* [46] (or to him who will bring this document), while in Spain it is *o a quien esta carta mostrare* [47] (or to him who will produce this document). The difference in the wording between the French and the Spanish clauses corresponds exactly to the difference in the Hebrew wording between the Jewish documents stemming from England and those stemming from Spain. In the Spanish-Jewish documents it is מוציא [48] (he who will produce), while in the Anglo-Jewish documents it is מביא [49] (he who will bring). Both of these Hebrew terms are used in the Talmud [50] with respect to legal documents and are certainly not literal translations of the corresponding Spanish and French words. While the Jews of Spain made use of one of these Talmudic terms, the Jews of England and France made use of the other, translating these, as the occasion arose, into the vernacular. Hence, the difference between the wording in the Spanish and French alternative bearer clauses.

In addition to the fact that the use of the promissory note with the alternative bearer clause is found among the Jews of Spain and of England at a considerably earlier time than it is found anywhere in Europe among non-Jews, there is other evidence which points to the Jewish origin of this type of note.

---

[44] See, e. g., BT, *Baba Bathra,* 44b.

[45] See, e. g., ספר השטרות of Rab Hai Gaon, no. 3; ספר השטרות of R. Judah Barzillai, no. 34.

[46] See Brunner, *Abhandlungen,* vol. 1, p. 508f.

[47] See document, dated 1285, quoted above.

[48] See documents cited in notes 55, 56, 57, below.

[49] See Davis, *ibid.,* nos. 28, 93, 207.

[50] *Mishnah, Gittin,* 1, 1 and 2, 1; *Kethuboth,* 13, 8-9.

Some of the special rules of law applicable to the negotiable promissory note seem to be traceable to Jewish law. One of these is the rule concerning protest. Thoel and Brunner are of the opinion that from the very beginning protest was nothing but evidence of presentment, which was necessary in order to put the debtor on a negotiable instrument in default.[51] Goldschmidt, on the other hand, maintains that protest was originally a warning to the debtor that upon default he will be liable to damages and expenses.[52] The earliest example of protest, cited by both Brunner and Goldschmidt, is a document from Pisa dated 1335.[53] The text of this document, in which the payment of damages and expenses is specifically mentioned, seems to support Goldschmidt's view. But the question may still be asked: why was it necessary to warn the debtor of the consequences of his default? The answer seems to be that the requirement of protest is of Jewish origin and is based upon the principle of Jewish law that no penalty is to be imposed upon a person without a previous warning.[54]

In a promissory note with an alternative bearer clause written in Hebrew and made by several Jews to Don Miguel Deca, banker of Pamplona, in the year 1325, there is a postscript in which the obligors state that in case of default they shall be liable, without protest, to a penalty equal to the amount of the principal obligation.[55] Similar clauses are also contained in two other Hebrew notes from Pamplona dated 1390 [56] and 1351,[57] respectively. The fact that as early as 1325 we find already a stipulation for a waiver of protest clearly indicates that the

[51] See Brunner in Endemann's *Handbuch des deutschen Handels-See und Wechselrecht,* vol. 2, p. 158, n. 15.

[52] Goldschmidt, *ibid.,* p. 457, n. 156.

[53] F. Bonaini, *Statuti inediti della Gitta de Pisa dal XII al XIV secolo,* vol. 3, p. 202f.

[54] See BT, *Zebahim,* 106b-107a.

[55] Baer, *ibid.,* p. 963f.

[56] *Ibid.,* 979f.

[57] *Ibid.,* 1003f.

requirement of protest in order to make the obligor liable to a penalty goes well beyond that date.

Another rule applicable to negotiable instruments which has a close parallel in Jewish sources is that of grace. Under the law merchant, the debtor on a negotiable instrument is entitled to several days of grace after the due date of the note.[53] A similar rule prevails in Jewish law and is known as זמן בית דין which may be rendered, somewhat freely, as judicial extension of time. Under this rule, a debtor in default may ask the court for an extension of time in order to enable him to raise the money necessary to pay the debt. This rule is stated by Maimonides as follows:

> "If the debtor said, 'I am willing to pay, but give me time, so as to enable me to borrow from another or to pledge my property or sell it, and I will bring the money', the court gives him 30 days' time. . . ".[59]

R. Asher b. Yechiel [60] quotes Nachmanides (1205-1270) to the effect that the rule about זמן בית דין is not a rule of strict law but one of grace (רחמים).

The similarity alone between זמן בית דין and grace is more than suggestive of the Jewish origin of this rule. But it is not this similarity alone which points to Jewish law as the origin of the rule of grace. The three Hebrew documents from Pamplona cited above [61] contain very significant evidence on this point. They are dated 1325, 1390, and 1451, respectively. The first one of these documents is a promissory note of the alternative bearer type made by several Jews, at the request of the Jewish community of Pamplona, to Don Miguel Deca. The instrument is drawn in the usual form of Jewish promissory notes of the time and contains the clause 'without asking for *zeman beth-din*". The second document, dated 1390, is also a promissory note of the

---

[58] See Goldschmidt, *System des Handelsrechts,* p. 280f.

[59] Malveh 22, 1. In English translation cited n. 35, p. 158.

[60] *Commentary on Baba Bathra,* 10, 25.

[61] See documents cited in notes 55, 56, 57, above.

same type as the first one and was made by one Jew to another. This document, too, contains the clause whereby the debtor renounces his right to ask for an extension of time. But to the usual without asking for *zeman beth-din"* is added the very significant and revealing phrase "without asking for grace" (בלי שאילת חן). The third document, dated 1451, is a promissory note made by two Jews to Miguel de Lorrencal, merchant of Pamplona. In this document, the phrase "without asking for *zeman beth-din"* is already omitted, and only the phrase "without asking for grace" is left.

The story of the development of the rule about grace is thus told most eloquently by the above three documents. In the oldest one of these, though the creditor was a non-Jew, the extension of time was still referred to only by its technical Hebrew name of זמן בית דין. The second document, though both parties were Jews, contains already both the technical Hebrew term of *zeman beth-din* and a literal translation into Hebrew of the Spanish term *gracia* by which the extension of time, apparently, came to be known. In the third document, drawn over a hundred years after the first one, only the Hebrew translation of the Spanish equivalent of *zeman beth-din* — *gracia* — is left.

CHAPTER XXIII

THE WRITING OBLIGATORY IN EUROPE IN THE LATER MIDDLE AGES

The clause binding the debtor's property, movable and immovable, present and future, which in England gave rise to the *Jewish gage,*[1] also becomes common about the middle of the 13th century in Germany, somewhat earlier in France and still earlier in Italy.[2] The form of security represented by the bond containing this clause was known in French law as *obligation* and its counterpart in German law is called by historians of German law *die juengere Satzung* — the newer gage.[3]

Franken,[4] who calls attention to the similarity between the French *obligation* and the German *juengere Satzung,* explains it by saying that legal institutions on either side of the Mosel river are equally traceable to a Frankish origin. According to Brunner,[5] the *juengere Satzung* developed from the procedure of *missio in bannum regis.*[6] Under this procedure, which was introduced by a capitulary of Louis the Pious, the property of a defaulting debtor was placed under the ban of the king. If the debtor failed to redeem the property by paying the debt within a year and a day, so much of the property as was necessary to satisfy the debt was turned over to the creditor. This capitulary

---

[1] See p. 252ff., above.

[2] See R. Huebner, *A History of Germanic Private Law,* p. 379ff.

[3] See J. Brissaud, *A History of French Private Law,* p. 607ff., especially p. 608, n. 1.

[4] A. Franken, *Das franzoesische Pfandrecht,* p. 2.

[5] H. Brunner, *Forschungen zur Geschichte des deutschen u. franzoesischen Rechts,* p. 466ff.

[6] MGH, *Legum Sectio* II, pp. 268-269.

of Louis the Pious, it is said, was the beginning of execution against land in the Frankish kingdom, from which, several centuries later, the *juengere Satzung* developed in Germany. The course of the development is described by Huebner as follows:

> "As the next step (to execution against the debtor's land) such executions against land in favor of creditors became free from their old association with the law of pledge. It became possible for the debtor to make a pledge of lands in such manner that he himself retained the possession and the profits while conceding to the creditor, in case of forfeiture, the rights of a credtitor 'who had obtained a judgment for the debt against his debtor, and for execution against the land'... This newer form of gage was therefore also designated an execution gage...".[7]

What is certain in all that Huebner, following Brunner and others, says is that the *juengere Satzung* represented an execution gage. But that it developed from the *missio in bannum regis,* which, according to Brunner,[8] stems from the primeval forests of Germany, is sheer imagination, to put it mildly. The Jews did not have the benefit of sojourn in the primeval forests of Germany, nevertheless they developed an execution gage which was in all respects identical with the German *juengere Satzung.*

Furthermore, in the light of what has been said above [9] about the *Jewish gage* in England and the form of the 13th century English bond it appears that England, too, had an execution gage. That this type of gage in England, which was known there as the *Jewish gage,* originated with the Jews can hardly be doubted. It is therefore likely that not only in England but also in France, Germany and Italy, where the part played by the Jews in the economy was similar to that which they played in England, the same type of gage was introduced by the

[7] Huebner, *ibid,* p. 381.
[8] Brunner, *ibid.,* p. 469.
[9] See p. 252ff., above.

Jews. This likelihood is greatly enhanced when the forms of the writing obligatory in France, England, Germany and Italy in the later Middle Ages are examined and unmistakable signs of copying from the Jewish bond are found there. But before proceeding to such an examination the writer must digress to say a word about the *missio in bannum regis,* which, according to Brunner, was an outgrowth of the Germanic outlawry.

It so happens that the capitulary of 816, which introduced the *missio in bannum regis,* is the first known European source which mentions the term of a *year and a day.*[10] There is apparently no trace of it in Europe prior to that time.

Much has been written by German scholars on the origin and meaning of the *Jahr und Tag.*[11] But none of these scholars was aware that this method of calculating the running of time was used among the Jews at an early time and that the Talmud is replete with references to it. "Thirteen years and a day", "twelve years and a day", "nine years and a day", "three years and a day" — are expressions found throughout the folios of the Talmud, as every student of the Talmud well knows.[12]

There is no mystery about the meaning of the extra day. It is merely a mode of reckoning the running of time. *A year and a day* simply means a full year. Traces of this mode of reckoning periods of time are also found in the Bible. Thus in Lev. 23:15-16, we read: "And ye shall count unto you from the morrow after the day of rest, from the day that ye brought the sheaf of the waving; *seven weeks* shall there be *complete;* even unto the morrow after the seventh week shall ye number *fifty days*".

It is interesting to note in this connection that the *year and day* is found already in an Assyrian legal document of the 8th century B. C. E. There is in this document a clause which,

---

[10] See Brissaud, *ibid,* p. 355, n. 2.
[11] See Huebner, *ibid.,* p. 15, n. 2 and authorities cited there.
[12] See, e. g., Mishnah, *Niddah* 5:4-6.

in German translation, reads: "Sobald er ueber Jahr und Tag das Silber gibt wir Manu-kisabi hinausgehen".[13]

This method of calculating time was apparently borrowed by the drafters of the capitulary from the Jews, and when its origin had been forgotten it gave rise to no little puzzlement and discussion.

That Louis The Pious' chancellor or scribe should have adopted ideas from the Jews is not at all surprising. The period of Louis The Pious' reign has been called by the eminent Jewish historian Graetz "the golden era for the Jews of his kingdom, such as they had never enjoyed and were destined never again to enjoy in Europe".[14] They were a thriving group of businessmen who enjoyed the protection of the emperor. Whatever international commerce there was was mostly in their hands, largely because they could more easily establish business relations with their brethren in other lands. The Jews also farmed taxes, and had free access to the royal court and held direct intercourse with the emperor and those near him.[15]

If it is to be assumed that the term of *a year and a day* was suggested by the Jews it may well be that the entire procedure of *missio in bannum regis* was also suggested by them. For the Jew in the 9th century the principle that a man's property, immovable as well as movable, is liable for the payment of his debts must have been in the class of self-evident propositions. This principle is assumed, without any discussion, throughout the Talmud.[16] Since disputes between Jew and Jew were subject to the jurisdiction of rabbinical courts and were decided in accordance with Jewish law, it is not unlikely that through the Jews Frankish judges and officials became acquainted with execution against land under Jewish law. Moreover, the Jews, as merchants, who probably engaged, at least to some extent, in

[13] Kohler und Ungnad, *Assyrische Rechtsurkunden*, no. 126.

[14] H. Graetz, *History of the Jews* (The Jewish Publication Society of America), v. 3, p. 163.

[15] *Ibid.*, pp. 161-162.

[16] See p. 253, above.

credit transactions, would be likely to seek the enactment of a
law which would give greater security to creditors.

All of the above suggests that the procedure of *missio in
bannum regis,* that is execution against the debtor's land, may
have been borrowed by the Franks from the Jews. But be
that as it may, this procedure is certainly a long way from the
execution gage of the later Middle Ages.

To return to the writing obligatory of the later Middle Ages.
In the 13th century there becomes frequent in the writing
obligatory throughout Europe a clause of far-reaching significance.
The borrower binds himself to pay to the lender his damages
and expenses as to the extent of which the lender shall be believed
on his mere word.[17]

The introduction of this clause in the bond made possible
a large expansion of credit, inasmuch as it afforded to creditors a
convenient and safe method of evading the strict canonical
prohibition against the taking of interest. Provision for the
payment of interest was made under the guise of compensation
for damages and expenses.

What is the origin of this clause? Here again Brunner has
the answer ready. The clause, according to Brunner, is an outgrowth of what he chooses to call a signpost of the Germanic
law of procedure (*ein Merkmal des germanischen Prozessrechts*).
Nowhere is Brunner's tendency to indulge in broad and unwarranted generalizations about the Germanic law of procedure
as having given rise to virtually every new and constructive idea
in European law of the Middle Ages better illustrated than in
this instance. It will therefore be instructive to quote at length:

> "In bonds for the payment of money the law
> of Steiermark of 1574 makes a distinction bet-
> ween those that contain the *Landesschadenbund*
> and those in which the *Landesschadenbund* is
> missing. The *Schadenbund, the* ordinary *Schaden-
> bund* or the *Landesschadenbund,* was a clause

---

[17] See, Brunner, *ibid.,* p. 646, n. 5.

consisting of two parts and customary in Steiermark. The first part was a provision concerning evidence of damages resulting from delay in payment. It provided that the extent of the damages which the creditor may suffer as a result of the debtor's delay in payment shall be established by the mere word of the creditor, his messenger or plenipotentiary... Also elsewhere this clause is not rare. As is well known, it is a signpost of the Germanic law of procedure that even the production of proof is subject to the principle of negotiation. Therefore, the parties are allowed to agree upon the mode of proof and to substitute their agreement, in their particular case, for the mode of proof established by law. Under Salic law, a defendant who was required to offer proof by ordeal, could, with the consent of his adversary, substitute for this proof by compurgation. According to Norman and Anglo-Norman law the parties could agree upon having the disputed issue decided by a jury (jurata ex consensu partium) even in cases to which the right to trial by jury was not applicable under the law. Similar agreements concerning the mode of proof could be made not only when issue was joined by the parties. The parties could provide at the time they entered into a transaction the rules of evidence which are to govern in case of controversy between them. Thus, in bonds for the payment of money it occurs very often that the contracting parties provide how the facts which concern the creditor-debtor relationship are to be proved. As a rule, it was naturally the creditor who secured to himself in advance certain advantages of proof. An example is furnished by the provision that the debtor may prove payment only *per instrumentum debiti cassatum vel per aliud instrumentum publicum*. Ever since

the old penalties imposed by law for delay in payment disappeared and the duty to compensate the
creditor for his loss occasioned by the delay became
limited to cases where there was an express agreement to that effect, we quite frequently find that
the debtor empowers the creditor to establish
the extent of his loss, thus occasioned, by his mere
word, without oath and without proof by witnesses.
For some time we find this clause throughout Central
and Western Europe. We find it in England, France,
Italy and Germany, as in general the medieval
bond, from the 13th century, has assumed an
international form".[18]

Let it be stated at once that, with the exception of the
substitution under the Salic law of proof by compurgation for proof
by ordeal, there is nothing in all the examples cited by Brunner
which is even remotely related to the Germanic law of procedure.
All of these examples represent instances of Jewish influence
upon European law. There is in Hebrew law even a technical term
for the principle underlying the examples cited by Brunner.
This principle is known in Hebrew law as נאמנות (credence).
In the standard code of Hebrew law, *Shulhan Aruk, Hoshen
Mishpat*, it forms part of the creditor-debtor law. A whole chapter,
containing twenty-three sections, is devoted to it. Little did
Brunner realize that in the above-quoted passage he was giving
a precise definition of נאמנות, namely, that the parties to a
transaction may agree in advance upon the rules of evidence
which are to govern any dispute that may arise in the future
out of that transaction, and that they will be bound by such
agreement.

The story of נאמנות is a fascinating one and is worth
telling in detail. It is spread over many centuries and many lands.

We shall begin from the end-product of נאמנות, namely,

---

[18] *Ibid.*, p. 645f.

the clause giving the creditor credence, on his mere word, as to the extent of his damages. This clause is found, among others, in a number of Hebrew bonds stemming from 13th century England and evidencing debts owed by one Jew to another. The following is a typical example:

> "And by his word alone, free of vow and free of oath, shall the said R. Yechiel be believed, if he should claim to have borrowed the said money through a Christian hand at usury. And the said R. Abraham shall be bound to reimburse him or his assign as to principal and interest which may accrue by reason of his failure to make timely payment, without suit and without dispute. And so long as this bond is in his hands, he (the debtor) shall not be believed, if he shall plead payment, or any other plea of acquittance, nor shall he (the debtor) be able to cause him (the creditor) to be subjected to an oath".[19]

There is in this bond a combination of two applications of the principle of נאמנות, namely:

1. That the creditor shall be believed on his mere word, without oath, as to the extent of his damages resulting from default in payment.

2. That so long as the bond remains in the hands of the creditor the debtor shall not be believed, if he interposes a plea of payment or any other plea of acquittance.

As to damages resulting from default, there is in the above document an element which is not found in the damages-and-expenses clause in non-Jewish documents from England, France or Italy. The writer is referring to the provision that in case of default the creditor may borrow the amount named in the bond through a *Christian hand* and that the debtor is bound to reimburse him to the full extent of the interest he may have to

---

[19] M. D. Davis, ed., *Hebrew Deeds of English Jews before 1290*, no. 83.

pay for the money so borrowed. This was obviously a fiction, designed to evade the strict Pentateuchal usury laws.

Interestingly enough, this fiction, which was apparently in general use among the Jews of 13th century England in their dealings among themselves, and was probably also in use among German Jews, found its way into bonds evidencing debts owed by Christian to Christian in Germany. By substituting a *Jewish hand* for the *Christian hand* of the Hebrew bond, it was used by Christian money-lenders to evade the canonical prohibition against usury. The fiction was known in Germany as *Geld auf Schaden nehmen* and was in wide use, particularly in South Germany. Huebner describes it thus: "It was also a favored practice, especially in South Germany, to permit the creditor to raise the money owing him at a Jew's, to whom the debtor must then pay the defaulted sum with interest (so-called *raising money on damages,* Geld auf Schaden nehmen)".[20]

Huebner apparently failed to perceive the true nature of the device. He did not realize that the Jew in the German bonds, like the Christian in the Jewish bonds from England, was but a fiction, and that it was never contemplated by the parties that in case of default the creditor should actually borrow the money from a Jew at interest. The payment of interest to the creditor was given the color of legality by representing it as reimbursement of interest supposedly paid by the creditor himself.

That the Jews of 13th century England did not borrow the credence clause from non-Jews becomes evident when we turn our attention to Jewish documents and formularies of other lands and other ages. There is hardly a Jewish document or a form of an obligatory nature, beginning with the Gaonic period (before the year 1000) and ending almost in modern times, in which we do not find the credence device in one form or another. Following are excerpts from some documents and forms:

> "And everything she will say concerning her *kethuba* she shall be believed by the word of her mouth" —

[20] Huebner, *ibid.,* p. 524.

From a form of a *kethuba* appearing in a collection of Gaonic responsa.[21]

"...And whenever this bond is produced uncut (uncancelled) or without payment being noted thereon, or when you have no witnesses of payment, N (the creditor) shall be believed when he will say 'I have not received payment', and it shall be incumbent upon you to pay him the whole debt, or what you will then owe him, by the word of his mouth, without oath..." — from a form of a bond, Formulary of Rav Hai Gaon.[22]

"...And if, Heaven forbid, I shall fail to pay at the time agreed upon, he (the obligee) may forthwith force me and compel me, in a Jewish or non-Jewish court, and may have recourse to the authorities and incur all necessary expenditures; and all the expenditures he may have to incur by reason of my default he shall exact from me, and from my representatives, all complete, in addition to his principal... and he shall be believed on his word..." — From a form of a surety's undertaking, Formulary of Rabbi Judah Barzillai (11th century).[23]

"...And all expenditures he may incur in compelling payment through the authorities shall come out of my property, and his principal shall remain undiminished. And so long as this bond shall remain in his hands, or in the hands of his messenger, whole, uncut (uncancelled) or without an acquittance being written thereon, he shall be believed against me by his word, even as a hundred witnesses, as to what he has collected and what remains owing to him..." — form of a bond, Formulary attached to

[21] A. Gulak, *Ozar Hashtaroth*, no. 114.
[22] *Ibid.*, no. 213.
[23] *Ibid.*, no. 237.

the Munich Mss. of the Babylonian Talmud.[24]

Further examples, literally by the hundreds, could be given from various Jewish sources. But the writer considers this unnecessary as it is abundantly clear, from the excerpts given, that נאמנות is a device found during the Middle Ages wherever Jews are to be found. However, some of the forms quoted above bear a little further analysis and comparison with corresponding non-Jewish forms.

In an Italian document, dated 1196, we find the following clause:

> "Ita quod non liceat ei producere testes de pagamento facto in toto vel in parte absque isto breve inciso reddito vel aliud de fine facto". (That he may not produce witnesses of payment made, in whole or in part, without this instrument having been returned with an incision, or without another instrument concerning settlement).[25]

This type of clause was apparently widespread in Italy, and its valdity was expressly provided for in certain town laws. Thus, in the Statutes of Pisa it is provided:

> "Si inter creditorem et debitorem in publico instrumento pactum seu conventio intervenerit, quod non possit probare solutionem debiti in instrumento comprehensi per testes vel aliam probationem nisi per instrumentum debiti cancellatum vel per aliud publicum instrumentum, tale pactum et conventio firmum et firma validumque consistat". (If it be agreed between creditor and debtor in a public instrument, pact or convention that he cannot prove payment of the debt contained in the instrument by witnesses or other proof save by the cancelled

---

[24] *Ibid.*, no. 216.

[25] *Historiae Patriae Monumenta*, v. 6, col. 1175. See also v. 3, col. 1164.

instrument, such agreement shall be valid and firm).[26]

It will be interesting, one might say amusing, to see what Brunner has to say about the clause, quoted above from the Italian document of 1196. Says Brunner:

> "As they began in Italy to apply Roman legal principles to obligatory documents it became customary — as a reaction against these principles — to incorporate in these documents a clause according to which the obligor could prove payment of the obligation only by producing the cancelled bond or through another public document, all other evidence of payment, and specifically proof by witnesses, being excluded by agreement".[27]

So, according to Brunner, the clause barring a plea of payment supported by the testimony of witnesses was introduced toward the end of the 12th century by the Germanists and nationalists of the day, who, in quite modern fashion, rebelled against the importation of foreign elements into their national law. Throughout his discussion of this clause Brunner speaks of the *Germanic legal custom* (*germanische Rechtssitte*), *the national law* and the *foreign law* — meaning Roman law. It is hardly believable that a scholar of Brunner's stature should have been so blinded by his nationalism as to become totally oblivious to the intensely practical considerations which dictate the form that a document evidencing a debt should take. Bankers and money-lenders are the most cosmopolitan group even in our own day. To suggest that in the 12th century they, or the notaries who served them, were motivated by nationalistic considerations is nothing short of absurd. The clause was a very convenient and desirable one from the creditor's point of view. He cared

[26] F. Bonaini, ed., *Statuti inediti della Citta de Pisa dal XII al XIV secolo*, v. 2, p. 800.
[27] Brunner, *ibid.*, p. 536.

not at all whence it came. It was good enough for him, even
if it came from the Jews, as long as it served his purpose.

That the clause came from the Jews and represents an
application of the Jewish principle of נאמנות can hardly be
doubted. Its very language reveals unmistakable signs of Jewish
authorship. It will be recalled that the form quoted above from
the formulary of Rav Hai Gaon, who died in Pumbeditha,
Babylonia, in the year 1036, some 160 years before the Italian
bond of 1196 was written, contains the clause "And whenever
this bond is produced uncut (uncancelled) or without payment
being noted thereon etc.".[28] It will also be recalled that another
form quoted above contains the similar clause "And so long as
this bond shall remain in his hands. . . uncut (uncancelled) or
without an acquittance being noted thereon etc.".[29] The phrase
the bond uncut in the Jewish forms obviously corresponds to the
phrase *absque isto brevo inciso* in the Italian bond. That the
phrase in the Jewish forms was not adopted from some non-Jewish
source becomes apparent from a reference to a certain rule of
Jewish law concerning the cancellation of legal documents. Cutting
or incision of a legal instrument is the method prescribed by the
Talmud for its cancellation. The Talmud goes so far as to prescribe the exact manner in which the incision is to be made,
namely, lengthwise and crosswise or in the place where the
witnesses' signatures appear.[30] קרע בית דין (a judicial incision)
was a *terminus technicus* among the Jews, and incision was among
them the standard mode of cancelling documents. Here, then, is the
origin of the *breve incisum* in the Italian bond.

And so the Italian bond of 1196 leads us not to the Germanic
law of procedure but, through the Jewish legal forms of the
Middle Ages, to the Talmud. Indeed, in the Babylonian Talmud,
Shebuoth 42a, a stipulation by the creditor with regard to the
method of proving payment of the indebtedness is mentioned,

---

[28] See p. 361, above.
[29] See *ibid.*
[30] See BT, *Baba Bathra* 168b.

and it is there stated that such a stipulation is valid. Maimonides, in his Code, formulates the Talmudic rule as follows:

> "If the borrower stipulated that the lender should be believed against him even as two witnesses, the lender collects without an oath, even though the borrower produces witnesses of payment, since the borrower gave the lender the credence accorded to two witnesses. Even if the borrower produces 100 witnesses who testify to payment, or to payment in their presence, the lender collects without an oath, two witnesses being like 100 witnesses".[31]

Finally, as we have pointed out in another connection,[32] a נאמנות clause barring a plea of payment by the debtor so long as the bond remains in the hands of the creditor, substantially the same as that found in Jewish forms in the Middle Ages, occurs in an Aramaic papyrus of 456 B. C. E.

Such, then, is the story of נאמנות which, from the Aramaic papyri and the Talmud, through Jewish medieval documents, found its way into the bond of the later Middle Ages throughout Europe. This, together with the fact that the *execution gage* had been a regular feature of the Jewish bond long before this type of gage was introduced in Europe, points to the conclusion that the European bond of the later Middle Ages was, in its essential features, Jewish in origin.

The reader will perhaps wonder how the various clauses of the Hebrew writing obligatory found their way into general use by non-Jews who did not understand Hebrew. The answer is twofold. In the first place, in the case of a writing obligatory executed by a non-Jewish debtor to a Jewish creditor the latter would probably insist that some of the clauses with which he was familiar and which contained provisions designed to afford the creditor adequate security, be included in the instrument.

---

[31] Jacob J. Rabinowitz, tr., *The Code of Maimonides, Book XIII, The Book of Civil Laws* (Yale Judaica Series, v. 2), p. 135.

[32] See p. 103, above.

Secondly, in the case of a loan by a non-Jew to a Jew the instrument would sometimes be written in Hebrew by a Jewish scribe in the style and form of the Hebrew writing obligatory.[33]

An example of a Hebrew writing obligatory, dated 1112 and executed by a Jewish debtor to a non-Jewish creditor, is found in a collection of Hebrew documents from Spain.[34] This document contains a clause binding the debtor's property, landed and movable, for the payment of the debt, a clause barring a plea of payment by the debtor so long as the instrument remains in the hands of the creditor *uncut* (uncancelled) and a clause providing for reimbursement by the debtor to the creditor of any expenditures the latter may have to incur in enforcing payment of the debt. The non-Jewish creditor, who undoubtedly knew the nature of the security he was taking, thus had occasion to become acquainted with three of the clauses of the Hebrew writing obligatory, which, in the 13th century, were to become the main constituent parts of the writing obligatory throughout Europe.

---

[33] See F. Baer, *Die Juden im Christlichen Spanien*, v. 1, p. 1053f.

[34] J. Millas i Vallicosa, *Documents hebraics de jueus catalans* (**Inst.** d'estudis catalans, Memories, v. 1, fasc. 3), no. XXI.

ADDENDUM I.

THE DEMOTIC DEED OF CESSION OF THE PTOLEMAIC PERIOD

In ch. XI we have expressed the view that the demotic deed of cession of the Ptolemaic period is a copy of the ספר מרחק of the Aramaic papyri. We have relied mainly upon the dates of the respective demotic and Aramaic forms, the latter being at least a hundred years older than the earliest known specimen of the former. We have since come upon a bit of evidence which confirms our view in decisive manner.

One of the clauses of the demotic deed of cession contains a peculiar phrase which engaged the attention of Griffith, Spiegelberg and Sethe, the foremost Egyptologists of the past generation, and which to this day has not received a satisfactory explanation. The last four clauses of the type-form of a deed of cession, based on several documents beginning with two dated 281 B. C. E., in Griffith's (GCD, 127) English translation, read:

9. No man in the land, nor I likewise, shall be able to exercise authority over them except thee from to-day onward.

10. He that shall come unto thee on account of them in my name, in the name of any man in the land, I will cause him to remove from thee.

11. Thou having claim on me by the right of the writing for silver which I made to thee concerning them in the year 5, Thoth, of the king ever living, to do unto thee its provisions at all times, beside (those) of the writing of abandonment which is above, making two writings.

12. And I will do unto thee their provisions at any time without a blow.

367

It is the phrase "without a blow" which is obviously difficult. Griffith interprets the word "blow" literally and takes the phrase to mean "without a blow with the policeman's club", that is "without compulsion". In his comment on the phrase (*ibid*, 128), he says:

> The blow is capable of two interpretations, viz. either physical resistance offered by the vendor when bound to quit the property sold, or the application of the bastinado upon his person. The latter meaning seems the most probable. It is clear that in ancient Egypt the bastinado had as well-defined a position in all police-work and tax-gathering as it had in the days of Muhammed Ali. 'Without a blow' when interpreted therefore really means 'without official compulsion'.

Spiegelberg (*Zwei demotische Urkunden aus Gebelên*, Recueil de travaux relatifs à la philologie et l'archéologie égyptiennes et assyriennes, 35, 88) translates the phrase as "ohne irgend eine Weigerung". Sethe (*Demotische Urkunden zum ägyptischen Bürgschaftsrecht*, 244f.) criticizes both, Griffith's and Spiegelberg's explanations, but hesitates about offering a definite explanation of his own.

It seems that the scribe who first used the phrase under discussion translated an Aramaic technical term literally, thereby causing Egyptologists of a later day to engage in a fruitless search after the exact meaning of the phrase. The phrase is a literal translation of בלא מחאה and should be rendered into English as "without protest". The basic meaning of the word מחאה is *a blow*, but in legal terminology it is used in the sense of *a protest*. In the former sense it occurs in the Story of Aḥikar, line 83 (APC, 215), in the phrase מחאה לעלים, which is rendered by Cowley (*ibid*, 222) as "A blow to a slave". In the legal sense of *a protest* it occurs a number of times in the Talmud. See JDT, 756b. The semantic development from *a blow* to *a protest* seems to have been as follows: The verb מחא with the complement ביד, which literally means *to strike at the hand* and hence *to interfere*, came to be used in the sense of *to protest*. The following example from Mishnah Baba Bathra 2:3 will illustrate this usage:

חנות שבחצר — יכול הוא למחות בידו ולומר לו: איני
יכול לישן מקול הנכנסין ומקול היוצאין. עושה כלים, יוצא
ומוכר בתוך השוק; אבל אינו יכול למחות בידו ולומר לו:
איני יכול לישן לא מקול הפטיש, ולא מקול הריחים, ולא
מקול התינוקות.

A man may protest against another that opens a shop within the courtyard and say to him, 'I cannot sleep because of the noise of them that go in and out'. He that makes utensils should go outside and sell them in the market. But none may protest against another and say, 'I cannot sleep because of the noise of the hammer' or 'because of the noise of the mill-stones' or 'because of the noise of the children'. (DM, 367).

The combination מחא ביד is also used in Dan. 4:32 (35) in the sense of *to protest*. See GB, 913a and p. 132 above. In the case of the noun מחאה, when used in the sense of *a protest*, the complement ביד is dropped. See JDT, *ibid.*

The phrase "without a blow" also occurs in some loan agreements from Gebelên (Ryl. dem. 21, Adler dem. 11, 12, 25). One of the clauses in Ryl. dem. 21 (112 B. C. E.), in Griffith's English translation (GCD, 151), reads:

> Thy agent is he that hath right to recover according to every word that he shall say against me; and I will do them at his summons without delay and without any blows.

In addition to "without a blow", there are apparently two other Aramaisms or Hebraisms in this clause. The Egyptian phrase which is rendered by Griffith as "thy agent is he" seems to be a literal translation from the Aramaic or the Hebrew with the emphatic הוא (he), which occurs quite frequently in the Bible and in the Aramaic papyri. One example from each will suffice to illustrate the point. Gen 15:4 — אשר יצא ממעיך הוא יירשך (the one that shall come forth out of thy bowls — he— shall

inherit you). In Brooklyn 7:35 — ענני הו ירתנה, which is rendered by Kraeling (APK, 207) as "Anani — he — shall inherit
her". The phrase that is rendered by Griffith in Ryl. 21 as "at
his summons" is rendered by him in Adler dem. 11 (*The Adler
Papyri*, p. 86) as "at his voice". קול (voice) is a familiar Hebrew
idiom for *command*. See Brown, Driver and Briggs, *A Hebrew
and English Lexicon of the Old Testament*, 877a.

Most remarkable is the fact that a formula meaning "without
protest and without delay" is contained in the form of a loan
agreement in the Formulary of Rab Hai Gaon (c. 1000 C. E.),
published by Assaf in Supplement to Tarbitz I, 3. In form No. 3
(p. 20), line 16, the debtor undertakes to pay the debt בלא ערערתא
ובלא אוחיריא (without protest and without delay). ערערתא =
ערעור is the equivalent of מחאה (protest). See JDT, 1122a.

Were it not for the fact that the phrase "without protest"
in the demotic loan agreement represents an Aramaism it would
be quite natural to assume that the demotic formula, which is
over a thousand years older than the Formulary of Rab Hai
Gaon, is the original. But with this and the other Aramaisms
noted above in the demotic formula, it is more reasonable to
assume that an old Jewish model is the source of both forms.
(For the formula "without delay" in Greek papyri in which the
debtors are designated as Persians of the Epigone, see p. 84f.,
above). Certainly *Reichsaramäisch* or "official Aramaic" will not
explain these forms in Egypt in the 1st century B. C. E. and in
Babylonia in the tenth century C. E. In the Aramaic papyri of the
fifth century B. C. E., that is in documents belonging to a period
when it is still plausible to speak of *Reichsaramäisch,* there is no
trace of any such formula as that discussed above, although
there are in these papyri three loan agreements (Cowley 10 and
11 and Brooklyn 11). Jewish notaries used Aramaic, with a
considerable admixture of Hebrew, as a medium of expression,
but they did not thereby become "Arameans" or "Syrians", nor
were the formulae they devised "Aramaic".

The phrase "without a blow", together with what seems to be
another Hebraism or Aramaism, also occurs in a demotic document

of 206 B. C. E. from the Thebaid (Sethe-Partsch, *Demotische Urkunden zum ägyptischen Bürgschaftsrecht* 703f.).In this document a woman gives her assent to a sale of certain property by her son. The son had apparently inherited the property from his father and his mother's assent to the sale was necessary in order to free the property from the lien she had on it by virtue of her marriage settlement. The document, in German translation, reads in part as follows:

> "Empfange Schrift aus der Hand des Chelo... meines obigen Sohnes... auf welches nämliches Schriftstück ich gerufen habe... Ich bin entfernt von dir in Bezug auf sie ohne jeden Schlag". (Receive the writing from the hand of Chelo... my aforementioned son... upon which selfsame writing I have called. I am removed from thee with respect to them without any blow).

Partsch (*ibid.*, 704) has attempted to make some sense out of the difficult phrase "rufen auf die Urkunde" (call upon the document), but without much success. The solution of the difficulty seems to be that we have here another literal translation of a Hebrew or Aramaic phrase. The word קרא, the basic meaning of which is *to call*, is also used numerous times in the Bible in the sense of *to read*. See GB, 723f. The woman states that she *has read* the document, that is that she knows precisely to what she is assenting. The scribe who adapted the formula to Egyptian rendered קרא by its basic meaning of *to call* — which makes no sense in the context — thereby unwittingly betraying the source from which he copied.

It cannot be too strongly emphasized that the evidence from the legal formulae in the papyri — which is not unlike archaeological evidence in the form of tools and objects of art — is of the utmost importance in the study of the history of the Jewish people in ancient Egypt.

ADDENDUM II.

THE GENERAL RELEASE IN TALMUDIC SOURCES AND
IN THE PAPYRI FROM ALEXANDRIA

At p. 264, n. 51, we have referred to Tosefta Kethuboth, 4:11, where part of a form of a General Release is quoted. The proposition in which this quotation occurs is reported there in the name of R. Judah (c. middle of 2nd century C. E.). This proposition also occurs in several other Talmudic texts, namely: Sifra, ed. Weiss, 72b; BT Nedarim 35b; Nazir 24a; Baba Metzia 104a; PT Yebamoth 15:3; Kethuboth 4:8. There is a great deal of confusion in the reading and interpretation of this proposition. It seems that the correct version is that of PT Kethuboth 4:8, where it reads:

וכן היה ר' יודה אומר פטרה אינו חייב בה שכן היא
כותבת לו ואחרן די אתיין לי עלך מן קדמת דנא.

This is to be rendered as follows:

> "And R. Judah also said: If he divorced her he is not liable (for the offerings to which she became liable during the existence of the marriage), for she writes to him thus: 'and the other (liabilities) which I have against you from before this (day)'".

R. Judah quotes here part of the General Release which the wife would execute to the husband upon being divorced and receiving from him what was due to her. After referring to the specific items which the husband owed to the wife, the document would further state that she released him of any other liabilities which she had against him up to the time of the execution of the release, which would include the liability for her offerings. The word אחרן means here, as everywhere else, *other*. This pattern of the General Release, in which the obligee releases the obligor of a specific obligation and of all other obligations "from former times to the present day", also occurs in a number of the papyri from Alexandria discussed in ch. 7, above. See P. BGU 1104, 1154, 1155, 1164, 1167, 1168, 1169. The document first cited is particularly revealing, as it furnishes an almost complete parallel to that part of the General Release which is quoted by R. Judah. In this document (lines 15-21) a widowed woman releases her deceased husband's mother, who was surety for her *pherne*, of the obligation of the *pherne* and of any other obligation "from former times to the present day". On the similar custom of the groom's father acting as surety for the *kethuba*, see Tosefta Kethuboth, 4:14 (ed. Zuckermandel 265.11f.) and BT Baba Bathra 174b.

The papyri from Alexandria in which the form of the General Release occurs are about 150 years older than the proposition reported in the Talmudic sources referred to above in the name of R. Judah. However, the Aramaic formula, which was apparently in common use among Jews at the time of R. Judah, is probably much older than the middle of the 2nd century C. E., and a close scrutiny of both formulae, the Aramaic and the Greek, will reveal that in all probability the former was the model and the latter the copy.

In the Greek formula, it will be recalled, the release includes all other obligations "from former times to the present day". The second part of this formula — "to the present day" — is obviously tautologous, the phrase "from former times" fully expressing the idea that the release relates to all other liabilities existing at the time of its execution. In the Aramaic formula, on the other hand, this tautology does not occur, the release relating to all other liabilities מן קדמת דנא (from before this time). Now, those who copy legal formulae are not in the habit of abbreviating them. Rather, in their desire to improve upon their models, they usually expand them, although, as in this case, improvement is not always the result. It would seem therefore that the Greek formula is a poor copy of a good Aramaic original. It is to be noted that the phrase מן קדמת דנה in the sense of *in past times* occurs in Dan. 6:11 and Ezra 5:11. It is possible that some scribe who translated the Aramaic formula into Greek was induced by the proposition מִן (from) to add the second part — "to the present day" — to his formula to make it more conformable with Greek diction.

Furthermore, as has been stated above (p. 264, n. 51), there is a formula of a General Release in P. Hib. 96 of 259 B. C. E., which relates to all claims "of former times" and which is almost like the Aramaic formula. This document, which is about 250 years older than the papyri from Alexandria, contains a definite indication that it was patterned after an Aramaic model. In line 3 thereof the document is called συγγραφὴ ἀποστασίου, (document of being distant) which is a literal translation of the Aramaic ספר מרחק (document of being distant). See p. 22, n. 10 and Addendum I, above.

ADDENDUM III.

PETITIONS TO THE KING IN JUDAEA, IN EGYPT UNDER PERSIAN RULE AND UNDER THE PTOLEMIES

Jer. 21:11-12 reads:

ולבית מלך יהודה שמעו דבר ד' בית דוד: כה אמר ד'
דינו לבקר משפט והצילו גזול מיד עושק.

("And unto the house of the king of Judah: Hear ye the word of the Lord; O house of David, thus saith the Lord: Execute justice in the morning, and deliver the spoiled out of the hand of the oppressor").

In this passage, it seems, the prophet is exhorting the House of David to perform the function — which by custom and tradition properly belongs to the royal power — of saving those who are wronged from the hands of the wrongdoers, that is of exercising royal equity in aid of the oppressed. In the light of Cowley 16, an Aramaic papyrus of c. 435 B. C. E., and of other evidence which we shall presently discuss, it is highly probable that the prophet was familiar with the practice of the royal chancellery and that he even used a term which was characteristic of a petition to the king by an aggrieved party.

Cowley 16 is a badly mutilated papyrus which Cowley calls "An Appeal to a Higher Court". The document is probably a petition to Arshem (See line 1 of the document and Cowley's comment thereon at p. 51 of APC), the Persian satrap of Egypt, by an aggrieved party who is asking for the intervention of the royal representative in his behalf. What the petitioners' grievance was is not apparent from the document because of its mutilated condition, but from the formula used at the end thereof the nature of the document as a petition may be inferred almost with certainty. In the last line of the document, line 9, there occurs the phrase כעשק אל יתעבד לי, which is rendered by Cowley as

375

"let wrong not be done to me". That this is a closing formula of a petition to the king or to his representative may be seen from a number of Greek papyri of the third century B. C. E. representing such petitions. In P. Cairo Zen. 59341 (a.) 33 (247 B. C. E.) = Hunt and Edgar, *Select Papyri* II, no. 267, for example, the corresponding closing formula reads [ἵνα] μὴ ἀδικηϑῶ ("in order that I may not be wronged"). See also P. Enteux. 26.15 (220 B. C. E.) = Hunt and Edgar, *Select Papyri* II, no. 268. The similarity between the Aramaic and the Greek formulae is so obvious and so striking that there can hardly be any doubt that the latter is an adaptation of the former. Cf. also כעשק עביד לי in lines 5 and 8 of Cowley 16 and the formulae in P. Cairo Zen. 59236.1 (254-253 B. C.E.) and P. Enteux. 82.1 = Hunt and Edgar, *Select Papyri* II, nos. 265, 269. It is to be noted that the verb עשק, which is used in Jer. 21:22 and in Cowley 16.9 is uniformly rendered by the LXX by ἀδικέω which is used in the Greco-Egyptian petitions just mentioned.

It seems that from the royal chancellery of Judaea, through the Jewish colony in Egypt, the practice of addressing petitions to the king or his representative to redress private grievances, together with the characteristic formula of such petitions, found its way into Egypt, first under Persian rule and then under the Ptolemies.

The picture presented by chapters V-XIII and by the three addenda is in accord with what Josephus (Antiquities XIV, 7, 2) reports in the name of Strabo:

> Now these Jews are already got into all cities, and it is not easy to find a place in the world that has not received this tribe of men and is not occupied by it. And it has come to pass that Egypt and Cyrene (as having the same governors), and a great number of other nations, imitate their way of living, and especially cherish many of these Jews, and grow to great prosperity with them, following the Jewish customs. — *The works of Flavius Josephus*, Whiston's translation revised by A. R. Shilleto, vol. 3 (1912), p. 20.

For Greek papyri the abbreviations used in Liddell-Scott-Jones, *A Greek English Lexicon* (1940) are followed.

APC.   A. Cowley, *Aramaic Papyri of the Fifth Century B. C.* (Oxford, 1923).

APK.   Emil G. Kraeling, *The Brooklyn Museum Aramaic Papyri* (Yale University Press, 1953).

AHDO.   *Archives d'histoire du droit oriental.*

AJS.   V. Scheil, ed., *Actes juridiques susiens* (Mémoires de la mission archéologique de Perse, vols. XXII-XXIV).

BASOR.   *Bulletin of the American Schools of Oriental Research.*

BIES.   *Bulletin of the Israel Exploration Society.*

BT.   *Babylonian Talmud* (cited by folio).

DM.   H. Danby, *The Mishnah* (Oxford University Press, 1933).

GB.   Gesenius-Buhl, *Hebräisches und aramäisches Handwörterbuch* (17th ed.).

GCD.   F. Ll. Griffith, *Catalogue of the Demotic Papyri in the John Rylands Library,* v. III.

GLS.   F. Pringsheim, *The Greek Law of Sale* (Weimar, 1950).

JDT.   M. Jastrow, *Dictionary of the Targumim, the Talmud Bavli and Yerushalmi and the Midrashic Literature.*

KRU.   P. Koschaker, *Ueber einige griechische Rechtsurkunden aus den östlichen Randgebieten des Hellenismus* (Abhandlungen der philologisch-historischen Klasse der sächsischen Akademie der Wissenschaften, XLII, Nr. 1).

MGH.   *Monumenta Germaniae Historica.*

MGP.   L. Mitteis und U. Wilcken, *Grundzüge und Chrestomatie der Papyruskunde,* zweiter Band, juristischer Teil, erste Hälfte, Grundzüge von Ludwig Mitteis (1912).

MRV.   L. Mitteis, *Reichsrecht und Volksrecht in den östlichen Provinzen des römischen Kaiserreichs* (1891).

OPU.   A. B. Schwarz, *Die öffentliche und private Urkunde im römischen Aegypten* (Abhandlungen der philologisch-historischen Klasse der sächsischen Akademie der Wissenschaften, Band XXXI, Nr. 3).

PMH.   F. Pollock and F. Maitland, *History of English Law* (2nd ed., 1891).

PT.   *Palestinian Talmud* (cited by chapter and section).

PWB.   F. Preisigke *Wörterbuch der griechischen Papyrusurkunden*, 3v. (1925-1931).

SP.   A. S. Hunt and C. C. Edgar, *Select Papyri*, v. 1 (1932).

UAR.   M. Schorr, *Urkunden des altbabylonischen zivil-und Prozessrechts* (1913).

UPBE.   *University of Pennsylvania Babylonian Expedition.*

———•———

Errata

Page 14, line 3 (from bottom), for derivately read derivatively.
Page 55, line 2 (from top), for commencing read commenting.
Page 72, line 13 (from bottom), for occured read occurred.
Page 80, line 1 (from top), for is read it.
Page 83, line 6 (from top), for occuring read occurring.
Page 96, line 3 (from top), for folows read follows.
Page 106, line 1 (from bottom), for occuring read occurring.
Page 116, n. 8, for 839 read §39.
Page 150, line 12 (from bottom), for vendee read vendor.
Page 286, line 5 (from bottom), for personality read personalty.
Page 320, n. 16, line 18 (from bottom), for to read of.

HOW TO SEE
MODERN PICTURES

AN EXTENSION OF THE DESIGN PRINCIPLE INTO THREE DIMENSIONS
AND AN EXPLANATION OF ITS BASIC APPLICATION TO THE WORK
OF THE MODERNS, THE PRIMITIVES, AND THE CLASSICS
OF BOTH EUROPE AND THE ORIENT, TOGETHER
WITH AN APPENDIX CONTAINING PRACTICAL
SUGGESTIONS FOR BRIDGING THE GAP
BETWEEN ARTIST AND PUBLIC

by

RALPH M. PEARSON

LINCOLN MacVEAGH
THE DIAL PRESS
NEW YORK · MCMXXV

PRINTED IN U. S. A.

THE VAIL-BALLOU PRESS
BINGHAMTON AND NEW YORK

TO MY WIFE, L. H. P.

PREFACE TO THE SECOND EDITION

Since the first edition of this book went to press several related contributions have considerably widened the perspective on the problem it attacks and incidentally revealed an ever-growing consciousness of the all-pervasive importance of educational effort in this direction. Among these the contribution of the psychologists probably bulks largest, though various new analyses of the arts of the museums which supplant the outgrown creeds of Berenson, Tolstoi, Ruskin and others may be of more immediate usefulness. On my central problem — the training of vision to see the actual architecture of pictorial design — there have been no further contributions so far as I know. The present approach, therefore, must stand for the time being with all its imperfections. The psychologists (see book list in appendix) corroborate this approach in the main but go further into its mental ramifications than I am equipped to go. For instance, in revealing more clearly the nature

Preface to the Second Edition

of the aesthetic experience they show a closer association with ordinary experience than I have shown, emphasizing it when derived from *fine art* as no more than an intensified form of that which is derived from a vivid choice of words, the right arrangement of a dinner table, the realization of the right design of a motor car, etc. This contradicts the separate compartment view of aesthetic experience and is a much more hopeful conception for the average observer, for it at once brings the possibility of realizing this experience within his immediate range. For the more extended analysis of the paintings of the galleries the new book by Albert C. Barnes, of the Barnes Foundation, is a valuable addition to present resources.

It is only fair to the reader to report that there is much difference of opinion as to the value of the Hambidge theory of dynamic symmetry briefly outlined in Chapter V. Charges of "mechanistic" have been brought against it from various quarters, charges which are based on the assumption that intuition instead of calculation is the only possible method of artists — that to use calcula-

Preface to the Second Edition

tion is to descend to the level of craftsmanship. Also the charge has been made that Hambidge would reduce all pictorial composition to flat pattern and thereby ignore those more important means to unified design that have three dimensional applications. To support this latter charge Hambidge is quoted as saying that "the use of deep space is a descent of art into photography."

Though my own acquaintance with dynamic symmetry is limited to its more obvious aspects and though I do not wish to over-emphasize its possible importance, there seems to be an irrefutable answer to these charges which applies to other mechanistic aids as well as this. If the mechanics or mathematics dominate when used in a work of art the result, of course, is mechanistic. But if the artist dominates the mechanics, making such aids subservient to his high purpose, then art also dominates. All the arts take their root to some extent in mathematics. That harmony in music, verse structure in poetry and the rhythms of the dance have mathematical implications could hardly be denied. Why, then, condemn mathematics unreservedly as a means to

Preface to the Second Edition

rhythms in visual art? The point should be made clear, however, as it has not been, perhaps, in the body of this book, that dynamic symmetry, diagonals with their independent uses, and all mechanical or mathematical aids are but so many individual items among a long list of the plastic means available to artists. The great work of art is a rounded out expression calling into play all the varied resources of its maker. The richer the resources, naturally, the richer the work. Intuition, with all the mechanistic aids in the calendar, still has every chance to function creatively. Leonardo proved it. Rheims Cathedral proved it. The Shelton Hotel proves it.

Those who make the flat pattern charge overlook the main Hambidge discovery that Greek and Egyptian temples, sculptures and vases were built, in the main, on the proportions of areas evolved thru dynamic symmetry, and that the fact that these works are three dimensional indicates the system to be capable of three dimensional application to pictures even if Hambidge has been so shortsighted as to make the statement quoted. Diagonals and rectangles as a means to

Preface to the Second Edition

dynamic symmetry or functioning independently can be utilized for three dimensional design purposes even when drawn on a two dimensional surface. This is the point these critics fail to see, as they apparently fail to see its proof in the paintings of Titian, Renoir, Seurat, Daumier and a long list of other masters of design, who knew nothing of dynamic symmetry but used diagonals and rectangles as structural guides. It is this lost comprehension of all potentialities of design that prompted the writing of this book and shaped its attack. If in it certain aids are overstressed I rely on the enlightened reader to restore a healthy proportion.

For preparing the ground for the change in the approach to pictures which must become general within our lifetime unless all signs fail, probably no one deserves greater credit than the late Arthur Dow and the art supervisors and teachers trained by him. These pioneers have substituted the design approach for the hitherto universal imitative approach to drawing in the public schools of the country. The importance of this teaching can hardly be overestimated and

Preface to the Second Edition

signs that it has been fruitful are evident in many directions — for instance, in the more spontaneously creative work shown in present-day school exhibits, in many applied design activities that have come to be part of most school programs, and in a quicker grasping of the design element in modern art by school children than by adults. Indeed the contribution of these public school art teachings, in the Dow manner, and of those art schools and colleges which have given a place to the same approach, is the yeast which is now at work among the youth of the country that will make it possible for them to *see* and *feel* modern (and ancient) art provided the growth is not checked, or destroyed, on their emergence from school, by the adult negativism so prevalent today among art "authorities" and "appreciators." The modern approach herein described is a carrying further of the two dimensional approach which Dow derived and made available from oriental art. It is to be hoped that the eager youth will have the chance to add it to their present equipment and thus fit themselves more thoroughly for those sensitive individual art

Preface to the Second Edition

judgments which will so enrich their own experience, and which are so sadly needed in all public art affairs.

Artists who are satisfied with their inheritance of suggestive representation are resisting the modern approach, or damning it bodily in a sort of blind self-defence. That their resistance and condemnation is instinctive and unthinking rather than rational is evidenced, I think, by the fact that there is not one iota of modern theory which they can logically denounce if they really grasp the significance of the classic art which they value so highly. If such will only turn their backs on the one concept of imitation, then there is not a single statement in this book which the balance of their art inheritance will allow them to deny. Artists who are dissatisfied with representation, on the other hand, but who have not yet assimilated the modern theory and are searching for the secret of the new vitality which they sense in modern work, can only be helped by such a laying open of basic principles as is here attempted.

I wish to acknowledge indebtedness for assistance in my own development from a rather hazy

Contents

ILLUSTRATIONS

Illustrations

HOW TO SEE MODERN PICTURES

CHAPTER I

THE NEW APPROACH TO PICTURES

THE modern movement in visual art offers, to-day, a new approach to pictures.[1] This new approach, in turn, offers to those who care to understand it, an important extension of experience, an increased capacity for appreciation, a different and more vital type of comprehension. It holds the capacity to do these things largely because it includes the past as well as the present in the widened sweep of its horizon, reëstablishing thereby numerous broken points of contact whose very existence had been forgotten in many quarters. The movement itself leans heavily on the past—is, in fact, such a marked going back to old standards that it could be called reactionary

---

[1] Since this inquiry will be confined chiefly to the field of pictures, that limitation will hereafter be assumed when the modern movement is mentioned. Sculpture may be included under pictures since, in a sense, it presents pictures to be looked at from all sides instead of one.

[3]

with more justice than is displayed when it is miscalled revolutionary. The new approach, therefore, must also be a return to a former type of approach. But to see it thus, a wide angle vision is needed, for the time gap to be spanned is certainly a good three hundred years—back to the days of Rembrandt or before. If the vision be narrower than that, if the approach to pictures be compared to the generally accepted approach of our own immediate past, the break is so radical that it can only be called revolutionary. But whatever its character or history may be, the important fact remains that just as the movement itself is a release for the artist into a wider experience, so, also, is the approach a release for the observer of works of art into wider experience. This quality alone makes exploration worth while for all those who prefer spiritual adventure to the comfort of spiritual stagnation. Let it be the reason for the present voyage of discovery and investigation.

The new approach is visual in character. It demands that pictures be seen as ends in themselves. It demands that a distinction be made

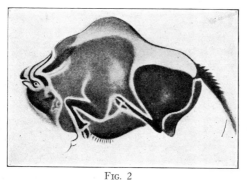

FIG. 2

PALEOLITHIC CAVE PAINTING
One of the Earliest Known Pictures.

American Museum of Natural History.

FIG. 3

ANCIENT MEXICO

This and figures 2, 4 and 5 are pictures from widely diverse civilizations
and ages in which highly developed design is inherent.

FIG. 4
ASSYRIAN

The New Approach to Pictures

between qualities in a picture whose only purpose it is to be seen, and qualities whose purpose it is to convey ideas or human emotions. It calls for the development of the sense of sight— the power of pure vision.[2] These demands will be emphasized continually as our journey proceeds.

But at the very outset, in order to eliminate needless antagonism, one point must be made clear. Just as visual qualities need not be the only ingredients of pictures, so the visual approach to works of art need not be the only approach. To segregate the visual from the literary and the human emotional approaches, is to segregate resulting experience from all practical entanglements. And this is exactly what should be done in order to better attain the main purpose of making the visual approach available to individuals for whom it is now sealed, double-locked,

[2] The term "pure vision" is not used in a scientific sense, for in such a sense there is, of course, no such thing. The human organism may respond to a great number of stimuli, which come to it through the sense of sight. "Pure vision" is here used to indicate that type of vision which results in a response to the purely visual aspect of things, as distinct from the response stimulated by various associated thoughts, ideas, etc.

How to See Modern Pictures

and covered with cob-webs. We do not see pictures, we think about them. For every one person who sees the lines, forms, and spaces, in a picture as *ends,* there are multitudes who see around them or through them to related *ideas.* Within the former experience of pure vision lies our only opportunity for knowing that crystalline form of esthetic emotion which is above and distinct from all human associations. The allurements of this pure experience of the ether above the mountain top are many, but so, too, are the allurements of the warm-blooded human experiences of the valley. The interweavings of art with life may not be denied. No choice need be forced. But here is emphasized a way which has been largely forgotten—a way which the modern movement of the day has rediscovered and laid open for those to travel who will.

Henry E. Krehbiel in his *How to Listen to Music,*[3] says "A tone becomes musical material only by association with other tones." *Similarly, a line becomes art material only by association with other lines.*

[3] Scribners, 1897.

[6]

The New Approach to Pictures

"Musical tones are related to each other in respect of time or pitch." *Art lines (or forms or colors) are related to each other in relation of space, movement, tonality, etc.*

"So far as music is merely agreeably coördinated sounds it may be reduced to mathematics and its practice to handicraft. But recognition of design is a condition precedent to the awakening of the fancy or the imagination."

So far as art is merely representative of nature, it may be reduced to imitation and its practice to handicraft. Recognition of DESIGN is a condition precedent to the awakening of esthetic emotion.

There is clearly an analogy. The modern movement has rediscovered the importance of design—the importance of the *relations* of lines, forms, colors, and spaces to each other and to the picture as a whole. Indeed it has discovered that this quality of design is one of the most essential qualities which determines a work of art —that without it the making of pictures may be "reduced to imitation and to handicraft." It is the recognition of design in a broadened meaning

[7]

of the word that may be said to be one of the basic principles of the modern movement.

Design, however, has been a basic quality in pictorial expression through countless centuries of human life. One sensitive to it is rewarded, in the briefest survey, by a thrilling discovery of its presence almost wherever he looks. Twenty thousand years ago, in the very dawn of known art, he finds it in certain of the paleolithic cave paintings. Coming to our own generation he finds it in the pottery of the Hopi Indians. Then a thousand years back he sees it in those master-pieces—the Aztec and Mayan reliefs, and, half around the world, in the equally marvelous carvings of Indo-China. He finds it in the decorations of Assyria, Crete, Egypt, Babylonia, China and Japan, in the supreme arts of Greece, in the recent totem-poles of the Alaska Indians, in Byzantine mosaics, marking its rebirth after the Roman debâcle, in carvings by African Negroes, in Persian paintings and textiles, in the master-pieces of Europe from the Twelfth to the Seventeenth Centuries, and in occasional work after that up to the true work of the modern movement of to-day. In all ages, in all places, he finds this same basic organization of elements built into the expression of the artist. A brief survey indicates its universality; a closer study proves it—with one exception. In work which copies nature—the so called representative work—it dies out and disappears.

Works of art from all the civilizations mentioned and many others, are preserved in our museums and are highly valued by society to-day. Archeologists give incalculable service in discovering, deciphering and cataloguing them. Institutions and private collectors, by purchase and gift, perform a great service in making them available to all in sumptuous buildings that are a fitting tribute to the great worth of what they contain. Historians and writers discuss them and interpret them and the great public gazes with awe and wondering reverence. But in all this appreciative activity, in all the discussion by learned authorities, in all the interpretative writings of historians and critics, in the mute teachings of museums through printed labels, in the lectures of museum docents, and of school teachers to touring students—in all the appreciation now bestowed on the art treasures of bygone ages, an overwhelming emphasis is given to consideration of facts and ideas relating to the works, an almost negligible amount of consideration to those visual qualities, the passionately apprehended space relations, which chiefly determine the art value of pictorial expression.

It is true that design is often mentioned in connection with such works, but, in a discussion of a Leonardo's *Last Supper,* there will be two pages about significance of subject matter to one sentence about significance of design. The emphasis is placed on matters of technic, or representation of life or of nature, on the story, on the deliniation of character or emotion, or whatnot, rarely on the crucible in which the artist has fused these various elements into a work of art—the crucible of design. Even though it may be said that design is taken for granted, the fact remains that the cumulative effect of such neglect is to lose for design the consideration which it deserves. The modern movement provides the opportunity to restore the balance, to vibrate to a forgotten chord, to *see* the thing which *is* art and has been art for twenty thousand years.

It should be then, a worth while aim to arrive at some comprehension of this strange, important quality called design, by excavating it, so to speak, from the accumulated mass of extraneous ideas under which it has become buried, and to apply such comprehension with great particularity in our study of pictures in order that we may gain the richest experience possible from them. Comprehension of design, along with comprehension of other qualities with which we are, perhaps, more familiar, means the attainment of discrimination. Discrimination means awareness, certainly a desirable state of being. The modern movement has opened a long-closed door. An open door invites entrance and exploration.[4]

[4] The following are fair examples of side-issue criticism. This from *Art and Archæology*. "Few are the people who see in a rag-picker anything suggestive of beauty. Mr.—— has, however, produced a figure that grips one. What a tale of object poverty it tells, a tale that cannot fail to touch the heart, and bring a clutching sensation to the throat. Everyone of these works tells a tale or preaches a sermon. They fearlessly typify those social forces and ideals which are the very root of society."

How to See Modern Pictures

And this sent to *The Arts* by a contributor signed B. P.:

"We were rude enough to follow a 'docent' as she was called, while she led a group of school children through a certain small city museum not long ago.

"From picture to picture they went.

"'Now children this painting is by Tryon. What is he famous for?' No answer. 'The name of an animal,' prompted the sweet docent. 'Horses,' said one little boy. 'Cows,' said another. 'That is right,' said the docent. 'Cows, Tryon, Tryon, cows.' 'Now next week I shall see which of you remembers best. And this is a particularly interesting Tryon because it has no cows.' At this there was a slight rumbling while Tryon took the opportunity to turn over in his grave.

"The next painting was called The Monarch of the Forest.

"'Now children what does the monarch of the forest mean?'

"'That's the big tree in the middle,' came in chorus.

"'You all know that, don't you,' smiled the docent, 'but you mustn't forget the little trees also. The forest has little monarchs as well as big monarchs.'

"In the foreground of the next masterpiece examined by the class were several domestic animals.

"Each one in turn was named by the bright little children. And to put the final proof of their profundity the dear docent said:

"'And what noise does the pig make?'

"'Umpf-umpf-umpf,' came in crescendo.

"'Sh, sh, sh,' admonished teacher, laughing. 'Not too much noise in the art gallery.'

"'Our hour is up now,' said the kindly lady, and merrily the children ran after teacher to the door of the museum."—B. P.

FIG. 5
AFRICAN NEGRO

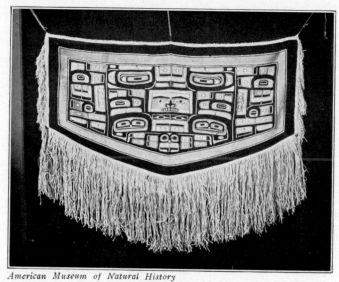

FIG. 6

APPLIED DESIGN. NORTHWEST COAST INDIANS

FIG. 7

CHAPTER II

APPLIED AND PICTORIAL DESIGN

THE modern movement in visual art (called Post-Impressionism) is a *return to style* —to a consideration of the *how it is done*. It might be defined as *pictorial expression of the felt nature of things built upon a passionate apprehension of line, space, texture, and color relations.* The word *design* is used in these pages as a compact label for these factors and must be understood to include all of them. This use extends its meaning beyond the limits associated with the word as used in applied design. The word itself when used in either the applied or pictorial field means more than is indicated by the term *composition*. Composition means the arranging, in a picture, of objects which are portrayed essentially as they exist in nature, whereas design includes the arranging or composing of objects which are transformed or conventionalized

How to See Modern Pictures

to meet its needs. Arthur Dow in his *Composition* [1] recognizes this larger meaning by saying he would prefer the word Design for the title of his book were it not for its associations with utilitarian application. But what does this definition of the modern movement mean in actual practice? How is it possible to progress from a more or less hazy comprehension of the dictionary meaning of its constituent words to a visual comprehension of its significance in pictures? To answer this it will be necessary to consider first what happens in ordinary, or applied, design, and then to compare such results with the happenings in pictorial design.

Fig. 7 is an example of ordinary applied design, its subject a vine in flower. A vine in nature is made up of stem, leaves, flowers, and

[1] Doubleday Page & Co. N. Y. 1916. Mr. Arthur Dow deserves great credit for his adaptation of the Oriental principles of design into his teachings so long before they were absorbed by Western artists or art schools. His influence on millions of children of grade and high schools through a method of teaching art which is built on the design approach, must have helped tremendously to free those children from the *imitation* thought-grooves, and, by so doing, prepare them for an understanding of the new art of their day. The value of such preparation hardly can be overestimated.

Applied and Pictorial Design

tendrils. Each of these parts, considered as a separate entity, is highly organized, or arranged, by nature. Nothing in a perfect flower, for instance, is accidental or superflous. The organization meets the functional needs of the flower as a living organism and at the same time arranges the various parts into an orderly pattern of great beauty. But—and this is the important point—as soon as one leaves the single unit in nature and looks at groupings of units, organization into pattern begins to disappear. In a simple, rigid plant like a geranium it is maintained to a large extent, but, as complexity of parts increase, orderly pattern changes into jumbled confusion. The ensemble of a wild grape-vine, for instance, while it maintains perfect functional organization, is a tangle of accidental and insignificant visual relations, which display a total lack of any pattern organization. The whole of nature is evidence of this condition. A forest or weed-patch, a mountain range or a pack of wolves, all spell visual confusion. The accidental or occasional exception certainly does not disprove this rule. But where nature stops the artist begins. When a designer wishes to use a vine as a motif for the decoration of a book cover, as in fig. 7, he begins at once to improve on nature. He studies the various parts carefully. He thinks of them as an assortment of raw materials out of which he is to create pattern (a picture). He changes or conventionalizes them to suit his needs. He reduces them to two dimensions, length and breadth, that they may take their places on the flat plane of the paper. He gives sensitive consideration to their proportions one to the other, and to their lines, textures, and colors, and to their spacing within set borders. He finds that ordered repetition pleases the eye and therefore repeats identical motives. In other words he creates a design by processes which may be summed up as follows:

DESIGN (in its ordinary meaning, and usually called applied design, because of its application to decorative purposes):

    1. Conventionalizes motives to suit its purposes.

    2. Repeats motives by rule.

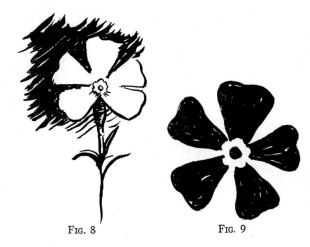

FIG. 8

FIG. 9

FIG. 10

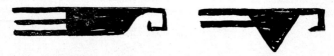

Fig. 11

Fig. 12

Applied and Pictorial Design

3. Gives sensitive consideration to line, space, texture, and color relations.
4. Is confined usually to two dimensions, length and breadth.

1. DESIGN CONVENTIONALIZES MOTIVES TO SUIT ITS PURPOSES

Fig. 8 represents a flower drawn essentially as it exists in nature.

Fig. 9 is a simple conventionalization of this flower, and fig. 10 a more complex or abstract one, for purposes of design. The function of applied design is to decorate—to treat some surface so that it will give a pleasing sensation to the eye through the medium of regulated lines, spaces, and colors. Subject matter, as such, ceases to be important, ceases to distract the attention of the observer from this purely decorative quality. The design exists as an end in itself. The actual flower of fig. 8 is a satisfactory organization so long as it is considered an entity pertaining only to itself. But, immediately it is associated with another flower, even a duplicate of itself, and

[17]

that association translated into a drawing for decorative purposes, then the actual forms become inadequate. Some of them are superfluous, some have too much detail, some are the wrong shape to harmonize with the border within which they must fit, or with other forms inside that border. Omission, selection, and transformation become necessary, and when applied are called conventionalization.

Applied design is radical in the conventionalizing of its motives. It may go so far that a bird is changed into a barely recognizable abstraction, as in the Hopi pottery motives in figs. 11 and 12, or, on the other hand, the process may go only as far as the simplification of figs. 9, 13 and 14. But however far it goes there is always change—abstraction, distortion, and conventionalization of subject to suit the needs of the organization.

Pictorial design, in the modern sense, has an equal range. It may practice only selection and omission; it may conventionalize without distortion, as in the Assyrian lion, fig. 15; it may practice distortion of recognizable subject matter as in fig. 16; or it may go the extreme length to

[18]

FIG. 13

FIG. 14

FIG. 15

FIG. 16

FIG. 17

FIG. 18

pure abstraction as in cubist painting, (see fig. 62). But whatever the degree the purpose remains the same—the moulding of subject matter into an harmonic entity, which, in the organized relations of its parts, thrills us through the sense of sight.

2. APPLIED DESIGN REPEATS MOTIVES BY RULE

The application of this statement is obvious. Fig. 17 is built up by repetition of the geometric flower pattern in fig. 10. Fig. 7 repeats the flower, leaf, and tendril motives. Fig. 13 repeats details within each bird as well as the entire birds themselves. Indeed, formal repetition is almost a universal quality of design.

Pictorial design also repeats motives, but by an infinitely more subtle rule. Instead of the exact and equally spaced repetition of fig. 17, it repeats only as dictated by the sensitive feeling of the artist. In "The Tea Party" by Gies, fig. 18, the wavy lines of the steam from the tea-pot are repeated twice, in reduced size and importance, in the wavy lines in the grass below, as are also

[19]

the circles of the cups in the circles of the flower-pots. The lines and forms of the two bodies repeat each other, but with variations, as in the forearms, which give emphasis and added interest.

In the works of the old masters the same type of sensitive repetition is universally made use of, as it is in the arts of Egypt, Assyria, China, etc.

3. APPLIED DESIGN GIVES SENSITIVE CONSIDERATION TO LINE, SPACE, TEXTURE, AND COLOR RELATIONS

If the lines of the design in fig. 7 (thought of, as marking the division between white and black masses) are looked at separately from all the other elements, it is seen instantly that they all have as definite a relation to each other as have the masses themselves. This relation is observed at once by a person with trained vision. If it can be seen or felt by an untrained observer, then that observer has passed the first grade in his journey toward comprehension of applied design.

In fig. 7, spaces can be considered in the same way. In seeing the spaces in a design it is neces-

[20]

sary to see the spaces around the motives as well as those taken up by the motives themselves. This is a tremendously important point. Every square inch of space within the borders of a picture should be so organized that it is a harmony, either as seen by itself or in relation to the whole. It is excellent practice to rule off into squares or diamond shapes, some picture by an old master and see how perfectly all spaces are organized. (See fig. 49). *Seeing* and *feeling* the right relation of spaces means passing the second grade toward comprehension of applied design.

Fig. 22 is a good example of texture relations. The word texture refers to the quality of a surface as to smoothness, roughness, hardness, etc. Texture relations in design are of the same importance as are the other relations just mentioned. Textures will be repeated for the sake of balance and rhythm, just as lines and spaces are repeated. Variety of texture is used to give variety of eye sensations.

Color relations in applied design comprise such a vast field that they can be only touched on here. Some idea of the complication of color combinations is realized when the "color organ" is mentioned. The thought of such an organ seems fantastical at first, but when the possibilities are studied the sense of strangeness in the association of the words "color" and "organ" begins to disappear, and a close kinship to be recognized. Colors play with and against each other just as notes do in music. Certain colors demand other colors in order to produce harmony exactly as one note demands certain other notes to complete an harmonic chord. If, for instance, there were one especially important spot of vermillion in a design, then one or more touches of the same color, or a lighter shade of it, would be demanded in certain spots for balance, and the true designer would be as pained by their omission or bad placing as a musician would by a discord. Color perspective is an important part of color design. The blues and purples are cold colors and appear to recede from the eye, while the reds and yellows are warm and appear to come toward the eye. Thus an appearance of movement forward and backward in a design, or picture, can be obtained by the alternate use of warm

Fig. 19

Fig. 20

FIG. 21

Examples wherein the sensitive line, space, and texture relations of applied design have been carried over into three dimensional pictorial design. Note the variation in the repetition of leg lines in Fig. 19, of curves in Fig. 21, of shapes in Fig. 20, and of lines in the two horses manes in 19 etc., etc.

Applied and Pictorial Design

and cold colors. By such is form or volume expressed. Color values (by which is meant the place of colors in the scale from light, or white, to dark, or black) are inseparable from color design. A design may be "played" all in light values of the same colors, (in a high key, as it is called), or in medium, or in low values, (a low key). Or it may run the gamut of the scale. Colors, then, are made use of in color design for four main purposes, as follows:

Harmony
Repetition
Perspective or volume
Values

When it is realized that possible combinations of colors are practically limitless and the resulting hues and values are as numerous as are the possible combinations of tones on a piano, then the immensity of the range of problems in color design begins to be understood.[2]

[2] Of course the comparison to music is not limited to color. All the other visual elements that go into the building of a design have their counterparts in music. Lines might be compared to the air in music, spaces to time intervals, textures to emphasis,

How to See Modern Pictures

All that has just been said about sensitive line, space, texture, and color relations in applied design is also true in pictorial design according to ancient and modern theory. (See fig. 19, 20, 21, 22, 23 and 24.) But the bridge that carries over in our minds from the one to the other has been washed out and must be rebuilt before we can see again these relations in pictures. The only method of rebuilding it, known to the writer, is, as has been said before, the method of hunting for the visual qualities in pictures—hunting intellectually, slowly and painfully, perhaps, but hunting with the object always in view of finally becoming visually, as well as mentally, aware of them, and thereby gaining the new and thrilling experience of visual esthetic emotion.

4. APPLIED DESIGN IS CONFINED USUALLY TO TWO DIMENSIONS

It is because such design is used for the decoration of surfaces that it is confined to two dimen-

forms to passages, etc. Control of the various relations in both cases determines the style.

Applied and Pictorial Design

sions, length and breadth. When a picture carries design over into three dimensions, length, breadth, and thickness, the meaning of the word is greatly stretched. In three dimensional creation the field of decoration is abandoned. Greater goals are hazarded. Instead of being a part of a decorative scheme, a picture becomes an entity in itself. All mental associations of usefulness, conformity to outside demands, etc., are lost. It is a source of experience within itself. There is no word in the English language to cover this extra meaning. Therefore we must force the word design to extra duty—as has been done in these pages. The question of how design in three dimensions is achieved and applied in pictures is probably the largest question to be considered and will be taken up in detail in the following chapters.

One point just raised, however, is worthy of a moment's further attention. Pictures were referred to as three dimensional sources of experience. This, to many, certainly will be an unfamiliar way of thinking of them. But why not think of them as just that? To object to

How to See Modern Pictures

this definition means that the objector thinks of pictures as pictographs, rather than as a means to visual sensation. His whole inheritance, of course, prompts him to think thus. It is the pictographic significance of pictures that is so constantly stressed in criticism, history, and every day discussion. When an individual is confronted with a picture it is almost an instinct to say, "That looks like——," or "That doesn't look like——," or "It certainly breathes the spirit of——," or "It is a powerful expression of——," or "It admirably suggests the——"; always the impulsive reaction is to something beyond or outside the picture itself, always the picture seems to be a sort of language for the transmission of facts or ideas to the mind. Applied design is about the only type of picture which does not have such extraneous connotations, though even in this field the authorities are continually explaining the religious siginificance of acanthus leaves, or that the break in the sky-band around a Hopi pot is to "let the spirits out." So nearly universal is this literary approach that one sometimes wonders if the race is

FIG. 22

An etching by Hopfer which is an excellent example of textures. Note the varying textures of hat, hair, fur coat, lettered panel and background. It has also very obvious design organization of big simplified lines, but the picture is built up in interest chiefly by the fascinating eye control with texture.

FIG. 23

THREE DIMENSIONAL DESIGN

FIG. 24

TWO DIMENSIONAL DESIGN

The above are good examples to show the difference between two and three dimensional design. Fig. 24 is not, of course, absolutely two dimensional for it suggests thickness but does so to such a slight extent that the contrast is evident. The design problem so admirably solved in the heads of the upper panel, (Fig. 23) is exactly the problem being solved by the moderns again to-day. It is French of the XIIth Century.

Applied and Pictorial Design

going blind—is losing the power to see objects as ends in themselves. Perhaps intelligence develops at the cost of the senses. Perhaps hearing will suffer gradually a like curtailment. It may be the day will come when we shall treat music as we now treat pictures and shall insist that a symphony "sound" like hens cackling in a barnyard or that it "express" this or "suggest" that. Of course, Wagnerian, and all other program music, is a big step in this direction. *Must intelligence destroy sensation?* Perhaps so. But consciousness of this tendency will make it possible to combat, at least, and probably to delay, its ravages in individual cases. Applied design is one field in which we are still allowed to see beautiful lines and spaces for no other purpose than that of pleasurable visual sensation (esthetic emotion). Pictorial design invites the extension of that experience into the field of paintings, sculptures, and prints. And, if one wishes to avoid extremes—does not care to experience pure, unadulterated sensation, he need only insist that, in pictures, the ideas and facts which he so loves, be presented to him through

How to See Modern Pictures

the medium of three dimensional design, so that he may gain a pleasurable visual sensation in looking at them *in addition to* a pleasurable intellectual sensation in thinking about their subject matter. It is the achievement of this double purpose that so enriches the work of the old masters, and it is well to realize that failure to react in either one of these fields means the loss of one half of our inheritance from them.

FIG. 25
HOPI INDIAN

CHAPTER III

VISION

SINCE vision has become such a neglected function, and yet is of such supreme importance as the one and only means of comprehending those visual qualities which are basic in pictorial design, it will be necessary to *think* a bit about *seeing*.

In the previous chapter it was hinted that knowing may prevent seeing. Here is an experiment suggested by Jan Gordon[1] which is

[1] *Modern French Painters*, John Lane, London 1923.

[29]

How to See Modern Pictures

most illuminating as a test of that possibility. A dozen persons without training in drawing are asked to draw a pail which is set on the floor in front of them so they may study it. A majority will draw it incorrectly with a flat

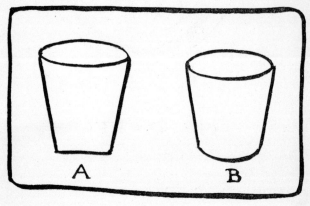

FIG. 26

bottom as in fig. 26 A. A minority will draw it correctly with an oval bottom, as shown in fig. 26 B. Why do the majority portray it thus incorrectly? The reason is this. They glance at the pail, then, with pencil poised over paper, begin to *think* about how to draw it. They *know* that the opening of a pail is round, and that such a round opening appears as an oval

[30]

Fig. 27

A picture in which cypress trees have been reduced to their simplest elements and woven into design.
From the original etching "Cypress Grove," by the author.

FIG. 28

An early American work by an unknown artist. Note the repetition of tree leaf textures, of small plants, the balance between large and small tree, the interesting play of land forms, the placing of the window squares and the contrast between them and the texture of round dots. The whole is most fascinating in the organization of its visual elements. Note how unimportant the story becomes in a picture like this.

in perspective. That is easy. No need even to look at the pail to find it out. So an oval is drawn. And the sides slope in toward the bottom. That is common knowledge. So the sides are drawn sloping in. Now, the bottom. How about the bottom? Why, the bottom is flat, of course. It sits on the floor. There is the pail to be looked at. Do their eyes tell them that the bottom repeats the oval of the top? No. Their minds tell them that it is flat and flat it is drawn. Their minds *know* so much about the bottoms of pails that their eyes cannot *see* a specific bottom directly in front of them. Their knowing prevents their seeing.

Here is another experiment. While inside a house in daytime, a piece of white paper is held up and compared to a black automobile on the street outside. The two extremes in value of the color scale are thus brought into contrast with each other, the lightest with the very darkest. It is positive and common knowledge that they are such extremes: there is no possibility of doubt. But, when looked at under the conditions stated, which *is* the darker? This question sounds so absurd to nine out of ten untrained people that they check their impulse to answer, that of course the automobile is darker, being black, because they suspect a trick. It is actually almost impossible to get many to answer. But, if they can be convinced that the question is serious and will finally give an answer, they will say invariably, even while looking at the two objects, that the automobile is darker. They do not *see* the actual condition, which is that the white paper, being in shadow, appears many times darker in value than the black car which is outdoors in strong light. In this case, also, knowing prevents seeing. If they did not know that black is darker than white, they would be forced to pause and gaze intently and then would *see* that white, in that particular situation, was much darker than black.

Blindness is defined as "lack of sight." The two experiments indicate lack of seeing. Does lack of seeing indicate blindness? If one stops to think of its ramifications this situation is appalling. If we are blind to the two actualities of the two experiments, we are blind to

Vision

thousands of other actualities. We know that the leaves of trees are green; we do not see that sky reflections may, in some cases, turn them to actual blue. We know a rose is red; we do not see the hundred changes in degree of red from noon to dark. Are we going through life literally as blind as bats, not realizing that we are missing a whole world of sensation through the sense of sight—that we are as visual cripples hobbling through a dark alley when the life and gayety of the boulevard is but half a block to one side of us?

No. We are not quite as blind as bats. We do see to a certain extent. We see life moving all about. We see beautiful sunsets, and mountain peaks, and butterfly wings, and roses, and other pleasing as well as repulsive sights. What kind of vision is it then that we do exercise?

There are four main kinds of vision. They are:

1. Practical vision.
2. Curious vision.
3. Imaginative or reflective vision.
4. Pure vision.

How to See Modern Pictures

1. PRACTICAL VISION

If an automobile stalls on a grade crossing, and up the track the driver sees an express train coming at full speed, he does not sit back and contemplate the design of the engine, he gives his complete energy to getting out of the way. In his able analysis of this type of vision, Jan Gordon designates it as "vision with resultant action." It is a very practical sort of vision. The same type of vision locates objects to be used in daily activities. There is the telephone, a table, a chair. One's eyes look at these objects and convey to the mind the information necessary to make them available for use. The objects are not seen as ends in themselves. Their actual forms and proportions are not studied, or even observed, and could not be described, or drawn from memory. In the words of Clive Bell [2] "the labels on the things are seen instead of the actual things themselves." This is practical vision with resultant action.

[2] Stokes. N. Y. 1924.

Vision

To continue Jan Gordon's simile, one may go to a movie and see a picture of an automobile stalled in front of an oncoming train. The need for resultant action is removed. There is time for a leisurely contemplation of the design of the engine, and for observing infinitely more of what is happening than was possible when the observer was himself an actor in the scene. The motion picture, then, calls forth a type of vision which is more observant and, therefore, is one step beyond the merely practical vision, though it still comes under that head.

If one looks at a street scene reflected in a mirror there is the same sense of detachment from actual physical participation in the scene itself. If a passing friend were recognized there would not be the same impulse to hail him as there would be were the vision direct. The scene in the mirror is unreal even though familar; it can be looked at as a picture of a scene instead of the scene itself. The need for resultant action is removed; objects and action will be observed much more accurately than if seen in

How to See Modern Pictures

life direct. So vision through the medium of the mirror, as that through the medium of the film, is also a step in development beyond the practical.

In both cases, however, the picture seen is absolutely true to life; it reflects all details as they actually exist; it changes the essential character of none. In other words it is a purely representative picture. And, since it is a human failing to get pleasure out of recognizing in a picture what is already familar in life, it is easy to understand the wide-spread popularity of all representative pictures—particularly the motion picture which allows just that recognition. A purely representative maker of pictures is attempting what the mirror and camera can do infinitely better than he, and his work is popular for exactly the same reasons. If art has to do with the creative changing of natural objects into design, then the pictures of the mirror, camera, and the strictly representative painter, have not started to approach the most outlying border of the province of art—have not, in fact even turned in that direction.

Vision

The most practical of business men, who habitually uses his eyes only to recognize labels on things, will often display an interest in some curiosity—a precious stone or an oddity of some kind—and he will observe this with a keenness of vision which he never bestows on ordinary or familar objects. The accurate, observing vision of the scientist, such as that of the botanist or ornithologist, might be included under this head since it is not common enough to warrant a separate classification here. But it is interesting to note that this keen, analytical vision, while it may see all the structural and scientific facts which come within its special department of knowledge, may, and probably does, remain absolutely blind to the pattern relations of the units observed. A scientist, for instance, whose special field is Archæology, and who has made a scientific study of particular works of art such as Hopi pottery, may see, in the designs he studies, all the historical, ethnological and symbolical significance, and be blind totally to

[37]

the art significance. The designs, as designs, stripped of all related facts and ideas, may leave him cold. It never may have entered his consciousness (from experience or otherwise) that they have an esthetic significance of their own. And not having experienced it, he may even go so far as to deny its existence.[3] This is the *curious* vision, which in spite of its limitations, is a big step beyond the practical. But it, like the practical, has not gazed even from afar upon the glorious country of art.

3. IMAGINATIVE AND REFLECTIVE VISION

If, after a motion picture performance, one goes home, and, during the quiet of the night, calls up in his "mind's eye" the picture he has just seen, or some similar event in his own experience, this becomes the imaginative or reflective vision. With it he has free play. He can review scene after scene from his past life,

[3] A most interesting example of this type of scientific mind is that of H. G. Spearing, who, in his *Childhood of Art* (Putmans, 1913), continually shows that he is unaware of the design significance in the very works about which he is writing.

[38]

and, if he has the imaginative ability, can add to them, color them, see fairies and goblins and things that never existed. Imaginative pictures, such as the illustrations of Arthur Rackham, and all historical pictures, grow out of this type of vision in the artist and stimulate it in the observer. It is a third big step beyond the practical and the first yet mentioned which is in itself a passport allowing its possessor to cross the borders of the world of art. Until it is achieved art is a foreign country with closed ports.

4. PURE VISION

This is the type of vision which is undeveloped almost universally and with which we are here chiefly concerned. It sees objects as ends in themselves, disconnecting them from all practical and human associations. To such vision a rusty tin can may be of more interest than a hundred karat diamond. For it sees the tin can and the diamond for what they actually appear to be, forms, textures, and colors. The form of the can, particularly if somewhat bent, may be more

intriguing to the eye in its irregularity than the
form of the diamond, in its geometric regularity.
And, on the other hand, the hard smooth texture
of the diamond, with its reflection of light and
color, may be more interesting than the texture
of the can. In either case, money value would
not enter into the consideration, for such value
is an extranous fact entirely outside the concerns
of the eye. If one looks at a chair with pure
vision, he does not think of the chair as something to sit upon; he observes it with wonder.
He sees its form, lines, and proportions. He
sees the patterns which the accidental lighting of
the moment makes upon it. He examines it as
one marvelling at a new discovery, for, though
he has seen hundreds of similar chairs in his life,
and even this one particular chair perhaps hundreds of times, he has never before seen it as
it now appears. Never before has it been in
exactly the same place on the floor, or been
turned exactly the same way, with exactly the
same degree of light on it, coming from the same
source. And if the chair be moved one inch, or
a different light be switched on in the room, the

whole design is changed instantly. This is pure vision and it is intriguing beyond words. When using it one's environment becomes of infinite variety and absorbing interest. The work of all artists, either representative or creative, is based on this type of vision. The representative artist puts into his picture what he sees while exercising it—the creative artist uses it to collect data which he later builds into his design.

Recognition of the existence of these four types of vision, then, makes it more possible to understand the common, habitual reaction to pictures and points the way to a possible enlarging of experience in that direction. The first three types, the practical, curious, and imaginative, because they are habitual in daily life, have become habitual in looking at pictures. And all three of them cause their owners to be interested in practical matters in the pictures—in the data which it records, in matters of skill, story, truth, etc. If anyone using these three types of vision looks at a picture in which the trees, let us say, have been made universal instead of particular —that is, in which the trees have had all their

How to See Modern Pictures

pictorially meaningless branches and wiggles omitted, and the essential shape then changed to meet the needs of design, (see fig. 27) he is at once more or less incensed. His practical vision at once asks, "What are they, cacti—or toad-stools—or sausages?" When told that they are trees, though the fact is of relative unimportance because the artist has aimed at another goal than that of copying, he is prompted, by this same practical or curious, or even imaginative vision, which latter is given to imagining additional facts or stories rather than pure forms, to great mirth and to the final absurdly obvious statement "But they don't *look like* trees!" Any other function than that of *looking like* something is entirely beyond comprehension. It simply does not exist for the person exercising only these three types of vision.

The attainment of further adventure in seeing pictures, therefore, depends on what we have called *pure vision*. In that direction, and in that direction only, lie the new horizons which have been revealed for us by the Modern Movement.

CHAPTER IV

RELATION OF LINES, SHAPES AND FORMS IN PICTURES

HAVING seen that the so-called pure vision is the type with which we are chiefly concerned in looking at pictures if we wish to see the design element in them, we can now take up the interesting question of how an untrained observer may develope this vision and make use of it. To attempt this goal it will be necessary to go further into the consideration of design in general, to dissect it down to the very bones of the skeleton out of which it is built—the interrelations of lines, shapes and forms, and their effects on the human eye. Since such analysis, however, is for the benefit of the observer of pictures rather than the maker of them, it will not be necessary to undertake a complete exploration of the fields entered. The aim will be to discover certain basic visual facts, familiarity

[43]

How to See Modern Pictures

with which will help one to see the visual content of pictures. If he here learns to recognize ten such basic facts on sight, his own interest and curiosity will lead him to the discovery and application of the next twenty.

Every picture which was ever made, or ever will be made, has two dimensional relations of

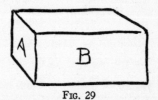

FIG. 29

its elements; every picture that deals with thickness, has both two and three dimensional relations. The inside of a room has three dimensions, length, breadth and height. A three dimensional picture represents, on a flat surface, the contents of a certain amount of space such as that contained in a room. Imagine a box, fig. 29, placed in this room. Any single side of this box, such as A, is itself a flat plane. The edges of that side, and the lines used to show

[44]

them, are naturally in the same plane of the side, and may be said, therefore, to be in two dimensional relation to each other. A different side of the box, such as B, is a different plane extending in a different direction, of which the same is true. Lines within, or bordering one plane, therefore, are in two dimensional relation with each other, whereas lines of one plane, when compared to lines of another plane, are in three dimensional relation to each other. It is well to remember, by the way, that there are no "lines" in nature. What is called a line, and is drawn as a line, is merely the edge which marks the actual or visual meeting of two planes.

A vertical line or form in nature gives a sense of stabilized power. It is dynamic, forceful, but poised. The eye observing it is impelled upward. A horizontal line gives an opposite feeling of repose, peace, absence of power. The vertical line suggests possible activity, that of tipping or falling; the horizontal one has fallen, is at rest, and allows the eye to travel leisurely back and forth along its length. A diagonal upright line is action itself. It is falling. And, like the vertical, it impels the eye positively in a certain direction. Let us now consider these lines as they are made use of in pictorial design.

Relation of Lines, Shapes, Forms

THE ALPHABET OF PICTORIAL DESIGN
LINES—SHAPES—FORMS

IN TWO DIMENSIONS—LINES

Varieties of Straight Lines

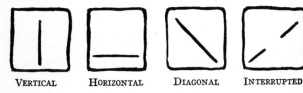

| VERTICAL | HORIZONTAL | DIAGONAL | INTERRUPTED |

These are the four main types of straight lines
that may be used in pictures.   They can be heavy
or light, long, short, or tapering.

Relations of Straight Lines

OPPOSED
EQUALLY

OPPOSED
UNEQUALLY

JOINED OR
ANGULAR

TRANSITIONAL

[47]

How to See Modern Pictures

RADIATING   CROSSED   RHYTHMIC

These are a few of the simplest combinations from the infinite number possible. One of the most basic of all laws of relations of lines in pictorial design is that any one dominant line in a picture needs another to stop the eye that follows its direction from going out of the picture— to turn it back within the frame. In the equally opposed lines shown above, the upper line does this, but, being at right angles, and equally spaced, it throws the eye either up or down. As placed in the next example, it throws the eye up. When two lines meet forming an angle, the eye is thrown in the pointed direction and again needs to be stopped and further controlled. Transitional lines lead the eye from one to the other with a series of breaks that are agreeable and give emphasis to the varied direction. Radiating lines draw the eye to a definite focus

Relation of Lines, Shapes, Forms

and are often used to concentrate interest on an important spot in the picture. Crossed lines attract and hold the eye, and give infinite possibilities for right arrangement, as is evidenced by the pleasing quality of plaid designs. Rhythmic arrangements of lines should affect us through the sense of sight exactly as rhythmic sounds do through the sense of hearing. The response of human beings to the rhythm of music, from the simplified form of the Indian drum, or the brass band, to the complex form of the symphony orchestra, is practically universal, but the response to the same quality in arrangements of lines and spaces is relatively slight because, and in the writer's belief only because, it has had insufficient opportunity for development.

Varieties of Curved Lines

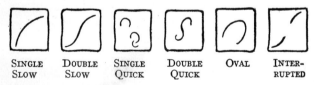

| SINGLE SLOW | DOUBLE SLOW | SINGLE QUICK | DOUBLE QUICK | OVAL | INTER- RUPTED |

All may be heavy, light, tapering, etc.

How to See Modern Pictures

Relations of Curved Lines

OPPOSED
EQUALLY

JOINED CURV-
ING ANGLES

TRANSITIONAL

RADIATING

SLOW WITH
QUICK

FLOWING

RHYTHMIC

Again infinite variations and all degrees are possible, and the control of the eye in these, and the following combinations, is the same as indicated above for straight lines.

Combinations of Straight and Curved Lines

OPPOSED
STRAIGHT
AGAINST
CURVED

OPPOSED
CURVED
AGAINST
STRAIGHT

OPPOSED
ANGLE
AGAINST
CURVED

OPPOSED
CURVED
AGAINST
ANGLE

RELATED

Relation of Lines, Shapes, Forms

In any picture there are many lines and in one sense they are all related to each other. The point is, are the relations intentional—are they *felt* by the artist? In a representative picture with, for instance, the fussy lines of tree branches copied as they exist in nature, it will be evident at a glance that the lines are *not* in relation.[1] When relations are considered, forms and lines are automatically simplified and controlled to that end. This is easily evident to one who looks for it.

SHAPES

Varieties of Shapes

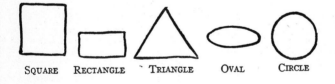

SQUARE   RECTANGLE   TRIANGLE   OVAL   CIRCLE

One or the other of the first two of these shapes is used in practically every picture as a border. Beyond such use they do not often occur in their pure shapes, but often in their essential shapes.

[1] See fig. 77.

How to See Modern Pictures

Variations are again infinite but should be seen for what they are essentially. When the eye looks into a square it travels across and back, up and down, and is equally rebuffed in any direction. In a rectangle the action is the same. In a circle, or oval, the eye travel is round and round, placidly—no rebuffs, no escape.

Relations of Shapes

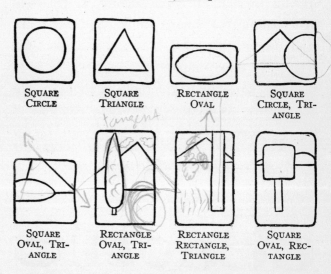

SQUARE CIRCLE	SQUARE TRIANGLE	RECTANGLE OVAL	SQUARE CIRCLE, TRIANGLE
SQUARE OVAL, TRIANGLE	RECTANGLE OVAL, TRIANGLE	RECTANGLE RECTANGLE, TRIANGLE	SQUARE OVAL, RECTANGLE

In addition to the elements named above, notice the additional shapes of spaces that are formed around the squares, ovals, etc. It can

[52]

Relation of Lines, Shapes, Forms

be seen at a glance at these simplest of all pictures that the problem of placing the most elemental shapes into a picture so that they seem *right* to the eye, is a serious problem and calls for exactly the same type of sensitiveness that governed a Titian when he was painting his masterpiece. And if an observer recognizes this quality in a masterpiece he will also recognize it, and respond to it emotionally, in the *right* arrangement of a square, an oval and a triangle. And, on the other hand, if he can sense the right relation of these simplest of all shapes, he is on the road to sensing the right relations of the masterpiece, as well as the wrong relations of inferior work.

IN THREE DIMENSIONS—FORMS

Varieties of Forms

| CUBE | PARALLEL-OPIPED AND TRI-ANGULAR PRISM | PYRAMID | SPHERE | CONE | CYL-INDER | OVOID |

How to See Modern Pictures

All forms in nature can be reduced to these primary geometric solids. A mountain is a cone or pyramid. A tree-top is a cube, sphere, or ovoid, its trunk a cylinder. A house is a parallelopiped plus a triangular prism. To so reduce such objects for purposes of pictorial design simplifies the problem to its lowest possible terms, both for the artist and observer, and, as a visual adventure, is most stimulating.

Combinations of Forms

HOUSE, PYRAMID, CONE, OVOID

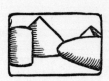

CYLINDER, CONE OVOID, PYRAMID

OVOID, PYR- AMID CYL- INDER, CUBE

The heavy problem of picture building is amply indicated in these three examples.

When a picture is looked at, the organized relations of its lines, spaces, forms, etc., should be felt emotionally rather than thought about in-

[54]

Relation of Lines, Shapes, Forms

tellectually. But since we, to-day, have almost lost the ability to respond to pictures emotionally (with that type of emotion called esthetic to distinguish it from the emotions of love, hate, etc.) it becomes necessary to bring this ability within the realm of consciousness again by actively *thinking about* the pictorial elements which exist to be *seen* and *felt*. Thinking in this case may lead to seeing and feeling. At least there is hope in that direction, whereas there is certainly no hope in a continued state of unconsciousness. Take the case of the simplified examples just shown. What is there to be seen and felt in the arrangement of shapes in fig. 30?

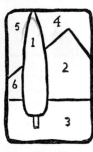

Fig. 30

Space 1 is essentially an oval.
Space 2 is irregular.
Space 3 is a cut-into rectangle.
Space 4 is irregular.
Space 5 is an irregular rectangle.
Space 6 is irregular.
Spaces 5, 4, 6, 2 make up a square behind space 1.

[55]

How to See Modern Pictures

The total space enclosed in border is a rectangle.

The making of this list is evidence of the intellectual recognition of the visual elements which make up this particular picture. The question now naturally arises, are these elements, or spaces, in the *right* relation to each other? Behind this question lies the very kernel of the hard-shelled nut we are trying to crack. What is a *right* relation of lines, spaces, forms, textures and colors?

In all frankness, it must be admitted that this supremely vital question cannot be answered in words. At least it is certain that it could not be answered in a hundred, or a thousand pages of words alone. It is tempting to say that it cannot be answered without training in drawing. It is obvious that comprehension comes most surely, after long training and practice, with attained pictorial expression. But,—and this "but " is the only justification of the present experiment—there is a chance, and certainly not a negligible one, that comprehension of the rightness of pictorial relations may come also through

[56]

Relation of Lines, Shapes, Forms

familiarity with right examples. Familiarity with good music breeds desire for good music where there was none before, and this desire can only grow out of some form of comprehension of rightness. The comprehension may be rudimentary and incoherent, inhabiting only the depths of the unconscious mind, yet it is there, it does exist. Perhaps training in expression makes comprehension more conscious and coherent, whereas familiarity only stirs blind desire. However the condition is explained, familiarity with great art in any medium does do something to the human soul—does release a blind hunger, a deep rooted need, that, even though it may lie dormant and ignored for most of a lifetime, is, nevertheless, as much a part of our human organism as the bones and blood vessels themselves. If familiarity, then, does have this possible power, it is the one great hope of the observer of art—the one chance for the individual who has not the time for training and practice in expression, to gain some degree of comprehension of works of art—to answer for himself the question, is this arrangement right? And if

How to See Modern Pictures

familiarity can give so much, then every possible extension of it is valuable—even the *thinking about* relations which should be *felt*.

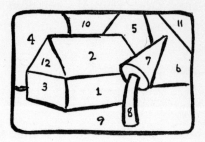

FIG. 31

When a picture progresses from two into three dimensions, the complication increases accordingly. In addition to the two dimensional relations of the parts of a single one-plane shape, there are the three dimensional relations of such a shape to others in different planes, as well as the three dimensional relations of the solid forms to each other. In fig. 31 what relations are there to be seen and felt? Here is a partial list.

IN THREE DIMENSIONS there are the relations to each other and the border of the picture of:

> House
> Pyramid

[58]

Relation of Lines, Shapes, Forms

Ovoid

Cone

Cylinder

IN THREE DIMENSIONAL relations of two dimensional shapes, there are such relations as those of:

Space 2 to space 5

Space 9 to space 10 and 11

Space 6 to space 4, etc., etc.,

Space 2 to the plane of border rectangle, etc.,

IN TWO DIMENSIONAL relations of lines forming parts of a single plane, or of lines to each other regardless of planes, there are such as:

Opposed equally

Opposed unequally

Curved opposed to straight

Angle against curve, etc., etc.

Here again the elements have been recognized, and the rightness of their relations may be thought about and felt. Is the house in the right proportion to the whole picture? Is the foreground space 9 interesting to the eye as a shape, and do the spaces 10 and 11 properly

How to See Modern Pictures

balance it? Is the tree 7 just the right distance from the side, and does it cut into the space 6 to just the right extent to make that space satisfying? Is the ovoid 4 the right size in relation to the pyramid and house? These and many other questions may be asked and their answer felt. Some trust may be placed in these sample pictures for they have been organized with considerable care and are essentially good designs.

BALANCE

There are many ways of obtaining balance in a picture. There can be color balance, where a small spot of intense color will balance a much larger spot of a subdued tint of the same, or other color; there is tonal balance, and balance of lines, shapes, forms, etc.

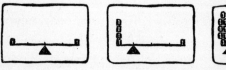

FIG. 32

Actual physical balance of fulcrum and lever is obtained in any of the ways shown in fig. 32.

[60]

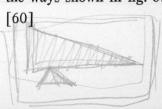

Fig. 35

Andrew Dasburg

Fig. 36

Henry McFee

Here are two paintings by contemporary Americans which reduce houses and mountains to geometric solids and build them into design. In the McFee note the three dimensional play of roof planes with each other. In the Dasburg note the transforming of fields into semi-abstract spots for purposes of design, also the weaving of color values. Note that both stand the test of being looked at upside down.

Fig. 37
GREEK VASE ABOUT 450 B.C.

Relation of Lines, Shapes, Forms

Pictorial balance may be illustrated in general by the diagram of fig. 33.

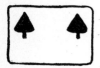  

Fig. 33

All three of these satisfy the eyes as balanced arrangements. The first is formal and stiff and would be used in such a picture as an Assyrian relief of a procession of standing figures, though the formality would always be relieved by controlled irregularities at intervals. As the near form increases in size and fills more of the space about it, it is balanced by a smaller form at a greater distance surrounded by a larger empty space. In color balance the small spot would increase in intensity and the large decrease as they changed in size. All good pictures, either representative or designed, use this law of balance. It is one of the shortcomings of the former that they stop with the application of such a law as this—do not go beyond it and change the forms represented to conform to farther laws of design.

[61]

How to See Modern Pictures

With the foregoing alphabet of design in mind it should now be possible to turn to works of art of any time or place and see more in them than is possible without such an understanding of their architecture. Take a simple partial abstraction such as fig. 34. Turn it upside down so the fact that it represents a bird may be forgotten, and the eyes look at it as an aggregation

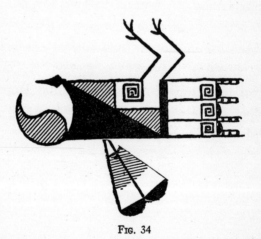

FIG. 34

of lines, shapes, and colors, (black, white, and grey being thought of as colors). Here in this one drawing by an unknown Hopi Indian lies the secret of all pictorial art of all the ages.

[62]

Relation of Lines, Shapes, Forms

With half closed eyes gaze at it for five minutes —ten minutes. Feel the relation of shape to shape and line to line. Note the large black triangle and how it is balanced by the lesser spots of black and by the extremely important angular line of the legs. See the repetition of curved lines, the slow and quick curve of the head, and the curving angles where head meets body, also the repetition of squares and rectangles. But also note the variation of repeated elements that differentiates pictorial from formal applied design, and adds interest by so doing. As complication in pictures increases, variation increases, adding richness of visual experience.

CHAPTER V

STATIC AND DYNAMIC SYMMETRY
AND THE DIAGONAL

S O far the very simplest A B C's of the design approach have been discussed. And, since the purpose of this book is to provide tools rather than carve paths, that general policy will be adhered to throughout. But an event has recently transpired in the art world that is of such vast importance to the highest development of contemporary design that it cannot be ignored in any type of investigation. That event is Jay Hambidge's rediscovery of the principles of what he calls dynamic symmetry, i. e., that type of symmetry which is present in the proportions of the human body, in growing plants, and in the arts of the Greeks and Egyptians.

As a result of his research, (some twenty years of it), Hambidge divides all design into two

Static and Dynamic Symmetry

classes, static and dynamic. Static design is that type which has been made use of in all ages and which has been considered heretofore in these pages. In contrasting the two types he says that the determination of the basic principles in a specific example of design means, in a sense, the elimination of the personal element. The residue then represents the planning knowledge of the artist. The higher and more perfect the art the richer the residue. Saracenic, Mahomedan, Chinese, Japanese, Persian, Hindu, Assyrian, Coptic, Byzantine or Gothic art analysis shows a conscious use of plan schemes, but with a type of symmetry different from that found in the growing plant or human figure, and which may be arrived at through the intuition of the artist. Greek and Egyptian analysis, on the other hand, shows a superior type which corresponds with that of the plant and the human, and which can only be arrived at through the geometric relations of areas computed with the aid of mathematics. The former is static, the latter living, or dynamic, symmetry.

Dynamic symmetry was discovered by the

How to See Modern Pictures

Egyptians and applied to temple proportions and bas-relief, was taken over by the Greeks about the sixth century B. C. and developed by them into the purest art expression ever attained by man. The Greek temples, sculptures and vases are built on it during the five hundred years of the golden age after which time the secret was totally lost until its present rediscovery. Dynamic symmetry, or living proportion, is strikingly exemplified in the position relations of the seed pods in a sun-flower. It can be expressed by a series of numbers, called the summation series, in which any one is always the sum of the preceding two, as 1 2 3 5 8 13 21 34 55 89 etc. It was developed by the Greeks through geometry, and the great lost secret of its application lay in the fact that, instead of depending on the proportion to each other of single lines, it depended on the proportion to each other of squares and rectangles of which any given line formed one side. Endless attempts to explain Greek symmetry in linear terms have been made during the Christian era, but no one had thought of explaining it in terms of areas.

Static and Dynamic Symmetry

Dynamic symmetry as applied, for instance, to a Greek vase governs every proportion of every least part from the height-width relation to the position of the handle and every fluting or curve of the stem. Given one of the correct over-all proportions, an infinite variety of correctly related sub-proportions becomes possible, just as in music, within one key, infinite harmonious creation is possible. In his book[1] Hambidge gives diagramatic analysis of many actual Greek vases taken from the collection of the Museum of Fine Arts, Boston, and elsewhere, which will give the reader a clear conception of the variety and complication of the design themes of these design masterpieces of all time. In temple architecture the application was as thorough, and the same doubtless held in sculpture, though the results of his investigations therein have not, as yet, been published. The application to the human body, and the possibilities of application to pictures are amply indicated in the pages of his too short-lived magazine, the *Diagonal*. Since our con-

[1] *Dynamic Symmetry and the Greek Vase,* Yale University Press, 1920.

How to See Modern Pictures

cern is with this latter field of pictures and lack of space forbids comprehensive study, we shall limit our investigation to the fundamentals and their application to that field, i. e., to the four most important dynamic rectangles, and to the diagonals by means of which they are determined.

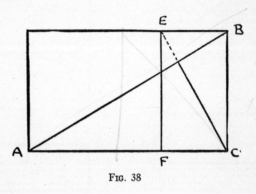

Fig. 38

The dynamic proportions of rectangles are arrived at by means of diagonals and verticals to the diagonals passing through a different corner, as in fig. 38 and extended to meet the side, as at E. The line EF is then drawn completing a small rectangle within the large one which is said to be "similar" to the large one because it has the same, though reduced, proportions. When the small rectangle is of such a size that

[68]

Static and Dynamic Symmetry

it is one half, third, fourth, or fifth of the larger then it is in dynamic relation to it.

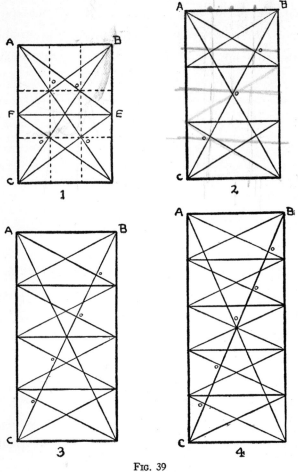

FIG. 39

How to See Modern Pictures

In the rectangle 1 of fig. 39 the square of which the end line AB is one side is exactly one half the area of the square of which the side line AC forms one side. In this case the ratio between the end line AB and the side line AC is 1.4142 which is the square root of 2. The rectangle is called, therefore, a root two rectangle. A moment's thought will indicate how impossible it would be to find this proportioned rectangle without considering areas instead of lines. The proportion of the lines to each other is incommensurate, (i. e. the one cannot be divided into the other without a fraction), whereas the proportion of the squares indicated by the lines is commensurate, or divisible evenly. This is the gist of the Hambidge discovery and its tremendous importance is seen at a glance even without knowledge of the elaborate geometrical data which supports it.

If a perpendicular to the diagonal CB is drawn through the corner A, and extended to meet the side at E, and the line EF drawn to complete the rectangle FB within the larger one, then, by this means, dynamic proportion has been established between the two. If the corresponding small

[70]

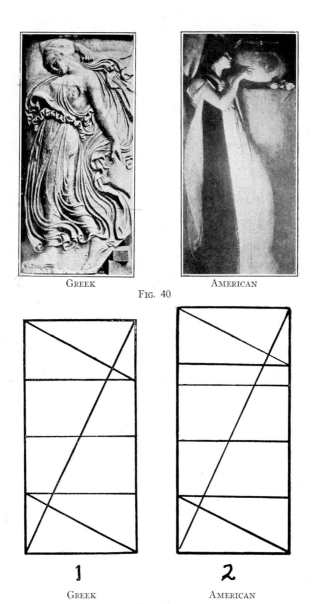

GREEK   AMERICAN

FIG. 40

1   2

GREEK   AMERICAN

FIG. 41

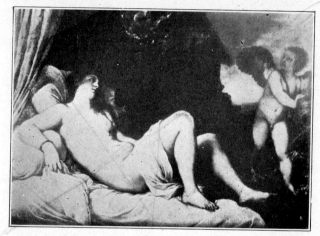

Fig. 42

Titian

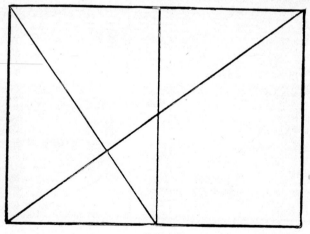

Fig. 43

rectangle EC is found at the opposite end of the large one, and lines drawn both ways through the eyes O, where the diagonals of the larger intersect the diagonals of the smaller, the larger rectangle will be divided both ways into three equal areas, as shown by dotted lines.

In the rectangle 2 the square of which the end AB forms one side is exactly one third of the area of the square of which the side line AC forms one side. In this case the ratio between the end line AB and side line AC is 1.732, or the square root of three. The rectangle is, therefore, a root three rectangle. If the other inside rectangles are found and lines drawn through the eyes O the large rectangle will be divided both ways into four equal areas.

In the rectangle 3 the end square is one-fourth the side square. In this case the ratio between the end AB and side AC is 2 or the square root of 4, and the rectangle is a root four rectangle. Lines drawn through the eyes O parallel to the side or end will divide the large one into 5 equal areas both ways.

In the rectangle 4 the end square is one-fifth

of the side square. In this case the ratio between the end and side is 2.236, or the square root of 5, which makes it a root five rectangle. This is the rectangle on which the Parthenon is built, and which was most often used in Greek architecture and vases. The locating of the similar root five rectangles within the large one, and of others within these, and various combinations of large and small, would determine the locations of rows of columns, wall divisions, etc.

This much of Hambidge's theory has been superficially reported because it bears most directly on the present subject of pictorial design. If significant proportions of rectangles, arrived at through the use of the diagonal and the perpendicular to the diagonal, are basic in architectural and vase design it would seem to follow that they will also be basic in picture design.

The diagonal, like the symmetry to which it is a means, has suffered a loss of identity during the Christian era, though its eclipse has been periodic and partial and not complete, as in the latter case. That the principle of the diagonal, if not of the complete theory, was fundamental

Static and Dynamic Symmetry

in the training of the old masters of Europe is obvious from a study of the work of such men as Tintoretto, Gozzoli, Raphael, Titian in the south, and Dürer, Rembrandt, Brueghel in the north. As representation gains in popularity through the 17th and 18th centuries the decline in vitality of design organization reveals itself also in the work. During these periods the spark is kept alive only by such individuals at Tiepolo, Goya and others who must have sadly passed the secret on from master to student as they watched the orgy of skillful imitation press against them from all sides. But it did live. The line held, up to Renoir, Seurat, Daumier and the rebirth of classicism of which they were a part. And in the last few years the teachings of Hambidge and a steadily increasing understanding of modern principles, have widened the understanding of the diagonal, though, since Hambidge's printed teachings have been confined largely to architecture and the Greek vase, it is a question how far it has been applied to pictures.

The four root rectangles just shown provide a skeleton framework of dynamic proportion into

How to See Modern Pictures

which a picture can be built which must, of necessity, absorb therefrom inherent dynamic quality. The question as to how many of the great pictures have been built into such proportions is an interesting one, and, since the testing of them is so simple a matter, easy to answer. One diagonal of the enclosing shape, and a perpendicular to it through the opposite corner, will tell the story. If, as has been explained, the rectangle formed by extending the perpendicular to the side, and completing it as in fig. 38, divides the whole rectangle into two, three, four, or five equal areas, then dynamic symmetry is present. Let us test several pictures of various periods to try out the theory.

First take a Greek example, Fig. 40 and compare it with an almost identical shape, "The Pot of Basil" by John W. Alexander. The shape of the rectangle enclosing the former is as shown in fig. 41 sketch 1, while the shape of the rectangle of the latter is as shown in sketch 2. The diagonal and perpendicular to it of the Greek rectangle divide it into four equal parts, or a

[74]

FIG. 44
JULES BRETON

FIG 45

FIG. 46
SISTINE MADONNA, RAPHAEL

root four rectangle. It therefore, has dynamic proportions. The Alexander shape divides into five unequal parts and misses dynamic proportions. To be accurate in such a process measurements should be taken from the original work. Measurements from photographs, as in these cases cannot be trusted as absolutely accurate, but will serve to demonstrate the process.

In Titian's "Danæ," fig. 42 the shape of the picture, from a photograph, is as shown in fig. 43. A diagonal and perpendicular divide the space into two equal areas. It is, therefore a root two rectangle, which would seem to indicate that Titian was aware of enough of the method to arrive at so much of the result, for these exact measurements could hardly be arrived at accidentally.

In "The Song of the Lark by Jules Breton fig. 44 the space divides as shown in fig 45 unequally, and therefore misses dynamic proportion.

Raphael, on the other hand, though he was a supreme master of diagonal organization, misses

How to See Modern Pictures

dynamic proportion in his *Sistine Madonna* (fig. 46) by a very small fraction of space, as shown in fig. 47.

Paintings of to-day made on stock sizes of canvas such as 12 × 14, 16 × 20, 24 × 30, 30 × 40, etc. and etchings and wood-blocks made on accidental shapes, would, of course, all miss these significant proportions.

We have been considering, in the above, the external shapes of pictures; now let us get inside the border and consider the architecture of the picture itself. If diagonals determine significant border proportions, they should determine also significant internal relations.

One of the laws of design is, as we have seen, controlled variation (which is another name for sensitive, as opposed to regular, repetition). If no more than the two diagonals of a picture were used, as in rectangle 1 of fig. 48 the relations of parts to them would be so limited that there could be no guide to controlled variation. If a picture rectangle is divided, however, into two, three, or four internal rectangles in both directions, width and length, and diagonals of each of these inner ones are drawn, then a pattern of diagonals is formed which becomes more intricate and varied as more spaces are used. By such multiplication ample guides would be found to which to relate the forms, lines, and spaces of the picture. In fig. 48 four rectangles are divided as suggested. They may, or may not, be dynamic rectangles. Since the diagonals will have significant relations to each other in either case, and since there are undoubtedly vast numbers of great pictures which are built on diagonal organization even though the outer shape is not dynamic, we will use in this case a non-dynamic, accidental shape. Rectangle no. 2 is divided into two parts each way, no. 3 into three parts, no. 4 into four parts. Each of these different patterns represents what might be called a different tempo. Pictures built into them would be in different keys—the keys of 1,2,3,4.

When a picture is to be tested to see if it is built on one of these key plans, and to find out which one, some experiment is necessary. If a straight edge is laid over a prominent diagonal line of the picture, and then moved across its

How to See Modern Pictures

surface without changing its slant till it meets
a corner, and the spot where it intersects the
other side noted, the key may be discovered. If
the point of intersection divides that side into
two, three, or four equal parts, the corresponding
key plan is indicated. If other picture lines,
of different directions, tested in the same way,
bring the same result, the case is proved. Then,
if the picture is consistently organized, every
lesser line and shape will conform in direction
or placing to the main di-
agonals or the diagonals
of the various equal divisions. Associated lines in
the picture will be parallel
to different diagonals thus
giving controlled variety
to eye movement. A
bending line, as in dra-
pery, will be parallel to
one diagonal, then change
direction and be parallel
to another. The thrill that comes from this *right*
control of the eye is called visual esthetic emotion.

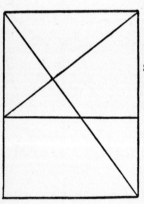

Fig. 47
TEST OF SISTINE MADONNA
RECTANGLE

[78]

Static and Dynamic Symmetry

"The Sistine Madonna," by Raphael, fig. 46, is a picture which conforms completely to diagonal organization. Since it is considered one of the world's masterpieces, and is familiar to all, we shall let an analysis of it indicate the process of analysis for all pictures. This painting does not have dynamic proportion, if measurements taken from its photograph are correct. But every item of the design alphabet of Chapter IV and

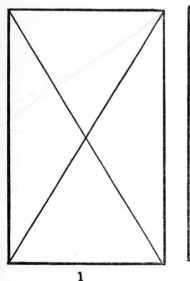 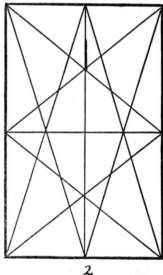

1   2

Fig. 48

[79]

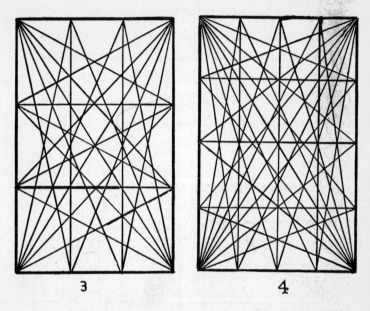

3   4

every attribute of design discussed in these pages, including the felt nature quality, is carried to supreme fulfillment in it. Careful study of it, and a painstaking search for its secrets, going far enough to include the reader's making his own application of diagonals by drawing them on a reproduction, will unlock sealed doors of the mind—may, in fact, open up a comprehension of the visual elements of all pictorial art.

The straight edge test, indicated above, at

[80]

Static and Dynamic Symmetry

once indicates the key of 4 arrangement in fig.
48.   First we will draw, over a rough tracing of

FIG. 49

[81]

How to See Modern Pictures

the main lines of the picture, the main diagonals and the diagonals to the four quarter sections of it. This has been done in fig. 49, with the dotted lines. Note that these dotted lines divide the main picture into four diamond shapes, which, in combination, give the pyramidal arrangement that was so common with the masters, and separately, enclose the heads and shoulders of the three figures. With pieces of paper cover up the surroundings of each diamond shape in succession, so that each may be seen as a separate entity. Note that each is a complete design in itself with satisfying relations of lines and spaces. Note the radiating and flowing curves, the curving angles, the combinations of curving and straight lines. And then note the lines of the composition which are parallel to these main diagonals.

In fig. 50, over the same rough tracing, have been drawn dotted lines dividing the picture into four equal rectangles both ways, and as many of the diagonals of both large and small as are *used* in this sketch. Every line in the picture has a definite relation to some diagonal, the

Static and Dynamic Symmetry

curved ones conforming in their general direction, while the straight ones either coincide

Fig. 50

[83]

exactly, or are exactly parallel. And note how many lines begin or end at the meeting of two diagonals, which is always a visually strategic point, or at their own meeting with a single diagonal. Do these relations seem accidental? Could they happen by chance? Did Raphael use such a plan scheme as here indicated? If one has doubt on this point the best answer will be to apply the same test to a representative picture and compare results.

Here again is the secret of the art of the ages, as it was in the Hopi Indian bird of fig. 36. The differences in the two cases are in the degree of complication, the one primitive simplification, the other sophisticated complication— both true works of art. And the Greek vase of fig. 37 completes the circle—the utmost of sophisticated complication attaining supreme simplicity.

So much explanation establishes the main facts of the application of dynamic symmetry and the diagonal to pictures, both to the border and the picture structure itself. Since farther study would go too deeply into the matter for

FIG. 51

BY TOYOKUNI

Japanese print in which the "felt nature" is expressed through design. The sweeping force of passion is indicated by the sweeping, hurried, lines·

any but the artist, we shall leave the discussion here. What has been said will testify to the writer's tested confidence in the theory, and will give, it is hoped, sufficient importance to it to prompt farther investigation. Our purpose, remember, is but to supply the tools.

CHAPTER VI

THE SOMETHING PLUS IN A
WORK OF ART

HAVING considered rather carefully that quality in pictures which is probably the most vital contribution of the Modern Movement to the world of art to-day—the quality of organization into design—it now becomes necessary to halt abruptly and take our bearings. For we must view this vein of new experience in relation to its surroundings, keeping a sense of values between it and other veins of related experience. To turn to it unreservedly would certainly be far more thrilling than, for instance, the thinking about the anecdotical content of pictures has been in the past; but, if there is experience beyond this, (and the almost universal love of the old masters is witness that there must be), it will be well to realize and welcome that experience also. What is the "something plus"

Something Plus in Work of Art

then—the something beyond design and beyond the bare literary content of subject matter, which distinguishes the great work of art?

This is, of course, the question which has occupied critics and philosophers as far back in human history, doubtless, as the time when man first began to examine into his own reactions. Many have answered it in many different ways. With the particulars of these answers, since this inquiry is neither historical nor philosophical, we are concerned only in a general way. Some thinkers have interpreted subject matter as an end in itself, or as a means to such ulterior purposes as the imparting of knowledge, or the picturing of good or evil, desiring the artist to be an educator, a missionary, or an historian. Many have recognized design but few have given it more than a very casual importance. Some have spoken of emotions and of the ability of the artist so to express his own as to recreate them in the minds of others. Some—and this division includes many of the representative artists themselves, who fall back on it because they feel the insufficiency of straight representation—

have thought that the expression of the personality of the artist is the end-all of art. Still others have spoken of life, and of the artist as interpreter of nature, and of man to man. And many have built theories of esthetics upon various interpretations of beauty alone, or of beauty and goodness, or of beauty and truth, as a means to spiritual well being. It is easy for us to-day, in looking back over such explanations in the past, and by relying on the extension of our comprehension of all art through the recent discoveries of arts which some fifty years ago were outside the horizon of Occidental society (particularly those of China, Japan, the Aztecs, the African Negro and many primitives), to discard the conclusions of the Ruskins, Tolstoys, and many others, as pitifully limited and entirely obsolete. But there is another angle to the matter. Perhaps art is great enough to mother all these activities of intellect. Perhaps all the writers and thinkers and philosophers and critics have been right in their explanations, or rather, perhaps they have all responded to a stimulus that is fundamental,

Something Plus in Work of Art

universal and unexplainable in works of art—
that has moved them all to a strange and more
or less conscious ecstasy which they have then
interpreted in the light of their own differing
personalities. Perhaps art is constant and man
variable. Perhaps art is the one great universal
language of the human race, timeless and
placeless—always understood—never explained.
Perhaps the varying explanations have explained
the explainers and left art untouched, supremely,
serenely omnipotent. Perhaps the thoughts
about art have been varying and temporary
fashions in which a universal *feeling for art* has
been dressed by different individuals and periods,
and in which its universality has been more or
less obscured.

If this be so—if the thing we call art is so
vast in its reach that it can be explained by all
explanations at the same time that it is unexplained by any of them, then the most we can
do in our attempt at comprehension, is to become
as unaware of ourselves as possible, and of the
processes which may be at work in us, which determine our relations to works of art, and of the

How to See Modern Pictures

degree and character of whatever amount of comprehension we do attain. Segregation of the various types of responses which pictures in general arouse, certainly makes us aware of our own particular response to a particular picture and therefore is a step in this direction. And, by becoming aware of the type of our own response, we become capable of valuing it and deciding whence it springs. All Southern Californians take great pride and delight in, and make pilgrimages to, a certain unique group of trees on the southern coast, called the Torrey Pines. Pictures of these trees are correspondingly popular—all types of pictures, from the penny post-card to the hand-colored photograph at five dollars, and the "hand" painting at five hundred. When a lover of the Torrey Pines buys a picture of a Torrey Pine, an excellent opportunity for awareness of processes is furnished. Is it the art quality in the picture (assuming there is one) which tempts his pennies or his dollars? If so he will talk of that and ignore or forget, or treat as a minor matter, the name and location of the trees. Or,

Something Plus in Work of Art

is the picture bought as a reminder of a loved object—as a *proxy* for the tree itself? If so a colored photograph probably is valued above a painting by a genuine artist, for it mirrors the beautiful tree more faithfully. Indeed any art quality in the picture, since it would necessarily, through transformation and transposition, alter the picture's truth to nature, would be considered a marked disadvantage and doubtless cause the rejection of the picture containing it. Awareness, in this case, would locate the source of the love felt for the picture, and identify the response to it. And so awareness of the many possible sources of delight in (or aversion to) pictures, identifies the many possible responses to them and furnishes invaluable data by which any individual may guide his further development.

The value of awareness being rather evident without unassailable proof, we come back to the main question of what it is of which we are to be aware. Design, with its ability to stimulate powerful esthetic emotion, is certainly one vitally important objective. Subject matter, even with its infinite possibilities for shunting interest into

How to See Modern Pictures

various by-ways and detours remote from art, is, still, an element in pictures of which awareness may well be profitable. The third, and most elusive of all elements, is the "something plus" which is sensed by the great number of serious, inquiring minds which build upon it those theories of esthetics which do not include design as the main constituent fundamental.

This "something plus" has to do with life. It is born of the artist's attempt to express the force underlying all things—the push of the sap upward in spring, the heave and give of muscles, the urge of love to the fusion that means birth of new life, the pull of the love that protects age and infancy. "When Carrière wrests from the matter of the universe a mother giving the breast to her babe, we shall not understand the value of that union if we do not feel that an inner force, love, dictates the bending of the torso and the curve of the mother's arm, and that another inner force, hunger, buries the infant in her bosom." [1]

Henry P. Bowie [2] thus describes Japanese

[1] Élie Faure, *History of Art*. Harper & Bros., N. Y. Introduction to Vol. I.
[2] *On the Laws of Japanese Painting*.

Something Plus in Work of Art

painting, "One of the most important principles in the art of Japanese painting—indeed a fundamental and entirely distinctive characteristic —is that called living movement, SEI DO, it being, so to say, the transfusion into the work of the *felt nature* of the thing to be painted by the artist. Whatever the subject to be translated, whether river or tree, rock or mountain, bird or flower, fish or animal, the artist, at the moment of painting it, must *feel* its very nature, which, by the magic of his art, he transfers into his work to remain forever, affecting all who see it with the same sensations he experienced when executing it." It is by expressing the *felt nature* of a thing, then, that the artist becomes the mouth-piece of the universe of which he is a part and reveals to man, through the "something plus" in a picture, the nature as well as the appearance, of the life and forms about him.

The old masters of Europe, the Chinese and Japanese, the Greeks, the Byzantines, the Assyrians, the African Negro, and many others, throughout history, embodied this felt nature of the thing in their works of art, and it is when,

How to See Modern Pictures

as in these cases, this divine fire is tempered and controlled by design, that deathless work is born —work which takes its place as part of the universal language of man.

CHAPTER VII

REPRESENTATION

REPRESENTATION in art means copying, imitating, or mirroring in a work, objects or facts, as they actually appear in nature or human life. It implies concern with detail—the slight, momentary, superficial aspect of things, such as the accidental shadows which reveal form at a particular moment in a particular light. The highest degree of perfection in representation might be assumed to belong to the color-camera, but the representative school of painting, in the works of such of its masters as Meissonier and Gerard Dow, has certainly pressed it to a close finish, matching skill of man against accuracy of machine, until it is hard, in the matter of fidelity to appearance, to award unassailable honors between them.

As a work of art, however, the picture by the representative painter will always have something the best of the honors, for the man picture-maker can never sink low enough as an artist not to omit, or select, or rearrange to some extent,—a thing which the camera unaided can never do. In other words, the representative artist, even though fidelity to nature be his aim, never reaches absolute representation. Assuming that art lies in the expression of the felt nature of things through organization into design, it is rather obvious that the skillful copying of external appearances, carried to its logical conclusion of absolute representation, is, because it is non-creative, of an entirely different world, one which does not even touch the world of art. But, when the slightest degree of selection or omission enters into the making of a picture, then, undeniably, the art instinct begins to work; and the degree to which these are employed successfully will determine the degree of art achievement in the result.

Straight representation is the very opposite of design. The two cannot exist in the same piece of work, for representation would cease to be representation, in the strict meaning of the word, as soon as design were brought in. But representation is not necessarily incompatible with composition. In painting a landscape in which a dozen trees appear, a representative painter may select three of the trees, and, omitting the others, place these three on his canvas in positions different from those which they occupy in nature, and then he may proceed to paint these three trees accurately, with all their insignificant as well as significant detail faithfully represented. Or he may apply omission and selection to the details of the trees, and to the clouds and hills. Such a process, which is called composition, is that, in fact, which is used to-day in what is called representative painting, etching, or sculpture. That it requires the use of some of the artist's peculiar powers is evident. But, to one who has experienced the greater thrill of creating design, this little experience, even though it demand great technical skill in the execution, is so tame in comparison, that to indulge in it becomes mere day labor or hack work.

How to See Modern Pictures

The degrees to which representative picture-making may call on the art instinct are limitless and may range all the way from the zero of photography to the supreme accomplishment of a Rembrandt, the representative quality decreasing as the art quality gains. In the past fifty or seventy-five years, since the art poverty of pure representation has been realized by Occidental artists (if not by the general public), various side-attractions have been depended upon to bolster up the sensed, if not acknowledged, insufficiency. The fact that these side-issues have been featured and exploited as vigorously as they have, is strong evidence that the fundamental insufficiency has been consciously realized. At any rate, whether recourse to them was conscious or unconscious, they have very generally monopolized the approach to art and thus served to distract the attention of picture lovers from the art content in the very pictures of which they were a part.

The *personality* of the artist, as revealed through his particular handling of representation, is one of these side issues, which has been spoken of with the hushed voice of awe and reverence for far too many years. The pushing of omission and selection to the point of *suggesting* facts instead of rendering them faithfully, thereby calling on the imagination of the observer to supply details that are but sketchily indicated, is another that has been a welcome stimulant to interest since the boredom of the documentary statement has been realized. The adventuring of the Impressionists into a new corner of the representative field by their catching and representing the essential quality of light, through the vibratory effect caused by the juxtaposition of broken spots of pure color, was another no less welcome diversion, even if it did arouse the customary howls of protest from the customary conservatives. Choosing of picturesque or poetical subject matter, and placing dependence on its subject interest to cover up lack of creative vitality in the picture itself was, and still is, an almost habitual resource of the hard-pressed representationists, and it charms the easily satisfied to-day as it did fifty and a hundred years ago. Anecdote has served its turn as entertainer, and the pleasure of the millions in *Saturday*

How to See Modern Pictures

Evening Post covers is evidence of its efficiency to-day, just as Paleolithic cave drawings of daily events of the chase, are evidence of its similar efficiency twenty thousand years ago. (Would that the former had even a fraction of the art quality of some of the latter!) Delineation of character or of moods of nature or of people, the use of sentimental titles, and considerations of technique, have aided the representative artist to stimulate interest in a type of picture which, be-because it is reflecting instead of creating, has been unable to dominate interest through its own inherent quality.

Since the above mentioned types of representative pictures furnish our own immediate background, and since the approach which they demand has become our habitual approach to all pictures, and has more or less completely blinded us to other and greater elements in some pictures, perhaps it will be well to think a little more fully about their character and its effect on us, so that by bringing this effect up from the unconscious to the conscious, we can more easily become aware of the kind of influence and of our response to it. Then, if we remain subservient to it, we shall do so from choice, not blindly. The qualities here mentioned, remember, are the ones constantly discussed by artists, critics and laymen as being important matters in representative pictures.

PERSONALITY OF THE ARTIST

As if any picture ever made could hide the personality of the artist! It is as much a part of the picture as the paint or canvas or lines. It is built in. It contributes to the result along with all other constituent parts. To single it out for special emphasis is to distract attention from the main issue of what the artist has accomplished with all the tools and building materials at hand. In appraising a cathedral or a Woolworth building one does not consider them as indices of the personality of the architect, one judges the result. The man gives himself to the work and dies. The work, if it is great, endures. The work absorbs the man, as the tree absorbs the sap that gives it life. It lives in its own right and gives forth again the vitality it has received. The work is what we are concerned with, the personality is an incident —a very minor one; and the heralding of personality implies a consciousness of sterility in greater and more vital content.

Whistler, particularly in his etchings, did much to popularize the suggestive method and there are those among his ardent disciples to-day for whom it still fills the entire horizon of art. How often, in an exhibition of etchings (for etching has inherited a larger portion of suggestive tradition than any other medium) one hears, "Ah! how admirably it suggests—" this or that. "How it stimulates the imagination!" "How subtly he indicates" the texture of a wall or the character of a woman. Suggestion, in a picture, has charm, without question, and because it usually is employed to concentrate interest on some focal point, makes an appeal to the eye

[102]

that is agreeable. Indeed a good suggestive picture such as any of those in Whistler's "Venice" set of etchings[1] is a really delightful piece of work which it is a pleasure to have about. But, if the degree and type of pleasure derived from it be compared to the pleasure gained from a picture expressing the felt nature of things through creative design, the result in the observer will be apt to be a reappraisal of pictures that are present day favorites. When one gains the ability to feel the power of design, the pleasant quality of suggestion dwindles into insignificance. This is not saying, however, that it cannot be made use of in a great work of art; only, when so used, it will be subservient to the main purpose in hand—not thrust to the head of the procession for its own minor merits.

THE IMPRESSIONISTS AS THE GRAND REBELS OF REPRESENTATION

The Impressionists made a great commotion for a time, which was for the good of the cause.

[1] Test any one of these etchings for design by turning it upside down and see what a meaningless jumble it becomes.

How to See Modern Pictures

But it was not too many years before it was realized that they were as strictly representative as
those who had gone before. Only, instead of
representing grapes so skillfully that the sparrows
pecked the canvas, the Impressionists represented light so admirably that it vibrated before
the eyes. They gave representation no more than
a temporary vitality. With the dwindling of
Impressionism into its true perspective as a step
in progress toward the real revolution which
followed it, i. e. Post-Impressionism, or the
Modern Movement, disappeared the prestige of
representation as a possible means to significant
achievement in art. The fact that some millions
of laymen and thousands of artists have not yet
learned that representation, as a means to art, died
with the Nineteenth Century does not alter the
record but must be laid to insufficient means of
communication. Twenty-four years, it seems, is
not time enough for the radio, the press, the tele-
graph, the pulpit, and the lecture to get such
news from Paris and distribute it throughout
America.

Representation

Shifting the burden of creation from the artist, where it belongs, to nature, where it has nothing to do with art, is what this process might be called. It is a lazy man's way out. Essentially, it is as if one should pick a beautiful shell from the beach and skillfully paint a near replica of it, and then hold this up to the admiring gaze of the multitudes, who had blindly tramped the original into the sand. The artist has "revealed" to the ignorant a beauty of nature to which they were before more or less blind.[2] The ignorant then become enthusiastic over the freshly discovered beauty, admiring nature's creation, but mixing the artist up in the matter and donating to him considerable of the credit which should, by rights, belong to God. The following words of Whistler, taken from his "Ten

[2] See the letter, quoted in appendix under *Beauty and Art,* from the head of an art organization as evidence of the acceptance of such a revelation as the proper function of the artist.

How to See Modern Pictures

O'Clock," [3] are illuminating in this connection.

"And when the evening mist clothes the riverside with poetry as with a veil, and the poor buildings lose themselves in the dim sky, and the tall buildings become campanili, and the warehouses are palaces in the night, and the whole city hangs in the heavens, and fairyland is before us—then the wayfarer hastens home; the working man and the cultured one, the wise man and the one of pleasure cease to understand as they have ceased to see and Nature, who, for once, has sung in tune, sings her exquisite song to the artist alone."

This is a vivid word-painting of an artist's sensitive response to the poetic beauty of nature. But this veiled mystery is a fact in nature, just as a pumpkin or warehouses in daylight are facts, and can be copied in a picture for its own poetic charm, or can be used by the artist to create charm which springs from his creation. A representative painter, keenly feeling the beauty, as Whistler

[3] And quoted by Charles Marriott (*Modern Movements in Painting:* Chapman & Hall, London, 1920) in his able analysis of the work of Whistler.

does, would copy the dim scene on canvas, trying to record it so faithfully that his picture would arouse the same emotion in the "blind" wise man that nature aroused in him. In other words he would employ his skill to reveal the beauty of twilight to the ignorant, and *would attempt no more than this*. The creative artist would never be satisfied with such an achievement. Instead of depending on the transforming twilight to create a poetic illusion for him, he would prefer to look at the warehouses in daylight and himself do whatever transforming was necessary to create his own illusion, suited to his own purposes. Instead of being an interpreter he would wish to be a creator.

All that has just been said applies equally to the element of the picturesque. For many years this quality has been a main resource of representative etchers. Old tumble-down structures and smoky scenes of industry make perfect etching subjects and have been copied by the thousand. Aged buildings of the Continent have been especially favored in this respect until even juries composed of representative etchers, wearied by the flood, have been known to remark (unofficially) that they wished there were fewer prints of old buildings.

A caution is necessary here. In discussing the anecdotical content of pictures, it is particularly necessary to stop and consider whether such matter is used for its own sake alone, or whether it is used as material for design. Most of the great masterpieces of the world are more or less anecdotical in character, relating incidents in private or royal or religious life, but, in them, the momentary anecdote is universalized by art with a resultant power so tremendous in itself that the story may be forgotten without consciousness of loss. But take the anecdote from a *Saturday Evening Post* cover and what is left? Skill and a mite of colored ink. And so all the attributes of representative pictures here mentioned, could be vitalized by the magic wand of art into deathless entities. It is only when they lack that

[108]

touch that they remain matters of temporary entertainment—nonentities of art.

TECHNIQUE AS A QUALITY TO BE FEATURED

Excellent technique, in any picture, as in any work of art, should be taken for granted as a matter-of-course necessity. Until an artist has mastered his technique, his works, even if they have true art quality in them, should be thought of as studies and experiments, and should not be presented in public exhibition unless for their historical interest as records of his development. This axiom applies with particular force to those embryo moderns who have not yet found themselves, and to the imitators and fakers of the superficial qualities of the true movement, who see, in the breakdown of the older tradition, only a chance to foist vulgarity and crudity, or their own immaturity, on a bewildered public. Such work is worse than negligible. It is an offence and should receive no mercy from critics or individuals of the public when once they detect its pretensions. The representative school stands for excellence and mastery of technique, and since, in far too many cases, this is about all of value that its pictures contain, it should receive full appreciation for it. Only, it should be borne in mind that mastery of technique is a self-forged tool with which a work of art is built, never has it any of the blood of art in its veins.

USE OF SENTIMENTAL TITLES AS A MEANS OF SUPPLYING A FICTITIOUS INTEREST IN PICTURES

A considerable number of representative artists, having learned from experience that their pictures must illustrate some thought in order to bolster up interest and appeal to public and buyers, have found that it is much easier to put the desired thought into the words of the title than into the picture itself, and that the charm works perfectly with this method. Since most observers and buyers look at a picture with their brains instead of their eyes, they relish a title that tells the whole story and thus saves all visual labor. An idea, once lodged in the mind by words, quite easily and automatically is imagined to exist in the picture. The message has arrived via the title; the picture, though it has had nothing to do with the process, gets the credit and everybody is happy. Take such a title as this:

"Smooth lakes where coyest wild-fowl whir"

Everyone likes to hear *"wild-fowl whir"* and "coy" wild-fowl! Memories of wild whirrings (if not of coy ones) rise in the mind of the reader of this title, and, when he glances at the attached picture, any spot of yellow ochre will "whir coyly" before his enchanted eyes. As a matter of fact the picture probably will begin to whir coyly before he even looks in its general direction. Or take this one:

"What gnawing thought, O ever-moaning sea,
Haunts thy perturbed breast."

But further comment is unnecessary.[4] "The song of the Lark," fig. 56 is another example of a sentimental title (and picture).

[4] The writer takes oath that these are actual titles taken from a printed catalogue of paintings. He could not have invented them.

How to See Modern Pictures

Here is need for the fullest power of discrimination. For the portrayal of character, or moods, or emotions, must spring from some degree of feeling for the basic nature of things. It is conceivable that a representative and creative artist both might experience identical consciousness of the inner reality of a human being, or of a storm, or an emotion. They might both allow the inner significance to permeate their entire beings; both might come to their work, after careful study of their subject, with a sense of suppressed power crying for expression. But, from the first laying of brush to canvas, all similarity in their mental states and in methods of approach would cease; from that instant their processes would be diametrically opposed. To understand more clearly the difference between them, it will be necessary to digress for a moment and realize the two possible types of artist vision.

CHARLES SHEELER
FIG. 52

FIG. 53

JUDSON D. SMITH

The boat design by Sheeler is a superb example of semi-abstract arrangement of curving forms and lines, with classic simplicity. The lower by Smith is a highly complicated arrangement of a multitude of small forms. Note repetition of curtain folds in table leg, abstract arrangement of window panels, and the play of forms and lines with each other throughout.

Representation

The kind of vision described in Chapter III, under the name of *pure vision,* perceives objects as ends in themselves, stripped of all associated facts and ideas. It is called *perceiving* or *perceptual vision.* As stated before, it observes accurately and can be used by both the representative and creative artist. The former uses it to observe facts which he then records in his picture. A child once defined drawing [5] by saying, "I think, then I draw a line around my think." This looking inward, seeing the image or concept of an object registered on the mind's eye, as it were, instead of the object itself, is called *conceptual vision.* The creative artist uses perceptual vision to collect data which he stores in his mind and later uses as material for his inward-looking conceptual vision, to build into design. To return now to the two types of artists.

The representative artist, all primed to deline-

[5] Roger Fry, *Vision and Design.* Brentano's, N. Y., 1920.

ate a certain human character or emotion, comes to his work, having used, and ready to use, perceptual vision. He poses a model to express, let us say, sorrow. He studies that model carefully, observing the drooping bend of the back, and begins to draw. He draws the significant bend of the back. He draws the bent arm. He comes to the elbow. Here is a wrinkle in the coat sleeve. Shall he draw that wrinkle? It is there, plainly to be seen. A wrinkle must exist in a coat sleeve even if that sleeve expresses sorrow. He draws the wrinkle. Then other details intrude. Some he omits, but many decisions must be made. He becomes occupied with drawing correctly. After a bit he is drawing freshly-shined patent-leather shoes. Suddenly he realizes his whole concern is with these glossy shoes—that he has forgotten all about sorrow. He tries to recapture his original fire, but original fire has a delicate constitution and dies easily of neglect. And even if he does recapture it, the process repeats itself. When finished, the picture records faithfully the external manifestations of sorrow, and probably

[114]

reflects some of the inner quality. Certainly it furnishes ample data by which the observer may recognize the existence of sorrow, but the record is one of a *particular sorrow* in a particular person, sitting in a particular light in a particular room.

The creative artist works differently. As a composer, at a piano, creates harmony while gazing into space, so the creative artist begins to draw with his conceptual vision turned inward searching the storehouse of his mind. That storehouse is well stocked for he has made preliminary studies in plenty—probably has drawn a model accurately in order to possess himself of all knowledge of details. And now he is ready to use his material—to create a picture. The inner fire burns. He comes to his canvas filled with a suppressed power that urges hands to vital, swinging, expression. Does he feel the bending weight of sorrow? His hand flows the bend of sorrow into line. No thought of detail, hardly a glance at the model. The *feel* of sorrow flowing into form! His problem becomes one of controlling the exuberance of spirit, of holding it to the slow, laborious process of organization, of conserving the force in him to hour after hour, and day after day, and week after week, perhaps, of controlled release. And when the day is done, he drops exhausted—an empty flagon from which the wine is drained. What was in him has gone into the work, where, if his power has been great enough, it will live forever. Thus is the felt nature of a thing eternalized into design.

Representation, therefore, may be more or less decked out with a number of interesting qualities, such as personality, suggestion, poetical subject matter, etc., which serve to color a type of work that would be as dry, in its strict application, as an inventory of merchandise. But, even in such gay attire, its essential function remains that of recording the particular, and this very characteristic, inherent in it, predestines it to a rôle of temporary and relatively insignificant service. Already this rôle is generally recognized and admitted in the world of art, and will be universally so recognized certainly in a very few decades. No. Perhaps not. Through all the history of man, there has been a majority that

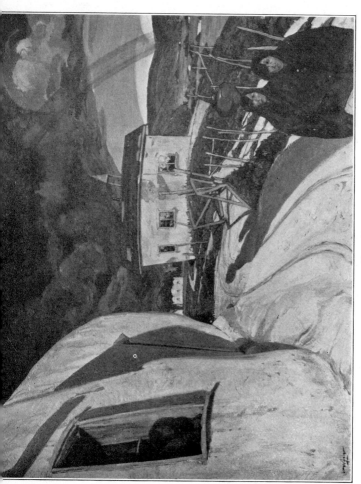

Fig. 54

A partial abstraction by Walter Ufer. Note the control of eye movement by the many lines and forms that focus on the small white house between the two large ones. Note also that the exaggerated movements obtained by this abstraction emphasize, and give variety to, this eye control, and therefore enrich the contribution of the artist.

Fig. 55

An etching by the author in which mountains have been treated as simplified forms in an attempt to organize their bulk-weight quality into design.

delights in the particular, and probably it is safe to guess that the majority will continue to do so till the end of human time. As a representative painter once said to a "modern" visiting his city, "Go to it, Old Boy. Show your work and get all the publicity you can. I'm not afraid of your getting my public away from me."—He knew.

The foregoing indicates, in a general way, the character of some of the main side-issues in representative pictures and attempts to estimate their value as contributions from the artist. Just a word about the responses they stimulate in the observer.

The personality of the maker of a picture may provide a most interesting study, involving psychology, heredity, neurology or whatnot, but it certainly has nothing to do with art, even in the narrow sense in which the word is used by the representationists. Suggestion in a picture stimulates the imagination, indeed, and such an operation has undoubted value—but to what does it stimulate? To the task of completing an unfinished inventory of facts—which is hardly an art activity. And, if it goes beyond this and aims to stimulate to a seeing or feeling of inner qualities, as in the case, for instance, of a representative portrait which might feature the "burning" eyes and subordinate the rest of head and body into sketchy indications, it, even then, is only directing forcefully the research of the observer into humanistic matters which are still extraneous to art. Impressionism, perhaps, did make a real and valuable contribution to the observer, for it taught him the fallibility of his own eyesight and that things *are* what they *do not seem.* Directing attention to, and forcing the recognition of, picturesque or poetical subject matter, to which in nature the layman had been blind, also has a value, in that it again extends the range of vision. But such value is educational. It helps to prepare for the appreciation of works of art; it does not, since its concern is with beauty of subject, provide art quality to be appreciated. Anecdote, without art quality imposed on it, amuses, but never thrills, a spectator. And delineation of character, or moods, or emotions, and the featuring of technique, all of them shunt interest on to a sidetrack where it

[118]

Fig. 56

BRANCUSI

Here is an expression of simplified form that compares in its unformal
classicism to the formal classicism of a Greek vase, though it has not,
of course, the dynamic symmetry quality of the latter.

FIG. 57
BRUNO KRAUSKOPF

Wir geben unser Blut
Gebt Ihr Euer Gold

FIG. 58
ADOLF RIEDLIN

FIG. 59
MATISSE

FIG. 60
ERIC J. SMITH

Examples in which design has been imposed on reluctant material with partial abstraction or distortion for the purposes of design. Incidentally they all express the felt nature of their subjects, and the caricature by Smith is probably the most obvious example in this book of a picture built on the laws of the diagonal.

may have a delightful time—and forget all about the main trunk line of art.

If this analysis of representation is fair, and the desire has been to make it so, then its net result is this:

Because it is particular instead of universal, and because the side-attractions which it calls to its banner have no blood-relationship to art, the sum total of the contribution which representation in pictures makes to the observer, is *entertainment* and *information* in various matters outside of art, and a *partial education in vision*. It is this general type of work which is distinguished by the term *romanticism,* and belongs to the romantic school of art. It is so called to distinguish it from classicism and the classic school, which we shall consider in the next chapter.

CHAPTER VIII

CLASSICISM

THERE are two ways in which design may be applied to the subject matter of a picture.

One is by making the demands of the design paramount to all other considerations, carrying the conventionalization or distortion of subject matter to any extreme to meet that need—even to the forfeiting of all resemblance to nature. This method leads to the partial or complete abstraction utilized by the Cubists, and, since, in the history of art, its use in pictures (as distinct from decorative design) has been very rare, it may almost be said to be, in that field, a discovery of the moderns. The other method by which design may be applied is by "imposing it on reluctant material" [1] without distortion. A

[1] This vigorous phrase belongs to my friend Jerome N. Frank.

human head is reluctant material, as is a mountain, a group of pots and pans, or a crucifixion. It is this method of imposing design on objects and relations of objects in nature, while employing only as much abstraction as is imperative in order to achieve universalization, which arrives at classicism in a work of art. It has been employed in all ages and places where classic work has been produced.

What is classic art? All that has been written so far is an answer to that question. At the end of Chapter VI this answer was summed up in the statement that when the expression of the felt nature of things is tempered and controlled by design, deathless work is born—work which takes its place as part of the universal language of man. Classic art is certainly that—deathless and universal. That it is arrived at through conceptual vision, and feeling the nature of things on the part of the artist, and through a certain amount of stylization or abstraction; that it is creative rather than imitative, that it always has a structural design comparable to that of music or architecture, that in its very highest manifestation this design depends on the laws of the diagonal and of dynamic symmetry—all these qualities seem so obvious as to make further discussion of them needless. And yet lecturers and critics on every hand are telling of a hundred other interesting matters and ignoring these. Intuition? Is that the means to an answer? Perhaps. But intuition works in established grooves and must be freed from the handicap of preconceived ideas. Take a particular case for a moment and consider how it must be treated by the artist in order to reach classic expression.

A mountain is a vast hulk of rock whose surface is furrowed and scarred, and partially dressed in a patch-work covering of foliage. In picturing a mountain, representation records the visible details which belong to the husk; while creative design, in searching for inner realities, is more concerned with the bulk and huge weight, which is sensed, rather than seen, under the husk. But the patch-work surface and the bulk-weight are both important characteristics of mountains. Both may be represented in a picture. Representation of the former can be obtained by straight,

Classicism

simple copying of appearances, whereas representation of the latter must rather obviously depend upon, first feeling the nature of the thing, then so presenting it in a picture that this felt nature, or vast weight, is sensed by the observer. To convey such a sense of inner weight the mountain must be drawn in a way that features this quality. Since surface details have nothing to do with bulk, but only with the outer plane to which they belong, they must be sacrificed to any method which portrays the inner quality. Such a method is the reducing of the mountain to its essential geometric form of cone or pyramid, or to some variation of these. But when surface is thus ignored, or altered, *abstraction* begins, for the slightest departure from visual truth to nature is the beginning of abstraction. A picture of a house, skillfully painted by a representative painter, who might decry the abstraction of a cubist as a monstrosity, is yet, in itself a partial abstraction, for it is not an absolutely accurate image of the house. And when one quality is to be emphasized at the expense of other qualities, as in the case of the weight of the mountain, abstraction in some degree is the only method by which this result may be gained. Creative design in picture making then, since it goes further than representation in recording the inner quality of things, must gain its end through a greater use of abstraction.

When it is realized that some abstraction exists in the most skillful of representative pictures, then a slightly greater degree of it than is conventionally accepted at the moment as proper, will not be so offensive to the picture lover as it may be otherwise. Indeed complete abstraction can then be looked on, and even welcomed, as an interesting experiment in which the laws of design function exactly as they do in a Raphael Madonna. And the partial degree of abstraction necessary to a forceful presentation of inner realities will be assumed as one of the essential resources of the artist.

The necessity and advisability of relying on some degree of abstraction in order to present the inner reality of things (as well as to attain expression through design) is not so hard to understand if one can open one's mind and eyes

Weyhe Gallery

Fıg. 61

A complete abstraction by Lyonel Feininger, that gives a powerful control of eye movement. This should be studied long and carefully, till the importance of shapes and lines and values are visually comprehended—which does not happen in a casual glance.

Fig. 62

A Cubist complete abstraction by Picasso.

to actualities, rather than confine them to beliefs. Those experiments in drawing the pail and comparing the white paper to the black automobile, described in Chapter II, prove that knowing and seeing are two very different functions that may cause one to deduce diametrically opposed conclusions from the same data. Recognition of this proven fact, (and the experiments certainly do prove it beyond dispute), should make a layman very modest about his ability to decide what are realities in nature or art. It should give him much of the uncertainity in the field of art or visible nature that he now feels, and readily admits, in fields of science and learning. It should send him to the artist with the same respect for his specialized knowledge that he now has for the specialized knowledge of the lawyer, doctor, or scientist. Abstraction beyond familiar limits offends to-day the layman and the artist of the representative school. Yet it is a necessity, if either inner reality or design is to be incorporated into a picture. If a work of art cannot be a work of art without employing abstraction, then comprehension of works of art is impossible without its acceptance. And when this is once admitted, as has been said, then the degree of abstraction is of minor importance.

In the complete abstraction method of applying design to pictures the artist's problem is greatly simplified since the design organization is all he need concern himself with. Heretofore this method obtained only in two dimensional design for decorative purposes. The Cubists, headed by Picasso, carried it over into three dimensions and applied it to pictures. By doing this they gained a complete release of their powers from the habitual limitation to faithfulness in representing the superficial appearances of things (a release which is unbelievably hard for an artist, trained in the representative school, to attain). This release meant freedom for invention, freedom to jump all restraining walls and hurl their trained abilities into pure creation, controlled only by the laws of design. These laws were so instinctive to these men, however, because of their years of discipline that they never thwarted the eager hand, but only guided

Classicism

it subconsciously. This release and call to invention was the great contribution of Cubism to Twentieth Century art. The artists, having once mastered it and exercised dormant creative abilities, as dormant muscles are exercised in a gymnasium, found themselves quite naturally more fit for creation again within set limitations.[2] Such limitations are imposed by the classic approach—by the necessity of portraying the inner realities. Pure abstraction is therefore, if our argument holds, a preparation for classicism—both from the point of view of the maker and observer of pictures.

Other elements of design which contribute to classicism have been elaborated elsewhere. Ab-

[2] Most of them have used Cubism as a phase of their development and to-day are applying their resultant freshened vision to a more traditional production. The abstract works (both complete and partial abstractions) produced by Cubism are certainly of great value to the layman, as well as to all artists, for, by reducing pictures to the sole function of creating esthetic emotion through the medium of organized visual elements, they simplified the problem of apprehending design—of seeing pictures as visual ends. It is only a proof of the general inability to see design that Cubist paintings have been so widely misunderstood and damned. When really seen (the genuine ones, of course,) they can only be warmly appreciated. It is to be hoped, because of their stimulative value, that the principles back of Cubism will soon become an important stage in all art training.

straction seems to be the root through which these others are able to assimilate the vitality of the artist, and therefore it is, perhaps, the most important single element. The non-visual qualities—that is, the humanistic source of the urge to expression, and of the interpretation of man to man—with all their ramifications in social, political, historical, religious, and economic conditions, are outside our field of inquiry, except as they come under the "felt nature" heading, although their importance in their own fields need never be forgotten.[3]

To some people the word *classic* refers back to the Greek art of the golden age and nowhere else. But this limitation in its application has been revised during the past fifty years as the enlargement of our horizon has progressed and corresponding new valuations have been applied. If we accept the definition of classicism here suggested, we must realize that there have been other classic periods in the history of Europe as well as in the history of many other civili-

[3] For this side of art as well as for the esthetic side, a book could hardly be more valuable than is Élie Faure's *History of Art*, Harper & Bros., 1921.

FIG. 63

MAURICE STERNE

Here is a modern work that has attained real classic quality. There is the felt nature of the woman universalized into design. If the result does not show the maturity of a Holbein or the Seurat or Daumier of Figs. 54 and 55 it does show at once that it is built on the same laws.

The Arts

FIG. 64

GEORGES SEURAT

This and the two following pictures conform to the definition of classicism here presented. This and the Daumier are obviously built on the laws of the diagonal and are masterly realizations of all classic elements.

Classicism

zations. Comprehension of classic qualities allows instant recognition of classic art whereever it is found, and however much it may be qualified by the individual traditions of a particular age and race. Thus, among examples of modern work, a Seurat "Young Woman at her Powder-box" (fig. 64), or a Joseph Bernard (fig. 66), or a Renoir, (fig. 70), or a Brancusi (fig. 56), all obviously spell classicism in their different styles as does the East Indian mediæval carving fig. 69, or the Chinese statuette of fig. 68; the British Columbian house-post, fig. 1, the Assyrian lion, fig. 15; and to come back to our own line of descent, the Daumier of fig. 65, the Raphael of fig. 46, beside endless others. It is no reflection of the classic Greek that is sensed in these widely diverse works; it is the fact that they are built on universal laws, that proves their right to the classic title. Differences in degree of mastery of these laws stand as just that—and may not bar the least of them from full appreciation of that inherent quality in them which makes them significant, *classic* works of art.

CHAPTER IX

CRITICISM AND THE STANDARD

THE function of the critic is that of a guide. He comes to a bewildered, confused, poorly informed public, beaten this way and that by the voice of every clamorer for attention, by prejudice crying its favorites, by commercialism exploiting craftily for profit, by sincere, misplaced enthusiasm proclaiming mediocrity, by the works of new schools that contradict the works of old; on every hand he finds the individuals which make up the public helplessly, almost hopelessly, muddled. What a tremendous opportunity here awaits him! What a privilege to guide in orderly progress through the intricacies of the maze, pointing out the sights to be seen, analyzing their character, affiliations, pedigree, aspiration, and, as he sees it, their degrees of accomplishment! To bring order out of confusion, to help to discrimination, to achieve comprehension!

M.lle Étienne Décente Quelegonde Bécassine de Constitutionnel, indigne suffoquée éblouïffée et reveicfuee à la répresentation d' Antony ou a poison de Dumas a ce l'immoralité de se moquer de la noble famille Bécassine de Constitutionnel

The Arts

Fig. 65

Daumier

Fig. 66

Joseph Bernard

Criticism and the Standard

Surely here is a position of responsibility and honor, to be looked on with respect, to be prepared for religiously, to be undertaken seriously and only after maturity of experience has allowed the attainment of a universal standard.

The standard is the back-bone of criticism. By it the works discussed are measured. By it alone are comparisons and placements, and, in fact, judgments of any kind made possible. The comprehensiveness of the standard determines the comprehensiveness of the criticism. If it is limited to a particular point of view, then the criticism is sufficient only within that limited scope. When it is universal, then only can the criticism have universal applications. The standard, then, is the main equipment of the critic, and, in conjunction with such other necessary equipment as sensitiveness to esthetic qualities, knowledge of technical problems, power of logical analysis, and familiarity with history both within and without his special field, gives him the power to be conscious of the comparative significance of his own reactions to the works he wishes to criticize and then to interpret these reactions in an orderly manner for the guidance of others. When he is sure that his standard is universal—that it is big enough to mother all the greatest works of all time, he may readily admit the uncertainty of the personal equation in his application of that standard to any given work. But, even though the very comprehensiveness of his vision causes him to feel and express doubt of his own infallibility in making applications, yet, because of the stability given him by his great standard, every one of his conclusions (assuming unfailing honesty in reporting them) will have value to his audience. Every one will help to produce a state of awareness of the character of an individual's own reactions, and of new qualities whose presence and importance were not even guessed.

In the field of pictorial art, the profession of criticism, like other professions in other fields, is honored by a pitifully small number of critics with the universal vision, and more or less unconsciously betrayed by a concourse without it. And since the few are so few, they are limited to the relatively small audience that searches out

GREEK

FRAGMENT FROM GOZZOLI

FIG. 67

CHINESE TEHUA

FIG. 68

Examples in which design has been imposed on nature without distortion, but with sufficient abstraction to meet the needs of the artist. These are classic works fulfilling the requirements of great art. The Chinese Tehua is a supreme example of the felt nature plus design. The rectangle containing the Greek figure is of dynamic symmetry proportions, and the figure and drapery a superb example of organized curves. The Gozzoli shows design imposed on landscape, particularly on rocks and trees. The Indian carving, fig. 69, is built on the laws of the diagonal.

FIG. 69

MEDIÆVAL EAST INDIAN

Criticism and the Standard

the high quality publications in which, alone, their criticisms appear. The very universality of their vision places them far enough ahead of their times and causes them to be objects of enough suspicion, to prevent their words reaching the public which needs them most.[1] The public is at the mercy of the hordes of near-critics with particular standards, or no standards but their own personal taste, who tickle the intellect with side-issue discussions, or the fancy with flowery gush.[2] These have ready admission to print,

[1] For instance, the "popular" magazines, with their policy of pleasing the public to get its money, would not publish such criticism on the ground that it would not be popular. In its issue of January 1923, the *Ladies' Home Journal* published an article on the "Crime Wave in Art" by Oliver Herford. In a four thousand word attempt to discredit the Modern Movement with ridicule, this article thoroughly disclosed Mr. Herford's own insensibility to the design principles that are basic in all art except the representative type, which is his standard. While to the informed reader his article only discredited Mr. Herford, to the public it could only add to the confusion. The editors, later, refused to publish an answer to it, which was a constructive explanation, on the ground that it "was more for the class-room than for a popular magazine." The idea evidently was that ridicule is good reading whereas explanation is too heavy. One cannot quarrel with the editors, of course, for conforming to what they consider a wise business policy but it is well to know, when one reads the magazine, what the policy is that determines the selection of the material there presented.

[2] Examples of flowery gush by art critic. "From the portraiture

How to See Modern Pictures

in magazines, exhibition catalogues and books. Their particular points of view are popular because the public, by its present satisfaction with the little side-issue field of representation, is eminently particular in its point of view. And so they amuse, or explore a circle within a circle, but have no plan for the whole labyrinth, and the net result of all their activity is to stimulate, and add to—confusion.

Within the great conglomerate mass of the "Public," however, are many who really care to understand works of art. They read the printed words of critics, or listen to lectures, or go on gallery tours, hoping to solve the riddle, hoping to find the magic key, hoping to find out what art is really about. What are such earnest ones to do? How are they to know whom to believe—whom to follow?

So far as the writer has been able to answer this question, after fifteen years of watching the

of beautiful women to the portrayal of beautiful flowers is but a step, and, as the portraits give forth that intangible something of the soul of the sitter, so the flowers bring to us the perfumes of Arcady. . . . An even lovelier picture is 'Memories,' a wistful, tender, exquisitely painted beautiful woman, who does indeed reveal her soul to us."

[134]

prevailing misconnection between public and works of art, there is but one possible method. And that is this:—to grab out of the air, or arrive at by reason, or intuition, or whatever means offers, some rudimentary realization of a universal quality in all works of art, and then, using this one fact as a test rod, to measure with it, the offered teachings. One's reasoning might run like this: "In all great works of art of the past, regardless of when or where, there is something common to all. It is not connected with subject or story, for differences of subject and story are infinite. It is not technique, for differences of technique are limitless also. If none of the tangible elements are universal, and yet there is some universal quality, then that quality can only lie in the method of arriving at tangible results. In the case of pictures the methods of arriving at results are visual and have to do with the kind and quality and relation to each other of lines, spaces, forms, and colors. There is a strong likelihood, then, that the universal quality lies in the *how it is done*—in the relationship of elements, which is called *design*. Ergo, I shall

How to See Modern Pictures

listen to those critics of art who talk of a universal quality (which they will call "design," the "grand tradition," "significant form," or "classicism"), and who connect this quality with universal relationships. From such I may learn the secret. From those who talk of particular contents I may learn many other things—but never the secret of the inner shrine." In other words, an individual, if he wishes to get anywhere in an understanding of art, must build his own standard and then have the courage to apply it—first, by criticising the critics and judging the judges, in order to choose the right guidance; second, by striving toward independent judgment, with modesty, perhaps, and considerable reliance on the trusted teaching—but without losing sight of his goal.

These pages have been an attempt to outline such a standard in a way that would help the reader to learn how to see modern pictures, or any pictures—to gain the power of discrimination necessary to courageous judgment and action in matters of art.

We found, in the preceding chapters, that the

Criticism and the Standard

type of vision called pure vision is the type with which we see the space relations of both applied and pictorial design. If we realize that the power of using this type of vision has been lost, to a large extent to-day, and then realize that this general loss probably means an individual loss covering our own case, and, if we then make the effort necessary to exercise it, (the fact that it can be exercised at will proves that it is dormant, not permanently lost) we shall have made, by that process, a first big step toward achieving a personal standard. Sensing the right relations of lines, spaces, forms, textures and colors is then the next big step, the attainment of which can be reached, let us believe, by familiarity with, and study of, right examples. There are certain examples at hand which are known to be right. Among them are the Greek and Egyptian classics, Japanese prints, the work of the old masters such as Dürer, Tintoretto, Raphael, Titian, Holbein, El Greco, the wall carvings of Assyria, the sculptures of old Mexico. Familiarity with the relations of visual elements in such work, arrived at through the use of pure vision and the elimination from consideration of all extraneous elements, will certainly develop the ability to recognize right relations wherever they are seen. When these two important steps are taken three fourths of the problem is solved. Sensing the "something plus" in a work of art, the expression of the felt nature, or inner reality of a thing, and accepting complete or partial abstraction as the only possible means to such expression, constitutes the other quarter of the problem. When these important steps are taken we have made our own the essential elements of a universal standard.

Achieving this standard in some degree is possible for anyone who cares to think and act seriously on the interesting problem. Partial achievement means partial power; supreme achievement, supreme power. Given a standard large enough to include all works of visual art of all ages, and a sensitive application of that standard, then the opinion of every serious individual about works of art, commands respect. It may be vulnerable to attack. What matter? It commands serious attention and respect be-

Criticism and the Standard

cause it records the esthetic emotional reaction of a human soul to a work of art. And among such reactions (provided they are true ones) there are no aristocrats—no authorities. The universal language has conveyed a feeling from man to man across the ages, or across a city, or a room. The recipient of the emotion is kin to all men and all women of all human time who have likewise received the "message" of an artist. He or she knows a sense of elation—of power. There is no doubt, or fear, or confusion, only the poise that comes of vital experience. The writer wishes to emphasize this point with all the power at his command. Given the ability to experience esthetic emotion from a visual work of art, the responses of the Italian section-hand, of the country school teacher, of the timid Texas ranch wife, of the art student, are exactly as valid—as important in every way—as worthy of respect—as are the responses of the critic, the museum director, the art editor, the college president. (Respect for the expression in words of such reactions is another matter and should go easily to the critic. We are speaking now of the value of the response, as such.) In this twenty-fifth year of the Twentieth Century the ability to experience this emotion is a very rare attainment. In every hundred thousand of population there may be ten people with the ability consciously developed, an unknown number in whom it is unconscious or intuitive, a vast majority in whom it is possible of development. The ten furnish the present audience of the creative artist—the others his future, potential audience. The point is this. Among the ninety-nine thousand nine hundred and ninety who do not, at present, consciously understand the meaning of visual esthetic emotion, are many so-called artists, art critics, college presidents, museum directors, and art editors. Among those who do know its meaning are simple, isolated modest souls who claim no distinction because of their gift. These last make their own judgments of works of art, instantly recognize the art quality wherever they see it, and smile with amusement at the side-issue discussions or airy persiflage of blind authorities and critics, or at gold medal awards to skillful

FIG. 70

RENOIR

A modern classic of great visual significance. It is an example of thoroughly organized three dimensional design—and is built on the same key of four scheme of diagonals as the Sistine Madonna of Fig. 46.

FIG. 71

A modern picture which tells its story powerfully, and is organized into design. From the painting by Erich Waske, contemporary German.

If magazine and book illustrations were built into designs, as this picture is, every one of them would be a work of art worthy of preservation, exhibition in art museums, and respect. The art would make valuable the presentation of the idea. Illustration that lacks the art has but a momentary and purely illustrative (in an intellectual sense) value. It is a document.

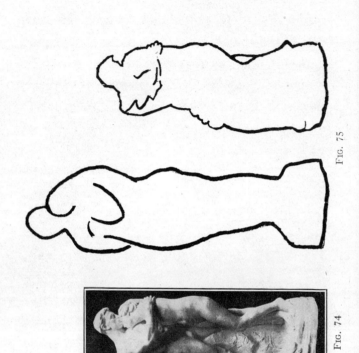

FIG. 75

FIG. 74

FIG. 73

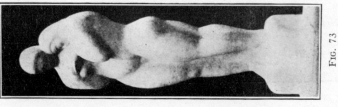

Criticism and the Standard

mediocrity. The power they know gives confidence and quiet authority. It is this power, gained in this way, that gives the courage to form individual judgments and courage to live up to them. It is this power that *is* the extension of experience, made possible for us to-day by the Modern Movement in the visual arts. It is this power that is available in some degree to any individual who cares to gain it, and it is this power, once gained, that makes its possessor a force in matters of art,—a force in the world of art. For discriminating judgment means discriminating purchase. And discriminating purchase, by its selection of significant work, shares the burden of creation with the artist and thus gives the layman his only possible opportunity of participating in the production of those works which will be the valued heritage of our age to succeeding ages, and by which, incidentally, our civilization will be appraised when million dollar corporations are forgotten. Much could be said in this connection of opportunities awaiting individuals, art associations, and women's clubs. When a higher standard than the present is adopted, however, such opportunities will be sought for, and that time will be a better one than the present in which to discuss them. The standard comes first. From its attainment will spring many significant events.

From the engraving by Marc Antonio

FIG. 76

AFTER RAPHAEL

Here is the opposite end of the design scale from that shown in the Indian carving of the frontispiece. Vast complication and sophistication against primitive simplicity. Yet every detail of the complicated mass perfectly controlled! Works like this probably mark the supreme three dimensional design achievements of man in complicated themes. For pure art power, however, the studied simplicity of the Greek vase undoubtedly surpasses this type of work.

FIG. 77

Realistic drawing of a cypress tree with all the visually meaningless wiggles, and spaces between wiggles, left as they are in nature. Compare this to the universalized cypresses in fig. 27.

CHAPTER X

CONCLUSION

SEVERAL of the matters we have been discussing probably constitute (that feared but unescapable word) the *science* of art. We have dared to examine a little into this science when many affirm such action to be a sort of sacrilege. That the curtain must not be raised, seems to be a rather general opinion; the inner sanctuary must not be profaned by vulgar eyes. Knowledge of the whys and wherefores of the art process is materialistic and therefore taboo. Intuition, mysticism, awe and reverence, and knowledge about knowledge, should be the avenues of approach, for so is dignity maintained. But—has the human body been profaned, or the appreciation of its beauty lessened, by a knowledge of anatomy? Or is the Parthenon less a masterpiece in our eyes because Hambidge has discovered its proportions to be based on a geometric relation of areas expressed by the square root of five? Or is a symphony less moving for recognizing the repetition and elaboration of motives that contribute to the design, or by knowing the organization of the orchestra? Such knowledge once acquired need not engulf sensation. It can be ignored at will, or it can serve its end subconsciously, or even consciously, while an enriched emotional response is made possible because of it. And if knowledge of the contributing science means gain in sensational experience in the cases of nature, and of such of the arts as architecture, music, poetry and drama (some study of versification and play-anatomy is deemed the normal approach to this art), why may it not be essential in the case of pictorial art?

Scientific knowledge in the field of art may be, however, a danger, as well as a blessing. That it has been a destructive influence is written into the record by the history of the past three hundred years since the scientific attitude of mind began to direct attention toward the mechanics of imitation, or truth to nature, and away from the emotion of pure sensation. The prevalence

[144]

Conclusion

of this scientific state of mind throughout society to-day is an alarming matter, if one wishes to be alarmed, and is certainly a direct cause of the prevailing esthetic malnutrition.[1] In this sense, to say that science has been the Nemesis of

[1] The prevalence of the idea that art has to do with truth can be estimated from the writings and sayings of persons in all walks of life, who have not yet comprehended the modern approach. The following quotation from an article on "The Art of Public Speaking" by Hon. Albert J. Beveridge in the *Saturday Evening Post* of April 26th, 1924, is one case in point:

"Oratory as a fine art. . . . For art is the most finished expression of truth in its myriad aspects, with the least possible obstruction in that presentation, so that those who hear or look, can get most easily the thing presented. It follows that art is the highest functioning of the mind and soul of man; and it follows, too, that it requires the utmost instruction, training and practise to become an artist of any kind."

The "come-back" of the new point of view on a pronouncement like this would be as follows:

The expression of "truth" requires knowledge and skill. Assuming the knowledge, skill may be taught, and learned with training and practice. The *how it is done,* wherein lies the art if there be any, cannot be taught, or learned by practice. It must be the creative contribution of the artist. Skill is the tool with which he expresses art, and always a valuable means toward that end. Art expressed blunderingly, with little or no skill, may yet have inherent power to move one emotionally (the function of art) whereas skill, without art, may arouse admiration but never emotion.

The Senator weakened his argument by unthinkingly adopting an inherited belief and applying it to his own field. He knows right well, if he stops to think, that skill in presentation of truth is a very secondary matter when it comes to moving an audience with oratory. There, as elsewhere, it is the *quality* of the presen-

How to See Modern Pictures

art is certainly no exaggeration. Witness the blighting effect wherever modern society has come in contact with indigenous art. England in India is an outstanding example, as is our systematic murder of the native arts of the American Indian. To blame commercialism entirely for this levelling process does not go deep enough. It is a state of mind that is guilty—a state of mind which, having lost the ability to respond emotionally to works of art, gives no *intrinsic* value to them, and allows commercialism to kill, either through competition or exploitation. England killed the East Indian textile art of the hand loom by the former method—by flooding India with the cheaper products of the machine loom. We have completely killed the weaving art, for instance, of the famous village of Chimayo in New Mexico, where the finest of Mexican blankets were woven fifty and a hundred years ago, by buying from the villagers in too large quantities, a cheapened, inferior, commercialized, though still hand

tation, of truth, or nonsense, or any subject matter, that *sways* the crowd emotionally. If he applied his own definition strictly, a professor of mathematics, because of his trained mind, would prove a greater orator than a Lincoln.

Conclusion

woven, substitute for the work of the past. If we had cared for intrinsic art value, we would have compelled the maintainance of the old high standard by buying only (at a higher price) blankets made of homespun wool and vegetable dye, and by refusing to buy the cheapened product made with Germantown yarn, store dyes, and ornate pattern. The Navajo Indians are now in the middle stage of this process of demoralization. The demand for inferior blankets has increased so fast that there is no need to do good work with the doubtful chance of a sale at a price that would pay for the extra labor. But profit can be made on good work as well as on atrocities. Works of art have always had their price, and been bought and sold at profit. No, it is not commercialism—entirely. It is the scientific attitude of mind that is guilty of demoralization in art, or worse than demoralization—of total annihilation.

Science is ordered knowledge. The scientific attitude of mind is concerned, to speak cautiously, with knowledge. Knowledge is objective. It must be about something—relativity, cake-baking, horses, art. There is an axiom hidden here. A person may *know* so much *about* a thing that he does not *know* the *thing itself*. A four year old child, knowing nothing about a thing, may know it vividly, that is, feel it, see it, sense it, while a professor of philosophy may know volumes about it, and not know it, in this meaning, at all. Take the case of the two school girls. "Come on out to the Zoo and see the animals," says one. "Can't," answers the other, "Got to study my zoölogy." The pail and dark paper experiments of Chapter II indicate that knowing may prevent seeing. We are now going a step farther and saying that knowing may prevent sensing. Or, if it does not prevent it (and it need not) it can exist without it. An extreme example of a man in this condition of mind is the before mentioned H. G. Spearing, who blithely calls the Egyptians children in art, and assumes maturity to lie in the imitative dexterity of his own time, as exemplified, doubtless, by a John S. Sargent. His is the well-stocked mind of the scientist, entirely unaware of the different world of visual sensation. To three scientists with whom the writer has broken lances, art was a

Conclusion

type of picture writing. To one its purpose was to convey information subtly and suggestively, his favorite work of art being the Greek "Discus Thrower" because in that statue the artist had portrayed a movement that was *about* to take place, the presumption being apparently, that this was a much more subtle achievement than the portraying of a movement actually taking place. To another its function was to record visual facts such as buildings and places, his home art gallery consisting of excellent records of Coliseums, Notre Dames, etc. To the third, its chief merit seemed to be accuracy—accuracy in reporting facts, of course. This man had bought an Eileen Soper etching because the proportions of the children's bodies were correct. Of the three, only the last, whose field was medicine, had any doubts, or modesty, as to the adequacy of his standard. The first, whose field at the time was art analysis, and the second, whose field was mathematics, had complete assurance of the sufficiency of their approaches. Not one of the three recognized either the existence, or possibility, of visual sensation as a matter of importance in connection with art. It was completely outside their consciousness. The scientist represents the highly ordered functioning of this type of knowing mind; the layman represents its foggy, incomplete functioning. The former may approach art with shrewd analysis, and miss the mark; the latter may approach it with strong accepted or inherited beliefs, that are probably vague in their application, and also miss. Both stages of development represent the same angle of approach, which we have called, with more or less accuracy, the scientific attitude. And it is this attitude which, in our time, notwithstanding its great value in other fields, loses all contact with art, and is dangerous from a cultural point of view, because its influence is negative and destructive.

The scientific attitude of mind, however, need be neither negative nor destructive. That it is so, results from concern with the wrong type of knowledge rather than from the fact of having knowledge. A misconception of the purpose of art canonized by the usage of three centuries, has diverted society onto a detour remote from the

Conclusion

world of sensation, and attendant knowledge has been, quite naturally, as foreign as the way itself. From such a situation there is no escape but by going back to the beginning and making a fresh start. Art leans on science. Design is ordered sensation. And, in its very highest expression, dynamic symmetry, it is built four-square on ordered knowledge. Therefore knowledge of the different world of sensation, even if it only goes so far as to recognize the fact of its existence, is an aid to comprehension, and, as has been said, when contact with that world has been lost, is apparently the only method of regaining it. A modern artist once wrote in a letter, "Work means nothing to me unless done with every intellectual sinew I possess brought to bear on rich emotional reactions to nature." Let that statement stand as the ideal of the work-method of the creative artist—as the definition of the means of attaining classicism. And let it serve also as the approach-method of the lay-man to a work of art. It covers the whole case. It is this book packed into a single sentence.

When all is said, however, science is only a

How to See Modern Pictures

means to an end. The end is design. Design in pictures has an entity of its own—has a value which must be recognized and appreciated wherever found, whether in the form of pure or partial abstraction, or when imposed on nature with the least possible abstraction. The degree must be overlooked, the essence observed. Only by such a process can the new approach be made one's own. By accepting this approach, the way is cleared for the appreciation of the greater achievement wherein the felt nature of life, or things, is expressed through design—the achievement which is the presupposed requisite in all great creative art.

In closing, a word about the source of this new means to vital experience. The so-called Modern Movement does not offer, at present, a clean-cut, obvious issue either to artists or laymen. Certain persons who have penetrated to the basic principle find themselves in an accord in their judgments and sensations which is quite thrilling to them in contrast to the babel of judgments that prevailed under the standard of representation. But others, who only grasp part

[152]

Conclusion

of the principle, or misunderstand it, find themselves confused between the two conflicting standards, and most unsure of their judgments. In this last classification are found all those artists who imitate the superficial qualities of the movement as exposed in the styles of the men who are its chief exponents. They flood the market and galleries with lifeless reflections of Cézanne and others, which give the critics the right to talk of the dwindling Movement and to surmise hopefully that out of the "insanity" something good *may* come in time. This, from the critics, soothes the somewhat disturbed complacency of the layman by reinstating his inherited beliefs in his own esteem, and thus delays any real clearing up of the confusion.

Confusion is needless. The Modern Movement has given us a basic principle. That principle can be isolated and understood unless the present research is all illusion. If there is such a principle outcropping in the work of Renoir, Cézanne, Seurat, Picasso, Dérain, Matisse, the Cubists, and others which correlates with the great arts of human history, then that is the superlatively important matter. It is the thing to be seized on avidly, to be examined, tested, questioned in the effort to make it available. It is the supreme contribution. Artists, by accepting it and making it their own, can then build on it in their own individual styles with endless opportunity for individual expression. Laymen may make it their measuring rod gaining from it assurance in their esthetic judgments. It is this contribution which the writer has found in "modern work." It is this contribution which he has tried to emphasize in these pages.

APPENDIX

SOME PRACTICAL SUGGESTIONS ON THE
APPLICATION OF THE STANDARD HEREIN
SET FORTH TO THE IMMEDIATE PROBLEMS
WHICH PRESENT THEMSELVES TO THE INDI-
VIDUAL AND WHICH DEPEND FOR THEIR
ANSWER ON HOW HE SEES PICTURES

BOOKS TO READ

ON RELATED THEORY

"How to Listen to Music," Henry E. Krebiehl, Scribners, 1897, $1.75.

"Enjoyment of Poetry," Max Eastman, Scribners, 1916, $2.00.

"Pictorial Beauty on the Screen," Victor O. Freeburg, Macmillan, 1924, $2.50.

These volumes cover their fields with a purpose very closely related to the present one and will greatly enlarge the horizon of any one not already familiar with their approach.

ON THE THEORY OF MODERN ART

"Art," Clive Bell, Stokes, 1914, $2.50.

"Vision and Design," Roger Fry, Brentano's, 1920, $2.50.

"Cubists and Post Impressionists," Arthur J. Eddy, McClurg, 1914, $5.00.

"Modern French Painters," Jan Gordon, John Lane, London, 1923, $7.00.

Appendix

"Primer of Modern Art," Sheldon Cheney, Boni & Liveright, 1924, $6.00.

"Cubism," Albert Gleizes & Jean Metzinger, T. Fisher Unwin, London, 1915.

ON RELATED THEORY

"On the Laws of Japanese Painting," Henry P. Bowie, Paul Elder, 1912, $3.50.

"Nietsche and Art," Ludovici, J. W. Luce, 1912, $1.50.

ON THE HISTORICAL DEVELOPMENT

"Modern Movements in Painting," Charles Marriott, Chapman & Hall, London, 1920, $7.50.

"The French Impressionists (1860 to 1900)," Camille Mauclair, Dutton, $1.50.

"History of Art," Élie Faure, Translated by Walter Pach, Harpers, 1921, 4 vols., each $4.50.

"Since Cézanne," Clive Bell, Harcourt, Brace, 1922, $2.50.

"The Masters of Modern Art," Walter Pach. N. Y. Huebsch. N. Y. 1924. $3.50.

"Georges Seurat," Walter Pach. N. Y. Duffield & Co. and The Arts 1923. $2.00.

TECHNICAL AND THEORETICAL

"Composition," Arthur Dow, Doubleday, Page, 1916. $5.00.

Appendix

"Dynamic Symmetry and the Greek Vase," Jay Hambidge, Yale Univ. Press, 1920, $6.00.

"The Diagonal," a magazine in 12 numbers, edited by Jay Hambidge. Yale Univ. Press, $5.00 set.

"Dynamic Symmetry and Composition," Jay Hambidge, $3.00.

GENERAL

"The Humanizing of Knowledge," James Harvey Robinson, Doran, 1923, $1.50.

"The Human Machine," Arnold Bennett, Doran, $1.50.

"Journalism Versus Art," Max Eastman. N. Y. Knopf. 1916, out of print.

"How to Appreciate Prints," Frank Weitenkampf. N. Y. Scribners, new edition, 1923. $4.00.

MAGAZINES SHOWING CONTEMPORARY CREATIVE ART

AMONG periodicals that are recording the history-making developments of their times in pictorial art by showing so-called modern work the following are probably the most important.

THE ARTS devotes its pages entirely to significant works of the present and past that are in tune with the "grand

Appendix

tradition" of all time. It shows no representative work. As a record of what is happening today it is most complete, and uncompromising, and therefore the most valuable.

THE DIAL is showing modern work and much that it shows is of lasting importance but unfortunately its standard is not so severe in the pictorial as in the literary field and it has in the past admitted many works to its pages that are too trivial to have lasting significance.

THE INTERNATIONAL STUDIO has, during the past several years, given an increasing amount of space to modern work, until the representative and modern schools have received about equal attention. As this book goes to press, however, a change in policy seems to have gone into effect which has resulted in the elimination of most modern work and a return to the standards of several years ago. It is to be hoped that this policy is only temporary.

THE SURVEY GRAPHIC is undoubtedly a pioneer among non-art magazines in that it has been the first to use modern works as illustrations to its text, and also as an independent means of interpreting contemporary life that is supplementary to its keen analytical literary approach. In doing this it undoubtedly points the way for magazine illustration of the future when all illustrations will be works of art as well as illustrations.

Appendix

VANITY FAIR has shown single pages of modern work for several years and, among popular magazines, has been a pioneer in this respect. Also its covers have long stood out in startling contrast to the prevailing candy-box level of the news stands pretty girls. Also its "chique" illustrations have borrowed much superficial flavor from modern art.

THE LITTLE REVIEW has always pioneered as courageously in the pictorial as in the literary field and with as little compromise to the public taste.

THE LIBERATOR, since its birth as THE MASSES, has probably published more vital modern drawings than any other magazine in this country.

THE BROOM, recently reborn, is entirely devoted to modern work. It is a striking example of an alive magazine that is too good to sell in quantity.

L'AMOUR DE L'ART, published in Paris, gives a comprehensive record of French modern work in all mediums.

THE PLAYBOY, a lively, modern magazine presenting the significant art of the day both pictorial and dramatic. It often includes tipped-in wood-block prints on Japan paper of significant modern work.

SHADOWLAND has presented considerable contemporary creative work and it is one of the few magazines that have used works of art on its covers.

L'ESPRIT NOUVEAU, of Paris, is a copiously illustrated

Appendix

record of contemporary history-making events in all arts.

DER QUERSCHNITT is similar in purpose to L'ESPRIT NOUVEAU—publishing articles in German, French and English.

BURLINGTON MAGAZINE, London, devoted to the great arts of the past with occasional articles on modern art.

DEUTSCHE KUNST UND DEKORATION, in German, has given a comprehensive record of modern developments as they have occurred.

DAS PLAKAT is of especial value as showing pictorial advertisements that are works of art.

The magazines here listed and others like them are making history in the magazine field, and are recording history in the making in the art field. It goes without saying that they should be available in every library and in every home. Without them a person who is away from the art centers of the country has no means of knowing what is happening in art during the year in which it is happening. They are supplementary to the more general survey of the books herewith listed, and furnish the opportunity to a student to apply the principles presented in the books.

Appendix

Two or three of these magazines come under the diagnosis of Max Eastman in his *Journalism Versus Art,* The reader can easily identify them by the character of their contents. The others quite decidedly do not so qualify.

SOME STUDY SUGGESTIONS

Many public libraries have collections of photographs of works of art of all periods which may be taken out, like books, and studied. In such study, frequent turning upside down should be resorted to in order to lose the meaning of subject matter and to see the lines, forms, spaces, etc., more easily. With thin tracing paper laid over such photographs, outlines can be drawn, as in fig. 75, which gives a most graphic means of seeing the essential character of the picture. Where two opposite types of work are thus treated, as in fig. 73 which is "modern," or highly organized into design, and fig. 74 which is strictly a representative work with no thought of design organization, the contrast between the two classes of work is striking. The one is simple, dignified, universal: the other fussy, accidental, particular.

After the ability is gained to recognize organized visual relations of elements it is interesting to study representative pictures and observe their unorganized elements—the meaningless relations of uncontrolled and copied nature.

Another excellent method of study is to take a piece of cardboard about post-card size, and cut an opening about one inch square near the middle of it. This can then be laid over a picture and the portion that shows through the opening studied apart from its context. In this case also the meaning of subject matter is largely lost and the quality of the work exposed. For instance when the branches of the tree in the realistic drawing of fig. 77 are thus observed their visually meaningless wiggles and spaces between wiggles are more obvious than when the entire drawing has its chance to convey the concept "tree" to the mind and thus distract attention from the essence of the thing itself. The same test applied to a highly organized work such as the "Sistine Madonna" of fig. 46 will reveal the perfect organization of every square inch of the picture. The same card, or another with an oblong opening, can then be used to observe forms

Appendix

in nature, thus supplying a boundary to the limitless spaces about one. By this simple means one of the problems of the artist can be realized.

With both these methods the entire list of the design elements of the design alphabet of chapter IV can be hunted for in turn in a given picture. By first tracing the border, then some three or four main lines or angles that seem related to it and to each other, and then studying, in the tracing, the relations of these elements, their design significance, or lack of it, can be felt. A course of study covering a wide range of pictures could thus be laid out, and by really *looking at* results with an effort to feel the relations, observation and sensitive reactions could be developed with surprising rapidity. Thirty minutes a day for a month would probably accomplish a revolution in approach to all pictures and open up forever this "mystery."

Since really seeing pictures depends on keen observation, any method which develops observation is a help toward that end. Under such a head come those games which children like, and which depend on remembering and describ-

Appendix

ing objects seen for one minute in a strange room, or on a tray, or in a certain spot outdoors. Seeing and reporting on insects, leaves, flowers, trees, clouds, fishes, dirty paper littering floor or street, clothes, faces, personal peculiarities, etc., etc., contributes to the same result as does the sudden asking of a person at dinner to describe the design on his dressing gown, or other familiar objects of daily use.

BEAUTY AND ART

The term that is most overworked in all usual approaches to art is "beauty." That term has been purposely avoided here because it has come to be entirely misleading through the generally accepted restriction of its meaning to beauties of nature such as sunsets, butterfly wings, roses, women, etc. When this application is entrenched in the mind, it is next to impossible to stretch the word to cover the different beauty that exists in the creation of an artist. The following extract from a letter to the writer from the head of an important art organization illustrates the restricted use. The italics are ours.

"I do not deny that there is a germ of something worth while in so-called modernism, but it certainly is not finding expression along the right lines to-day, and will not so long as it contents itself with contortions and vulgarities. To my mind, art which does not concern itself with beauty is not worth considering, for that is the mission of art—to add more beauty to the world. I know that at present you scorn representative art, but you will not, I hope, mind my saying that the art that has enabled you, in the past, to *transcribe and make manifest* certain beauties of nature, is an art which is essentially worth while, and I hope that you will not cast it aside completely. The world to-day stands in great need of visions of beauty."

This is an excellent statement of the general point of view which would have the artist "transcribe and make manifest" the beauties of nature. Since this entire book has been an attempt to present the artist as a creator of beauty in his own right, instead of a transcriber of natural beauty, there will be no need to reopen the argument here. It seems pertinent, however, to make it plain that the word beauty is omitted, not because it might not cover both approaches, but because the inherited limitation of its meaning to one will not let it cover both. By "contortions and vulgarities" the writer, doubtless, refers to departure from truth to nature,

Appendix

or abstraction. The fact that he does not see design in abstract works proves that he does not see it in the old respectable masterpieces of which he most approves for other reasons. If one sees design, contortions plus design never could be vulgarities.

OFFICIAL ART

Official art pronouncements, such as awards of honors or prizes, commissions for statues or murals, and selections of works for official exhibits, need to be looked into and the forces at work back of them understood, before blind confidence is placed in their infallibility. If such pronouncements are made by juries of artists it is pertinent to know by what group these juries were controlled, whether conservative or radical. Decisions can then be qualified. Instead of saying that such a work, having received first prize, is the *best* in the exhibition, one can, and should, say it is the best in the opinion of the conservative artists in control of the jury, or in the opinion of the radicals, or whatever the case may be. From such a course clarity of understanding is possible.

When judgments are made by public officials several facts must be borne in mind. In a

Appendix

democracy such as ours, officials are either elected by a majority of citizens, or appointed by another official who is so elected, or chosen by boards of directors who are conservative business men. In any case they and their views are apt to personify the majority standard. In the field of public commissions, this type of official judgment has reared monuments to itself all over the country, in its statues to soldiers and sailors and its choice of decorations and designs of public buildings, but its crowning glory is probably the MacMonnies statue "Civic Virtue," which it has prominently installed in City Hall Park of the city of New York. Representing, as it does, a very earthy nude "he-man" of the policeman type trampling the writhing, be-garlanded form of a woman, this official conception of virtue is not only degraded and degrading in idea, but commonplace in its unrelieved realism. Yet there it stands proudly advertising to all beholders that New York City, America's center of culture, officially believes in the standards of 1880. This statue and all art judgments of like calibre stand as memorials of our dark age of art—the lowest

Appendix

ebb of the art tide possible in human expression. Let us give thanks that there are many Americans besides such officials and the majority that elected them and that these have long since climbed out of this abyss.

Among the exceptions to the worst official judgments stand those that are near enough in tune with the times to commission good representative murals or monuments with some art quality. When work such as fig. 73 is commissioned we shall have reached the beginning of our golden age.

The layman, therefore, must pause a moment when he hears of the latest thousand dollar prize award, or the latest commission for a statue commemorating man's combative qualities, and question: Who decided? Why the particular decision? What standards were in power? To what age do these standards belong? The necessity is hard to face but there simply is no easy way out. The individual layman has got to do his own thinking—and a considerable amount of his own judging.

ON BUYING PICTURES

Individuals who are too modest to act on their own judgment in buying pictures must choose their source of advice. The available sources of advice throughout the country are the museum, the art association, the women's club art department, the art and popular magazine, the art critic, the art lecturer, the artist, the art dealer, and the interior decorator.

Enough has been said to the effect that caution is advisable in accepting the offerings of "art critics" and other teachers of the subject. That the same sifting process must be extended to the pronouncements of artists, goes without saying when one, an academician, defines art as "anything well done," and fine art as "anything extremely well done," while another may elaborate a contrary definition even to the length of these pages. Artists are not often coherent in two mediums, and are too prone to talk in their

[174]

Appendix

own special language. They are likely to give too little credit to the layman for whatever gains in appreciation he does make, and too much blame for obvious inherited shortcomings. Indeed, misunderstanding is the usual situation between artist and public, so much so that direct communication is almost impossible. An intermediate agency to translate each to the other is a virtual necessity, if there is to be any understanding. That agency is increasingly to be found in the woman's club, the art association, and the museum with the open-door educational policy.

That these three agencies are coming to supply this connecting link more and more adequately is one of the encouraging signs of the times. The chairmen of art departments, the secretaries of associations and museums, through their management of exhibition, lecture and study activities, become a focus of interchange that must mean growth. To these active, interested, unselfish persons come the inquiries of those who want to know about pictures—What to see in this? Is this one good to buy? Why is it bad?

Appendix

Why is it good?[2]   Art chairmen and secretaries are not always infallible in their pronouncements, of course, but their interest is rooted in either a real love, or a desire to know (speaking generally), and their judgments can only be biased by inherited beliefs (an honest bias), and not by considerations of profit. The inherited belief, when outgrown, breaks down in time— is vulnerable to knowledge, which makes growth possible. As they grow, their members grow with them. By going to these agencies to question and to buy, the individual is sure of sincere advice, which is probably sounder than his own judgment, especially if that is undeveloped, and his act, and the nominal commission from his purchase, stimulates and helps finance further activity. Purchasing power is a great force. Let it act in the field of the arts through organi-

[2] A first loan print exhibit staged by the Woman's Club of a Southwestern city forced on the art chairman the necessity of decisions between genuine artist proofs and commercial prints of commercial etchings. She was not sure and went about questioning. The questioned ones were not sure but began investigating. The resulting interest crowded the hall at an exhibition of very high quality originals—and no commercials.

Appendix

zations which *can afford to educate*. Commercialism, by its complacent prostitution of art wherever it touches it, has long forfeited all right to consideration. The two interests are opposite. On the women's clubs, art associations, and museums of the country rests the responsibility for education in art.

To these organizations come, during the year, many local and travelling exhibitions in all mediums which represent the art productions of the year. In a highly civilized state of society these exhibitions would be the table talk of the entire population of the city or town in which they occurred. Buyers would watch them as brokers watch the stock reports, and depend on them for paintings, sculptures, architectural designs, prints, and all kinds of handicrafts. Prices in such exhibitions are properly fixed, without juggling, profiteering, or excessive commissions to middlemen. A small fee goes to the organization, usually from 10% to 15%, to help defray expenses, the rest goes to the working producer. To buy from such exhibitions is a

Appendix

sure and quick method for the layman to enter into the world of art.[3]

Organizations of this kind have to practice an open-door policy, since they are public agencies, and accept for exhibition all schools of art so long as they are non-commercial and sincere expressions. This is as it should be. All serious work has a claim to a showing. Sometimes even commercial work creeps into the museums, to which, of course, it is always laying siege. Public criticism and lack of purchase is the most effective means of elimination of such,

[3] The following incident is illuminating in this connection. A wealthy man saw a very good realistic painting of an animal reproduced in color on the cover of an art magazine. He liked it and went to the editor, saying that he wanted to buy the original. The editor referred him to the "exclusive" dealer from whom he had borrowed it. In any museum exhibit a painting of this class would be priced at from $300.00 to $500.00. The man paid the dealer $2500.00 for it. Such an event seems almost tragic. If the man had had knowledge, or judgment, he would have indignantly refused such a price, or, if he was willing to spend so much money, would have gone to a museum exhibition and bought five or more paintings of equal merit, kept one for himself and given the others to some public school whose empty walls cry for them. Possession of wealth surely involves some responsibility in this, as in other, directions. Even more than other people, the person of means needs a standard of wise expenditures, both for his own satisfaction and for the beneficial result on society.

Appendix

and other inferior work. This again means discrimination. Always discrimination.

One other desirable method of purchasing works of art is to go direct to the artist. A feeling on the part of the layman that artists are "aloof," or "haughty," or disdainful of their timid knowledge need not prevent going to them to buy. The true artist is aloof from his public because practically every contact with it forces the fact into his consciousness that his work is not valued (when it is valued at all) for its intrinsic worth but for other side-issue reasons, that his best work is nearly always misunderstood and ignored, and that, as a result of this situation, he is virtually an outcast. Social honors when prompted by his "interesting personality," or his fame, or his value as a social asset, are empty and do not dispel this deep-rooted hurt. Communication under such circumstances is impossible. Aloofness is his only refuge and means to peace. But when a layman comes to him to buy—the very act spells valuation of work, the heart is warmed, and communication becomes spontaneous. Such a visitor earns the right to

Appendix

benefit from the specialized knowledge of the artist, as he earns the same right to specialized knowledge, when he pays a retainer fee to a doctor, or lawyer, or when he buys a ticket to a concert, or lecture. He is welcome because he brings with him the means to more production.[4] The commercial artist is deferential to a buyer solely for monetary reasons; the true artist feels kindly to a buyer for proving his "love of art" by action as well as words—and for the material support.

The art dealer and decorator as sources of buying advice will be considered separately.

[4] In his experience the writer has heard of only one case of an artist repelling a visiting buyer because of her "ignorance." And in this case the act proved to the writer's satisfaction his earlier impression that this man was a posèur aping the eccentricities of Whistler.

THE ART DEALER

In appraising the art dealer, a little analysis will illuminate his position and the resultant character of his influence. First of all, it must be remembered that he is a business man in business to make money. To do this he must sell the greatest possible number of the most profitable pictures. The easiest means to that end is to give the buyer what he wants. The answer of a certain dealer when asked why he displayed colored photographs in the front window and kept his original etchings in a drawer in the back room, covers this point. "A colored photograph sells itself in three minutes whereas it would take an hour of argument to sell an original etching." Then he added the classic remark of all art dealers, "It's not my business to educate the public. I give them what they want." He did not add, in this case, that a profit of 400 or 500% on the photos, as against some 30% on the etch-

Appendix

ings, had anything to do with the relative positions. Color reproductions are as profitable as color photos. The great average public wants colored pictures that "look like" nature. The article in demand is the seller's harvest. The result is that in every commercial art or department store machine-made reproductions are featured, and sold in quantity. In the "high class" trade there is a difference. The wealthy buyer too often wants the vicarious distinction of ownership of famous rarcties.[5] Such cost money. The more they cost, the more famous and rare they must be,—the more they are wanted, and the more profit they return to the dealer. Therefore the Fifth Avenues of the country display original old masters in the window instead of chromos. But they are there, not because they are great works of art, as they often are, but for the chromo reason—profit.

[5] A person who really "loves art," loves all art regardless of when, where, who, and how much. When a collector says he is not interested in contemporary art, but only old masters, he means that he is not interested in art, but in some derivative of art—such as respectability. Famous art is more respectable than contemporary.

Appendix

In the case of contemporary original pictures the artist usually gets from one-half to two-thirds of the selling price, the balance being a reasonable selling commission about large enough to cover selling costs. Sale of such work is difficult—the more creative it is the more difficult because the smaller the number of its appreciators. The ordinary commission on such sales is not large enough to be "very attractive" to the dealer. Suppose, then, a dealer knows and likes significant work, and "would like to sell it," but is "not in business for love," and fills his store with what he himself will often classify (privately) as "junk." A customer with thirty dollars to spend, asks his advice. On his answer hinges his profit. Shall it be $20.00 or $8.00? The pressure is too much. Can he, does he, give an honest answer and take the loss?

THE DEALER WHO LIVES UP TO AN IDEAL

There are in the country a small total of dealers who do take the loss—who do live up to their ideal—who do give true advice as they see

[183]

it, and who make good financially in the end by
slowly, painfully, building on the confidence of
individual customers which they have fairly won.
These few among thousands deserve the support
of every agency for good in their community.
They perform true service, they give themselves
to the cause of education. All honor to them.
They will not be found, by the way, on the
costliest Fifth Avenue corners, but on side streets,
or upstairs—a fact which rather measures the
American public. They can be identified without difficulty. Their shops will display "un-
popular" originals—works that are ahead of
average understanding. If one enters such a
shop with intellectual and emotional curiosity he
will feel distinction in the air—and the stimulation of something beyond his immediate grasp.
In charge he will find a man who has an ideal
and is living up to it, and who is ready and willing to "educate" if a question extends the invitation. Such dealers really earn their commission on sales and should have (and do have)
the loyal support and appreciation of both artists

Appendix

and individuals of the public whom they serve so constructively.[6]

There is a class of dealer between these two extremes who sells original contemporary work in paintings, sculptures, prints, etc. This class caters to a public which is above the chromo and photograph stage, and not rich enough to buy old masters. It is the individual buyers from this group who contribute to the development of their age by helping, through purchase support, to make the production of contemporary work possible. This is the hopeful group—the one that deserves every educational help and right direction. Its members, however, like all of modern society, are the inheritors of the representative tradition and the great majority quite naturally think a contemporary original should either "look like" something or "be like" some accepted work of the past. In painting, the work of twenty-five

[6] The writer knows and respects six such print dealers in the city of New York and as many more in the rest of the United States. Of those who partly compromise with business expediency, he knows several dozen, and of those whose policy is "strictly business" too many to count.

Appendix

to fifty years ago, or similar contemporary work, is understood and bought. The work of to-day, grown out of Post-Impressionism, is still strange and misunderstood and shunned. In prints, Rembrandt and Whistler are fountain heads, therefore most of them buy prints by contemporary "second Whistlers," or Rembrandts, forgetting that imitative work is always weaker than its source, and always esthetically insignificant. The dealer supplying such buyers, therefore, meets the same type of money pressure that works on the chromo dealer. Impressionistic representation is wanted, easy to sell, and therefore profitable to feature. Work that is "like" dogs, or ducks, or mountains, or dancing girls, or Inness, or Whistler, or that is nature suggestively presented, with only enough variation from the standard to display "personality," sells in quantity, and insures a revenue from the more modest commissions that obtain on living artist's work. Such dealers will gladly supply any work that is asked for, but "cannot afford" to give the time and expense necessary to introduce new, unfamiliar creative work that needs education to

Appendix

put over. "It is not their job to educate the public."

The result of such analysis as this should not be to place general blame on the dealer. The fact that his is a business enterprise probably justifies all profits, and most of the means of obtaining them. The object lesson is that, except in a very few extreme cases, his advice is thoroughly prejudiced by matters of profit and cannot be depended upon, and his stock is always chosen for its salability—never for merit. A buyer with his own standard may make use of the dealer's machinery of supply, indeed, if he is after good things, may find the dealer a ready ally in obtaining them, for many dealers have a conscience and really would like to sell good work, and are pleased if they are forced to do so by an intelligent buyer. In looking over walls full of framed commercial trash at fifteen to thirty dollars in one shop, the writer came upon a very good original color aquatint, the ordinary price of which would be twenty-five dollars. But it was marked twelve dollars. "Why so cheap?" he asked the dealer. "Why the original less than

Appendix

the commercial reproductions?" "Ah!" was the sad answer, "Nobody knows; nobody cares." [7]

Slow improvement is to be noted in the dealer field, however. Many of the leading department stores in addition to having tons of the usual trash in their "art departments" are opening real galleries in which they show only originals, and some are carrying out a regular program of monthly one-man shows by contemporary artists. One New York store is even showing radical creative "modern" work. These departments are, in some cases, in charge of men or women with an ideal who would like to go much farther in this direction than the general manager, with

[7] If the individual buyer of any art object from a Christmas card to a couch cover, could only realize that the *prevailing* (not the exceptional) standard of taste to-day is almost as degraded as it has ever been in the entire history of man—that it is infinitely below that of the unspoiled Indian and many savages, (for such create while we imitate), and could then reason from this fact that to just the extent to which his own taste coincides with the average taste, it also must be low and undeveloped, then a start toward improvement could be made. For then he would realize that business, to gain profit from pleasing the average taste, must present and sell bad art. When he entered the cheap department store or the sumptuous sales room, he would know why imitations, fakes, copies, veneers, bad colors, bad designs were displayed on all sides. He would understand what went on behind the scenes in every store of the kind, how the buyers would reject quality in design for popularity in design,

[188]

Appendix

his eye on dividends, will let them. Buying power has undoubtedly created this change and will govern future developments. The matter is all in the hands of the buyers.

reject good art for bad art. And then perhaps he would realize a sense of responsibility in purchasing—that buying mediocrity causes the production of mediocrity. May that time come.

THE INTERIOR DECORATOR

In so far as it bears on pictures, the creed of the decorators and their resultant advice seems to be quite uniform in character, even though the personal equation among members of the profession varies the severity of the application in given cases. An extreme manifestation of this creed was rumored recently as declaring for "no more pictures." But that policy seems not to have gone beyond the rumor stage, at least it is not yet law, and we shall therefore ignore it. A more accurate appraisal can be made from such an article as one that appeared in *Good Housekeeping* magazine recently, called "Choosing the Right Picture." Following is the sub-title, caption to the illustrations, and opening paragraph of the article. The italics are the writer's.

Appendix

"ACCORD BETWEEN HISTORIC ELEMENT IN FURNITURE BACKGROUND AND PICTURES IS ESSENTIAL"

"To the right, a representative Corot landscape, a charming thing for a Georgian living-room, or to incorporate into a panel over a dining-room fireplace. Below is Drouais' painting, "The Flutist." It typifies the French feeling of that period, the gayety and irresponsibility, and the correct surroundings in which to place it would be a Louis XV music-room, a French bedroom, or any feminine apartment done in the modern manner."

"The Rembrandt portrait below is the perfect accompaniment for William and Mary furniture, or even for the somewhat older period, Jacobean. It represents the transition epoch when decoration was turning from massive to more graceful lines. The *old English* print at the foot of page is the *natural choice* for *American* colonial rooms. It would be in keeping with English rooms done in Sheraton, Heppelwhite, or Adam style."

[191]

Appendix

"In choosing the pictures for any room *the most important consideration is the matter of accord,* or the historic and artistic relation between furniture and decorations. This accord is not hard to obtain. It means simply a recognition of the historic element in furniture and background."

The point of view here presented has several characteristics that are immediately obvious.

1. It is entirely backward looking.

2. It treats pictures exactly as it treats textiles—as spots of decoration to be judged in relation to an harmonious room scheme, and as *no more* than that.

3. It bases the harmony, or "accord" solely on the historic element, (though harmony of color is undoubtedly assumed).

4. It advocates the use of commercial reproductions (without saying so) since the pictures recommended could hardly be had in the original.

5. It advocates borrowing instead of earning respectability.

Appendix

This advice tells all people to live in the environment of the respectable courtly past, to ignore the arts of their own day, to take no part in the great adventure of creating contemporary art by commission or purchase, to dare nothing individual in their home decoration but to conform to a set standard called "proper" by authorities. It would have them think of pictures as historic documents with decorative possibilities, and live with commercial copies produced by machinery instead of with original prints.

Such advice is entirely negative, of course. It neither has, nor could have, any cultural result, for to accept something that has no connection with present-day life or with the individual, merely because someone else says it is "proper," is a little below zero as a means to individual culture. It invites standardization, the every-home-the-same idea that means spiritual stagnation, dead-level monotony.

Against such negative advice we oppose the following:

1. Pictures are entities in themselves; they are sources of experience.

[193]

Appendix

2. They should receive the respect to which such a position entitles them.

3. When articles of furniture in a room are works of art, pictures (which are also works of art) should be related to them, but only as aristocrat to plebeians; for in pictorial art the creative instinct has greater play than in the purely decorative application to furniture. In this sense, pictures become the focal point of the decorative scheme.

4. Harmony may exist between a picture and its surroundings, but it should be based on a kinship of art expression rather than on a matter of dates. There are wood-block prints or etchings made to-day with which a Heppelwhite table would "go" perfectly. To make such a selection becomes a vital cultural experience.

5. Original prints (i. e. wood-blocks, etchings, and lithographs) have the distinction of coming to the owner direct from the hand of the artist, in necessarily limited editions, with no intervention of commercial or mechanical processes. As such they have an inherent value that is obvious,

recognized, and that increases with time if they are significant works. Their modest prices (from five to thirty dollars, the same range as is charged for commercial reproductions) put them in reach of every home. Commercial reproductions, on the other hand, have a reference value which should make them, like books, available in a library. They are produced at small cost, in unlimited quantity, and their money value deteriorates from the date of purchase.[8] To give them the dignity and permanent importance of frames and wall-space is a cheap and colorless experience.

Of course, interior decorators are fulfilling an important function in their proper field, without question. It is only when they enter the field of pictorial art, and treat pictures like pieces of

[8] The president of a large printing house once told the writer that no ordinary sized color reproduction could possibly cost to produce anywhere near one dollar. In Europe the finest of such reproductions around 10 x 14 inches in size and up sell for from 25 to 75 cents, American money. In this country prints of the same size and of inferior quality sell for from 10 to 30 dollars. And because such tremendous profits can be taken from an ignorant public that demands them, they are featured in every commercial "art" store in the country. American prices include the frame worth $3.00 to $5.00.

Appendix

cloth, that they lay themselves open to attack and to the charge of obstructing cultural development.

PICTURES IN THE HOME

Many homes harbor pictures that were wedding gifts a quarter of a century ago, or that are proxies for fish, roses, sunsets, grapes, lovers, old homesteads or lovely maidens. Some of these are valued because Aunt Sally, or George, or Isabel gave them, others because they have watched family events for so long that many romantic associations cling to them. Others stay because no one has thought of removing them and still others because no one ever thinks about them at all. Probably 96% of the pictures on the walls of American homes serve only as happy reminders of some *thing* or some *body* else, and rate exactly at zero as *sources of experience* in themselves.

An inventory of all pictures in the home is an excellent thing. With it quite naturally goes an appraisal and a reassortment. For those that are valued as gifts from departed or present

Appendix

loved ones, and have no claim to value in their own right, an appropriate method is to fit up a private museum in the attic where all such can be hung in style and pilgrimages made to view them whenever a member of the family, or group of friends, wishes to "reminisce." The remainder will then have no sentimental cobwebs attached and can be judged on their merits. If they are mirrored reflections of some thing in nature or human life, two methods of treatment apply. They can be removed from their frames and pasted into a scrap-book which can thereafter be easily accessible in the library to any one who wishes to refresh his memory as to the appearance of nature, or the model. Or they can all be destroyed and reliance placed on one's own imagination for reference to facts in nature—a process which is a much more stimulating and interesting experience than merely glancing at a complete record.

The sentimental and reflecting pictures having thus been disposed of, there remain the reproductions or photographs of works of art including the work of the masters. These must not be de-

Appendix

stroyed. They have real value and more right to frame and wall space than any yet mentioned. But, if the experiment of living with originals is to be tried, they will become more and more unsatisfactory as contact with original work grows keener, and so they must not be made too permanent. A compromise method would be to provide a beautiful portfolio for all of them, and then two frames with demountable backs into which two reproductions could be placed and hung for a time and changed on occasion. In the portfolio the others will be instantly available for those delightful and profitable study-hours when one enlarges his horizon by study of great work. In this form the collection of reproductions can be greatly increased, as it should be, and, by buying them unframed, a considerable saving can be made (i. e. the difference between prices under 50 cents and prices of $10.00 to $30.00). Such a collection can include magazine reproductions, which if they are taken from the high-quality art magazines will soon constitute a very valuable addition to the home library besides affording an exciting occupation to all

Appendix

members of the family (including children) in the collecting.

The reproductions having now been taken care of, there remain only the original works of art. Discrimination is necessary here. In fact discrimination, and periodic change, is an invigorating program for all originals. In the process of selection free play is allowed for all the family critical faculties. In the weeding out, discussion may rage hot and heavy. Movies and dances will be forgotten. In fact the home life will probably be quite demoralized in the excitement —in which happy state the writer exits—with the rolling-pins crashing after him. Perhaps he has served just a tiny bit, however, by providing the frames and wall space for the new collection of original works of art.[9]

[9] A large variety of reproductions of works of art in photographs, half-tones and color prints, can be obtained from museums, especially from the Metropolitan of New York and the Art Institute of Chicago. Prices of these range all the way from two to fifty or seventy-five cents—the right price for such works. Also advice can be had from museums and public libraries as to where other such prints are obtainable.

ART IN THE SCHOOLS

There has been a movement under way for many years to put pictorial and sculptural art in the schools. Until very recently, that effort has largely resulted in the installation of reproductions of the master-pieces of the past. Since about the beginning of the century, however, a counter movement to install contemporary original works has gained slow headway. The plan put in operation by the Chicago Art Institute, of having its advanced students paint murals for the public schools at the cost of the materials, was probably the start of this movement, or certainly one of its earliest manifestations. Since then interest in school exhibits of American work has grown. It has been fostered by women's clubs, parent-teacher associations, art departments and principals. The response from the children has been so thrilling that enthusiasm has been contagious and spread

[201]

Appendix

rapidly, until we must now be on the threshold of a very general awakening to the great importance of this opening of the doors of the art world to children.

The question as to the type of works which should go into the schools has many angles, of which only one or two can be touched on here. Since the question of cost between the different types need not enter in, original prints being available at practically the same price level as the larger mechanical reproductions, and paintings and sculptures being obtainable at a great range of costs from the free work of art students up, the questions of relative merit and the principle at stake become the important matters. Relative merits of originals and reproductions have been discussed elsewhere in this book, but to the evidence might be added the pride, keen interest and sense of direct contact which children instantly display in work of their own living artists, a contact which is lacking between them and artists of the past, regardless of the greatness of the work. The principle at stake centers in this. Has a nation an ethical

Appendix

right to associate *only,* or *principally,* with the art of other ages and civilizations—in other words, to borrow instead of create its culture?   Borrowing evidences lack of internal resources, if not of poverty, and borrowing peoples become negligible in history.   Borrowing is the vogue at present because it is a means to display of wealth, because it is an easy way of escaping individual judgment and the attendant chance of making mistakes, because vicarious respectability attaches to it, and because former art is, in many cases, greater than our own of to-day.   Shall the children be taught to borrow their art, or to share in its creation, or both?

ART AND THE "MOVIE"

What to do about the "Movies" is a question which cannot be entirely passed by in these pages, for the minute minority who cannot enjoy bullets and biffs and *simon pure* love, villainy, and righteousness, every night in the week have some rights—the right of protest at least. Yet is a protest really justified? We live in a democracy. The box office is the voting booth. We vote for the dime novel level, and we get it. What is there to say? The producers meet the demand and pocket the cash. They are not "in business for love." And why should they educate?

There was a test case recently. The film play, "The Cabinet of Doctor Caligari," came over from Germany with both stage sets and acting the work of artists. The former were creative semi-abstract designs with a visual emotional significance that illuminated, with their weird

[204]

contortions of line and form, the weird soul-contortions of the scheming hypnotist. The art force of this harmony between setting and play was compelling beyond belief and, as an accomplishment, was far beyond anything the writer had ever seen, or heard of, on the screen. Enthusiastic reports of it first came from Paris, where war hates were forgotten (two years after the armistice) by crowds that stood in line to buy tickets. Then there was excitement here among artists and others who went to see it two and three times and called it the first work of visual art in the movies. Then came reports of not pulling a crowd in San Francisco, of not paying in Chicago, of being suppressed in this and that city by the American Legion because it was German, of no special interest shown here, no press comments there. Such was America's vote. To an insider at Hollywood was put the question, "Will Caligari have any effect on American production?" And with the usual cynical smile came the answer, "They've been watching it, all right, and with interest. They know its quality—and that it *lost money*. No,

Appendix

it won't have any influence on American production."

Pictorially the motion picture of to-day is straight representation. It, therefore, calls forth in the observer only practical vision—does not go beyond ordinary daily visual experience. Though there have been a few outstanding productions in this country in which there has been art in the acting, there have been none, so far as the writer has been able to learn, among commercial productions at least, that have made use of visual art in the setting. And, as the public is eminently satisfied with this situation, no change in policy in commercial productions is in sight.[1]

The answer, then, of those who would like to see visual as well as dramatic art in the movie, must be to carry over the revolt of the little

[1] This should be qualified by the admission that there have been commercial productions that made use of many of the good qualities of representative art, such as composition, tone harmony, centralized interest, etc. "The Covered Wagon" and Coogan's "Oliver Twist" are examples. See Victor O. Freeburg's "Pictorial Beauty on the Screen" for an able presentment of what has, and can yet be done in this direction. The above plea is for creative visual design in settings.

Appendix

theater movement from the speaking to the silent stage. Caligari is said to have cost but $7000.00 to produce. Small independent producers with an ideal beyond profit could finance such an investment. Independent little theaters in clubs, schools, museums, neighborhood centers, etc., could present regular programs using the best films already in existence and engaging such independent productions as would surely spring into being once such a movement gained headway. Here again is a logical opportunity for the women's clubs and other educational agencies to take coördinated action to help break the throttle-hold of commercialism on our cultural life, and give a constructive program in its stead. The intellectual educational possibilities of the screen are already widely recognized and made use of; its possibilities in the field of education in visual art have not yet been touched.

Charles Chaplin, in an article "Does the Public Know What it Wants," in the *Ladies Home Journal* for October, 1923, refers to Caligari in these words:

"And therefore we all argue about what 'they'

the material from which a work of art is built. Any pictorial subject-matter may be transformed into a work of art. So also may any dramatic subject-matter, whether tragedy or comedy, be transformed—by an artist. Charles Chaplin has the reputation, and it is evidently deserved, of being one of the few artists in the "Movies." An artist, by the very definition of his high profession, is a leader of taste—an establisher of spiritual values. He cannot be these things and compromise with the public demand. When a pictorial artist so compromises, he is labelled commercial. When a screen artist so compromises he surely earns the same title. Is Chaplin really satisfied with the accomplishment indicated by his words when he has the greater one within his reach—the one which would give him an enduring place in history as an establisher of higher values in his profession? From the commercial producer there is no hope. From the artist producer there should be. Perhaps some day the much loved Charlie will forget his public entirely and produce a work of real art—and take the loss, if there is one, as a matter of minor importance, as artists in the visual and other fields are always taking it. And he will do it from choice, selfishly, as they do, because he will *get more* from such a course than he can from only taking the money.

But there is another angle to the matter which is even harder on the producers than the foregoing prescription of altruism, and leaves them not one rag of excuse for their present program. That is that the work of art can be, and often is, a "success." Caligari failed more because of its nerve-racking story than because of its art quality. The artists who were thrilled by it thought of the story as a means to an end, whereas the public, unconscious of the art, thought only of the story and was frightened away. When a comedy, for instance, is a work of art, it wins everybody in sight—the ignorant who perceive only the comedy, the "high-brow" who attends only to the art, and a middle class who enjoy both. There are examples enough on the speaking stage, and we who are a bit discriminating crave this whole-hearted surrender to fun and art. We want to find it in the "movie" as a

Appendix

quick and convenient release from ourselves and our work. To impose art on comedy, or tragedy, or a popular story with human situations, is a way to success. History proves it. And the sets need not be cubist abstractions, as in Caligari. There are a thousand ways of creating emotional illusion with form, space, and color without offending the layman. Why do the producers fail to "succeed" in this direction?

ART AND ADVERTISING

American pictorial advertising is a barometer of prevailing standards in pictures. The following table tells the story by recording an analysis of all pictorial "ads" in six chance copies of current popular magazines.

PICTORIAL ART IN MAGAZINE ADS

Magazines	Ads that were works of art as herein defined.	Ads showing touch of representative artists and having some art quality.	Ads with no touch of art quality.	Total ads counted.
Saturday Evening Post	0	1	80	81
Ladies Home Journal	2	8	268	278
Woman's Home Comp.	0	5	138	143
Good Housekeeping	0	4	263	267
Asia	0	4	29	33
Butterick Quarterly	0	0	26	26
Totals	2	22	804	828

Appendix

No comment is necessary unless, perhaps, to emphasize the outstanding indication of the American business man's apparent ignorance of the distinction inherent in the contribution of the artist to a picture, or an "ad," or whatever he touches creatively. When one considers that a great number of advertisements aim to give their wares distinction in the mind of the prospective buyer, their failure to employ the most potent known means to that end is indeed surprising, and can only be explained as resulting from the prevailing broken contact between artist and public.

During two months of observation of street-car, subway, elevated, billboard and store advertisements in the city of New York, thousands of cheap glaring crudities were seen daily, and, in the entire time, just one lone, solitary example of a group of display "ads" that were the work of an artist. See fig. 78.

Germany, Switzerland, and to some extent France, make constant use of ads that are works of art. America will probably do so in time.

FIG. 78

The only example of a display "ad" that was the work of an artist found during two months of observation in New York City. One of a series of Hale posters for Saks & Co. Compare this with any one of the thousands of familiar realistic "ads" and see which has the greater advertising force and distinction. If this wins in these respects it should follow that its superior quality will gradually be recognized and the entire field of pictorial advertising be gradually revolutionized.

Appendix

familiar standard. Blame for the degrading can by no means be placed carelessly on either group alone and certainly not on the public alone; for artists, as a class, have had a first-hand part in the pulling down process, and are therefore, if anything, more to blame. No, blame must be shared by artists and public alike, or else placed squarely on the state of mind which has produced the most materialistic civilization in the world's history. But blame and causes are both backward-looking. Results and futures are more to our point.

That there is need of coöperation between artist and public is indicated by all of human history. The public needs it as an escape from materialism, for the release from self made possible by spiritual adventure, for the joy in life to be found in this release, and, for the healing joy of experiencing pure sensation which accompanies it. Increased capacity for the enjoyment of natural beauty is an additional side-issue perquisite to be gained from the larger experiences mentioned, as is also the keener visual sensitiveness to the visual quality of

Appendix

environment, such as gowns, room decoration, house or wall-paper designs, etc. The artist needs the coöperation for the stimulation resulting from a sensitive response to his work, because it fulfills his inherent human need to serve, and because from it comes the material means of living and working. When the coöperation is present the relation is normal and fruitful in both directions. Both sides give and both receive.

The present situation of divorce between the two thwarts all these mutual needs and the results are abnormal, disease-breeding and wasteful to a dangerous degree. As it works on the public, the loss of this esthetic emotional outlet turns the individual back into his material self and his material activities. Some consciousness of the futility of physical comings and goings and thinkings must be in all of us, for widespread boredom is a sign of the times, and the usual frenzied hurry—the ever present urge to *go* somewhere and *do* something, instead of quietly to pause and see, hear, or feel, can only be the result of a blind desire to fill in the void

Appendix

—to kill time (pathetic expression). Religion fulfills a similar emotional need to that fulfilled by art, and highly religious people find in it a substitute for art. Those that are cut off from both safety outlets are ships without ballast rolling fitfully in the storm of life—even welcoming the excitement of war and killing for the chance they offer of an escape from the deadly monotony of physical self.

On the artist the results of the divorce are probably as devastating as is possible from any human disaster. The condition immediately divides all artists whose development is above that of their public into two classes, those who compromise with the public taste in order to get money, and those who do not so compromise. The former again divide into two classes—those who hate themselves for their prostitution of their higher abilities, probably carrying this hate over against society, and those who accept the situation with a cynical laugh, abdicate the function (though not the title) of artist, and proceed to give the public what it wants and take the money—the price of selling their souls. The

Appendix

entire class of the sellers-out is tragically large to-day and, of course, highly honored and rewarded by those among the public and the art officials whom it pleases. Yet let us be slow to blame. One must live—and support a family. But the great waste of it all! The perverted abilities! The withered, starved, or still-born possibilities! The bitterness, the hate, the disgust, the hollow sham, the falsehood, the cynicism!

The artist who does not sell out and yet has to earn a living—let us pass him by. Analysis here cuts too deep into quivering flesh. Read the biographies of the creators of the race. It has always been thus, of course, only never before as it seems, has the chasm been quite so deep as during the last hundred years.

The artist whose plane of development is the same as that of his public has the most placid life of all artists, and, if placidity is the goal, is the most to be envied. He goes his way peacefully without question or conflict. He is understood and appreciated and honored and his work is purchased. He lives in ease and comfort and

Appendix

can afford to have a family, and a new car every two years. He is popular at the club, at church and at dinner. No repressions—no aloofness. Yes, he is most to be envied—if placidity is the goal.

Nothing new has been said in this scratching of the surface of artist and public relations. Everyone knows the conditions. Commercial age. Industrial democracy. There is nothing to be done. The tide is too strong. Yes, but does every individual know just how much he gains and loses from this situation? There is food for thought here. Even if no general change can occur, individual change is possible. That is the main point.

How can the change be made in an individual case? How can the coöperation of the ages be reëstablished? There is an answer to that which may not solve the entire question but certainly is a starting point toward the solution. That answer is:

Appendix

BUYING POWER

Buying power works for good in two directions by automatically reëstablishing coöperation. Just as the purchase of mediocrity stimulates the production of mediocrity, so the purchase of works of art at least allows works of art to be produced. An individual program might be this: In every field where art touches life such as the fields of pictures, sculptures, textile and costume design, lamp shades, iron ornaments, jewelry, etc., stop buying mediocrities, demand works of art—the productions of creative artists. Whether the artist work through the machine, in the case of industrial products, or direct in original creations, demand, through purchase, that he, not the average layman, be the arbiter of taste. Such an act does as much as one person can do to force commercialism to raise its standards, and supplies the food and drink that makes possible more production. And such action reacts on the buyer. Association with works of art breeds understanding of art and desire for it. The keen, sure means to familiarity

Appendix

is through the sacrifice entailed by ownership. Buy works of art—the best according to your present judgment. Buy them even if they may later prove to be only half good. Successive purchases will increasingly gain better and better works. Knowledge grows with the thought and interest essential to selection. Buy works of art in every department of sensation. It is the sure way to spiritual adventure.

Lest he be accused of prejudice in giving such advice, because he belongs to the camp of the artists, the writer submits that he is also a buyer of art and knows whereof he speaks, and what he has gained from the buying experience. On one occasion when his total worldly cash capital amounted to one hundred dollars, he "foolishly" spent sixty-five of these dollars for works of art, and then had to travel nine hundred miles in his car and live for one month in a strange city on the balance with no accessions of wealth, without selling his purchases and, needless to say, without regret. The food he didn't eat during that month would only have given momentary satisfaction whereas the works of art have already contributed three years of unfailing satisfaction.

He knows of many similar cases—the two girls on a hundred dollar a month income who bought an eighty dollar book of color reproductions of early Chinese paintings—the print collector who cut down his daily lunch bill from the usual seventy-five cents to thirty-five cents and put the balance into his print fund until he had gathered some fifteen originals of high merit which were later invited by his local museum for exhibition—the rich widow who dispensed with servants, automobile, and all such expensive physical luxuries, and lived in a small cottage spending her income of some thousand dollars a month on works of art for

[222]

Appendix

herself and to be given to her town library museum—the two country school teachers buying original prints with five dollar per month installments, etc., etc. It is not sacrifice to do these things though it is so labeled. The real sacrifice lies in not doing them and thereby earning the wages of boredom. Only some people have never found it out.

CONCLUSION

THE purpose of this book resolves itself into two main functions, an explanation of a method of seeing all pictures, which method is built on a universal standard, and the presentation of evidence to show that sensitive individual judgments built on such a standard are sorely needed in everyday life.

To an individual equipped with this ability to judge, a new and entirely different set of experiences from those he can know without it, is bound to come during the ordinary course of events. For instance:

He will visit an exhibition of paintings. Instead of experiencing muddled confusion, he will observe keenly and let himself enter into the spirit of different works with the will to see and feel the best they have to offer and to give full credit to that best, but not to overestimate it or give more appreciation than is deserved. In

Appendix

one painting he will see superb craftsmanship and give it credit, then look for the contribution of the artist. If the picture rivals the color photograph he will find none, or almost none. The more creative it is, the more it shows design organization of all the elements, the more of the felt nature he senses in it, the more is its art power. He can test it mentally and emotionally, watching the type of his reactions and being conscious of their derivation. Visiting an exhibition will become, under these circumstances, a real event. Tea and talk may cease (for him) to be the main attraction to a display of works of art.

After the exhibition he will drop in at an art dealer's gallery. From the window display he will know the type of dealer before entering, whether he is entirely commercial, semi-commercial, or educational. A glance around the walls will tell him the type of pictures displayed. If there are no works of art in sight, a question will discover whether or not they are stored in drawers waiting to be shown to the rare, above-the-average buyer. And when such are brought out they will be recognized for what they are—imitative, academic, suggestively representative, creative. If the shop specializes in significant work, the dealer will readily respond to even a hesitating interest, and will bring out his treasures, and forget salesmanship in his real enthusiasm for them. And, if a purchase is made to add to the home collection, the buyer will thank the dealer and make him promise to let him know when more examples of So-and-so's new style arrive.

In the evening at home the new purchase will be examined and criticized by the family, and the So-and-so's, who also have an example of this artist's work, will be called over to see his latest —and to learn incidentally, during the talk, that their example, bought four years ago, has increased in price. The children will know all about the artist for an exhibition of his work visited the school last month and they wrote essays, and are clipping reproductions for their scrap-books, and the class bought one of his pictures for the permanent collection in assembly hall.

Appendix

Then Mrs. So-and-so will laughingly tell of her decorator's advice about installing French prints in the new east room and her ensuing argument with that authority on the question of contemporary originals. And mother will report her altercation with the head buyer of Smith's furnishings department about crétonnes —how he tried to tell her that their re-hashes of French rococo and Chinese mandarin were "the most popular this year," and how she insisted on seeing new creative designs by American artists, and when he said he had none, how she had said, Very well, she would wait to buy till he got some in. And then the talk will turn to the latest decision of the Art Commission and the pressure the Club is bringing to bear on the officials to force them to buy a better design than the one they favor, and to the Parent-Teacher Association's program for bringing better "movies" to town, etc., etc., etc.

Dreams, dreams, dreams. Yes, but sometimes dreams come true—which is the only excuse for so much concern with them. Art touches life in a thousand places every day. There are no

Appendix

limits to the possibilities of using it. The key
is discrimination. You, friend Reader, are
judge, jury and court of appeals. The decision
is yours. You have the right, and the privilege,
and the opportunity to do—exactly as you wish.